POWERSCORE®
ACT & SAT
READING BIBLE

The only book you need for the
ACT & SAT Reading Sections!

POWERSCORE®
TEST PREPARATION

Published by
PowerScore Publishing, a division of PowerScore Incorporated
57 Hasell Street
Charleston, SC 29401

Author: Victoria Wood

Editorial Assistance: Terry Bray

Manufactured in Canada

06 01 20 17

ISBN: 978-0-9908934-8-6

MIX
Paper from
responsible sources
FSC® C004071

Guess what?

We offer **ACT Prep Courses** too!

In Person and Online options available.

"I GOT IN!"

You can do it. We can help.

PowerScore®
ADMISSIONS CONSULTING

CONTENTS

CHAPTER SIX: THE FUNDAMENTALS OF ACT AND SAT READING

CHAPTER SEVEN: GENERAL READING STRATEGIES

CHAPTER EIGHT: STRATEGIES FOR SINGLE PASSAGES

CHAPTER NINE: STRATEGIES FOR PAIRED PASSAGES

CHAPTER TEN: ANSWER CHOICE ANALYSIS

CHAPTER ELEVEN: WORDS-IN-CONTEXT QUESTIONS

CHAPTER TWELVE: LITERAL COMPREHENSION QUESTIONS

CHAPTER THIRTEEN: EXTENDED REASONING QUESTIONS

CHAPTER FOURTEEN: EXCLUSIVE SAT CONTENT

CHAPTER FIFTEEN: REVIEW AND PROBLEM SETS

CHAPTER SIXTEEN: TEST READINESS

APPENDIX: VOCABULARY: REPEAT OFFENDERS

INDEX

Acknowledgements

Full text of the passages and excerpts used in *The PowerScore ACT and SAT Reading Bible* can be found in the original sources:

Page 69, Passage: Bullen, Ross. "George Washington at the Siamese Court," *The Public Domain Review*, < https://publicdomainreview.org/2016/04/21/george-washington-at-the-siamese-court/>, published under a Creative Commons Attribution-ShareAlike 3.0 license.

Page 72, 304, 318, 356, Passage: OpenStax, Biology. OpenStax CNX. Mar 23, 2016 http://cnx.org/contents/185cbf87-c72e-48f5-b51e-f14f21b5eabd@10.8. Published under a Creative Commons Attribution License 4.0.

Page 98, Passage: Rosengarten, David. "We Are What We Eat: We are a Nation of Immigrants!," *eJournal USA: Society & Values*, July 2004: 8-9. December 2011. < http://www.ait.org.tw/infousa/zhtw/DOCS/ijse0704.pdf>

Page 132, 144, Passage: Kosman, Joshua. "A New Music for a New Century," *eJournal USA: Society and Values*. June 1998: 22-23. December 2011. < http://www.4uth.gov.ua/usa/english/arts/ijse0698/kosman.htm>

Page 156, 158, Passage 1: OpenStax Astronomy, Astronomy. OpenStax CNX. Jan 13, 2017 http://cnx.org/contents/2e737be8-ea65-48c3-aa0a-9f35b4c6a966@10.13. Published under a Creative Commons Attribution License 4.0.

Page 156, 158, Passage 2: Rowbotham, Samuel Birley. *Zetetic Astronomy*. 1881. Public domain.< https://archive.org/details/zeteticastronom00rowbgoog>

Page 199, Passage: Kamenetz, Anya. "Freedom and the Web." 2011. < http://learningfreedomandtheweb.org/Mozilla_LFW.pdf>. Published under a Creative Commons Attribution License.

Page 270, Passage: Somma, Angela. "The Environmental Consequences and Economic Costs of Depleting the Oceans," *eJournal USA: Economic Perspectives*. January 2003: 14-15. December 2006. <http://usinfo.state.gov/journals/ites/0103/ijee/somma.htm>

Page 280, Passage: Hale, Sarah Josepha. "Mary Had A Little Lamb." Public domain. < https://en.wikipedia.org/wiki/Mary_Had_a_Little_Lamb>

Page 282, Passage: Austen, Jane. *Emma*. 1815. Public domain.< https://www.gutenberg.org/files/158/158-h/158-h.htm>

Page 291, Passage: OpenStax, Introduction to Sociology 2e. OpenStax CNX. Jan 13, 2017 http://cnx.org/contents/02040312-72c8-441e-a685-20e9333f3e1d@7.9. Published under a Creative Commons Attribution License 4.0.

Page 312, 314, Figure: "Carbon Dioxide Emissions from Fossil Fuel Burning in Industrial Countries and the Rest of the World 1751-2012". Earth Policy Institute. <http://www.earth-policy.org/indicators/C52/carbon_emissions_2013>

Page 330, Passage: OpenStax Economics, Principles of Economics. OpenStax CNX. May 18, 2016 http://cnx.org/contents/69619d2b-68f0-44b0-b074-a9b2bf90b2c6@11.330. Published with a Creative Commons Attribution License 4.0.

Page 346, Passage: Wharton, Edith. *Ethan Frome*. 1911. Public domain. < https://www.gutenberg.org/files/4517/4517-h/4517-h.htm>

Page 348, Passage: Polk, Noel. "Faulkner at 100," Humanities September/October 1997. Volume 18/Number 5. December 2011. < http://www.neh.gov/news/humanities/1997-09/polk.html>

Page 350, Passage: Silberg, Bob. "The Big Question: The Reason for the Genesis Mission," NASA's Solar System Exploration. 28 June 2011. December 2011. < http://solarsystem.nasa.gov/scitech/display.cfm?ST_ID=2397>

Page 354, Passage: Reidy, Joseph P. "Black Men in Navy Blue During the Civil War," Prologue Magazine. Fall 2001, Volume 33, Number 3. December 2011. < http://www.archives.gov/publications/prologue/2001/fall/black-sailors-1.html>

Page 358, Passage: Clinton, Hillary. Address to the United Nations Commission on the Status of Women. March 12, 2010. UN Headquarters, New York City, New York.

Page 359, Figure: "Distribution of Male & Female Employment, by Sector". Food and Agriculture Organization of the United Nations. ©FAO. February 1, 2017. <http://www.fao.org/gender/infographic/en/>. Adapted with permission.

Page 362, Passage 1: "Evaluating Online Learning: Challenges and Strategies for Success," U.S. Department of Education. July 2008. December 2011. < http://www2.ed.gov/admins/lead/academic/evalonline/report_pg6.html>

About PowerScore

PowerScore is one of the world's fastest growing test preparation companies. Headquarted in Charleston, South Carolina, PowerScore offers GMAT, GRE, LSAT, SAT, and ACT preparation courses in over 150 locations in the U.S. and abroad. For more information, please visit our website at www.powerscore.com.

About the Author

Victoria Wood is a test preparation expert, specializing in the ACT and SAT. With over 20 years of experience in education and test preparation, she has assisted thousands of high school and college students in exceeding their standardized testing goals in reading, writing, and mathematics. She is the author and co-author of many acclaimed PowerScore publications, including *The GMAT Sentence Correction Bible, The GRE Verbal Reasoning Bible, The GRE Quantitative Reasoning Bible,* and *The SAT Bible Trilogy.* Currently, Ms. Wood serves as a Senior Curriculum Developer at PowerScore Test Preparation. You can reach her at vwood@powerscore.com.

CHAPTER ONE
INFORMATION FOR PARENTS

NOTE FOR TEST TAKERS: If you are a high school student preparing for the ACT or SAT, skip this chapter and start with Chapter Two. This chapter is strictly for your parents or guardians, written to help them understand the current climate of the ACT and SAT as well as the state of college admissions. Don't worry—we're not sharing any test secrets with them that we won't share with you. But we *are* going to urge them to be a supportive advocate rather than a nagging tyrant over the next few months, and we will offer them suggestions for the best ways to assist you as you prepare for the test and college admissions. Really, we promise—we are doing this for you. Trust us and jump to Chapter Two now, but be sure to show this chapter to a parent or guardian if they haven't discovered it on their own already.

↳ GRATUITOUS VOCAB
advocate (n): supporter
tyrant (adj): an oppressive ruler

A Message from the Author

Dear Parent or Guardian,

Thank you for choosing PowerScore for your child's test preparation! He or she will soon have the tools needed to unlock the secrets of the Reading tests on the ACT and the SAT. I assure you that your student is in good hands; I have been working in education for over two decades, and most of that time has been spent in standardized testing for college admissions. By now, I have taught, tutored, and counseled thousands of high school students on their quest to higher ACT and SAT scores.

But even more importantly, I, too, am a parent. I understand your desire to help your child reach his or her full potential. I know the urgency you feel to provide your child with an edge that will secure admission to the best colleges and result in the brightest future. Whether the *PowerScore ACT and SAT Reading Bible* is your first foray into test prep with your advanced sophomore or a last-minute supplemental resource for your mid-year senior, your commitment and attentiveness are evident. This chapter aims to help you focus that devotion so that it is interpreted as enthusiasm and best assists your child on his or her journey through the college admissions process.

If you ever have any questions, please do not hesitate to reach out to me through email at act@powerscore.com or sat@powerscore.com. I am always happy to help both parents and aspiring college students.

Sincerely,
Vicki Wood

Help Select a Test

With practice and dedication, all students are capable of achieving significant score increases and reaching their realistic admissions goals. While most of the responsibility for this preparation lies with students, parents must encourage and guide these active teenagers to be committed to their preparation. I know it's difficult, though, to give advice about a constantly evolving process, especially when you have little experience or have been removed from the practice for so many years. That's why I have created this chapter just for parents.

Following each section of this chapter is a summary of "How you can help" and "How you can hinder" your child in the standardized testing process. These are not meant to discourage your involvement. In fact, their intention is quite the opposite: they are provided to help you understand how you can best assist your child without adding undue pressure or implied criticism. Let's get started!

Choosing between the ACT and SAT used to be as simple as stating your home address; students on both coasts favored the SAT while the Midwest promoted the ACT. But as the tests have changed, so have students' and colleges' preferences. These days, colleges do not favor one test over the other. This is often hard for parents to believe, especially if they themselves attended an Ivy League school, but I assure you that Harvard is not subtracting points from a student who submits an ACT score. This is wonderful news for students, as it allows them to select the test that best accentuates their strengths.

But for many students, it also creates the first overwhelming decision in the college admissions process: which test to take. This is where parents are an integral asset to their children; by helping them make informed decisions, you not only teach them how to pragmatically face future dilemmas, but you relieve much of the stress surrounding college applications. Notice, however, that I use the word *help*, both in the previous sentence and in many of the headings of this chapter. It is extremely important that your child be an active participant and principal decision maker in all aspects of college admissions. You should not take over his applications, you should not write his essay, and you should not select his prospective schools. Your child will not only resent the imposition, but also "check out" of the process, which will *hinder* him in meeting his own personal goals and your goals for him. Make sure that your son or daughter is the captain of this ship, but as always, provide the wind that he or she needs to fill its sails and move forward.

So which test should your child choose? At first glance, the current ACT and SAT look quite similar. Closer inspection, however, reveals some differences

Colleges no longer have a preference for one test over the other. All 4-year colleges accept both the ACT and the SAT.

Confidence Quotation

"Parents can only give good advice or put them on the right paths, but the final forming of a person's character lies in their own hands."
-Anne Frank

that may sway students one way or the other. This book will clearly demonstrate the differences on the Reading Tests of both tests, and Chapters Three and Four will outline the disparities between the other sections. We suggest that you read these two chapters so that you understand the formats of the two tests, as much has changed on them since you were in high school. Having strong Math and Science skills and living in New England are no longer reasons to pick one test over another. Make sure that your child also reads these two chapters so that she can see if one test appeals more to her than the other.

If, after researching both tests, a student does not feel compelled to take one test over another, suggest that he take a free online practice ACT *and* SAT. You can find these free, printable tests at www.ACT.org and www.CollegeBoard. org. It is important that your child takes each test under timed conditions, all in one session, in order to mimic testing conditions as closely as possible. After scoring the tests, the concordance tables on ACT's and College Board's websites will help you see whether the ACT or the SAT best accentuates his strengths. For example, Charla scores a 26 on a practice ACT and a 1310 on a practice SAT. According to the concordance tables, a 26 ACT is equivalent to a 1270 on the SAT. Charla thus scored 40 points better with a 1310 on the SAT, and PowerScore would recommend that she pursue this test.

> By taking both a practice ACT and a practice SAT, students can get a feel for which test will best accentuate their strengths.

Of course, many students will still want to take both the ACT and the SAT, which some test prep experts and high school counselors do recommend. If your child decides to try both tests, make sure that he studies for one at a time, starting with the test that he feels will generate the best results. Because the tests are so similar, a student's preparation for one will also get him ready for the other, but he should only attempt the second test when he feels he has reached his maximum score on the first one. And he should carefully study the format differences before attempting the second exam.

> Students should focus on one test at a time and only take the other test when they feel they have maximized their score on the first one.

With the recent changes to the ACT and the SAT, there is no longer a simple way to determine which test a student should attempt. Every decision now needs to be tailored to each individual student based on his or her strengths, preferences, or performance.

How you can help:
- Understand the format of the two tests so you can participate in discussion about which test accentuates your child's strengths.
- Print out a free practice ACT and a free practice SAT.
- Proctor the test for your child at a time of his or her choosing. You can use the Virtual Proctor in the PowerScore Free Help Area to help you keep and call time.
- Print out an ACT/SAT concordance table available online so your child can compare his scores on the two tests.

> PowerScore has a Free Help Area at www.powerscore. com that offers test prep material, virtual proctors, and admissions information.

Confidence Quotation
"We fluff them and fold them and nudge them and enhance them and bind them and break them and embellish them beyond measure; then, as we drive them up to the college interviews that they've heard since birth are the gateway to the lives they were destined to lead based on nothing more than our own need for it to be true, we tell them, with a smile so tight it would crack nuts, 'Just be yourself.'"
-Heather Choate Davis, "Elijah & the SAT"

We recommend that students register online (rather than by mail) because scores are released earlier into online accounts.

How you can hinder:

- Force your child to take a practice test. He needs to be a willing participant in this process.
- Critique your child's performance on either test. These practice tests will provide "before" scores; he can (and will) improve these scores by studying for the exams. If the score is below your expectations, it is likely also below his expectations. Bringing attention to your disappointment will only chip away at his self-esteem and thus his test score; high scores are built on confidence and encouragement.
- Choose the specific test for him; this must be his decision if he is going to "buy in" to the plan.
- Insist that he prepare for both tests concurrently. The second test should only be attempted when he feels his score is maximized on the first test.

Help with Test Registration

Both the ACT and the SAT have an online test registration deadline about a month before the official exams. Registering after this date can result in late fees or in having to take the test at a non-preferred test center. Even though you have likely outfitted your teenager with a fancy phone that has incredible calendar capabilities, you should keep on top of registration and application deadlines to make sure that none are missed.

Students should register for the tests online at www.ACT.org and www.CollegeBoard.org. While both organizations still allow students to register by mail, the mail deadline is earlier and the score release is later. For these reasons, we highly recommend registering through the tests' websites.

You child must register for the test. A tutor or test prep service cannot complete the registration for her, as the tests require personal information, such as a social security number, college preferences, and an identifying photograph.

How you can help:

- Maintain a list of registration deadlines.
- Ensure that your child completes test registration at least a month prior to the test to ensure a seat at the preferred testing center.
- Provide your child with a credit card in order to pay for registration.

How you can hinder:

- Complete the registration process for your child. She will be asked questions about her current courses and college plans and accuracy is important. Plus, as I stated previously, she must be a willing and active participant.

Help Set a Target Score

Once your child has a practice test score, you can use it to help him set a realistic target score for his official test administration. The key here is the word *realistic*. A 1300 is an admirable SAT goal and it's certainly attainable if he's starting at an 1150. But if his initial test score is an 800, a 500-point score increase is not very pragmatic. Sure, it can be done, but the average student does not have 30-hours a week to invest in SAT prep for months at a time. And that's likely what it would take to make such a drastic increase.

The first step in determining a realistic score increase is to count up the number of questions your child answered correctly in each section. For example, consider Ari's results on a practice ACT:

	Score	# Correct
English	19	39/75
Math	24	35/60
Reading	22	24/40
Science	25	27/40
Composite	23	

Next, your child should set a goal for how many more questions he believes he can answer correctly in each section after serious preparation. Take Ari again. Based on these results and his confidence level in each subject, he sets realistic goals: he wants to answer 11 more questions correctly in the English test, 7 more in Math, 5 more in Reading, and 3 more in Science.

Finally, note the new score that will result should your child meet his goals. Consider Ari's projections as an example:

	Score	Correct	Increase	Goal	Goal Score
English	19	39/75	+11	50/75	23
Math	24	35/60	+7	42/60	27
Reading	22	24/40	+5	29/40	26
Science	25	27/40	+3	30/40	26
Composite	23				26

By setting a goal for increasing the number of questions he answers correctly, Ari is able to calculate a projected score for each section and thus an average of those scores, called a composite score. While he scored a 23 composite on his practice test, his projected composite goal is now a 26.

Once your child determines a realistic composite score increase, tack an extra point or two onto his ACT projection and an extra 50 points onto his SAT projection. For example, Ari's ACT target score would go from a 26 to

After completing a practice test, your child can set a goal by determining how many more questions he believes he can answer correctly in each section.

a 28. These are "reach for the stars" points; students often exceed their own expectations, so it's important that they challenge themselves to attain even more.

By setting a target score based on the number of questions he wants to answer correctly, you child has concrete goals that can be measured and evaluated. It gives him ownership in his preparation and helps him maintain focus through the process.

How you can help:
• Explain how your child can set goals for increasing the number of questions answered correctly in each section of the test.
• Discuss what realistic score increases look like.

How you can hinder:
• Insist on an unrealistic score increase.
• Insist he apply to a college with average test scores well above his target score.
• Compare his goals and scores to those of his siblings or classmates.

Help Create a Study Schedule

Despite the fact that most test takers are on the verge of adulthood, many struggle to organize their time and formulate a plan that allows for ACT or SAT preparation. Some do not even know how to effectively study! This is a perfect opportunity for a parent to assist.

Some parents choose a test preparation course or a tutor at this point so that a study schedule is generated by an expert. But if this is not an option for your child, you can certainly create a personalized schedule using this book and all available official questions.

Students should expose themselves to as many real test questions as possible during their preparation.

It's important to supply your child with as many *real* test questions as possible. There are a number of materials available that use "simulated" questions, which are created by test prep companies to mimic actual test content. While the quality of these certainly varies, as a general rule they're a poor substitute for the real thing: questions designed by the test makers and administered on previous ACTs and SATs. Real ACT questions are only available in *The Official ACT Prep Guide*, on the ACT website, and on official previously-released tests online. For the SAT, the real test questions in *The Official SAT Study Guide* are the same ones available for free on the College Board's website. PowerScore's Free Help Area is a one-stop shop that contains all of these available online ACTs and SATs.

The number of real questions available for each test is constantly changing; new editions of the *Official Guides* often include new tests and either organization may add practice tests to their websites at any given time. So it's impossible for me to provide a definitive schedule based on a prescribed number of questions for your child. Plus, I know from experience that all students are different; they come to me at different times in the process with different schedules, different skills, and different attitudes. Study plans must be individualized based on the test taker and the material available.

So to begin creating a schedule for your child, count up the number of tests and timed sections that she has available as well as the number of chapters to read in study books. Then take the time available for study and assign tasks to each week. For example, Elena is taking both tests, but she is starting with the SAT, which she will take in 12 weeks. She has six official full-length SAT practice tests, which means she has 6 Writing and Language sections, 6 Reading sections, and 12 Math Sections (6 No Calculator and 6 Calculator). She also purchased *The ACT and SAT Reading Bible* and *The Official SAT Study Guide*. Elena's schedule might resemble the following:

To help your child create a study schedule, determine the number of timed practice sections and study guide chapters available and divide these evenly among the weeks available prior to the official test.

Week 1
- Read and complete Chapters 1-5 in *The Official SAT Study Guide* (introductory material).
- Visit www.CollegeBoard.com to learn about the test and see sample questions.
- Visit the PowerScore Free Help Area to print supplemental resources.

Week 2
- Read and complete Chapters 6-12 in *The Official SAT Study Guide* (Reading Test).
- Read and complete Chapters 2-4 in *The ACT and SAT Reading Bible*.
- Take a timed Reading section from an official test (1/6).

Week 3
- Read and complete Chapters 13-17 in *The Official SAT Study Guide* (Writing and Language Test).
- Read and complete Chapters 5-7 in *The ACT and SAT Reading Bible*.
- Take a timed Writing and Language section from an official test (1/6).

Week 4
- Read and complete Chapters 18-21 in *The Official SAT Study Guide* (Math Test).
- Read and complete Chapters 8-10 in *The ACT and SAT Reading Bible*.
- Take a timed Math section from an official test (1/12).

Week 5
- Read and complete Chapters 22-24 in *The Official SAT Study Guide* (Math Test).
- Read and complete Chapters 11-12 in *The ACT and SAT Reading Bible*.
- Take a timed Math section from an official test (2/12).

Week 6
- Read and complete Chapter 13 in *The ACT and SAT Reading Bible*.
- Take a full-length timed practice test, all in one sitting. This will deplete her second Writing and Language section (2/6), her second Reading section (2/6), and her third and fourth Math sections (4/12).

Week 7
- Read and complete Chapter 14 in *The ACT and SAT Reading Bible*.
- Take a timed Reading section (3/6) and a timed Writing and Language section (3/6).

Week 8
- Read and complete Chapter 15 in *The ACT and SAT Reading Bible*.
- Take a timed No Calculator Math section (5/12) and a timed Calculator Math section (6/12).

Week 9
- Read and complete Chapter 16 in *The ACT and SAT Reading Bible*.
- Take a timed Reading section (4/6) and a timed Writing and Language section (4/6).

Week 10
- Review previous chapters in *The ACT and SAT Reading Bible*.
- Take a timed No Calculator Math section (7/12) and a timed Calculator Math section (8/12).

Week 11
- Review previous chapters in *The ACT and SAT Reading Bible*.
- Take a timed Reading section (5/6), a timed Writing and Language section (5/6), a timed No Calculator Math section (9/12), and a timed Calculator Math section (10/12).

Week 12
- Review previous chapters in *The ACT and SAT Reading Bible*.
- Take a full-length timed practice test, all in one sitting. This will deplete her last Writing and Language section (6/6), her last Reading section (6/6), and her last Math sections (12/12).

A couple of notes about this schedule: first, notice that Elena has weekly goals instead of daily goals. Because high school students have busy schedules, it is best to set a goal for the week rather than for each day. That way, unexpected events that arise will not cause her to go off schedule. And second, it is not enough to just take timed practice sections and timed practice tests. Students must review EVERY question that they missed or guessed correctly. They must understand why they missed it and how to avoid the same mistake in the future. These tests assess the same content, over and over. If your child misses a Writing and Language question which tests her knowledge of the use of *its* and *it's*, you can be sure she will see this concept again. Students must review these missed questions in order to produce substantial score increases, but in my experience, few take the initiative to do so without guidance from a teacher, tutor, or parent.

The point of these study schedules is to divide the material up as evenly as possible and to ensure that the test taker has constant contact with real test questions. If Elena crammed everything into eight weeks, she would have four weeks without any materials to study, which could cause her to forget many of the strategies and tips in the study guides. Obviously, the amount of work assigned to each child will vary based on her academic and extracurricular schedules and the number of books and practice tests she has available. Academic work ALWAYS comes before ACT and SAT preparation, but the more exposure she has to real test questions, the greater the resulting score increase.

How you can help:
- Amass as many resources with real test questions as possible.
- Create a schedule with your student that evenly distributes work over the weeks available for preparation.
- Proctor timed sections and timed practice tests (and you can use the Virtual Proctor in the PowerScore Free Help Area to help you keep time).
- Remind your child to review the questions she missed or guessed correctly after each timed section or timed practice test.
- Allow the schedule to be flexible, accepting changes as needed to accommodate your child's activities and moods. Having weekly goals instead of daily goals assists with this, as it allows for days off and breaks.

How you can hinder:
- Force your child to study a certain amount of time each day. She needs to be a willing participant in order to learn the material.
- Grade or review your child's work in her presence. This is a process she must do herself and your involvement may be interpreted as critical or overbearing.

Set weekly work goals instead of daily work goals to allow for flexibility.

Students must review questions that they missed or guessed correctly in order to maximize the value of practice tests.

Homework should always come before ACT and SAT prep.

Why should students review questions they guessed correctly? It was only through luck (and possibly the process of elimination) that they received a point on the question, so they need to review the fundamental concepts in order to avoid guessing in the future.

Help Locate Supplemental Material

If your child is like most teenagers, he probably doesn't go above and beyond what is expected of him. He's never vacuumed the car when you asked him to wash it or folded the laundry when he got his socks out of the dryer, right? It's okay—he's completely normal. And we see this in students' ACT and SAT prep, too. Even the best students rarely search out more work and additional supplements. But once again, the more a student prepares for a test, the higher the score increase. If you feel that your child's study schedule is lighter on some weeks than on others, you may want to seek out additional, brief activities to supplement his preparation.

One suggestion we have for students is that they read several articles each week from magazines that publish material that is typically more dry and difficult than that in the standard high school curriculum. You can find a list of such magazines—such as *Scientific American*, *Atlantic Monthly*, and *The Economist*—in our Free Help Area online. Print articles from assorted magazines and give him one when he has five minutes of down time, such as at the breakfast table or in the car. He doesn't have to read the whole thing— just the first 500 to 900 words—but he should be able to identify the main idea and the author's attitude when he's done. Because Reading is the most difficult section to improve upon on both tests, it's important that you start this activity early in your child's preparation. It will help him build stamina and maintain focus while reading dull passages.

Another five-minute activity is the ACT or SAT Question of the Day. Both organizations offer this service, currently in the form of an email from ACT and as an app from the College Board. Encourage your child to subscribe to these services and attempt the daily question.

You can also advise your child to use the supplemental materials in our Free Help Area. We offer flash cards, official practice tests, practice questions, and more.

There is a fine line here, though, between being seen as supportive and being seen as domineering. You would be wise to discuss supplemental materials with your child while setting up the study plan and tell him your ideas for extra help. Ask him if this is something you can assist with and then respect his decision; if he isn't on board with the plan, the extra work might actually do more harm than good.

How you can help:
- Ask your child if you can find brief, supplemental resources to help fill out his study plan.

Your child should prepare for long, dull reading passages by reading magazine articles from sources previously used on the test.

- Look for some activities or supplements that teach or reinforce the material in a new way, such as flash cards. Students learn best when material is presented in several different fashions.

How you can hinder:
- Find supplemental resources after your child tells you he is not interested.
- Find too many supplemental resources or resources that take too long to complete.

Encourage Positive Thinking

In our extensive experience with test preparation at PowerScore, from the ACT and SAT to the LSAT, the value of confidence and positive thinking is often overlooked by students and parents alike. But a confident attitude and positive thoughts can help a student increase their score by many, many points. Just search "positive thinking quotations" on the internet to find the hundreds of successful, famous individuals, both past and present, who have written about the notable effects of a positive attitude. They must all know something to have been so successful in their careers. We have strewn many of these quotations throughout the sidebars of this book. Find one or two that really resonate with you and your child and print them on an index card. Hang it where he will see those inspiring words every day.

Speak of the ACT and the SAT in a positive way around your test taker. Do not insinuate that the test is hard or difficult or that your child is not prepared. Say things like, "You have learned everything you need to know to succeed," and "I am confident that you will do well on the SAT." If you hear your child speak negatively about his abilities, make him change those words. If he says, "I am terrible at math," ask him to add "but I am great at ACT math!" If he says, "I am going to bomb this thing," make him stop and repeat "I am going to ace the SAT." Students who do well on the test never go into it thinking they are going to perform badly. It is important that you remind your child of his potential and his preparation every day.

How you can help:
- Speak positively about the test and about your child's abilities to master the test.
- Inspire him with quotations about positive thinking from famous people he admires.

How you can hinder:
- Speak negatively about the test and your own abilities or experience with the ACT or SAT. If you believe that you are "bad at math," your child rationalizes that he is genetically predisposed to also struggle with math.

Thinking positively is one of the most important--and overlooked-- strategies in test preparation.

For more information on the effects of positive thinking and pressure on standardized testing, check out the next chapter.

- Speak negatively about your child's abilities or his progress. Words have power, and if you have labeled him a poor test taker or a weak verbal student, he will believe you.

Avoid Exerting Excess Pressure

I have discussed this point a bit already in this chapter, but it's important enough that it deserves its own heading and section. The pressure surrounding college admissions tests can be paralyzing and has certainly been known to affect test scores. Students face pressure from teachers, counselors, friends, coaches, and even themselves—but what they fear most is extra pressure from Mom and Dad, the people whose opinions ultimately matter most (even if subconsciously).

When you first sit down with your child to discuss ACT and SAT planning, explain that you want to be proactive in the process but that you do not want to add pressure. Tell her that your job is to act as her ACT and SAT personal assistant, keeping her on task and helping her locate resources for study. If at any time she feels that your participation feels more like pressure than support, she needs to tell you immediately. This open discussion alone will remove so much of the pressure—imaginary or not—that your child feels comes from you.

It is also important to note to both you and your child that the entire college admissions process does not ride solely on a student's test scores. Her transcript, activity list, essays, recommendations, and interviews can offset a subpar test score. The ACT and the SAT measure very few of the attributes desired by an admissions committee; they don't reveal your child's integrity, dedication, passion, kindness, persistence, or personality. Remind her that she can shine in other areas if her testing goals are not met. Knowing this—and that she can take the test again—often helps to relieve pressure.

Again, avoid citing your own score or the scores of your other children. If those scores were lower, your child may feel bound by genetics or become complacent and accept a lower standard for herself. If those scores were higher, your child has additional pressure to try to measure up, and it's likely that she has felt this pressure throughout her academic career. All children are different, with different strengths, weaknesses, and abilities, and she needs to know that you believe and understand this.

During practice tests or timed sections, avoid expressing any disappointment in results or in your child's ability to grasp a certain concept. Never make statements like, "How could you miss this?" or "This is an easy one." What is easy for one person may be extremely difficult for another, and statements like

Give your child an 'out' by asking them to tell you if you're becoming too involved in the process.

Confidence Quotation
"While this test has some ability to predict student performance in the first year of college, it falls far short of predicting overall academic or career success and a host of other aptitudes that educators and society value, such as intellectual curiosity, motivation, persistence, leadership, creativity, civic engagement and social conscience."
-Joanne Creighton, President of Mount Holyoke College

these can kill a child's confidence. Instead, assure them that all questions are valid and that it's okay to make mistakes.

If your child is invested in attending college, she will do her best on test day, even if she isn't the most motivated or serious student on a daily basis. While she may not have the life experience that you do (and thus not understand natural consequences in the same way), she still has goals and aspirations and she knows that the test is the gateway for meeting many of those goals. Ensure her that you have confidence in her abilities and then have faith that she will perform to the best of her ability.

How you can help:
- Have an open, frank discussion with your child about your role in the process and how you want to be perceived as supportive instead of overbearing.
- Remind your child that the test is not the only factor in admissions and that she can retake it if needed.
- Have confidence and faith in your child on test day.

How you can hinder:
- Make your child feel inadequate by commenting on her performance on practice tests.
- Compare your child's scores to your own scores or to the scores of her siblings.

Help Prepare for Test Day

There are a few things you can do in the 24 hours prior to the ACT or SAT to help your child perform to the best of his ability. For one, make sure that he eats a dinner high in complex carbohydrates the night before the test. Just as athletes will use a spaghetti dinner to fuel their athletic performance, students can benefit from carbohydrates in the same way for an academic performance.

It is important that your child gets at least eight hours of sleep for the two nights preceding the test. Too often we hear students say that they were tired and lost focus during the rigorous three to four hour testing period. We know that many sporting events and extracurricular activities take place on Friday nights, but urge your teenager to be home as early as possible.

This next tip is extremely important and often hard for parents to follow: do not allow your student to study the day before the test. The brain is like a muscle, in that they both benefit from a break before strenuous competition. It is okay to study two nights before the test, but the final 24 hours should be ACT- and SAT-free and composed of relaxing activities. By taking a break, your child will be mentally refreshed and at the top of his game on test day.

When a child misses a question and someone comments that it was "an easy one," the child feels inadequate. These feelings can be toxic to ACT and SAT prep.

Confidence Quotation
"If my future were determined just by my performance on a standardized test, I wouldn't be here. I guarantee you that."
-Michelle Obama, Former First Lady of the United States

As in most of their endeavors, teenagers need sleep and healthy food to perform well on the ACT and SAT.

Did you ever struggle with a crossword puzzle clue, only to come back to it days later and realize the answer immediately? Your conscious brain took a much needed break, but your subconscious was still on the job. We want students to come into the ACT or SAT alert and rested after a similar hiatus.

On the morning of the test, ensure that your child eats a healthy breakfast. We recommend something high in protein to help the student stay energized and full. Many students complain of rumbling stomachs during the test, so send them with a bottle of water and a granola bar, bag of carrots, or other healthy snack which they can consume during a scheduled break. Try to avoid any breakfast or snack with excess sugar, as it will inevitably lead to the dreaded energy crash.

Finally, make sure your child has all of his required materials before he heads out the door on test day. He will need all of the following:

- Test Admission Ticket: This was emailed upon registration, but a new one can be printed by logging into his ACT or College Board account.
- Photo ID: Acceptable photo IDs include a driver's license and school ID. For a more detailed list of acceptable identification, see the tests' websites.
- No. 2 Pencils: Send a minimum of two pencils in case one breaks during the exam. I usually take five or six to avoid having to sharpen them after every section. Pens and mechanical pencils are not allowed.
- Eraser: Make sure that the erasers on the pencils are not stale so that mistakes can be erased completely. Stray marks can be interpreted as wrong answers.
- Calculator: Each test's website provides a list of acceptable calculators. Be sure that your child's calculator is approved and has fresh batteries.
- Watch (optional): Students cannot always depend on the clocks working at the testing center, so we suggest that they bring a wristwatch. Just make sure that it does not have any alarms, or your child can be dismissed from the test.
- Snack (optional): Help your child avoid a grumbling stomach by sending a healthy snack and a bottle of water, which he can consume during testing breaks.
- Backpack: Because food, beverages, and books are not allowed in the testing room, make sure your student takes a backpack in which to store these items. Backpacks can be placed under the desk during testing.

The following items are prohibited, so make sure your child does not take any to the testing center.

- Cell phones and other electronic devices: All electronic devices (other than permitted calculators and simple wristwatches) are prohibited and, if detected, will result in dismissal from the test. As much as we warn students to leave their cell phones and portable audio players in their cars, we repeatedly hear of violations and subsequent dismissals. The test makers are very serious about this rule.

Confidence Quotation
"The best substitute for experience is being sixteen."
-Raymond Duncan, artist and philosopher

Cell phones are not allowed at the testing center and the discovery of one will result in immediate dismissal.

- Textbooks: Obviously students cannot use a textbook or dictionary during the test. But there is often 30 to 40 minutes of downtime while they wait for the test to begin, so I recommend taking *The ACT and SAT Reading Bible*, their notes, or another test prep resource to read while they wait (provided they have a backpack to store it in when the test begins). By looking over their study material, students can help their brain "warm up" and review any last minute strategies or formulas they need for the test.
- Highlighters, colored pens and pencils, or other office supplies: If it's not on the acceptable list above, it's prohibited!

How you can help:
- The night before the test, ensure that your child eats a dinner high in complex carbohydrates.
- Encourage your child to get a minimum of eight hours of sleep the two nights before the test.
- Remind your student not to study the day before the test.
- Advise your child to eat a healthy, high-protein breakfast the morning of the test.
- Ensure that your child takes his admission ticket, photo ID, pencils, eraser, permitted calculator, watch, snack, and backpack.

How you can hinder:
- Allow your child to stay out late the night before the test.
- Force or encourage your child to "cram" in the days leading up to the test.
- Insist that your child take his cell phone in the event that you need to reach him. He will be dismissed if his phone is discovered or makes any noise.

Help Plan the Number of Test Attempts

Once your child navigates her first standardized test, a whole new set of questions is sure to arise about her results and what they mean to colleges. I will address some of that in this section, but I also suggest that you read Chapter Five, which will help you make sense of your child's ACT or SAT score.

Most high school students take the ACT or the SAT three times between their junior and senior years, which is perfectly acceptable to college admissions officers. They understand a student's desire to improve or retake a test that may not have gone well. And statistics show that most students do improve when they retake the test.

Many students come to us after receiving their first test scores. The official score report can be a sobering experience, alerting both parents and students alike to a test taker's weaker subject areas. If your child's first test scores

Chapter Five covers the scoring scale of the ACT and SAT in detail.

are not in range of the target score she set, it may be a good time to consider private tutoring or prep courses. But even if you do not enlist the help of a professional, PowerScore highly recommends that all students take their chosen test at least twice, being sure to continue studying in between attempts. It may be more difficult to decide whether a third attempt is needed. If your child's first two scores were similar, she may be feeling discouraged and doubtful about improving it. In this case, help her analyze her efforts. Did she maximize her opportunity to improve her score? Did she study as much as she could? Did she exhaust every option and resource? If the answer is "yes," then it may be time to try the other test—the ACT if she took the SAT or the SAT if she took the ACT. If the answer is "no," then she needs to recommit herself to improvement and pursue a third attempt. But as I stated in the previous section, she has to "buy into" this idea and be the one to make that decision. If you force her to take the test for a third time, I can say with a degree of certainty that her score will not improve.

Students should plan on taking the test two or three times.

Most admissions experts will caution a student not to attempt a test more than three or four times, because too many attempts can raise red flags on applications. Admissions officers will assume that a student is either not taking each attempt seriously or that she *is* serious but unable to improve. If your child has taken the ACT four times and is not seeing the improvement she wants, it may be time to look at the SAT (and vice versa).

How you can help:
• Help your child evaluate her efforts and determine whether another attempt is warranted.

How you can hinder:
• Force your child to take the test again.
• Insist your child take the test more than three or four times.

Understand College Score Policies

It's important to understand how your child's prospective school will interpret his test scores. Most colleges have policies for how applicants are to submit their test scores, and will likely fall into one of the following categories:

1. **All scores required**
   If a college requires all scores, your child MUST submit scores from all testing dates. So if he took the SAT in May, October, and December, all three sets of scores are to be submitted. This worries some parents, especially if there is a particularly low score in the child's record, but schools that require all scores usually do so in order to benefit the applicant through superscoring or taking the highest score from each section, which is explained below.

2. **All scores recommended**

Colleges that recommend all scores would prefer to see them all, most likely because they will also superscore or take the highest score from each section. This is not a requirement, however, and the student has some discretion in selecting which scores to send.

3. **Single score required**

Colleges that require students to choose a single score to submit participate in what is commonly referred to as "Score Choice."

Let's look at how each of these policies would be applied to an applicant. Consider Tony's SAT results below:

January SAT		June SAT		October SAT	
Reading	**650**	Reading	620	Reading	640
Writing	510	Writing	570	**Writing**	**590**
Math	560	**Math**	**610**	Math	600
Total	1720	Total	1800	Total	1830

If a college has an **all scores required** policy and examines all three, the admissions officers will see an overall improvement in the composite score. But more often, schools that ask for all scores will "superscore" Tony's results, meaning that they will take the highest score in each section to create a new composite score. In this case, Tony scored highest in Reading in January (650), highest in Writing in October (590), and highest in Math in June (610). His composite superscore then is 1850. It is easy to see why students, parents, and counselors often prefer colleges that superscore!

It should be noted that while many schools superscore the SAT, some of these same schools do NOT superscore the ACT. This disparity is odd and unexplained. Test prep experts and applicants have taken to social media to protest the inconsistency, and thus some colleges are starting to come around and change their ACT superscore policy. It is important to research a school's policy for both the ACT and the SAT when applying with both tests.

So back to Tony's results. If he were applying to a school that had an **all scores recommended** policy, there really is no reason for him to hold back any of the score reports. The progression shows gradual improvement, and he has a high score in each area from a different test date; to hold one of those dates back is to delete his highest score in a section.

Tony's Superscore:

Reading	650
Writing	590
Math	610
Composite	1850

Colleges have long used superscoring for the SAT, but many are just starting to superscore the ACT.

But what if Tony's results looked like this?

January SAT		June SAT		October SAT	
Reading	640	Reading	620	**Reading**	**650**
Writing	510	Writing	570	**Writing**	**590**
Math	560	**Math**	**610**	Math	600
Total	1710	Total	1800	Total	1840

Now his highest Reading score is in October, and the January test holds no high scores in any section. In this case, Tony might consider only submitting his June and October test dates. I would personally not recommend it, though: he wouldn't be following the school recommendations *and* he'd fail to reveal an important personality trait. He went up 130 points over ten months, which shows the admissions officers that he is dedicated to improvement and to his education.

When a college has a **single score required** policy, students should choose the score with the highest composite. In Tony's case, he would submit his October scores. Luckily, few schools have such stringent policies.

If you have read your child's prospective college's score reporting policy on its website and are still unsure about whether they consider scores by section (superscoring) or by date (single test scoring), have your child call the admissions department. It is extremely important that your child—not you—make this call. It serves as an impromptu interview, as the admissions officer with whom your child speaks will likely make a note about the call and put it into his admissions folder. Appearing polite, inquisitive, and interested in the university can go a long way in helping him achieve acceptance to the school. But having a parent call can send the opposite message, mainly that he is disinterested in the school and too immature to call himself.

You should never call an admissions office on your child's behalf. This is an opportunity for him to show maturity and express interest in the school, which can set him apart from other applicants.

How you can help:
- Help your child research the score policies at his prospective colleges. Be sure to note any differences between ACT and SAT policies as needed.
- Discuss with your child the benefits—or lack thereof—of submitting only some scores to schools that allow students to choose which test administrations to submit.
- Encourage your child to call a school's admission office with any questions about score reporting policies.

How you can hinder:
- Call a college's admissions department on your child's behalf.

Be Aware of Grade Inflation

On the day that ACT or SAT scores are released, I wait for the inevitable phone call: the one from a distraught parent who cannot understand why her daughter with a 4.5 GPA received an 18 on the ACT. Teachers and administrators at her daughter's school are often quick to jump on the test anxiety bandwagon, even though the girl clearly does well on her classroom tests given her high GPA. In situations like this, however, the most likely culprit is grade inflation.

Due to federal educational reform, there is enormous pressure in public schools to pass all students. In many private schools, teachers feel pressured to give higher grades than a student has earned because B's and C's can ruin her chances at top universities. This in turn spoils the private school's track record of students accepted into highly selective schools, which is often the school's strongest selling point to prospective families. What results in both public and private schools may be grade inflation, where a student's grades do not accurately reflect her true abilities.

Some grade inflation occurs from weighted classes, to which colleges may or may not give weight themselves. It can also occur from elective courses, like art, phys ed, and music (colleges usually remove these courses when determining a GPA for core classes). But much of grade inflation occurs when students are assigned higher grades than they would have earned on the traditional GPA scale so that a school's students seem more competitive to prospective colleges.

Most of today's parents are unaware of this harmful trend. When they were in high school, grade inflation was not as rampant. If they hear that their daughter has a 4.2 GPA, they assume she's in the top 5% of her class and that the ACT and SAT should be easy tasks given her aptitude. After all, the valedictorian with the 4.0 from their own high school pulled in a 34 ACT and 1520 SAT. But when their high-GPA child comes home with sub-par standardized test scores, the gig is up, for the unsuspecting parents at least. Admissions officers, on the other hand, know the deal. They keep tabs on high schools and they are well aware of which ones blow up grades and which ones do not.

So how can you tell if your child's GPA has been subject to grade inflation? There is no sure-fire way to know, but you can get a sense of whether it has occurred by looking at where students at her high school from her current class and from the past few years are being accepted to college. If her classmates all have 4.0s or higher but are only being accepted to less selective regional schools, there's a good chance grade inflation is present at the school. But if all those 4.0s are getting acceptance letters from highly selective

Confidence Quotation
"The federal emphasis on standardized assessments has become so excessive that it has modified state and district behavior in troubling ways."
-Randi Weingarten, President of the American Federation of Teachers

Grade inflation is occurring frequently in the United States. It's important to recognize so that your child does not have undue expectations placed on her.

By comparing your child's class rank percentile to her GPA, you may be able to determine whether grade inflation is occurring at her school.

schools, then grade inflation is probably not an issue. Also, ask the guidance counselor for your child's class rank. If he or she says the school does not compute class rank, this is a red flag. Admissions officers often use class rank to determine whether grade inflation is occurring, so high schools who knowingly have too many 4.0 students may slyly choose not to compute class rank.

If your child *is* provided with a rank, you may be able to determine whether grade inflation is occurring by turning it into a percentage. For example, if her rank is 50th out of 200 students, she is in the top 25% of her class (50/200 = 0.25 or class rank/total number of students = percentage). Her GPA puts her in the 75th percentile because it is higher than 75% of the student GPAs in her class (but lower than 25% of her class). Does her class rank seem to correlate with her GPA? If she is ranked in the 50th percentile but her GPA is 3.5 or higher, there is probably some grade inflation. By comparison, in the past only the top 10% of students received A's.

If you find that your child's GPA is inflated, you probably have unrealistic expectations for her ACT and SAT scores. To determine a more reasonable target score, return to her class rank and percentile and compare them to the ACT and SAT percentile tables available online. If she is in the top 25% at her high school, a corresponding ACT score is 24 (74th percentile) and an SAT score is 1160 (76th percentile). While this is not a guaranteed way to determine your child's potential on these standardized tests, it's likely to be more reliable than an inflated GPA.

How you can help:
- If you suspect that grade inflation is occurring at your child's school, adjust your expectations for her test scores.
- Understand that admissions officers are aware of grade inflation; in such cases, grades are often adjusted in a student's admissions file.

How you can hinder:
- Expect your child's ACT or SAT scores to reflect her GPA when grade inflation is suspected. This puts pressure on a test taker to perform at a level that may very well be impossible for her.

Continue Your Research

Applying to college is a daunting process for both you and your child. If you'd like to continue your education on both standardized testing and general admissions information, I recommend the following books and websites.

Books

A is for Admission:
The Insider's Guide to Getting into the Ivy League and Other Top Colleges
By Michele A. Hernàndez
Hernàndez, a former admissions officer at Dartmouth, shares secrets about how Ivy League admissions committees evaluate applicants.

Admission Matters:
What Students and Parents Need to Know About Getting into College
By Sally P. Springer, Jon Reider, and Joyce Vining Morgan
From writing essays to getting financial aid, *Admission Matters* leads parents through the process from start to finish. A great starter book for a parent new to the journey.

adMission Possible:
The "Dare to Be Yourself" Guide for Getting into the Best Colleges for You
By Marjorie Hansen Shaevitz
Another step-by-step guidebook to college admissions, Shaevitz's book sets itself apart by reminding students to be themselves and select colleges that best match their interests and personalities.

The Gatekeepers: Inside the Admissions Process of a Premier College
By Jacques Steinberg
A New York Times Bestseller, *The Gatekeepers* follows a diverse group of students applying for admission at the nation's most selective colleges, as told by a *New York Times* education reporter who was granted access to the admissions process at Wesleyan University.

Where You Go is Not Who You'll Be:
An Antidote to the College Admissions Mania
By Frank Bruni
Another *New York Times* reporter offers a new perspective on the admissions process, this time reminding students that other life decisions are more important than where they will attend college.

Confidence Quotation
"When I was a boy of fourteen, my father was so ignorant I could hardly stand to have the old man around. But when I got to be twenty-one, I was astonished at how much he had learned in seven years."
-Author unknown, but often attributed to Mark Twain

Websites

The ACT
The home of the ACT test is www.act.org. Here you can download a practice test, register for the ACT, and learn more about scoring.

College Board
The College Board, at www.collegeboard.org, is the owner of the SAT. Students can register for the test, print several practice tests, and learn more about College Board programs.

College Board Big Future
The college search on Big Future is the internet's most trusted source of information for the nation's colleges an universities. Use this site for comprehensive facts and data about your child's prospective schools, including their freshman class mid-range ACT and SAT scores.

College Navigator
The government's own college search engine, produced by the National Center for Education Statistics, with information similar to Big Future, including tuition rates, admissions information, and majors and programs.

College Confidential
The world's most savvy students use the forums on College Confidential to discuss the ACT and SAT, and the world's most savvy students' parents have a forum of their own, as well, to discuss all aspects of college admissions.

FairTest
The National Center for Fair and Open Testing works to "end the misuses and flaws of standardized testing," in part by offering a list of schools where the ACT or SAT is no longer required.

PowerScore
Visit our website for a Free Help Area, complete with test preparation materials and admissions information.

Once again, thank you for entrusting PowerScore to help raise your child's Reading score. College admissions standards and practices have changed drastically since most parents were in high school and it's much more difficult to gain admission now than it was twenty years ago, so it's important that students present their best possible ACT and SAT scores on their applications. While the brunt of this preparation falls on your child, you play an integral role in encouraging him to succeed and helping him navigate the process. And PowerScore is available to guide both of you by email at act@powerscore.com or sat@powerscore.com. We look forward to assisting you!

CHAPTER TWO:
INTRODUCTION FOR STUDENTS

Welcome to the PowerScore ACT and SAT Reading Bible! The purpose of this book is to introduce you to the types of questions you'll encounter on both the ACT and SAT Reading Test and to teach you new strategies for approaching those questions on the tests. We are certain that you can increase your Reading scores with close study and application of the PowerScore techniques.

Because access to accurate and up-to-date information is critical, we have devoted a section of our website to Reading Bible students. This free online resource area offers supplements to the book material, answers questions posed by students, suggests study plans, and provides updates as needed. There is also an official book evaluation form that we strongly encourage you to use. The exclusive PowerScore ACT and SATReading Bible online area can be accessed at:

www.powerscore.com/readingbible

The concepts and techniques discussed in this book are drawn from our live ACT and SAT courses, which we feel are the most effective in the world. If you find that you need a more structured learning environment, or would just like to participate in a live classroom setting, please visit our website to learn about our course offerings.

If we can assist you in your ACT and SAT preparation in any way, or if you have any questions or comments, please do not hesitate to contact us via e-mail at act@powerscore.com or sat@powerscore.com. Additional contact information is provided at the end of this book. We look forward to hearing from you!

This chapter and the next three chapters of this book cover the format of the ACT and the SAT and their Reading sections. While the text may be heavy at times, we recommend you thoroughly cover these chapters first so that you understand the construction of the test. However, if you are anxious to begin studying for the tests, you can skip to Chapter Six, provided you return to these introductory chapters at a later date.

Please do not hesitate to write in this book! Take notes, underline important sentences, and complete the problems presented. Your test success depends on your understanding of the concepts presented here, and achievement will only come with study and application.

Test Twins: The ACT and the SAT

With a renewed national focus on standards in education, both the ACT and SAT were subjected to changes in the 2015-2016 school year. The ACT experienced some minor alterations, which most test takers didn't even notice, while the SAT underwent a major overhaul, changes that were impossible for students to ignore. The result was a pair of tests that are now so similar in Reading that the untrained eye would be unable to distinguish them if the formatting were removed.

There are, however, subtle contrasts between the Reading tests, which we will explain in subsequent chapters. These differences, though, are not enough to warrant our students spending time and money on a second book. As one of our senior instructors said, "They are twins with different haircuts." The ACT and SAT Reading Bible will fully prepare the student taking only the ACT, the student taking only the SAT, and the student taking both tests. Throughout the book we will alert you to strategies and ideas that only apply to one test or the other so that you can focus on a specific test or understand how the tests differ if you are planning to take both of them.

In the next two chapters, we explain the format of the two tests in detail, but let's take a brief look at how the tests compare:

♣ *GRATUITOUS VOCAB*
subtle (adj): difficult to detect
subsequent (adj): coming later
warrant (vb): to justify

The ACT and the SAT are so similar now that it doesn't make sense to buy two different books if you are taking both tests.

General Test Information	
The SAT	The ACT
Three subject areas: Reading, Math, and Writing/Language	Four subject areas: Science, Reading, Math, and English
Composite score from 400-1600	Composite score from 1-36
Optional essay section	Optional essay section
Four answer choices	Four answer choices
No penalty for guessing	No penalty for guessing
3 hours, 45 minutes without Essay or 4 hours, 35 minutes with Essay	2 hours, 55 minutes without Essay or 3 hours, 35 minutes with Essay

Science	
The SAT	The ACT
No dedicated Science section; science questions occur randomly in Math, Reading, and Writing	One scored section 40 questions 35 minutes

Reading	
The SAT	The ACT
One scored section	One scored section
5 passages; 1 set of paired passages	5 passages; 1 set of paired passages
52 questions	40 questions
65 minutes	35 minutes
Question types: Words-in-Context (13%-17%), Literal Comprehension (20%-30%), Extended Thinking (30%-40%), Science Synthesis (10%-12%)	Question types: Words-in-Context (5%-10%), Literal Comprehension (30%-40%), Extended Thinking (50%-60%)

Math	
The SAT	The ACT
Two scored sections	One scored section
Calculator allowed on one section	Calculator allowed
Some formulas provided	No formulas provided
58 questions	60 questions
80 minutes	60 minutes
Content tested: Pre-Algebra and Data Analysis (28%), Algebra (35%), Algebra II (27%), Geometry and Trigonometry (10%)	Content tested: Pre-Algebra (20%-25%), Algebra (15%-20%), Algebra II (15%-20%), Geometry (20%-25%), Trigonometry (5%-10%)

Writing/Language and English	
The SAT	The ACT
One scored section	One scored section
4 passages	5 passages
44 questions	75 questions
35 minutes	45 minutes
Content tested: Grammar/usage (45%) and rhetorical skills (55%)	Content tested: Grammar/usage (45%-60%) and rhetorical skills (40%-55%)

Confidence Quotation
"Whatever the mind can conceive, it can achieve."
-W. Clement Stone, businessman and author

As you can see, the tests are remarkably similar, testing identical content often in nearly identical format. In the next two chapters we will fully explain each test's Reading format, but before we look closely at the details, let's address your attitude toward the two tests.

Rethinking the ACT and SAT

↳ GRATUITOUS VOCAB
undermine (vb):
to weaken

The ACT and SAT are unlike any classroom exams you have ever encountered, and your potential for success depends on your ability to change your mind-set about the tests. Most students enter a test center with several assumptions that affect the way they approach the test. If believed, these toxic thoughts can undermine your confidence and poison your final results. It is imperative that you begin thinking about the ACT and the SAT in a new way, and avoid saying or believing any of the following toxic thoughts:

Toxic Thought #1:
"I am not good at taking reading comprehension tests."

Reading tests from high school are designed to measure your comprehension of material that was previously read in school. Often you are assigned a text to read in a given period of time and the test occurs days or even weeks after you complete your reading. If you struggle with these tests, it is most likely because you have forgotten what you read. And given the normal schedule of a typical high school student, it's no wonder you cannot remember some boring story or article you read last week.

↳ GRATUITOUS VOCAB
curriculum (n):
course of study

The reading passages on the ACT and the SAT are not designed to test your knowledge of high school reading curriculum or your long-term memory. Instead, you are asked to immediately answer questions about a text that you have just read. Because these are standardized tests, there are patterns to the questions and to the right and wrong answers, all of which we will teach you in this book.

It is important to stop saying, "I am not good at taking reading tests." This thought has more power than you know, and once spoken, its negative potential can spread like a virus. You must begin thinking and saying, "I am great at answering ACT and SAT Reading questions." Just as a negative statement can negatively influence your performance, a positive statement can help boost your achievement. If you slip and think or say "I am not good at taking reading comprehension tests," counter the negative energy by adding, "but I'm great at answering ACT and SAT Reading questions."

Test anxiety is often caused by toxic thoughts.

Toxic Thought #2:
"I am not good at vocabulary or reading."

If you believe the toxic thought, "I am not good at vocabulary or reading," it's quite likely that someone—a teacher, a parent, or even a peer—once said or indirectly told you that you were not good at language arts. These words are especially influential during middle school, when students are the most susceptible to evaluation by others. Maybe it was a 'C' you received from

Mrs. Crawford in Literature class, or maybe it was your father saying, "I read *Hamlet* when I was much younger than you," or maybe it was even your best friend telling you she received a 98% on the same test on which you scored a 78%. Whatever they said, you heard, "You are not good at vocabulary or reading." And, as we noted previously, words have power. You internalized this sentence, and began your life as a person who is not good at reading the English language. You likely never did well in English class again and shied away from any elective courses that focused on reading or language skills. You believed you weren't good at language arts, and this toxic thought spread to your teachers, parents, and peers. They did not think you were very good at reading either, and thus didn't expect very much from you when it came to any language arts course. One bad writing experience led to many more, which led to other people indirectly telling you that you were not good at reading. Someone might even be telling you right now to concentrate on the Math sections of the ACT and SAT because you have a better chance of improving in the math portion than in the verbal portion.

What a sad situation to have resulted from one simple statement so long ago! Can you imagine where you might be if someone had told you that you were good at language arts? Think about your classmates who *are* good at their verbal courses—I bet you can remember specific instances in which people praised them for their abilities in reading and writing. Thoughts and words are so powerful.

It is time to stop thinking that you are bad at reading. For one thing, you may have misunderstood the person whose words or actions led you to believe they thought you were bad at language arts. What if Mrs. Crawford gave you a 'C' because you talked too much in class? What if your dad brought up early Shakespearean readings simply to make a comment about how much school has changed since he was a student? What if your friend lied about her 98% because she was embarrassed about her real score?

If you can pinpoint the moment that you were first "told" you were bad at reading, can you think of any alternative meanings the speaker might have had? Can you look back and see how things might have been different if you had taken the comment a different way?

Another reason that you must stop putting down your reading abilities is that the ACT and SAT are much different from high school writing and grammar tests. Like we said on the previous page, the questions test your immediate recall and interpretation of the text. We will give you the tools you need to succeed on the Reading section and improve your scores.

You must banish all negative thoughts concerning your abilities in language arts. If you believe that you are not good at reading, you will not be receptive to the new techniques covered in this book. You must also begin thinking

Confidence Quotation
"A successful person is one who can lay a firm foundation with the bricks that others throw at him or her."
-David Brinkley, newscaster

Learn to think and speak positively about the test and your abilities to master it. No perfect scorer ever went into the test hating it. They saw it as a challenge that would showcase their strengths.

✦ GRATUITOUS VOCAB
receptive (adj): open or willing to ideas

positively about reading and vocabulary. Anyone can be good at the Reading section of the ACT or SAT with a little practice. If you slip and think, "I am bad at reading," add a positive clause at the end: "but I am great at ACT and SAT Reading."

Toxic Thought #3:
"I have to do well on the ACT and SAT."

The pressure surrounding your performance on college entrance tests can be colossal. It may seem like everything—from admissions to scholarships to pride—is riding on those few hours spent huddled over a bubble sheet. But the very thought that the test *can* cost you everything *will* cost you everything.

One of our instructors takes the SAT at least once a year in order to keep up with any new trends on the test. There is no pressure on her to do well, as she has already attended college and no one will ever see her results unless she chooses to share them. She usually scores above a 750 on each section of the test. One year, however, her friends started making wagers on how they thought she would do. One friend had so much confidence in her, he made a hefty wager that she would score a 1550 or better. He promised to give the instructor half his winnings if she could win the bet. She didn't think it would be too difficult, as she had already made that score several times. But on test day, the pressure started to get to her. She made it through the Reading section and the Writing & Language Arts section, but when she reached the first Math section, she panicked when she didn't know how to solve a question in the middle of the test. As she tried to find a solution, a little voice in the back of her head started saying, "There goes the money! He's going to kill me. I can't believe I can't solve this medium-level question!" The more she panicked, the more questions she started to misread or misunderstand. When time was called, she still had three questions unanswered and she had guessed on four others. She went into the hallway and regrouped; by leaving three questions blank and possibly missing more, it was impossible to now get a 1550. The money was gone and there wasn't anything she could do about it. She took a deep breath and went back in, knowing the pressure was off.

When she got her score report a few weeks later, she contacted us to share her story and her interesting results. She did indeed miss the 1550, as she suspected, but what was so intriguing was her location of errors. In the Reading section, which she thought she had aced, she missed three questions. In the first Math section, she missed the three omitted, two of the four that she guessed on, and two more that she thought she had done correctly. After that section, the pressure had been relieved, and her remaining sections had a direct consequence: she did not miss another question on the test.

GRATUITOUS VOCAB
colossal (adj): huge

Confidence Quotation
"It's not who you are that holds you back, it's who you think you're not."-Denis Waitley, productivity consultant

She wanted to share her story with us because it reminded her how students feel when taking the ACT and SAT, and revealed to her how the slightest bit of pressure can endanger a test score. Adults sometimes forget about the pressure surrounding this test, because they haven't taken it in so long and because they are no longer under the illusion that the test is the ultimate element for college admissions. If one of our instructors was so affected over a friendly bet, we can only imagine how our students feel when admissions and thousands of dollars of scholarship money are on the line.

Many students want to blame the pressure on their parents, their future college, their teachers, or even the test itself. But the truth is that you are the one creating the pressure. If you did not care about your future, nothing your parents or teachers said about the importance of the ACT and SAT would matter at all. You would simply shrug them off. In fact, you would not be reading this book right now. Your parents would have purchased it for you, and you would have thrown it on your desk or under your bed with no intention of reading it, because college entrance tests are not a priority for you. Just the fact that you are reading this sentence assures us that you are the creator of any pressure you are experiencing concerning college admissions. You want to go to college. You probably want to go to a specific college. You may even want to win scholarship money based on a test score. The very existence of these desires creates a fear of not fulfilling the desires, which in turn creates pressure. Marcus Aurelius the Wise, one of the last great Roman Emperors, wrote "If you are distressed by anything external, the pain is not due to the thing itself, but to your estimate of it; and this you have the power to revoke at any moment."

> You control the stress you feel surrounding the ACT and SAT. Learning to control the pressure takes effort, but will be rewarded on the test and throughout your life.

Marcus Aurelius knew the secret to ACT and SAT success over 1700 years before these tests were even invented: you must revoke the power you have given the ACT and SAT in order to avoid the pressure associated with them. You cannot make these tests the single measure of your achievements and you cannot believe that they have the ability to ruin your future.

Your test score is only one component of your college admissions folder. Admissions officers will also be looking at your application, transcript, other test scores, activity list, essays, recommendations, and possibly even an interview. A college is looking for the most dynamic individuals to fill their hallowed halls, and while test scores can reveal a person's potential academic success, they do little to show character and integrity. For this reason, some schools—especially those that specialize in liberal arts—no longer require the ACT or the SAT. And in most schools where the ACT and the SAT are required, students can offset a subpar test score or average grades by documenting initiative in an academic pursuit or passion for a single extracurricular activity.

> ✿ GRATUITOUS VOCAB
> *dynamic* (adj): marked by productive activity and change

> For a list of colleges that do not require the ACT or SAT, visit www.fairtest.org.

You should also remember that this is not your only chance to take a college entrance test. If your score does not meet your expectations, you have options. Both ACT and College Board offer programs designed to relieve test anxiety and maximize student achievement that allow you to choose which individual test administration you would like to send to colleges. This means that an uncharacteristic score never has to be revealed to any admissions program. Or, if you choose not to use these programs, many colleges will "superscore" your ACT or SAT results, using only your highest scores on each section. For example, say you take the SAT in January and receive a 630 on Math and a 480 in Evidence-Based Reading and Writing. You retake the test in June and score a 600 on Math and a 590 in Evidence-Based Reading and Writing. Colleges that use this policy will only look at the 630 in Math and the 590 in Evidence-Based Reading and Writing, giving you a total of 1220 on the SAT. The lower scores are ignored. Similarly, let's say that your first attempt at the ACT landed you a 19 in Math, a 24 in English, a 22 in Reading and a 27 in Science. When you took the test a second time, you scored a 25 in Math, a 25 in English, a 27 in Reading, and a 24 in Science. Your superscore would be a 25 in Math, a 25 in English, a 27 in Reading and a 27 in Science, for a composite of 26. To find out how your prospective colleges view multiple test scores, call their admissions departments. Knowing that you have other options and opportunities should relieve much of the stress surrounding the test.

Also, don't forget that the ACT and the SAT are standardized tests, meaning that every ACT is similar to other ACTs and every SAT is similar to other SATs. Similar tests have patterns, as there is a finite number of concepts tested on both tests. If you learn all of these patterns and concepts, you will have no problem mastering the test. This knowledge should give you the confidence you need to do well and banish any fear or anxiety surrounding the tests.

Finally, remember that the ACT and SAT are not IQ tests, nor are they predictors of how well you will do in college. The makers of the test would like you to believe otherwise, but test prep instructors can give you many examples of students with average IQs and exceptional test scores. The ACT and SAT are beatable tests. The concepts can be learned and mastered by every student. The ACT simply tests how well you will do on the ACT and the SAT simply tests how well you will do on the SAT; they do not indicate how well you will do in the rest of your life. Do not overinflate their importance.

The moral of the story is that you do not *have* to do well on the ACT and SAT. It would be great if you did, but there is not an obligation to do so, and even if your score is below your expectations, you can take the test again. To obsess on a particular score will only keep you from reaching your ultimate potential on the test. You must change your mantra for the ACT and SAT. Instead of worrying about what you *have* to do, assert what you *will* do: "I will do well

For more information on how colleges interpret multiple test scores, see pages 16-18 of Chapter One.

♣ GRATUITOUS VOCAB
prospective (adj):
potential; of the future

♣ GRATUITOUS VOCAB
mantra (n):
repeated phrase

on the ACT and SAT." Recite this sentence several times a day throughout your preparation. Write it down and hang it from your bathroom mirror so you see it every morning and every night. If you begin to panic during the test, take several deep breaths while remembering you always have options. You will do well on the college entrance exams.

Power Thoughts

As you work through this book, there are three thoughts on which you should stay focused. These thoughts empower you:

> *"I am great at taking the ACT and SAT."*
> *"I am great at ACT and SAT Reading."*
> *"I will do well on the ACT and the SAT."*

If any toxic thoughts begin to seep into your conscious, immediately recite an empowering thought and then reread this section. If you begin to feel pressure, think about how you can gain control of the situation while reciting an empowering thought. We cannot adequately stress the power of positive thinking. You must believe in yourself and in your abilities if you want to do well on the ACT and SAT.

To aid you in your visualization of success, we have placed a series of quotations on positive thinking and confidence in the margins of this book. If certain quotations particularly inspire you, rewrite them on index cards and hang the cards on your mirror, locker, refrigerator, bulletin board, or somewhere else that you can read them every day before the ACT and SAT. Learning to visualize your full potential takes practice and repeated affirmations.

Confidence Quotation
"Confidence is preparation. Everything else is beyond your control." -Richard Kline, actor

✦ GRATUITOUS VOCAB
affirmations (n): positive assertions

About This Book

The PowerScore ACT and SAT Reading Bible is organized into several sections. The first six chapters offer an introduction to the ACT and SAT and their Reading sections, highlighting basic information and the fundamentals of success on the tests. The following seven chapters cover the Reading sections in depth and offer specific strategies for improvement. Chapter Fourteen explains content that is exclusively tested on the SAT, and the last two chapters offer practice problem sets and a final review.

Throughout the book, we use the margins to highlight important information. Some of these margin notes have specific topic names to help you organize your review of the book. The notes titled "Tips and Tricks" call attention to shortcuts and tricks designed to save time on the test. The notes called "Caution: Test Trap" warn students about common wrong answer choices and mistakes made by previous test takers. Finally, the sidebars designated "Gratuitous Vocab" provide the definitions of vocabulary words used in the text. While neither the ACT nor SAT advertise themselves as vocabulary tests, you can expect several questions using academic-level words, so a little extra vocabulary help will not be wasted study time. You will also find an appendix of commonly used vocabulary words on both tests at the end of this book.

The ACT Reading Test and the SAT Reading Test are so similar that this book will prepare you for both tests. If content is tested on only one test, we will alert you with an "ACT ONLY" or "SAT ONLY" note in the margin. Chapter Fourteen thoroughly covers aspects of the SAT Reading Test that are not included on the ACT.

Because access to accurate and up-to-date information is critical, we have devoted a section of our website to ACT and SAT Reading Bible students. This free online resource area offers supplements to the book material, questions posed by students and their answers, and updates as needed. There is also an official book evaluation form that we strongly encourage you to use. The exclusive ACT and SAT Reading Bible online area can be found at:

www.powerscore.com/readingbible

We strongly recommend purchasing *The Real ACT Prep Guide* and/or *The Official SAT Study Guide*, depending on which test or tests you are planning to take. These are the only books with real test questions, and it is imperative that you practice with tests produced by the test makers.

If we can assist you in your ACT or SAT preparation in any way, or if you have any questions or comments, please do not hesitate to contact one of our helpful instructors via email at act@powerscore.com or sat@powerscore.com. We look forward to hearing from you!

≋TIPS and TRICKS≋
Look to Tips and Tricks for shortcuts and time-saving techniques.

⚘ CAUTION: TEST TRAP
Don't fall into the traps set for you by the ACT and College Board. Learn to avoid these traps with these margin notes.

⚘ GRATUITOUS VOCAB
gratuitous (adj): free

◎ ACT ONLY ◎
When something applies to only one of the tests, watch for ACT ONLY and SAT ONLY bulletins.

CHAPTER THREE:
INTRODUCTION TO THE ACT

If you haven't yet taken an ACT or a PreACT, you may be wondering about the general format of the test. This chapter will explain the fundamentals of the test and look briefly at the English, Math, and Science sections to give you a clear view of the "whole picture."

This chapter addresses the ACT only. If you are planning to take the SAT but not the ACT, you should skip to the next chapter.

◎ ACT ONLY ◎
If you are taking the SAT but not the ACT, move on to Chapter Four.

If you are intimately familiar with the format of the test or if you are anxious to begin preparing for the Reading portion of the test, you can skip to Chapter Six where we begin discussing the Reading test in depth. But we would encourage you to return to these introductory chapters before taking your ACT.

The ACT debuted in 1959 to compete with the SAT. While the SAT assessed critical thinking, the ACT was developed to more accurately test what students were learning in high school. Because the exam was created in Iowa, the ACT dominated the Midwest and Central regions of the United States and this fact remained true until the turn of the millennium. As more universities began to accept either test, students in SAT-traditional testing areas began to take both tests and by 2012, the ACT had overtaken the SAT for the most number of test takers.

The ACT was originally considered a "Midwest test" but is now taken by students all over the United States.

This, along with new state standards for curriculum, led to changes for the SAT and then the ACT. Now the two tests are extremely similar and assess the same content. It was once rumored that the ACT was "easier" than the SAT—a brilliant marketing ploy that contributed to the rise in ACT test takers—but the two tests resemble each other so much now that you cannot really argue that one is less difficult than the other. The SAT is more text-heavy but provides much more time per question than the ACT, so it really comes down to a preference at this point. Most guidance counselors will advise you to take both tests to find the one on which you perform best, since all US colleges and universities now accept both tests.

The Format of the ACT

The ACT, which assesses a student's knowledge of English, Math, Reading, and Science skills learned in school, is a standardized test used for college admissions. The goal of the test is to predict a student's success at the university level, which helps admissions officers select applicants who will prosper despite the rigors of their school. The ACT is written by testing experts called psychometricians, who consult with high school and college teachers, for a company called ACT, Inc. The ACT has 4 sections, which takes students a total of two hours and fifty-five minutes to complete:

The ACT was first administered in 1959 and originally stood for "American College Testing Program." Now the acronym has no meaning.

Section	Question Types	Time Limit
English	75 multiple-choice questions (based on five sets of passages)	45 minutes
Math	60 multiple-choice questions	60 minutes
Reading	40 multiple-choice questions (based on four sets of passages)	35 minutes
Science	40 multiple-choice questions (based on seven sets of passages)	35 minutes
Writing (Optional)	1 essay analyzing arguments and developing an opinion	40 minutes

The four scored sections are always presented in the same order:

Section 1: English
Section 2: Math
Section 3: Reading
Section 4: Science

The optional Writing section is given at the end of the test.

◎ ACT ONLY ◎
The SAT does not alternate choices between odd- and even-numbered questions. For the ease of discussion, we will use A, B, C, and D as answer choices in all questions after this chapter.

The multiple-choice questions in English, Reading, and Science have four answer choices. Odd-numbered questions in these sections have choices A, B, C, and D, while even-numbered questions have the options F, G, H, and J. The Math test uses five answer choices: A, B, C, D, and E in odd-numbered questions and F, G, H, J, and K in even-numbered questions. The test makers use the alternating answer choices to make it easier for you to bubble in your answer sheet and to help prevent "bubbling mistakes" when skipping questions.

Other ACT Subject Areas

THE ENGLISH TEST

The English score is determined by 75 multiple-choice questions that accompany five passages containing grammatical and rhetorical errors. The passages span a wide variety of topics and styles, from informal personal anecdotes to formal biographies of famous people, but they are usually very easy to read. Each passage has numbered underlined portions; in some cases, a single word is underlined, and in others, a phrase or entire clause is underlined.

Each numbered underlined section corresponds to a same-numbered multiple-choice question with four possible answers. The questions will line up visually with the corresponding text. Let's study an example paragraph and question set:

⁂ GRATUITOUS VOCAB
rhetorical (adj): used for style
anecdotes (n): short, amusing story

The North and South having fought
——————
1

the Civil War with a drastically different

set of assets. The South had the advantage

of fighting the war on the home field where

the vast majority of citizens supported the

Confederacy. 2 Not only were Northerners

1. A. NO CHANGE
   B. fought
   C. had fought
   D. OMIT the underlined portion

2. The writer is considering deleting the preceding sentence. If the writer does this, the paragraph would primarily lose:
   F. background information about the causes of the Civil War.
   G. evidence of different assets for the North and the South.
   H. a description of battle fields during the Civil War.
   J. reasons why the war was not fought in the North.

divided in there support of the war, but
——
3

they had to fight in enemy territory where

military orders from Washington were slow

to arrive, if they made it through enemy

lines at all. This, however, is essentially

where the Southern advantages ended.

3. A. NO CHANGE
   B. they're
   C. their
   D. one's

The ACT English Test, which is always the first section of the ACT, assesses your ability to identify and correct grammatical, mechanical, and rhetorical errors in context.

To reveal the secrets of the English section on the ACT, visit www.powerscore. com to learn about our courses and other publications.

Curious about the answers? 1) B, 2) G, 3) C

The ACT Mathematics Test, the second section of the ACT, includes content from Arithmetic, Algebra, Geometry, Algebra II, Trigonometry, Coordinate Geometry, Data Analysis, and Statistics.

THE MATH TEST

The Math score is determined by 60 multiple-choice questions, which have five answer choices:

1. If $3^y = 5$, then what is the value of 3^{2y}?
    A. 2.5
    B. 5
    C. 10
    D. 20
    E. 25

2. There are 496 employees in a company, one of whom is to be selected at random to win a car. If the probability that a supervisor will be selected is $\frac{3}{16}$, how many supervisors work at the company?
    F. 31
    G. 64
    H. 93
    J. 165
    K. 403

3. In the figure below, a square with sides of length 10 is inscribed in a circle. What is the area of the circle?

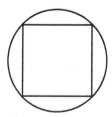

    A. 10π
    B. 25π
    C. 50π
    D. 75π
    E. 100π

Certain calculators are permitted but formulas are not provided.

To learn more about how to ace the Math section of the ACT, check out our website for courses and publications at www.powerscore.com.

The Reading section, which we begin to discuss in Chapter Six, follows the Math potion of the ACT.

Answers: 1) E, 2) H, 3) C

THE SCIENCE TEST

Following the Reading section is the Science test. The Science score is determined by 40 multiple-choice questions in six or seven different science-themed "passages." The passages typically include a brief explanation and two or three tables, charts, or diagrams. Consider a basic example:

> Many bird species are migratory. A team of ornithologists undertook a study in which they counted migrating bird species passing through the area, capturing them in mist nets (nylon mesh nets nearly invisible to birds). The results for three months of their study are given in Figure 1 (average number of species captured daily in mist nets during spring migration).

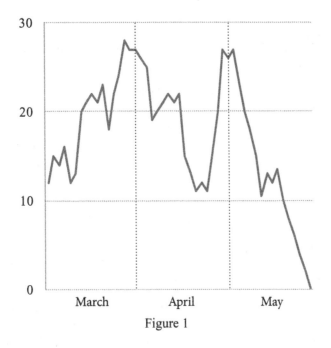

Figure 1

1. According to Figure 1, at which point in the spring migration were the fewest number of species present in the area?
   A. Mid-April
   B. Early March
   C. Early May
   D. Late May

To learn more about the intricacies of the Science test, check out our website for courses and publications at www.powerscore.com.

The Science Test assesses reading comprehension and data analysis skills, not knowledge of biology, chemistry, physics, or other sciences.

Answer: 1) D

THE OPTIONAL WRITING TEST

Students have the option of paying an additional fee to take the ACT Writing Test, which is an essay question that occurs at the end of the test. Some colleges require Essay results, so it's important to check with your prospective schools before registering for the test.

If you chose to take the Essay, you will have 40 minutes to write a response that analyzes three different perspectives of an issue and provides your own view of the topic. The task is similar on each ACT, and is followed by the prompt and three perspectives. Consider an example:

Check with your prospective colleges to see if they require the Optional Writing Test.

Essay Task

Write an organized, rational essay in which you analyze three perspectives on new kindergarten educational standards. Ensure that you:

- explore and assess the three perspectives
- record and develop your own view of the topic
- explain how your view and perspectives given are related

You may agree fully, partially, or not at all with the given perspectives. Be sure to support your views with evidence and specific examples.

Kindergarten Requirements

New kindergarten educational standards have become much more demanding than ever before. By the end of the school year, five and six year old students are required to be reading basic texts and writing simple sentences. The amount of time dedicated to literacy has increased by over 200% in some school districts, while the time dedicated to play—both outside and in the classroom—has been reduced significantly, with a single recess reported in most schools despite a full-length school day. Given the importance of education, it is necessary to analyze the implications of increased demands in kindergarten.

Perspective One
Young children learn best through play. Removing play from the classroom will lead to older students with limited knowledge and who are unable to reason critically.

Perspective Two
Students who are not exposed to print before kindergarten can benefit from intense literacy education during their first year of school. By teaching them to read in kindergarten, they can "catch up" with the other students.

Perspective Three
Children are not developmentally ready to read until ages 6 or 7. Forcing kindergarten students to read before this time can cause burnout and a dislike for learning.

⚑ GRATUITOUS VOCAB
implication (n):
something suggested or naturally understood

Testing Schedule

The ACT is offered six times a year, usually in September, October, December, February, April and June.

You should take your first ACT during the spring of your junior year, making sure that you have completed Algebra I, Geometry, and Algebra II. If your high school offers a grammar course, also take this class prior to registering for the ACT. Because the ACT is considered a junior-level test, it is wise to take the exam when junior-level material is still current and fresh in your mind. The test is offered in April and June; choose the administration that works best with your end-of-school-year schedule.

Although PowerScore recommends taking the test during your junior year, it is extremely important that you are fully prepared prior to taking the ACT. Be sure to download and take the free practice tests from the ACT website. The accompanying score report will help you determine if you are ready for the ACT. If you find that you need additional help, consider a prep course or private tutoring. You can learn about the courses and tutoring packages that PowerScore offers at www.powerscore.com.

If your spring score does not meet your expectations, you have several more opportunities to try again during the fall of your senior year. In fact, most students take the test two or three times. Note, however, that most colleges do not accept scores from the February administration from seniors applying for the fall of that same year.

Confidence Quotation
"A man is but the product of his thoughts; what he thinks, he becomes."
-Mahatma Gandhi, Indian activist

The PreACT

The PreACT is a standardized test program used to help students gauge their performance on the ACT. Although it is a program owned by the ACT, the PreACT is administered to sophomores by local high schools any time between September and June.

The PreACT is a shorter and slightly easier version of the ACT. Most of the concepts tested on the ACT are also tested on the PreACT, and you will receive a score from 1 to 36 just as on the real ACT.

Most students take the PreACT because they want to practice for the real ACT. Unlike the PSAT, the preliminary test for the SAT, there are currently no scholarships associated with the PreACT.

Studying for the PreACT with this book

Because the ACT and PreACT are so similar, students studying for the PreACT Reading section will greatly benefit from studying this book. All of the material covered in the following chapters can and may appear on the PreACT.

Because there are no scholarships associated with the PreACT (as there are with the PSAT), there is no reason to study for the test.

Yet we urge you not to study for the PreACT. Since there are no scholarships associated with your results, there is really no reason to try to beat the test. It would be better to take the PreACT without any preparation so that you can get an accurate "before" score; your results will reveal your strengths and weaknesses and you will be able to create an effective plan of attack then for the real ACT.

High school has enough tests for you to worry about; the PreACT should not be one of them.

Chapter Summary

Format of the ACT

- There are four tested subjects in a specific order: 1) English, 2) Math, 3) Reading, and 4) Science.
- The test takes a total of two hours and fifty-five minutes to complete.
- The odd-numbered questions have answer choices A, B, C, and D (and E in Math), while the even-numbered questions have answers labeled F, G, H, and J (and K in Math).

Other ACT Subject Areas

- The English test has 75 questions about five passages, covering grammar and rhetoric rules for standard English. You have 45 minutes to complete this section.
- The Math section includes 60 questions in 60 minutes about Arithmetic, Algebra, Algebra II, Geometry, Coordinate Geometry, Trigonometry, Statistics, and Data Analysis.
- The Science portion has 40 questions about 6 to 7 passages with tables, graphs, and figures. There is a 35 minute time limit for the section.
- The Writing test is optional and requires you to analyze three different perspectives of an issue and provide your own view of the topic

Other Information

- The test is offered six times a year, typically in September, October, December, February, April and June. Most students should take the test for the first time in the spring of their junior year.
- The PreACT is great practice for the ACT but you should not study for it as there are currently no scholarships associated with it.

Confidence Quotation
"All you can do is plant your seed in the ground, water it, and believe. That is what allowed me to be in this position right now. I would not stop believing."
-Tyler Perry

CHAPTER FOUR:
INTRODUCTION TO THE SAT

It's important to understand what is tested on all sections of the SAT and not just on the Reading test. In this chapter, we are going to look at the general format of the SAT and PSAT, including the Math and Writing sections, so that you have a clear understanding of the test as a whole. We will begin talking about the Reading section of the SAT in Chapter Six, but if you are anxious to get started, you can skip ahead and return to these introductory chapters at a later time.

This chapter addresses the SAT only. If you are planning to take the ACT but not the SAT, you should skip to the next chapter.

The SAT, developed and administered by the College Board, was the first American college entrance test, premiering in 1926 as the Scholastic Aptitude Test. It has undergone many changes since that time, the most recent occurring in 2016 when it was redesigned to align with state standards for high school curriculum. These changes also brought the SAT more in line with the ACT so that the tests have extremely similar Reading and Writing/English sections and test the exact same concepts in Math.

When the ACT debuted in 1959, it secured the Midwest and Central regions of the United States as its main market, so the SAT was preferred in the South and the West and was particularly popular in the Ivy League-laden Northeast. As the millennium approached, however, more and more colleges and universities began accepting ACT scores, and thus the number of ACT test takers increased. By 2012, the ACT had overtaken the SAT as the most popular college admissions test. This, along with the state standards reform, prompted the SAT to make the changes that caused the two tests to so closely resemble each other.

So which one should you take? Most guidance counselors and test prep experts would say "both" now that all colleges accept results from either test. The questions on the SAT have more words-per-question on average than those on the ACT, but there is more time per question on the SAT than on the ACT. We recommend taking a practice test for both tests and seeing on which one you perform better. Then you can focus your effort and preparation on the test that will best reveal your potential.

◎ SAT ONLY ◎
If you are taking the ACT but not the SAT, move on to Chapter Five.

The SAT was first administered in 1926 and originally stood for "Scholastic Aptitude Test." Now the acronym has no meaning.

The Format of the SAT

The SAT is a standardized test used for admission to thousands of colleges in America. It assesses a student's ability to demonstrate skills learned in school and to reason critically in math, reading, writing, and in some sense science and social studies, ultimately predicting his or her success at the university level. It is written by high school teachers, college professors, and testing experts for a non-profit company called the College Board. The SAT has 4 sections, given over three hours:

Section	Question Types	Time Limit
Reading	52 multiple-choice questions (based on five sets of passages)	65 minutes
Writing & Language	44 multiple-choice questions (based on four sets of passages)	35 minutes
Math– No Calculator	15 multiple-choice questions 5 grid-in questions	25 minutes
Math– Calculator	30 multiple-choice questions 8 grid-in questions	55 minutes
Experimental*	An unscored section of reading, writing, or math	20 minutes
Essay (Optional)	1 essay analyzing an argument	50 minutes

* The experimental section is distributed randomly to some students who do not take the optional Essay. Note that not all students who opt out of the Essay will have an experimental section.

In all, there are 52 Reading questions, 44 Writing and Language questions, and 58 Math questions (45 multiple-choice and 13 grid-in questions). Students who choose to take the optional Essay will answer a single essay question. The scored sections are presented in the order above in released practice tests, but the College Board has said the sections can come in any order, so we hesitate to say that this will always be the order of the test.

All multiple-choice questions on the SAT have four answer choices, labeled A, B, C, and D.

The test contains:
• 52 reading questions
• 44 writing questions
• 58 math questions

Other SAT Subject Areas

THE MATH SECTION

The Math score is determined by 45 multiple-choice questions and 13 Gridded-Response questions from two math sections; one in which calculator use is permitted and one in which calculators are not allowed.

Multiple-Choice Questions

The most common type of math question is a four-answer multiple-choice question:

> **1**
>
> If x is an integer and 2 is the remainder when $3x + 4$ is divided by 4, then which of the following could be a value of x?
>
> A)   0
> B)   3
> C)   4
> D)   6

The No Calculator Math section has 15 multiple-choice questions, while the Calculator Math section has 30 multiple-choice questions.

The SAT Math Sections test content from Arithmetic, Algebra, Geometry, Algebra II, Trigonometry, Coordinate Geometry, Data Analysis, and Statistics.

Gridded-Response Questions

Both Math sections include Gridded-Response questions, which are often called "grid-ins." You will find 5 of these question types in the No Calculator section and 8 of them in the Calculator section. For grid-ins, students are not given any answer choices, and they must correctly fill in the answer using a four-grid answer box:

> **2**
>
> A negative even integer x is randomly chosen from the negative integers greater than or equal to –20. What is the probability that $2x + 10 > -10$?

There are very specific rules for completing the grid. Be sure to memorize these rules before test day so that you don't spend valuable test time reading the directions.

To learn more about the Gridded-Response Questions and the Math sections of the SAT, check out the SAT website at www.collegeboard.com.

THE WRITING AND LANGUAGE SECTION

The Writing and Language score is determined by 44 multiple-choice questions that accompany four passages containing grammatical and rhetorical errors. The passages span a wide variety of topics and styles, from informal personal anecdotes to formal biographies of famous people. Each passage has numbered underlined portions; in some cases, a single word is underscored, and in others, a phrase or entire clause is underlined.

Each numbered underlined section corresponds to a same-numbered multiple-choice question with four possible answers. Let's study an example paragraph and question set:

The SAT Writing Test assesses your ability to identify and correct grammatical, mechanical, and rhetorical errors in context.

The North and South **1** having fought the Civil War with a drastically different set of assets. **2** The South had the advantage of fighting the war on the home field where the vast majority of citizens supported the Confederacy. Not only were Northerners divided in **3** there support of the war, but they had to fight in enemy territory where military orders from Washington were slow to arrive, if they made it through enemy lines at all. This, however, is essentially where the Southern advantages ended.

1
A) NO CHANGE
B) fought
C) had fought
D) OMIT the underlined portion

2
The writer is considering deleting the underlined sentence. Should the writer do this?

A) No, because it provides background information about the causes of the Civil War.
B) No, because it offers evidence of different assets for the North and the South.
C) Yes, because it contains a description of battle fields during the Civil War.
D) Yes, because it fails to explain why the war was not fought in the North.

3
A) NO CHANGE
B) they're
C) their
D) one's

Expect scientific tables and charts to appear in one or two of the Writing passages on your SAT. But don't worry--the questions about these graphics will test your reading and writing abilities rather than your knowledge of science.

To learn more about the Writing and Language section of the SAT, check out the SAT website at www.collegeboard.com

THE OPTIONAL ESSAY SECTION

Students have the option of paying an additional fee to take the SAT Essay, which occurs at the end of the test. Some colleges require Essay results, so it's important to check with your prospective schools before registering for the test.

If you choose to take the Essay, you will have 50 minutes to write a response that analyzes an author's ability to develop an argument. The prompt is always the same, and can be summarized as follows:

> As you read the following excerpt, examine how the author uses
>
> - evidence, such as facts or examples, to justify his or her argument.
> - reasoning to develop beliefs and to link opinions and evidence.
> - rhetorical or persuasive components, such as diction or appeals to emotion, to add power to his or her assertions.

Following the prompt will be a 650 to 750 word passage which you must read and analyze as instructed in the prompt. At the end of the passage is the assignment, paraphrased below:

> Write an essay in which you describe how the author develops an argument to convince his or her readers that [author's assertion]. In your response, explain how the author uses one or more of the elements listed in the box above (or other elements of your own selection) to strengthen the reasoning and persuasiveness of his or her claim. Your analysis should focus on the most relevant elements of the text.
>
> Your response should not reveal whether you agree with the author's argument, but rather describe how the author develops an argument to persuade his or her readers.

The passages that students are asked to analyze in released examples have included Martin Luther King Jr.'s speech in which he argues that American involvement in the Viet Nam War is unjust and Jimmy Carter's book forward in which he urges readers to prevent development of the Arctic National Wildlife Refuge.

It's extremely important to check with your prospective schools to see if the Optional Essay test is actually a requirement.

✦ GRATUITOUS VOCAB
diction (n): word choice
assertion (n): a statement made confidently

The basic Essay directions are always the same; only the author's name and argument will change from test to test.

THE EXPERIMENTAL SECTION

Some students who do not take the optional Essay will be required to take an unscored 20-minute section. The experimental section may be an additional Math, Reading, or Writing and Language section, but it is never an additional Essay. Sometimes called the variable or equating section, this section is used to collect data, such as difficulty level and validity, about specific questions that will be used on future SATs.

Since the College Board needs so many questions for future tests, test takers in the same location may have different experimental sections. Some students feel that the experimental section is more challenging than the other sections, which may be true since these non-operational items are not part of a full section and thus not equated for difficulty.

While the College Board has always had an experimental section on past versions of the SAT, the test maker has been very vague about the section on the newest edition of the test. Students who are not taking the Essay are assigned to separate testing rooms than students who are taking the Essay, so this experimental section could come at any time during the test. Since no other section is only 20 minutes, however, it should be easy to identify as the portion of your test that is unscored.

The experimental section is only given to students who do not take the optional Essay, and then only to some of those students.

The experimental section can occur at any time on the test, but it is easily identifiable because it's the only 20-minute section on the test.

Testing Schedule

The SAT is offered seven times a year, usually in October, November, December, January, March, May, and June. Starting in 2018, however, the January test date will be dropped and an August test date added.

You should take your first SAT during the spring of your junior year, making sure that you have completed Algebra I, Geometry, and Algebra II. If your high school offers a grammar course, also take this class prior to registering for the SAT. Because the SAT is considered a junior-level test, it is wise to take the exam when junior-level material is still current and fresh in your mind. The test is offered in May and June; choose the administration that works best with your end-of-school-year schedule.

Although PowerScore recommends taking the test during your junior year, it is extremely important that you are fully prepared prior to taking the SAT. Be sure to download and take the free practice tests from the College Board website. The accompanying score report will help you determine if you are ready for the SAT.

If your spring score is lower than you anticipated, you have several more opportunities to try again during the fall of your senior year. In fact, most students take the test two or three times. The test is offered four more times during the fall and winter of your senior year, although some colleges may not accept scores from the January administration.

Confidence Quotation
"If I have lost confidence in myself, I have the universe against me."
-Ralph Waldo Emerson, poet and essayist

The PSAT

The Preliminary SAT (PSAT) is a standardized test program used to help students gauge their performance on the SAT. Although co-sponsored by the College Board and the National Merit Scholarship Corporation (NMSC), the PSAT is administered by local high schools and is generally given to sophomores and juniors.

The PSAT is a shorter and slightly easier version of the SAT. Most of the concepts tested on the SAT are also tested on the PSAT, as you can see on the following page.

	THE SAT	THE PSAT
No-Calculator Math Section	20 questions 25 minutes	17 questions 25 minutes
Calculator Math Section	38 questions 55 minutes	31 questions 45 minutes
Math Concepts	Arithmetic, Algebra I & II, Geometry, Trigonometry, Data Interpretation	Arithmetic, Algebra I & II, Geometry, Data Interpretation
Reading Section	52 questions 65 minutes 5 passage sets	47 questions 60 minutes 5 passage sets
Reading Concepts	Words-in-Context, Literal Comprehension, Extended Thinking	Words-in-Context, Literal Comprehension, Extended Thinking
Writing and Language Section	44 questions 35 minutes 4 passage sets	44 questions 35 minutes 4 passage sets
Writing and Language Concepts	Grammar & usage and rhetorical skills	Grammar & usage and rhetorical skills

Most students take the PSAT because they want to practice for the real SAT. Others register in order to submit their names to colleges as prospective students. For these reasons alone, the test is well worth the small fee charged by your high school. Additionally, students who take the PSAT are also qualified for several scholarships or recognition programs, including the National Merit Scholarship Program.

Take the PSAT in your junior year even if you already took it as a sophomore. Only your junior-year results are submitted to scholarship organizations.

The PSAT is only given once a year, usually in the second week of October. Because the test contains sophomore-level material, you should take it after the completion of your second year of high school, in the fall of your junior year. Many students also take the PSAT in their sophomore year; if you choose to take the test as a sophomore, be sure to also take it as a junior in order to qualify for any junior-level scholarships or recognition programs, such as the National Merit Scholarship Program.

Studying for the PSAT with this book

Because the SAT and PSAT are so similar, students studying for the PSAT Reading section will greatly benefit from studying this book. All of the multiple-choice material covered in the following chapters can and may appear on the PSAT.

Chapter Summary

Format of the SAT

- There are three tested subjects and four sections on the SAT: 1) Reading, 2) Writing and Language, 3) Math–No Calculator, and 4) Math–Calculator. These sections appear in the same order on practice tests but the College Board states that they can appear in any order on an official test.
- The test takes a total of three hours to complete (without breaks), but possibly longer if you opt to take the optional Essay or are assigned an experimental section.
- There are four multiple-choice answers for every question on the test.

Other SAT Subject Areas

- The Math portion of the test has two sections: one in which a calculator is not allowed (25 minutes) and one in which it is allowed (55 minutes). There are a total of 45 multiple-choice questions and 13 Gridded-Response questions about Arithmetic, Algebra, Algebra II, Geometry, Coordinate Geometry, Trigonometry, Statistics, and Data Analysis.
- The Writing test has 44 questions about four passages, covering grammar and rhetoric rules for standard English. You have 35 minutes to complete this section.
- The Essay test is optional and requires you to analyze an author's ability to develop an argument.

Other Information

- The test is offered seven times a year, typically in October, November, December, January, March, May, and June. Starting in 2018, however, the January test date will be dropped and an August test date added. Most students should take the test for the first time in the spring of their junior year.
- The PSAT is great practice for the SAT and provides scholarship opportunities for top performers.

Confidence Quotation

"Champions aren't made in the gyms. Champions are made from something they have deep inside them-- a desire, a dream, a vision."
-Muhammad Ali, American boxer and heavyweight champion

CHAPTER FIVE:
ACT AND SAT SCORES

An ACT or SAT score is often called "The Great Equalizer" among college admissions officers. It is the only tool in your admissions file that truly compares you to other applicants. Grade point averages, class ranks, and extracurricular activities are important, but they are difficult for anyone to judge in comparison with another student from another school. For example, the amount of work it takes to achieve an 'A' in Mrs. Jones' English class in San Diego may only equate to a 'B–" in Mr. Smith's English class in Boston. And Lincoln High School in Minnesota may only allow one student to be ranked number one in the class, while Washington High School in Louisiana allows all students with a GPA higher than 4.0 to receive a class ranking of one. While admissions officers maintain school files with information about class rankings and course difficulty in order to try to more adequately compare students from different schools, this system still presents great difficulty and potential unfairness. Therefore, because the college admissions tests are standardized and taken by all applicants, they are used to directly compare students in math, reading, writing, and science.

Most everyone knows that the top score on an ACT is a 36 and a top score on the SAT is 1600. But your score report is going to contain a lot of other data, including individual test scores, concordance tables, percentile ranks, and score ranges. It can be intimidating to both students and parents who are not familiar with all of the data included on your official score report, so we will explain each component in this chapter.

↳ GRATUITOUS VOCAB
concordance (n): agreement; in this case, a conversion table that compares ACT scores and SAT scores.

Scoring the ACT

On each section of the ACT, you can determine your raw score by simply counting the number of questions you answered correctly. This raw score will be converted to a scaled score, from 1 to 36, to account for slight differences between test administrations. The average of the four subject area scaled scores, rounded to the nearest whole number, will produce your composite score. Consider an example:

English	25
Math	28
Reading	20
Science	23
Total	96

Composite (96 ÷ 4): 24

The average composite ACT score among all test takers varies from year to year, but is typically between 20 and 21.

Each multiple-choice question that you answer correctly earns you 1 point toward a raw score. There are no penalties for wrong answers. Questions that are omitted and left blank neither receive points nor lose points. Once a raw score is calculated from the points earned, test makers use a conversion table to produce a scaled score for each section. Each ACT test has its own conversion table, but they are usually quite similar. Here is a partial conversion from a practice test in *The Real ACT Prep Guide*:

This partial conversion table offers some sample scaled scores. For example, if you answered 38 math questions correctly, your scaled score would be 24.

Scaled Score	Raw Score			
	English (out of 75)	Math (out of 60)	Reading (out of 40)	Science (out of 40)
36	75	60	38-40	39-40
32	70	56	34	35
28	63-64	48-50	29-30	31-32
24	53-54	37-39	24-25	26-27
20	42-44	31-32	20	20-21
16	33-34	20-22	16	14
14	28-29	13-15	13	11-12
10	20-21	6	6	7

Remember, this is a raw score conversion table for a single test; the conversion table for your test will be slightly different, but this one gives you an idea about how many questions you need to answer correctly in order to receive a certain scaled score.

ACT Subscores

In addition to scaled scores, your ACT student report will include several other scores, subscores, and relevant information, both for your own use and the use of college admissions officers.

Two scores will be prominently displayed with your Math, Science, English, and Reading score. The first is a STEM (Science, Technology, Engineering, and Mathematics) score, which is simply an average of your Math and Science Scores. The second is an ELA (English Language Arts) score, an average of your Reading and English, and if applicable, Writing scores.

Your scaled scores in each subject area will be compared to College Readiness Benchmarks. These benchmarks are the minimum scores that the ACT believes you need to achieve in order to have a high probability of success in corresponding college courses. For example, the Reading benchmark score is 22; if you score a 24 on the ACT Reading test, the test makers believe that you have a high chance of succeeding in a college Social Sciences course in which there will be copious reading.

↳ GRATUITOUS VOCAB
copious (adj): plentiful; a lot

Under the "Detailed Results" portion of your score report, English, Mathematics, Reading, Science, and the optional Writing tests will be further broken down to help you pinpoint your weaknesses on the test. For example, the Reading test will show your achievement on (1) Key Ideas & Details, (2) Craft & Structure, (3) Integration of Knowledge & Ideas, and (4) Understanding Complex Texts. Each of these subcategories will show the total number of questions and the number you answered correctly, which will correspond to a percentage bar graph. The bar graph will indicate whether you are in the ACT Readiness Range for that particular subcategory.

On the second page of the official score report is information about career planning based on your ACT results.

Confidence Quotation
"Make a choice. Just decide what it's going to be, who you're going to be, how you are going to do it. Just decide. And from that point, the universe is going to get out your way."
-Will Smith, actor and performing artist

ACT Percentile Ranks

Each scaled ACT score places a student in a certain relative position compared to other test takers. These relative positions are represented through a percentile that correlates to each score; the percentile indicates where the test taker falls in the overall pool of test takers.

For example, a score of 26 on the Math test represents the 84th percentile, meaning a student with a score of 26 scored better than 84 percent of the college-bound seniors who have taken the test in the last year. Only 16 percent of test takers scored better. The percentile is critical since it is a true indicator of your positioning relative to other test takers, and thus college applicants.

The ACT has also prepared a composite score percentile conversion. For example, a student who has earned a 26 average of all four sections receives an 83rd percentile ranking. This student has performed better than 83 percent of test takers.

The percentiles may vary slightly from year to year, but a recent representation is available for your study on the next two pages. First, though, consider a summary of some benchmark scores:

Percentile ranks for each section score are listed on the next page; percentile ranks for composite scores are on the page after that.

1% of test takers score 33 or higher.
8% of test takers score 29 or higher.
21% of test takers score 25 or higher.
44% of test takers score 21 or higher.
57% of test takers score 19 or higher.
76% of test takers score 16 or higher.
96% of test takers score 12 or higher.

ACT Individual Section Percentile Table

Scaled Score	English Percentile	Math Percentile	Reading Percentile	Science Percentile
36	99	99	99	99
35	99	99	99	99
34	99	99	98	99
33	97	98	97	98
32	95	97	95	97
31	93	96	92	96
30	92	95	89	95
29	90	93	86	94
28	88	91	84	92
27	85	88	81	90
26	82	84	78	87
25	79	78	75	83
24	74	73	71	77
23	69	67	66	70
22	64	62	61	63
21	58	57	55	56
20	52	53	48	48
19	45	49	42	40
18	40	43	36	33
17	36	37	31	27
16	32	27	25	22
15	27	15	21	17
14	21	6	16	13
13	16	2	11	9
12	13	1	7	6
11	10	1	4	4
10	7	1	2	2
9	4	1	1	1
8	2	1	1	1
7	1	1	1	1
6	1	1	1	1
5	1	1	1	1
4	1	1	1	1
3	1	1	1	1
2	1	1	1	1
1	1	1	1	1
Average	**20.3**	**20.9**	**21.3**	**20.8**

Say you scored a 17 on the Mathematics test and a 17 on the Science test. This equates to the 37th percentile for Math but only the 27th percentile for Science.

ACT Composite Percentile Table

Scaled Score	Composite Percentile
36	99
35	99
34	99
33	99
32	98
31	96
30	95
29	92
28	90
27	87
26	83
25	79
24	74
23	68
22	63
21	56
20	50
19	43
18	36
17	30
16	24
15	18
14	12
13	7
12	4
11	1
10	1
9	1
8	1
7	1
6	1
5	1
4	1
3	1
2	1
1	1
Average	**21.0**

A student who scored a 28 English, 26 Math, 25 Reading, and 22 Science Reading would have a composite score of 25:

28 + 26 + 25 + 21 = 101

101 ÷ 4 = 25.25

Round to the nearest whole number: 25.25 → 25

A composite score of 25 ranks in the 79th percentile.

Scoring the SAT

You will receive two scaled scores on the SAT: a Math score of 200 to 800 and an Evidence-Based Reading and Writing score of 200 to 800. The two scores are added together to produce a total score. The average SAT score varies from year to year, but is usually around 1080. The lowest score a student can receive is 400 (200 Math and 200 Reading and Writing) while a perfect score is 1600 (800 Math and 800 Reading and Writing). Consider an example:

Math	630
Reading & Writing	560
Total	1190

◎ SAT ONLY ◎
This section applies only to the SAT.

You may hear some older test takers refer to their score out of 2400. This is because a perfect score was 2400 from 2005 to early 2016, when the Writing section had its own, separate scaled score from 200 to 800. In March of 2016, however, the College Board changed the test and combined the Reading and Writing scaled score, thus reverting back to the pre-2005 scale of 200 to 800 for the entire verbal section.

Each multiple-choice question that you answer correctly earns you 1 point toward a raw score. There are no penalties for wrong answers. Questions that are omitted and left blank neither receive points nor lose points. For the Math section, the raw score is directly plugged into a conversion table to produce a scaled score (200–800). Each SAT test has its own conversion table, but they are usually quite similar. Here is a partial conversion of a Math section from an official practice test:

Raw Score Math (out of 58)	Scaled Score
58	800
53	750
48	700
41	650
36	600
30	550
24	500
19	450
15	400

This partial conversion table for the SAT Math test offers some sample scaled scores. For example, if you answered 36 math questions correctly, your scaled score would be 600.

The Reading and Writing score is handled a bit differently since the two subject areas are combined to produce a scaled score. Each individual raw score is assigned a "Test Score" from 10–40 based on a conversion table.

Once the Reading Test Score is added to the Writing Test Score, the "Reading and Writing Test Score" will be between 20–80. To find your scaled score, simply multiply this by 10. Here is a small sample of the conversion table (in which the Reading and Writng scores must be added together) from that same practice test:

The Reading and Writing score conversion is a bit more complicated. It may be helpful to look at a complete conversion table, which you can find at the College Board's website or in The Official SAT Study Guide.

Raw Score		Test Score	Scaled Score
Reading (out of 52)	Writing (out of 44)		
52	44	40	400
50	42	38	380
47	40	36	360
43-44	38	34	340
39-40	35	32	320
35-36	32	30	300
31-32	29	28	280
28	25-26	26	260
23-25	22	24	240
19-20	18-19	22	220
15-16	15-16	20	200

To better understand the scoring system for the Evidence-Based Reading and Writing score, let us analyze one student's test results:

Of the 52 Reading questions, Gabriel answered 35 correctly and 15 incorrectly, and left 2 blank. Therefore, he earns 35 points for the questions he answered correctly. He does not gain or lose any points for the incorrect or omitted questions. Gabriel's raw score is 35.

According to the conversion chart, a raw score in Reading of 35 equates to a test score of 30 and a scaled score of 300.

Gabriel answered 29 Writing questions correctly and missed 15 questions, so his raw score is 29.

According to the conversion chart, a raw score in Writing of 29 equates to a test score of 28 and a scaled score of 280.

Now add the Reading and Writing scaled scores together:

300 (Reading) + 280 (Writing) = 580 (Reading and Writing Score)

Gabriel would add this 580 to his Math scaled score to compute his total SAT score.

SAT Subscores

Your SAT student report will include additional subscores and information to help you understand your performance on the test.

The College Board includes benchmark scores to help you determine your college and career readiness. The Math benchmark is 530 and the Reading and Writing benchmark is 480. The test makers believe that you if you attain or exceed those scores, you have a 75% chance of earning a grade of C or higher in corresponding college courses.

In addition to the Test Scores for Reading, Writing, and Math mentioned in the previous section, you can expect Cross-Test Scores for "Analysis in History/ Social Studies" and "Analysis in Science." These will also be reported on the 10 to 40 point scale and will be based on questions throughout all portions of the test that focus on the applicable subject area.

Finally, you will see a series of subscores. Some of these subscores pertain to a single subject area: "Heart of Algebra," "Problem Solving and Data Analysis," and "Passport to Advanced Math" in Math and "Expression of Ideas" and "Standard English Conventions" for Writing. The remaining two—"Command of Evidence" and "Words in Context"—are derived from both Reading and Writing. These scores will range between 1 and 15 and are meant to help you pinpoint specific weaknesses within a section or sections.

And while it's important to be your own critic and research which areas are causing you the most difficulty, the College Board will assist you with the process through use of the Skills Insight portion of your official online score report. This score evaluator explains exactly which concepts with which you need further practice in all tested subject areas. It's an under-used tool that can have valuable benefits to the discerning student.

↳ GRATUITOUS VOCAB
benchmark (n): a standard of excellence that other things are measured against.

be sure to check out the Skills Insight portion of your score report. This valuable tool offers suggestions for improvement.

SAT Percentile Ranks

Like an ACT score, an SAT score provides admissions officers with a number that can be used to most accurately compare you to all of the other applicants from around the globe. Despite what high school counselors and even college admissions departments might claim, a standardized test score is the most important piece of data in your application.

The College Board also releases percentile tables which allow students and admissions officers to see how their score compared to other test takers. Each scaled SAT score places a student in a certain relative position compared to other test takers. These relative positions are represented through a percentile that correlates to each score; the percentile indicates where the test taker falls in the overall pool of test takers. For example, a score of 650 on the Math section represents the 86th percentile, meaning a student with a score of 650 scored better than 86 percent of the students in a research study sample of U.S. college-bound juniors and seniors. Only 14 percent of test takers scored better. The percentile is critical since it is a true indicator of your positioning relative to other test takers, and thus to college applicants.

The College Board has also prepared a composite score percentile conversion. For example, a student who has earned a combined 1250 on the Math and Evidence-Based Reading and Writing sections receives an 80th percentile ranking. This student has performed better than 80 percent of test takers.

Percentile tables for individual sections and their composites are available on the College Board website. Currently these tables—provided on the following pages—are based on research data but that may change after the company collects enough data from current test takers. Here is a summary of some benchmark scores:

> 1% of test takers score 1510 or higher.
> 7% of test takers score 1380 or higher.
> 20% of test takers score 1250 or higher.
> 40% of test takers score 1130 or higher.
> 50% of test takers score 1080 or higher.
> 60% of test takers score 1030 or higher.
> 80% of test takers score 920 or higher.

GRATUITOUS VOCAB
correlates (vb): to have a mutual relationship or connection

An example of a composite conversion table follows the individual subject conversion table on the following pages.

The average SAT score is around 540 in each of the sections, for a 1080 composite average. Note that this is 80 points higher than the average prior to the test change in 2016 if you are comparing your scores to those of older friends or siblings.

SAT Individual Section Percentile Table

Scaled Score	Math Percentile	Reading and Writing Percentile
800	99+	99+
790	99	99+
780	98	99+
770	98	99
760	98	99
750	97	99
740	96	98
730	95	97
720	95	96
710	94	95
700	92	94
690	91	92
680	89	91
670	88	89
660	87	86
650	86	84
640	83	81
630	81	78
620	79	75
610	76	72
600	73	69
590	70	66
580	67	63
570	64	60
560	60	56
550	57	52
540	53	49
530	49	45
520	45	42
510	40	38
500	34	35
490	30	31
480	27	28
470	24	25
460	21	22
450	18	20
440	16	17
430	14	15
420	12	13
410	10	11
400	8	9
390	7	7
380	5	6
370	4	5
360	3	3
350	3	3
340	2	2
330	1	1
320	1	1
310	1	1
300	1	1-
290 or less	1-	1-
Average	**541**	**543**

Say you scored a 600 on the Reading and Writing section. This equates to the 69th percentile. But if you scored a 600 in Math, you earned a spot in the 73rd percentile.

SAT Composite Percentile Table

Scaled Score	Composite Percentile		Scaled Score	Composite Percentile
1600	99+		1100	55
1590	99+		1090	52
1580	99+		1080	50
1570	99+		1070	48
1560	99+		1060	46
1550	99+		1050	44
1540	99		1040	42
1530	99		1030	40
1520	99		1020	38
1510	99		1010	36
1500	98		1000	34
1490	98		990	32
1480	98		980	30
1470	98		970	29
1460	97		960	27
1450	97		950	25
1440	96		940	24
1430	96		930	22
1420	95		920	20
1410	95		910	19
1400	94		900	18
1390	94		890	16
1380	93		880	15
1370	92		870	14
1360	91		860	13
1350	91		850	12
1340	90		840	11
1330	89		830	10
1320	88		820	9
1310	87		810	8
1300	86		800	7
1290	85		790	7
1280	83		780	6
1270	82		770	5
1260	81		760	4
1250	80		750	4
1240	78		740	3
1230	77		730	3
1220	76		720	2
1210	74		710	2
1200	72		700	2
1190	71		690	2
1180	69		680	1
1170	67		670	1
1160	65		660	1
1150	64		650	1
1140	62		640	1-
1130	60		630 or less	1-
1120	58			
1110	57		*Average*	**1083**

A student who scored a 570 Math and 650 Reading and Writing would have a composite score of 1220 and rank in the 76th percentile.

SAT to ACT Concordance Table

If you have taken only one of the tests—either the ACT or the SAT—you may be wondering how you would score on the other test. Or if you've taken both tests, you're probably trying to determine which one produced the "better" score. The College Board has created a concordance table to help you compare your test results.

SAT Composite	ACT Composite	SAT Composite	ACT Composite	SAT Composite	ACT Composite
1600	36	1250	26	900	17
1590	35	1240	26	890	16
1580	35	1230	25	880	16
1570	35	1220	25	870	16
1560	35	1210	25	860	16
1550	34	1200	25	850	15
1540	34	1190	24	840	15
1530	34	1180	24	830	15
1520	34	1170	24	820	15
1510	33	1160	24	810	15
1500	33	1150	23	800	14
1490	33	1140	23	790	14
1480	32	1130	23	780	14
1470	32	1120	22	770	14
1460	32	1110	22	760	14
1450	32	1100	22	750	13
1440	31	1090	21	740	13
1430	31	1080	21	730	13
1420	31	1070	21	720	13
1410	30	1060	21	710	12
1400	30	1050	20	700	12
1390	30	1040	20	690	12
1380	29	1030	20	680	12
1370	29	1020	20	670	12
1360	29	1010	19	660	12
1350	29	1000	19	650	12
1340	28	990	19	640	12
1330	28	980	19	630	12
1320	28	970	18	620	11
1310	28	960	18	610	11
1300	27	950	18	600	11
1290	27	940	18	590	11
1280	27	930	17	580	11
1270	26	920	17	570	11
1260	26	910	17	560	11

Note that this table was created by the makers of the SAT and while it has been shown to be accurate, it has not been verified by the makers of the ACT.

Let's say you only plan to officially take one test, and you score a 23 on an ACT practice test and a 1250 on an SAT practice test. You've clearly done better on the SAT practice test, as a 1250 SAT scores equates to a 26 ACT score, three points higher than your actual ACT practice score. It would be wise to concentrate on the SAT given your results.

Chapter Summary

Scoring the ACT

- You earn one point for every correct answer. There is no penalty for wrong answers.
- Raw scores for each subject area are converted to a scaled score of 1–36.
- The average ACT composite score is between 20 and 21.
- Your official score report will contain several subscores to help you and college admissions officers understand your strengths and weaknesses.
- Your scaled scores will determine your ranking compared to other test takers using percentiles.

Scoring the SAT

- You earn one point for every correct answer. There is no penalty for wrong answers.
- Raw scores for each subject area are converted to a scaled score of 200–800.
- The average SAT composite score is about 1080.
- Your official score report will contain several subscores to help you and college admissions officers understand your strengths and weaknesses.
- Your scaled scores will determine your ranking compared to other test takers using percentiles.

CHAPTER SIX:
THE FUNDAMENTALS OF ACT AND SAT READING

Finally, we get to the real reason you are here—to learn how to improve your Reading score! The previous chapters contain a lot of information about test formats and policies, and it's extremely important that you return to them if you skipped to this chapter. But for now, let's get right into the heart of ACT and SAT Reading.

There is a single scored Reading test on both the ACT and the SAT. On the ACT, it is always the third section. On the SAT, it has been the first section on released tests, but the test makers state that the sections may come in any order. Both Reading tests are composed of passage-based reading comprehension questions, which assess how well you understand written language. This skill is used more than any other in college, so your Reading test score is usually considered the most indicative sign of your readiness for higher education. Admissions officers know that in college, your ability to carefully analyze passages will help you much more than your ability to execute basic ACT and SAT math skills, such as finding the length of a hypotenuse, so extra weight is given to Reading and Writing scores in comparison to your Math score when admissions decisions are being made.

The other reason that Reading scores are so impressive is that the skills required to score well are usually developed over time. You begin preparing for the ACT and SAT Reading tests in preschool or kindergarten when you summarize the plot of the book your teacher read aloud during Story Hour. Students who go on to read independently for their own enjoyment tend to score well on standardized reading tests without any last minute preparation because they have spent the better part of a decade prepping for the test without even realizing it.

While Reading test scores may be the most difficult to improve of all the subject areas on the ACT and SAT, it is certainly not impossible. With careful study of the strategies in this book, you can raise your score. You must also adjust your attitude toward the section and think positively about the sentences and passages you will read, no matter how difficult or dry they seem at first glance. To begin your analysis of the ACT and SAT Reading sections, it is important to study the format and directions of each test prior to an official administration.

↳ GRATUITOUS VOCAB
indicative (adj):
showing or indicating
execute (vb):
to carry out

You have been practicing for the ACT and SAT Reading tests since you learned to read over ten years ago.

ACT Reading Test Format

◎ ACT ONLY ◎
This page and the next two pages cover information only about the ACT; the same information about the SAT is discussed immediately following.

The ACT Reading test features several passages, each of which is followed by questions that assess your understanding of the author's message or the author's writing style.

The directions for the Reading test can be summarized as follows:

> Each of the passages in this test is followed by several questions. Read each passage, select the best answer to each question, and mark the corresponding oval on the answer sheet. You can return to the passage as often as you like.

Consider an overview of the Reading test before we discuss each component in further detail:

Number of passages:	Five; three single passage sets and a paired passage set, for a total of four passage "sets"
Questions per passage set:	10
Total number of questions:	40
Total time:	35 minutes
Passage length:	Approximately 500 to 900 words
Reading complexities:	Estimated 8th grade to 12th grade

There are four "sections" of passages; three of these sections contain an individual passage followed by 10 questions. The fourth section features a set of paired passages that discuss a related topic and the two passages are followed by 10 questions. The individual passages tend to be closer to 800-900 words while the paired passages are usually nearer to 400-500 words, for a total of 900 words between the two.

The text complexity varies from passages similar to what you might encounter in 8th grade to those you may read in 12th grade. The ACT does not publish text complexity levels, but these estimates cover all of the passages in *The Official ACT Prep Guide*.

ACT Passage and Question Format

The questions that follow each passage are multiple-choice questions with four possible answer choices. Some questions will direct you to a specific line reference while others will assess your knowledge of the passage as a whole. The following passage is shorter than a true ACT passage, but it will give you an idea of the types of text and questions you may encounter:

SOCIAL STUDIES: This passage is taken from the article "George Washington at the Siamese Court," by Ross Bullen in The Public Domain Review (2016).

In October of 1856, readers of the *New York Daily Times* were eager for news from Siam. In the 1850s, most Americans would only be familiar with the Southeast Asian nation now known as Thailand through its most famous citizens, Chang and Eng Bunker, the original

5 "Siamese twins," who had been living in the U.S. since 1830. But the Kingdom of Siam itself—its geography, its government, its culture—was a total mystery. However, a new treaty between Siam and the United States, negotiated in 1856 by Townsend Harris, the first U.S. Consul General in Japan, kindled a public interest in all things

10 Siamese. In an article titled "From Siam," the *Times'* correspondent does not hesitate to dampen the public's enthusiasm. "The importance of a commercial treaty with such a people has been and will be overrated in the United States," he writes. "The present prospects of Siam are not flattering." Seemingly without any sense of irony, the

15 author of "From Siam" criticizes the widespread practice of slavery in Siam, and states his belief that "The kingdom is in a state of unrest… which may end in a civil war."

If the *Times'* correspondent failed to see the shared potential for civil unrest in both his own country and Siam, other points of

20 comparison between Siam and the U.S. were harder to ignore. The author reports that "we had a Siamese Prince to visit our ship a short time since, who went by the proud name of 'Prince GEORGE WASHINGTON.' During George's rambles around the ship, if any of his inferior subjects came in his way, they would sprawl themselves

25 out instanter far down and wriggle themselves out of the way like a worm."

A Siamese prince, demanding that his "inferior subjects" prostrate themselves before him, and adopting the name of the United States' first President, was too odd a figure to ignore; indeed, descriptions

30 of Prince George Washington would become a regular feature of American writing about Siam from the mid-1850s to the turn of the century. But who was this unusually named prince? And what did the Americans who wrote and read about him think he could teach them about Siam? Or about America?

ACT passages are not typically known for their exciting topics.

Notice the spaces between paragraphs and how the line numbering does not include these spaces.

1. The passage mentions which of the following as something most Americans would associate with Siam prior to 1856?

    A. Prince George Washington
    B. Siamese twins
    C. The commercial treaty between the United States and Siam
    D. The geography of Southeast Asia

2. The quotation in lines 21-26 identifies Prince George Washington as being:

    F. excessively talkative.
    G. charismatic but peculiar.
    H. demanding of his attendants.
    J. charitable and compassionate.

3. As it is used in line 9, the word *kindled* most nearly means:

    A. charred.
    B. revived.
    C. extinguished.
    D. stirred up.

Confidence Quotation
"The positive thinker sees the invisible, feels the intangible, and achieves the impossible." -Unknown

While test takers can often predict the level of difficulty of each question in the Math test based on its location in the section, the difficulty levels of the ACT Reading questions are randomly distributed in each question set. It is impossible for you to know the difficulty level of a question while you are taking the test.

Notice that there spaces between the paragraphs in an ACT passage, but yet that the line references do not count the space and refer only to lines with text in them. This is a minor difference from the SAT, where there are no spaces between paragraphs in passages.

As you can see in the three questions above, the ACT alternates between answer choices A, B, C, and D in questions 1 and 3 (odd-numbered questions) and F, G, H, and J in question 2 (even-numbered question). This is to help prevent students from mis-bubbling their answer booklet. The SAT is not as magnanimous and only uses A, B, C, and D, and so for the sake of discussion, we will only use A, B, C, and D elsewhere in this book.

Curious about the answers?
1. B
2. H
3. D

SAT Reading Test Format

The SAT Reading test has multiple choice questions that assess your comprehension of an author's message or writing choices based on six passages.

The directions for the Reading test can be summarized as follows:
- Each passage is followed by questions about its content.
- The correct answers are based on information that is <u>stated</u> or <u>implied</u> in the introduction, the passage, or accompanying figures (e.g. charts or graphs).

Let's look at an overview of the SAT Reading test:

Number of passages:	Six; four single passages and a set of paired passages, for a total of five passage "sets"
Questions per passage set:	10 or 11
Total number of questions:	52
Total time:	65 minutes
Passage length:	500 to 750 words
Reading complexities:	9th grade to early undergraduate

There are five sections or "sets" of passages; four of these sections contain an individual passage followed by 10 or 11 questions. The fifth section features a set of paired passages that discuss a related topic and the two passages are followed by 10 or 11 questions. The individual passages tend to be closer to 650-750 words while the paired passages are usually nearer to 350-400 words so that the two together are about 750 words.

The text complexity varies greatly. You may find a basic passage similar to the type of text you read in 9th grade, and another that is quite challenging and typical of the text presented to freshman and sophomores in college. The College Board states that the text complexity range extends from 9th grade to early postsecondary, but some experts who have evaluated the most difficult sample passages have stated the complexity is closer to grade 16, or college senior-level material.

◎ SAT ONLY ◎

This next three pages cover information only about the SAT.

Note that "500 to 750" is the official College Board word count. But some passages in released tests are actually slightly over that word count.

SAT Passage and Question Format

The questions that follow each passage are multiple-choice questions with four possible answer choices. Some questions will direct you to a specific line reference, others will assess your knowledge of the passage as a whole, and a couple will ask you to analyze a table, chart, or figure that accompanies a passage. The following passage is shorter than a true 500 to 750 word SAT passage, but it will give you an idea of the types of text, graphics, and questions you may encounter:

This passage is adopted from *Biology*, a textbook by OpenStax. The authors discuss how the environment affects an animal's body plan.

Animal body plans follow set patterns related to symmetry. They may be asymmetrical, radial, or bilateral in form. Asymmetrical animals are animals with no pattern or symmetry, such as a sponge. Radial symmetry
Line describes an animal that has an up-and-down orientation: any plane cut
5 along its longitudinal axis through the organism produces equal halves, but not a definite right or left side. This plan is found mostly in aquatic animals that attach themselves to a base and extract their food from the surrounding water as it flows around the organism. A sea anemone is an example of an animal with radial symmetry. Bilateral symmetry occurs
10 when animals can be divided into two equal halves. Over 99% of animals are bilaterally symmetric, including most mammals, and the goat provides an example of an animal with mirror image halves. A plane cut from front to back separates the animal into definite right and left sides. Bilateral symmetry is found in both land-based and aquatic animals, and it enables
15 a high level of mobility.

Animals with bilateral symmetry that live in water tend to have a fusiform shape, which is a tubular shaped body that is tapered at both ends. This shape decreases the drag on the body as it moves through water and allows the animal to swim at high speeds. Certain types of sharks can
20 swim at 50 kilometers an hour and some dolphins at 32 to 40 kilometers per hour. Aquatic organisms are constrained in shape by the forces of drag in the water; land-dwelling animals do not have the same limitations because air has a lower viscosity than water, and the land-dwellers are thus able to move with less resistance. Land-dwelling animals are instead
25 restrained by gravity and have movement adaptations that reflect this. For example, most adaptations in birds are for gravity rather than for drag.

Viscosity of Liquids and Gases		
Substance	Viscosity (dyne-sec/cm^2)	Temperature (°C)
Blood	0.04	37
Water	0.01	20
Air	0.00018	20
Water vapor	0.00013	100

The most noticeable difference between the ACT and the SAT is the inclusion of infographics on the SAT. We will address these charts and graphs in an SAT-exclusive chapter near the end of the book.

1

According to the passage, bilateral marine animals have a fusiform shape because the shape

A) allows the animal to move through the water with less drag.

B) helps the animal attach to a base, such as rocks or dock installations.

C) divides the animal into two definitive halves.

D) limits the restrictions of gravity on the animal.

2

As used in line 21, "constrained" most nearly means

A) repressed.

B) restricted.

C) stressed.

D) amplified.

3

Which statement is best supported by the data presented in the table?

A) The viscosity of air at 20°C is greater than the viscosity of water vapor at 100°C.

B) The viscosity of water increases as the temperature increases.

C) The viscosity of blood is less than the viscosity of water at the same temperature.

D) The viscosity of air is over 50 times greater than the viscosity of water at the same temperature.

Only two of the passages will have an accompanying table, graph, or figure, and you can expect two to four questions to address the graphic. The rest of the questions will be about the passage itself. We will address these graphics in greater detail in a later chapter.

While test takers can often predict the level of difficulty of each question in the SAT Math sections based on its location in the section, the difficulty levels of the SAT Reading questions are randomly distributed in each question set. It is impossible for you to know the difficulty level of a question while you are taking the test.

Answers:
1. A
2. B
3. D

ACT and SAT Time Management

It is important to plan an approach to the Reading section before arriving at the test center.

Passage Management

We recommend that you aim to **read each passage or set of passages in about 2½ minutes on both the ACT and SAT**. This allows you sufficient time to gather the main ideas without getting bogged down by details, and we'll discuss your reading speed in more detail later in the book. As you practice, use a timer to record how long it takes you to read passages and then work on cutting that time to under 2 minutes and 30 seconds.

ACT

If you can meet this time limit on all four passage sets, you'll spend a total of 10 minutes reading ACT passages.

SAT

If you can meet this time limit on all five passage sets, you'll spend a total of 12 minutes and 30 seconds reading SAT passages.

Question Management

As you can see below, you will have 37.5 seconds per question on the ACT and 60 seconds per question on the SAT, provided you read each passage in 2 minutes and 30 seconds. Obviously some questions might take longer than others, since there are many different types of comprehension questions, but on average, try to answer them in this time frame. Practice with a timer so you get a "feel" for how long 37.5 seconds takes and how long a minute takes when you are tackling questions. When the time is up, make a guess and put a star next to the question in your test booklet so you know to return to it if there is extra time at the end of the section.

Complete all of the questions about one passage before moving on to another passage. The different topics force you to quit thinking about a previous passage, so it is best to tackle these questions in complete sections. You should plan only to return to the questions you struggled with for longer than the allotted time (37.5 seconds or one minute, depending on the test).

ACT

If you read each passage in 2 minutes and 30 sections, you will have 25 minutes for the 40 questions, meaning **you'll have 37.5 seconds per question**.

SAT

You are left with 52 minutes and 30 seconds for the 52 questions, meaning **you'll have just over a minute per question**.

Silent countdown timers are available at www.powerscore.com. Although they are not allowed at the official ACT or SAT administrations, timers are still valuable tools for practice.

The SAT has more passages and questions, but also offers more time per question than the ACT.

Remaining Time

Never stop working before time is up. Our instructors always come back from real ACT and SAT administrations with stories about students at the testing centers who finished a section and put their heads down on their desks. This is outright lunacy! You are never done on an ACT or SAT Reading section (or any section for that matter). If you answer all questions before time is called, you should **spend the remaining minutes reviewing your answers**. Double check every problem, but especially those that gave you the most difficulty. Almost all of our students have reported finding errors when checking their work.

It is important to practice time management before approaching the actual ACT or SAT. By taking several timed sections in *The Official ACT Prep Guide* or *The Official SAT Study Guide*, you will become comfortable with budgeting time on each question and double checking your answers.

ALWAYS go back and check your work if time remains at the end of a section.

ACT and SAT Guessing Strategy

While older versions of the SAT penalized test takers for incorrect answers, the newest incarnation no longer penalizes for guessing and the ACT has never penalized for guessing. Thus, **you must guess on every question** to which you do not know the answer on both the ACT and the SAT. If possible, separate answers into "Contenders" and "Losers" by crossing out the letter that corresponds with each wrong answer choice so that it is easy to make a guess from among the Contenders. If you are unable to complete the Reading test in the allotted time, blindly guess on the remaining questions in the last minute of the section. Never leave a question blank in the answer booklet!

↳ GRATUITOUS VOCAB
incarnation (n): form

⋮TIPS and TRICKS⋮
ALWAYS make an educated guess when you do not know the answer on the ACT and SAT.

ACT and SAT Passage Subjects

The ACT and SAT use passages from sources in similar or identical subject areas. The only real difference is the terminology each test uses to describe the type of passage. Consider the following table of the subject areas cited by each test and the number of corresponding passage sets that appear on each test:

ACT		SAT	
Passage Subject	Number of passage sets	Passage Subject	Number of passage sets
Literary Narrative	1	Literature	1
Natural Science	1	Science	2
Social Studies	1	Social Studies	1
Humanities	1	History	1

Confidence Quotation
"Properly, we should read for power. Man reading should be man intensely alive. The book should be a ball of light in one's hand."
-Ezra Pound, American poet

As you can see, the passage subject areas are identical or extremely similar. The main difference is the ACT's inclusion of Humanities, which we will discuss in the following section.

On the ACT, the test makers identify which subject area a passage comes from in the introductory text before each passage. For example, this ACT passage is labeled "Natural Science":

NATURAL SCIENCE: This passage is taken from the article "Turtles Invading Japan," by Erin P. Davis in *Global Science Weekly* (2016).

> In the 1970s, pet turtles became a novelty in Japan. The most common species, red-ear sliders, were imported from the United States and sold in pet shops and at *matsuri*, local festivals that... .

🍂 GRATUITOUS VOCAB
explanatory (adj): serving to explain

This is not the case on the SAT, but the introductory text tends to be more explanatory and thus the subject area should not be too hard to determine. In this example, it is clear from the name of the source (*Scientist Now*) and description of the passage that the topic is Science:

> This passage is adapted from Kara Isley, "How Does Your Garden Glow" from *Scientist Now*. The author is describing fluorescence, the property that causes some flowers to glow under black light.
>
> Humans perceive light from red to violet, but many animals can see light beyond violet—or ultraviolet light. Some plants have ultraviolet markings that attract pollinators that can see... .

The paired passage set can occur in ANY subject area on the ACT and SAT.

On both the ACT and the SAT, the paired passage set may occur in any of these subject areas.

Literary Fiction

Literary Fiction passages are referred to as Literary Narrative or Prose Fiction on the ACT and as Literature on the SAT. Despite the variation in name, these passages are the same on both tests.

Literary Fiction passages are excerpts from novels, short stories, and memoirs. While a memoir is technically non-fiction, it is written in a style that mimics fiction, so you should treat it as a literary fiction passage when applying reading strategies. Fiction passages most often appear as single passages, but on occasion they are used in the paired passages.

Memoirs are actually non-fiction but they are written in a style that mimics fiction, and thus should be read like other Literary Fiction passages.

> *Source examples:*
> An excerpt from a Charles Dickens novel
> An excerpt from a short story by Sandra Cisneros
> An excerpt from Maya Angelou's autobiography

On the ACT, these passages are typically adapted from fiction written during the last fifty years, making them fairly easy to read. The SAT tends to pull from literature written during two time periods: the last fifty years, so that they are extremely similar to the ACT passages, or the late 19th and early 20th century, making them more challenging for most students.

Relatively recent fiction passages on the ACT and SAT are sometimes written by authors who are members of historically underrepresented groups, such as women or Mexican Americans, and these passages typically feature characters from the same background. The text will often address cultural differences. Previous ACT or SAT passages have come from the works of Amy Tan, Randa Jarrar, Rita Dove, Albert Murray, Gabril Garica Marquez, and Donna Tartt.

Classic literature passages themselves are not difficult to read, but some of the text may be hard to understand given the differences in culture and daily life over 100 years ago. Previous SAT passages have been taken from the novels and short stories of E.M. Forster, Charlotte Brontë, Daphné Du Maurier, Stephen Crane, Edith Wharton, and many others. Note that the ACT does not typically use classic literature, but you should be prepared for anything on standardized tests.

The Literary Fiction passage is always the first passage of the Reading test on the ACT. It is also the first passage on all of the tests in *The Official SAT Study Guide*.

Science

The remaining passages on the ACT and SAT are all non-fiction passages. With these, your goal is to determine the main idea of the passage and the author's attitude toward the topic. We will discuss this in more detail in the next chapter.

Science passages on the ACT and SAT cover scientific topics from fields such as biology, ecology, physics, geology, and astronomy. They may explain a scientific phenomenon or the effects of science on society.

> *Source examples:*
> Wolf communication compared to human communication
> The composition of lava
> How images from the Hubble Telescope are used in school curriculum

Most test takers prefer Science passages to Social Studies passages and History passages, especially if a passage is more about science and less about humans. If the author does not inject his opinion that often, as is the case with some scientific passages, then you are mostly dealing with facts, which are easy to find and prove when you are answering questions. Plus, these types of passages often have an impartial or matter-of-fact tone, making questions about the author's attitude easier to answer. But still, even though most science passages are stacked with facts, be on the lookout for the author's point of view. He likely has an opinion on the subject.

Science passages may contain some unknown vocabulary, but this should not worry you, as it is always explained. The author might define the term in a surrounding sentence, as in this example with the word *cyclotron*:

> The cyclotron, built in 1963, is located in a laboratory on the campus of Michigan State University. A cyclotron is a machine used to accelerate charged particles making them useful for nuclear physics experiments.

Scientific vocabulary is always defined or explained on the Reading test.

You may also be given a footnote at the end of the passage that defines a marked term:

> Bats are chiropters*, a classification that seems unnecessary given that they are the only members of the group. The other mammals that are said to fly—including the flying squirrel, the sugar glider, and the colugo— actually glide using the skin between their limbs and torso. These animals can only glide downward, while bats can truly fly in all directions using real wings.
>
> *A chiropter is a winged mammal.

There will be a single Science passage on the ACT and it is always the final passage on the Reading test. There are two Natural Science passages on the SAT. In the *Official SAT Study Guide*, these two passages are the third and fifth sets of passages.

One of the Science passages on the SAT will be accompanied by a table, graph, or figure. Since the test does not have a dedicated science section, questions about infographics are peppered throughout the Reading, Writing, and Math sections. We will cover these charts and graphs in Chapter Fourteen.

Social Studies

Social Studies passages address current or past events with a focus on how those events affected society. Topics may be drawn from such fields as sociology, economics, psychology, education, and business.

> *Source examples:*
> The long term-effects of state standards in education
> The impact of 3-D televisions on buying trends
> The role of African-American women in the Civil War

On the ACT, "history" is considered a part of Social Studies while the SAT makes it a separate topic. We will discuss how it exclusively applies to the SAT next.

In Social Studies passages, the author will likely provide her point of view of a particular event. She may cite an expert who agrees with her to bolster her main idea, or she may reference an expert who disagrees with her to refute his point of view. Either way, be sure to document any multiple viewpoints that may be provided.

Social Studies passages are typically written in a relatively recent time period, often making them easier to read than historical pieces. They are always the second passage on the ACT. In the *Official SAT Study Guide*, they occur as the second of the five passage sets on practice SATs.

History

History passages on the ACT are described under the previous "Social Studies" heading. This section pertains only to the History passages on the SAT.

These passages are typically pulled from historical documents or texts that the College Board has dubbed the "Great Global Conversation"; specifically,

◎ SAT ONLY ◎
The ACT does not have tables, graphs, figures, or related questions in its Reading section.

♣ GRATUITOUS VOCAB
bolster (vb): to support and strengthen
refute (vb): to prove to be false

◎ SAT ONLY ◎
On the ACT, "History" falls under Social Studies and the passages resemble all other Social Studies passages. On the SAT, History passages are a bit more difficult because they are selected from historical sources.

you can expect history passages from speeches, letters, essays, government documents, books, or other sources of historical content.

Source examples:
The farewell address of Dwight D. Eisenhower warning against the influence of the defense industry on the military
A letter from Harriet Ann Jacobs about her childhood in slavery
A portion of the Articles of Confederation about states' rights

Historical texts frequently contain an author's strong opinion on a topic that was debated during that particular time period. Think slavery in the 1860s, women's rights in the 1920s, and the Viet Nam War in the 1960s. There is an abundance of documents in which authors take different sides of an issue so they make perfect paired passages.

Because of the formal language used in past centuries, history passages are often deemed the most difficult by test takers. In released SAT practice tests, historical passages are the fourth of the five passage sets.

Humanities

The SAT featured Humanities passages in the past, but the test currently focuses more on History and Social Studies. Certainly these subjects can intertwine, such as in a Social Studies passage on the Mona Lisa's influence on the "selfie" trend, but only the ACT has a dedicated Humanities passage on every test.

Humanities passages cover topics with a cultural interest, such as literature, art, dance, music, television, and theater.

Source examples:
The architecture of Aldo Rossi
The characters of Shakespeare's comedies
Developments in jazz in the 1970s

In the majority of the humanities passages that we analyzed, the author viewed his subject in a positive light. In a paired passage, it is possible that one author will praise a work of art while the other criticizes the same piece, but in single passages, the author usually views the topic favorably.

Some Humanities passages are taken from memoirs and read just like Literary Fiction. If you find a passage such as this, treat it as fiction instead of as nonfiction when applying the PowerScore strategies discussed later in this book.

Two conflicting opinions about a period in history make excellent paired passages.

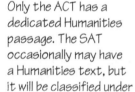

Only the ACT has a dedicated Humanities passage. The SAT occasionally may have a Humanities text, but it will be classified under "Social Studies" or "History."

General Test Strategy

Order of Passage Subjects

It is important to pinpoint which passage subject areas cause you the most difficulty and which you find easiest, as you should attack them in an order which will earn you the most points.

Most students report that they struggle with completing the ACT Reading test in the allotted 35 minutes and the SAT Reading test in the allotted 65 minutes. For this reason, you should **leave the most difficult subject areas for the end**. It doesn't make sense to spend time grappling with a Social Studies passage only to leave unanswered questions from an easier Science passage.

Let's look at an example of how some students should approach the passages. First, consider the definitive order of ACT passages:

Order of Passages on the ACT
1. Literary Fiction
2. Social Studies
3. Humanities
4. Science

Marcus, an ACT test taker, prefers the Social Studies passage and struggles with the Humanities passage. His section order might resemble the following:

Marcus's Preferred Order:
1. Social Studies
2. Literary fiction
3. Science
4. Humanities

Marcus should work on these sections in his preferred order, skipping the Literary Fiction passage and attacking the Social Studies passage first. He will save the Humanities passage for the end of the section.

Now consider the likely order of passages on the SAT (remembering that this order could change without notice):

Order of Passages on the SAT
1. Literary Fiction
2. Social Studies
3. Science I
4. History
5. Science II

÷TIPS and TRICKS÷
By leaving your most difficult section for last, you will be sure to earn points for all of the "easier" sections you might not otherwise have reached in the allotted time.

Dani knows that the Literary Fiction passage is the easiest for her, while the "Social Studies" passages—particularly the History passage—are the most difficult for her. Her section order would look like this:

Dani's Preferred Order:
1. Literary fiction
2. Science I
3. Science II
4. Social Studies
5. History

Dani can start with Literary Fiction but then skip the Social Studies passage to tackle the first Science passage. She should save Social Studies and History for the end. This ensures that she answers as many questions as possible before getting to the questions that will be most difficult—and thus time-consuming.

You may also want to take into consideration your comfort level with the paired passages. If you do well on these passages or struggle with them, you will want to locate them as soon as the Reading test starts so you can adjust your planned section order.

✦ GRATUITOUS VOCAB
synthesis (n): combination

On the SAT, Shondra prefers the Science passages and dreads the Social Studies passage, but she also has a hard time with the synthesis questions on the paired passage set. When she gets her test, she realizes that the first Science passage is the paired passage set, so she has to assign it lower priority:

Shondra's Preferred Order on the SAT:
1. Science II
2. Literary Fiction
3. History
4. Science I (paired passage set)
5. Social Studies

Shondra is also taking the ACT, where the paired passages occur in the Literary Fiction section. She will have to decide which is more difficult for her—a Social Studies passage or a paired Literary Fiction passage— and plan accordingly:

Shondra's Preferred Order on the ACT:
1. Science
2. Humanities
3. Literary Fiction (paired passage set)
4. Social Studies

When following this passage order strategy, it is imperative that you carefully "bubble in" your answer booklet. If you skip questions 1 through 10 in the test booklet, you must also skip them in the answer booklet. Be sure to practice this method with real answer sheets prior to taking the ACT or SAT.

Only you can determine which order to tackle each subject area on your ACT or SAT, but you must be ready to adjust your order based on where the paired passages fall and your ability to master them. By preparing now, you will not waste any time on a test where time is such a valuable commodity.

If you already know which sections accentuate your strengths and which sections expose your weaknesses, complete the plans below for the test(s) you will be taking. Otherwise, return to this page after reading this book or completing a practice test.

ACT Preferred Section Order

Current Order of Passages on the ACT
1. Literary Fiction
2. Social Studies
3. Humanities
4. Science

If Literary Fiction is the paired passage set, I will attack the sections in the following order:

1. _____
2. _____
3. _____
4. _____

If Humanities is the paired passage set, I will attack the sections in the following order:

1. _____
2. _____
3. _____
4. _____

If Social Studies is the paired passage set, I will attack the sections in the following order:

1. _____
2. _____
3. _____
4. _____

If Science is the paired passage set, I will attack the sections in the following order:

1. _____
2. _____
3. _____
4. _____

☠ CAUTION: TEST TRAP
You must carefully bubble your answer sheet when skipping a passage set!

✒ GRATUITOUS VOCAB
imperative (adj): crucial

commodity (n): a valuable thing

You may not yet know which areas are most difficult for you, in which case you should return to this section after completing the book.

SAT Preferred Section Order

Current Order of Passages on the SAT
1. Literary Fiction
2. Social Studies
3. Science I
4. History
5. Science II

If Literary Fiction is the paired passage set, I will attack the sections in the following order:

1. _____
2. _____
3. _____
4. _____
5. _____

If History is the paired passage set, I will attack the sections in the following order:

1. _____
2. _____
3. _____
4. _____
5. _____

If Social Studies is the paired passage set, I will attack the sections in the following order:

1. _____
2. _____
3. _____
4. _____
5. _____

If Science II is the paired passage set, I will attack the sections in the following order:

1. _____
2. _____
3. _____
4. _____
5. _____

If Science I is the paired passage set, I will attack the sections in the following order:

1. _____
2. _____
3. _____
4. _____
5. _____

Vocabulary on the ACT and SAT

It's no secret that the SAT used to feature difficult vocabulary words in Analogy and Sentence Completion questions. But what surprises most people is that both the ACT and SAT test vocabulary words in reading comprehension questions and answer choices, even now, long after the Analogy and Sentence Completion questions have been removed from the SAT.

When the latest version of the SAT was unveiled, the College Board declared that it would no longer feature "obscure" words, but rather "relevant words in context." The problem with this is that the definitions of *obscure* and *relevant* depend on whom you ask. For example, despite these statements from the College Board, official practice tests feature the words *didactic*, *egregious*, and *promulgated*, which the average high school student would certainly deem both obscure and irrelevant.

But good news—words like these are rare on the SAT (and nonexistent on the ACT), and for that reason, we do not recommend that students study long lists of higher-level vocabulary words. Instead, we have created a list of 300 of the ACT's and SAT's most commonly occurring high-utility words—such as *diplomatic*, *synthesis*, and *undermine*—which are featured strongly in academic text but not in everyday conversation. Most of these words appear on the Common Core State Standards Tier II vocabulary list, and thus are natural vocabulary words for two tests that are often marketed as statewide Common Core assessments.

Both the ACT and the SAT have a penchant for words that have multiple meanings. Take, for example, the adjective *acute*. It has several definitions:

1. *sharp or intense*
   The patient reported <u>acute</u> pain in her abdomen.
2. *critical or serious*
   There is an <u>acute</u> shortage of teachers at the high school.
3. *extremely perceptive*
   The <u>acute</u> detective knew that the suspect was lying.
4. *of an angle less than 90 degrees*
   The architect worried that the <u>acute</u> wall made the room too small.

The tests will use a word like *acute* in context so that you can determine its meaning by the surrounding text. We will look into how these words are tested in depth in the chapter on Words-in-Context, but for now, we would recommend that you start studying the high-utility vocabulary words in appendix of this book.

> ❧ GRATUITOUS VOCAB
> *obscure* (adj):
> not clearly understood
>
> *didactic* (adj):
> intended for education
> *egregious* (adj):
> extraordinarily bad
> *promulgated* (vb):
> announced; made known

> ❧ GRATUITOUS VOCAB
> *penchant* (n):
> a strong liking

> You will find 300 of the most commonly occurring ACT and SAT vocabulary words-- including definitions and example sentences--in the appendix of this book.

Chapter Summary

ACT Reading Test Format

- There are four "sets" of passage: three that contain single passages and one that contains paired passages about a related topic.
- There are ten questions per passage set for a total of 40 questions.
- Passages are 500 to 900 words in length.
- The reading level of the passages varies from 8th grade to 12th grade.
- Passages are pulled from four main subject areas: Literary Fiction, Science, Social Studies, and Humanities.

SAT Reading Test Format

- There are five "sets" of passage: four that contain single passages and one that contains paired passages about a related topic.
- There are ten or eleven questions per passage set for a total of 52 questions.
- Passages are 500 to 750 words in length.
- The reading level of the passages varies from 9th grade to early undergraduate.
- Two of the passages will have an accompanying table, graph, or figure.
- Passages are pulled from four main subject areas: Literary Fiction, Science, Social Studies, and History.

Time Management and General Strategy

- Aim to read passages in 2½ minutes or less.
- On the ACT, you have 35 minutes to complete the Reading Test. Budget 10 minutes for the four passage sets and 25 minutes for questions. This gives you 37.5 second per question.
- On the SAT, you have 65 minutes to complete the Reading Test. Budget 12½ minutes for the five passage sets and 52½ minutes for questions. This gives you just over a minute per question.
- Practice using a timer so you get the feel for how long you have worked on a question.
- Always guess when you do not know the answer before moving on to the next question. There is no penalty for wrong answers.
- If you finish a section before time is called, review your answers. Never finish early on the ACT or SAT.
- Determine the order to attack passages prior to taking the test and be sure to bubble your answer sheet carefully when skipping around.
- Do not focus on the occasional obscure vocabulary word that may appear but instead study common academic words that frequently appear.

Confidence Quotation
"The words 'never,' 'can't,' 'quit,' and 'fail' are not in my vocabulary."
-Robert Cheeke, American bodybuilder

CHAPTER SEVEN
GENERAL READING STRATEGIES

Reading is a skill that most people first learn in kindergarten or first grade. It is one that is continually honed through many years of practice, although the fundamentals of reading are rarely taught past elementary school or middle school, and almost never addressed in high school—at least not in a way that students understand they are reinforcing their reading proficiency. Students who read for pleasure continue to polish many of these basic skills, often unconsciously, but students who only read when obligated by schoolwork almost never fully develop the skills needed to be a proficient reader.

This chapter is dedicated to correcting that oversight. By practicing the strategies here, students can improve their comprehension, retention, and reading speed. This is not only important for your ACT and SAT preparation, but also for your success in college, since college textbooks and course packs are often loaded with dry, dense articles like the ones used on the ACT and SAT.

You should practice reading college-level texts every day from now until your test date. Even spending ten minutes a day familiarizing yourself with dry, difficult passages will translate into higher scores on the ACT and SAT. The Reading Bible website (powerscore.com/readingbible) has links to magazines and novels that have been used as sources for previous ACT and SAT passages. You can print articles from portions of these works to use as your daily practice.

We will discuss strategies for attacking questions and answer choices in subsequent chapters, and we will address test-specific reading strategies in the following chapter. The information provided in this chapter, however, will simply address how to approach academic passages on standardized tests.

Confidence Quotation
"Resolve to edge in a little reading every day, if it is but a single sentence. If you gain fifteen minutes a day, it will make itself felt at the end of the year."
-Horace Mann, reformer of American education

Adjust Your Attitude

Have you ever done well at anything you hated to do? Probably not. People who excel at a sport, skill, or art usually love what they do. Beethoven was a musical genius because he loved to play the piano. Shakespeare is the world's most famous playwright because he loved to tell tales. And Georgia O'Keeffe is one of the most celebrated artists in history because she loved to paint.

It's unlikely that your score will improve if you go into the test hating the reading passages. We admit that they are dry and boring. We know that they use prose that is difficult to read. But we insist that you love them just the same.

TIPS and TRICKS
By pretending to love the passage you are reading, you will increase comprehension and retention.

You must attack each ACT and SAT reading passage as if it is an exciting novel you have been waiting to read for months. Enjoying a passage, and even pretending to enjoy a passage, can increase your comprehension and retention of the material you are reading. For example, what are you most likely to remember: an article in your favorite magazine or the reading assignment in history class? Plus, it is easier to read material in which you are interested. Even if the magazine article and history text are written for the same reading level, you are likely to breeze right through the article, but slow down, stumble, and lose focus in the history passage. Stimulating passages both hold our attention and increase our retention.

So **you must pretend that the test passage you are about to read is interesting**. Tell yourself it is exciting. Act like it's a best seller. Do whatever you have to do to expel those negative thoughts and beliefs, because they do nothing to improve your results. Lou Holtz, longtime Notre Dame football coach and commentator, once said "Ability is what you're capable of doing. Motivation determines what you do. Attitude determines how well you do it." Change your attitude toward the ACT and SAT reading passages and you will improve your performance.

Confidence Quotation
"Nothing great was ever achieved without enthusiasm."
-Ralph Waldo Emerson, American poet and essayist

Adjust Your Reading Speed

Good readers are like good drivers who adjust their speed according to the design and conditions of the roadways. They slow down through curves and on wet roads, and they speed up on straightaways and in good weather. Similarly, the best readers adjust their speed according to the design and conditions of the material. They slow down for the main idea and obscure sentences, and they speed up for supporting paragraphs and easier text.

Most students mistakenly believe that they need to slow down their normal reading speed in order to fully understand an ACT or SAT passage. But research shows that there is little correlation between your reading rate and comprehension; how well you understand the passage depends on how well you pull information out of it, not on how slowly you work through it.

You should aim to complete long passages in under two and a half minutes. Taking any more time makes it much more difficult to complete all of the accompanying questions. It is imperative that you practice with a stopwatch or timer (most cell phones have these functions) so that you can begin to adjust your reading speed accordingly.

To improve your pacing through the passages, it helps to study the differences between good readers and inefficient readers. Good readers process groups of words at one time, allowing their eyes to stop only a few times on each line (usually at punctuation marks like commas and periods). Inefficient readers, on the other hand, study every word and their eyes slow or stop many times on every line of text. They may also move their lips while reading; this is a huge mistake because their very nimble brains can suddenly move only as fast as their lagging lips. You do not have the luxury to read every single word of a long passage. By learning to read groups of words, you can increase your speed exponentially.

You should also be conscious of when to read more slowly and when to read more quickly on a passage. Good readers read the main idea and topic sentences slowly, usually more slowly than inefficient readers, but then those experienced readers process the supporting details quickly—much more quickly than their less successful counterparts. Begin at your normal reading rate because the main idea is almost always in the first paragraph. **Slow down when you find the main idea and read it carefully**. You may also note any of the author's prevalent feelings toward the subject.

Once you locate the main idea, **read the supporting paragraphs more quickly**. Good readers usually slow down for the first and last sentence of all supporting paragraphs, but read the details in between quite rapidly. The topic sentence of the supporting paragraph usually provides enough information to

⬳ GRATUITOUS VOCAB
correlation (n):
mutual relationship

⧉TIPS and TRICKS⧉
Aim on completing
passages in less than
2½ minutes each.
Use a stopwatch
or countdown timer
while you practice to
determine your reading
speed and practice
improvement.

⬳ GRATUITOUS VOCAB
nimble (adj): quick

exponentially (adv):
more and more rapidly

help you quickly process any other details in the paragraph. It's unlikely that you will understand all of the information in the supporting paragraphs, and that's okay, too. You might not be asked about that specific portion of the text, and if you are, the test will usually provide a line reference so that you can come back and study it more closely. By reading the less important details quickly, you are preserving time to carefully read the questions and answer choices, which is imperative for your success.

Although it is acceptable to skip difficult supporting details, you must ensure that you understand the main idea of the passage. If you finish the first paragraph and do not yet understand the main idea or the general meaning of the paragraph, do not continue reading. The remaining paragraphs are likely to confuse you even more, rather than help you make sense of the first paragraph. At this point you have two options:

1. Skip to the last two sentences of the passage to see if the author summarizes his argument in a more straightforward manner.
2. Reread the first paragraph more carefully.

Always try option 1 first. If you find that the last two sentences do indeed explain the main idea, you can go back and begin reading the second paragraph. If these final sentences do not clear up your confusion, you are forced to reread.

For most students, this suggestion of reading slowly for main ideas and quickly for supporting details will seem foreign or unnatural. That is why it is extremely important that you practice this technique, preferably with a timer or stopwatch.

Practice Active Reading

You might remember "Active Reading" from your elementary school days, as it is commonly taught in early grades. Maybe your teacher had a poster hanging in the room, outlining the most important active reading skills:

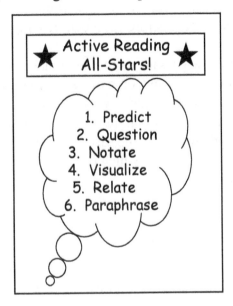

As basic as these skills might be, they are worth reviewing for the ACT and SAT. Good readers continue to practice active reading long after elementary school, but the average student leaves these skills behind with recess and show-and-tell.

1. Predict

Remember when your reading assignments had supplemental pictures? Your teacher would ask you to look at the pictures before you began reading and predict what you thought the story was going to be about.

Unfortunately, the ACT and SAT do not have pictures to go with the passages. But each passage does have an introduction at the beginning that you can use to make predictions. The blurb provides context and often reveals who wrote the passage. After reading the introduction, ask yourself, "What predictions can I make about the passage based on this information?" Spending just a few seconds making these predictions can help you better understand and connect with the passage. Let's look at an example for an SAT passage:

> The following passage is adapted from the 2014 memoir, *Blue Kites Above*, by Indu Khanna. The author, the daughter of Indian immigrants, attended high school in both Mumbai, India, and San Francisco, California.

Confidence Quotation
"A book burrows into your life in a very profound way because the experience of reading is not passive."
-Erica Jong, American author and teacher

⚓ GRATUITOUS VOCAB
supplemental (adj): additional

Based on this introduction, what predictions can you make about the text? You might surmise that the author will discuss the differences between the value placed on education in Indian and American cultures. You may predict that the author's parents are educated based on their travels. You may guess that the author herself is quite educated given that she has published a memoir. Whether your predictions are right or wrong is irrelevant; what matters is that you are thinking about the text before you begin reading.

Once you begin reading the passage, continue to make predictions about the author's beliefs or the outcome of a situation, especially if you encounter foreshadowing, those hints of what is to come. You might make conjectures between paragraphs when transitions suggest the next topic, or predict within paragraphs when a comparison leads to a contrast. Making predictions engages you in the text, which is the ultimate goal for increasing comprehension and retention.

2. Question

Good readers ask themselves many questions while reading ACT and SAT passages. The two most important questions are asked at the end of the first paragraph:

1. What is the main idea?
2. How does the author feel about the situation?

As you continue to read, stop briefly after each supporting paragraph and ask two more questions:

1. What is the topic of this paragraph?
2. How does this paragraph develop the main idea?

You should also ask questions about individual sentences and ideas throughout your reading. Some of your questions will be answered by subsequent text, others may go unanswered, and the rest you might just answer yourself when drawing conclusions.

3. Notate

It is impossible to remember all of the details from an ACT or SAT passage. Our short term memory is like a guard whose sole purpose is to allow only five or six facts into our brains at one time and deny entrance to any other new information. Most students read an ACT or SAT passage once and then have to reread each paragraph when they return to answer specific questions.

Good readers take measures to prevent time-consuming, redundant rereading by constructing a "Sidebar Summary." After questioning themselves about the main idea and topic of each paragraph, they write a short, three or four word summary next to each long paragraph or each group of related paragraphs. The key word is *short*; writing full sentences is time consuming. Consider an example of a sidebar summary:

≝TIPS and TRICKS≝
Taking a couple of seconds to create a short sidebar summary for each paragraph can save you minutes once you reach the questions.

Sociologist Angela Lieto, for example, cited in an interview in 1998, did not agree that such behavior was always fostered in the home. There are thousands of children, she reasoned, who exhibit bully behaviors but
Line
5 have not been exposed to such harassment either by the parents or other caretakers. She contends that bullying, a learned habit, results from the intrinsic rewards of childhood hierarchies. In her view, students who gain confidence and influence by tormenting others will continue
10 to be bullies. It is only when other children determine that bullying is "uncool" that these dominant members of the group will relent.

bullying is learned

This test taker summarized the sociologist's viewpoint in three words: *bullying is learned*. A simple note like this one will keep your short term memory from becoming overcrowded and unreliable and also help you easily identify the structure of the passage at the completion of your reading.

Some students prefer to underline key points from the passage. While this can be a valuable strategy in your classroom reading, it is not always an effective time-saving solution on the ACT and SAT. The main ideas are often contained in sentences using challenging vocabulary and sentence structure, so understanding these complex sentences after reading the entire passage may require you to read surrounding sentences as well. Consider the main idea in the paragraph above: "She contends that bullying, a learned habit, results from the intrinsic rewards of childhood hierarchies." It may take two or three re-readings of this sentence just to make sense of it! If the main idea is as simple as "Bullying is learned," by all means, underline the sentence. But when a topic sentence is not so clear, like the one above, be discriminate when choosing portions of the text to underline.

Only employ underlining if the main idea sentence is easy to understand. Otherwise, sidebar summaries work best.

↳ GRATUITOUS VOCAB
intrinsic (adj): natural; essential

4. Visualize

As you read a passage, visualize the setting. This is especially easy to do with Literary Fiction passages. Imagine what the scene looks like and how the characters' faces and gestures change during conversation. For non-fiction passages, you can picture events from the passage taking place or reactions the author might have to certain situations. Even imagining the author delivering a reading of the text can help you pick up on emphasis, mood, and style.

5. Relate

As you read, ask yourself if there is anything in your background or experience that can help you relate to the people or the situations in the passage. For example, if the passage is about the preservation of a historical building, try to think of something you have tried to save or preserve or imagine a building in your town being threatened by demolition. If the author recounts a moment when her father was disappointed by her actions, try to remember a time that you let down a parent or authority figure. How did it feel?

If you can find similarities between your own life and a dull, obscure ACT or SAT reading passage, the text will not only become easier to read, but also easier to remember. Comparing your feelings to those of a character or author helps you understand the tone and mood more effectively.

6. Paraphrase

When good readers come to an important sentence that is complex or difficult to grasp, they paraphrase the sentence using their own words. Which of the following is easier for you to understand and remember?

> *Original from passage:*
> An anthropological search that is indiscriminate will occasionally meet with promising, if not revolutionary results, but typically such developments are dependent on definitive, premeditated exploration.

> *Paraphrased:*
> An anthropology experiment that is not well-planned may sometimes have good results but usually good results come from well-planned experiments.

Remember, important sentences are main ideas, either of the entire passage or of individual paragraphs. There is no need to paraphrase a sentence that contains trivial details, but by paraphrasing a topic sentence, you can quickly read the rest of the paragraph.

Active reading strategies may seem quite basic, but they are utilized by good readers of all ages and skill levels. Relearning these skills and applying them to ACT and SAT passages will ease your reading and boost your comprehension of important passages.

Identify Non-Fiction Passage MAPS

When reading non-fiction passages (Social Studies, Humanities, History, and Science), you should have four main goals, which you can remember by using the mnemonic device "MAPS." Each letter stands for an element of the passage you should identify:

M   Main Idea

A   Author's Attitude

P   Purpose

S   Structure

The two most important elements of a passage are the Main Idea and the Author's Attitude. Let's look at them, as well as Purpose and Structure, more closely.

Main Idea

Your primary goal on every non-fiction passage is to determine the main idea, or the central idea of an entire passage. Sometimes this theme is a fact that the author explains throughout the piece, but more often it is an opinion that the author is trying to prove.

Because the main idea usually occurs near the beginning of a passage, you should notate it as you read. Do not wait until finishing the passage to try to determine the main idea. Understanding the main idea as soon as it is introduced will help you understand the rest of the passage. We will discuss in detail the location of the main idea and separating it from other viewpoints later in this section.

Author's Attitude

The author's attitude toward the subject about which he is writing is called the tone of the passage. Because students often confuse tone (which is very important on the ACT and SAT) with mood (which is not important on the ACT nor SAT), we think it is easier to remember the word *attitude* when interpreting the author's feelings. After all, according to most parents of high school students, teenagers know all about attitude, right? Many of you have probably been accused of being sarcastic, rude, bitter, indifferent, flippant, or contentious at one point since turning 13. These are words that can also describe an author's attitude toward the topic about which he is writing.

<u>Confidence Quotation</u>
"To read without reflecting is like eating without digesting."
-Edmund Burke, Irish author and philosopher

The main idea of an ACT or SAT passage is usually at the beginning. We will look at common passage openings later in this chapter.

⚲ GRATUITOUS VOCAB
flippant (adj): disrespectful
contentious (adj): tending to argue

The tone of a passage is constant; that is, it is maintained throughout the passage, and not just specific to one paragraph or section. If the author starts out showing his respect for a sculptor's work, he will not suddenly become critical halfway through the passage. He may present the viewpoints of a person or group of people but his personal opinion will not change.

Unlike the main idea, the author's attitude cannot always be determined at the beginning of a passage. You may need to read the entire article before you are able to step back and determine the author's feelings. On both the ACT and the SAT, authors usually leave clue words to indicate their feelings toward the topic, and we will examine this later in this chapter. We will also discuss identifying the author's attitude when looking at question stems that inquire about tone.

Purpose

Some test questions will ask you to provide a reason that the author wrote a passage. Is she trying to stop the closing of an art museum? Or hoping to gain support for the use of stem cell research? Maybe she is encouraging her readers to write in cursive instead of print.

There are many reasons that people write, and identifying the specific reason that an ACT or SAT author might be writing a passage can help you when you have to answer the questions. Like the author's attitude, you will probably need to finish the passage before you are able to name the purpose with certainty. For many passages in Humanities, History, and Social Studies, the author is writing to persuade. She wants her readers to change their minds or take action against something about which she feels strongly. Many Science passages are simply meant to inform the reader about a phenomenon. But these generalizations are simply that—generalizations. You might come across a passage on the architecture of Frank Lloyd Wright that simply explains his style or a passage on the three toed sloth that implores you to protect their habitat.

You should not spend more than a few seconds considering the purpose of a passage. Once you finish reading, and before moving on to the questions, review the main idea and identify the tone. Then briefly consider why the author wrote the passage and move on to the final element of MAPS, the Structure.

The author's attitude will not change during a passage.

Many Humanities, History, and Social Studies passages are written to persuade.

⚓ GRATUITOUS VOCAB

phenomenon (n): an occurrence, often which is impressive or unusual

generalization (n): an opinion formed from only a few facts or examples

Structure

Some ACT and many SAT questions will send you back to the passage with a specific line reference, so you know exactly where to return to find the answer. But other questions ask about particular information without providing line references. Consider an example:

1. The author cites all of the following as components of a community EXCEPT

    A) supportive relationships
    B) membership drawn by a common interest
    C) a location common to all members
    D) a population with diverse backgrounds and interests

This question asks the reader to find three specific details in a passage without directing the reader to any specific locations. Students who do not pay attention to the structure of a passage will waste time skimming the entire passage again, while students who notate the organization can quickly pinpoint the three examples in the text.

The structure of the passage refers to its organization. How did the author arrange the information? Many passages open with the main idea and each subsequent paragraph contains an example or supporting evidence. Some body paragraphs may also provide reasons for, consequences of, or solutions to a particular issue or event. Finally, you may also see a paragraph that compares a related idea or one that offers a contrast to the main idea.

You do not need to physically notate the development of a passage; instead, mentally recognize the organization as you read. This will save you time when faced with questions like the one above. Often your sidebar summaries will help you determine the structure, too, which will also help when searching for answers.

Reading actively and finding the passage MAPS are not skills that you develop overnight. It takes repeated practice, which you can begin on the next page. As you read, predict, question, notate, visualize, relate, and paraphrase, all while attempting to identify the main idea, author's attitude, purpose, and structure.

The ACT tends to provide fewer line references than the SAT, so notating the structure is an especially important strategy on the ACT.

Confidence Quotation
"Force yourself to reflect on that you read, paragraph by paragraph."
-Samuel Taylor Coleridge, English poet and philosopher

Identify Non-Fiction Passage MAPS Mini-Drill

> Read the following passage and identify the Main Idea, Author's Attitude, Purpose, and Structure. Suggested answers begin on page 120.

By the latter half of the 19th century, the stage was set for the most important period of gastroimmigration in American history—when the Chinese immigrants and the Italian immigrants
5 arrived. I call it supremely important, for if you go to any American city today, and open the phone book to check on the restaurants, you will find that Chinese restaurants and Italian restaurants, despite the rise in popularity of many other ethnic cuisines, still
10 dominate the restaurant culture.

Chinese food in America, of course, has a secondary position behind Italian. It came to this country with the Chinese immigrants who arrived to work on the railroad in the West—or, rather,
15 who came to feed those who were working on the railroad. The cooks didn't have much to work with, but they imaginatively threw together little bits of meat and vegetables in their large pans and gave it a name: chop suey. As this type of cooking hit the
20 big cities, and spread across the country, a whole new cuisine emerged: Chinese-American, replete with Egg Rolls, Wonton Soup, Fried Rice, Chicken Chow Mein, and Spare Ribs. It never had quite the reach of the Italian-American food that was spawned
25 a little bit later—because, though most Americans ate this food, they didn't usually try to cook it at home. However, it did accomplish something extremely significant—it opened up the minds and palates of almost every 20th-century American to the
30 exotic allure of Asian food, paving the way for the absorption of many Asian cuisines into our national eating habits.

A bit later came the big one: Italian-American food. Around 1880, the first wave began—
35 immigrants from Naples, arriving at Ellis Island. Before long, they were living around Mulberry Street in Manhattan, where they desperately tried to reproduce the food of their homeland. They failed, because they could not obtain the ingredients that
40 they used back in the old country. Through sheer ingenuity, however, they made do with what they had. So what if the new dishes used dried herbs instead of fresh, canned tomatoes instead of fresh, more sauce on the pasta than is traditional, and more
45 meat in the diet? The Italian-American cuisine that they created was magnificent—though, if you were born after 1975, you'd never know it, because the best "Italian" chefs in America today eschew Italian-

American cuisine, preferring to climb ever-higher
50 mountains of radicchio, anointed with ever-older bottles of balsamic vinegar.

But the real triumph of the cuisine is in the American home—where pizza, lasagna, manicotti, meatballs, veal parmigiana, through frozen food, or
55 delivery food, or home cookin', or routine items such as hot dogs and hamburgers play a tremendously vital role in the everyday fare of Americans. And, I daresay, what we learned from Italian-American food is extremely important—that food with
60 origins in another country can not only become an interesting diversion here, but solidly part of our mainstream fare.

Main Idea:

Chinese and Italian cuisine dominate over other ethnic foods today. It was caused by the immigration from east & west.

Author's Attitude:

Informative, positive

Purpose:

To show the reader how significant the effects of chinese & Italian cuisine on american foods & culture are.

Structure:

1. Introduces the immigrants & states how dominant they are

2. How Chinese started cooking & how it affected American cuisine

3. How Italians came, how they made their food

4. Italian food became an important part of American food

Recognize Patterns in Non-Fiction

Learning to recognize specific patterns in Social Studies, Humanities, History, and Science passages can help you more easily identify the main idea and the author's viewpoint. Note that the strategies here do not often apply to fictional passages or passages taken from memoirs, which usually read like fictional passages. We will discuss specific strategies for those passages later in the chapter.

Passage Openings

Most ACT and SAT passages open in one of five ways. Understanding these five patterns can help you quickly pinpoint the main idea.

1. The first sentence is the main idea.

While we like to think of the test makers as nefarious villains, our paranoia often causes us to overlook the benevolence of the ACT and College Board. Their kindness in the Reading section most often occurs in the first sentence of a reading passage, where they spoon-feed us the main idea. The rest of the paragraph then elaborates or explains the thesis. If the author cites a contrary opinion, expect her to reiterate her personal point of view—the main idea—in the final sentence or sentences of the paragraph. Consider an example:

↳ GRATUITOUS VOCAB
Nefarious (adj): extremely wicked
Benevolence (n): kindness

To devotees accustomed to the narrative style and moral rectitude of Alexandra Tharrington's nineteenth century novels, the newly discovered autobiographical text from the author will come as a great surprise. ← Main Idea

While her fictional pieces use lyrical language to paint stories of honorable, courageous women, this biographical document exposes the character of an unprincipled, insecure woman in a style that is discordant and terse. These personal accounts from Tharrington herself—such as the anecdote in which she steals from her bed-ridden mother—reveal a much different temperament than previously thought by fans and critics alike. ← Main Idea Elaboration

Some of these critics argue that this nonfiction text was written toward the end of her life when she was left destitute and alone, thus altering her outlook on morality and self-sufficiency. They contend that Tharringon was both scrupulous and intrepid, like her heroines, when she was publishing novels. ← Contrary Opinion

However, they cannot dispute that this new biographical evidence will both astonish her fans and shake the foundation of her legacy. ← Restated Main Idea

This style of passage opening is common in Science passages and in the paired passages, no matter the subject area, but can appear in Humanities and Social Studies passages as well.

2. The main idea is the answer to a question.

If a paragraph opens with a question, expect the answer to that question to be the main idea. This answer may come immediately after the question, so that the rest of the paragraph elaborates or explains the thesis. Or the answer may not come until the last sentence of the paragraph or the first sentence of the second paragraph. If this is the case, the preceding information will hint at the answer, explain the answer slowly, or offer contrary opinions. Let's study an example:

What predictions can you make about this passage based on the first paragraph? How does the author feel about snakes? Can you predict the topic of each supporting paragraph given the last sentence?

> Why does the sight of a snake cause instant terror for most people? These reptiles get little credit for eliminating rodents, bugs, and other household pests that may also induce fear and loathing. Snakes are not valued, either, for
> *Line 5* the food source they provide for more appreciated owls, hawks, herons, and carnivorous mammals. And the fact that many poisonous snakes provide venom used in medicines and research is ignored by most snake detractors, even those who benefit from such medicine. Unfortunately,
> *10* most people's opinions of snakes have been influenced by terrifying myths, fictional media, and negative religious stories, resulting in a population that fears these wonderful creatures.

← Question

Contrary Opinion

← Main Idea

This style of passage opening may occur with any subject area.

♣ GRATUITOUS VOCAB
proverb (n):
  a wise saying
maxim (n):
  a principle

3. The main idea explains or disputes an opening proverb or quotation.

When a paragraph opens with a proverb, maxim, or quotation, expect the main idea to be a restatement of the saying or its direct counterargument. The main idea will usually occur in the second half of the first paragraph or in the first sentences of the second paragraph, after a brief explanation of or a commentary on the quotation. Examine a sample:

> H.L Mencken once remarked, "Looking for an honest politician is like looking for an ethical burglar." It's difficult to believe that even in his day, many politicians did not uphold the very laws and values to which their constituents
> *Line 5* were held, and it is downright disappointing that changes in our political system were not made then, when media did not yet have such tremendous influence. Yet here we are, nearly a century later, still dealing with unethical lawmakers and power-hungry leaders.
> *10*   That is why Carson Sykes, the candidate for governor, is such a refreshing change. He is an honest politician in Mencken's dishonest world, hoping to change an unethical and outdated system. He first began fighting his one-man war on political corruption in 1988 when....

← Quotation

Commentary

Main Idea (contrary to quotation)

This type of passage opening may also occur with Social Studies, Humanities, History, and Science.

4. The main idea follows a story, anecdote, joke, report, or comparison.
In this style of passage opening, the story may account for one, two, or several paragraphs, depending on its length. The main idea occurs in the first paragraph *after* the completion of the anecdote. Consider this type of opening:

October 30, 1938. In living rooms all over America, families were gathering to listen to their favorite dramas on the popular radio program, *Mercury Theatre on the Air.*

Line 5 Instead, they heard a seemingly-real weather report that was interrupted by a news bulletin claiming explosions on Mars. Then new developments arose, with a meteorite crashing in New Jersey which contained a martian that incinerated all onlookers. As each minute passed, the news bulletins grew more disturbing; armies of aliens were landing on Earth and
10 obliterating any human being in their paths.

Panic ensued. The listening public inundated police stations and newspaper offices with hysterical phone calls, asking about gas masks and evacuation. Families retreated to cellars and basements with survival supplies and loaded
15 guns. Thousands were treated for shock and hysteria.

Little did they know, they were simply listening to an adaptation of H. G. Well's fictional *The War of the Worlds.* It was a fabrication. A hoax. A Devil's Night prank.

Although the after effects were eventually deemed
20 relatively innocuous, one thing was made clear by the broadcast: <u>media has the power to influence millions to act</u> ← Main Idea <u>instantaneously</u>. This discovery was limited to radio and print at the time, but has since proven true of the power of television and the internet as well. <u>These sources of media</u> ← Restated
25 <u>have the ability to propel the masses into action, and in the</u> Main Idea <u>process, change the course of history.</u>

⌐ Story

The story or anecdote is usually easy to read, and occasionally over-dramatic. You can progress through it quickly, without worrying about finding important ideas, since these ideas will come after the story itself. The story will likely be an example that illustrates the main idea.

✦ GRATUITOUS VOCAB
conventional (adj):
following accepted
customs and behaviors

5. The main idea follows opposing conventional wisdom.

When a paragraph opens by citing the opinions of critics, researchers, scientists, experts, or the general public, expect the main idea to disagree with this conventional wisdom. The thesis will follow these opinions in the final sentence of the first paragraph, or the opening lines of the second paragraph. Consider an example of this final type of passage opening:

> For centuries, historians held that Christopher Columbus discovered the Americas when he landed in the Bahamas in 1492. His accomplishment was commemorated with a federal holiday, state capital, national capital, and even a country named in his honor. Millions of America's school children have been taught to revere the courageous explorer, despite a self-written journal that paints a portrait of a man who was heartless and inhumane toward the resident population. His character was not of importance; we were to idolize the man simply because he discovered our country and made European settlement possible.
>
> Now, however, this theory is under investigation, as new evidence suggests that the Phoenicians first visited the Americas in 1600 B.C. Archaeologists believe that an ancient coin depicts a map of the world, which includes two land masses that cannot be anything but North and South America. If true, these coins not only provide the oldest....

Line 5, Line 10, Line 15 (line markers)

Opposing Conventional Wisdom ⟵ (annotation)

Main Idea ⟵ (annotation)

If faced with this type of opening paragraph, watch for words that show contrast, such as *however, conversely, despite, but,* and *though.* The author's point of view or main idea will follow words like these.

We have presented the five most common ways that ACT and SAT passages begin. This is not an inclusive list; you might come across a passage that does not open in one of these manners. If you find yourself confused or unable to find the main idea, there are four key sentences to check:

1. The first sentence of the first paragraph
2. The last sentence of the first paragraph
3. The first sentence of the second paragraph
4. The last sentence of the second paragraph

If you still cannot locate the main idea, look at the last two or three sentences of the entire passage to see if the author summarizes his main idea at the end.

Confidence Quotation
"All that a man achieves
and all that he fails to
achieve is the direct
result of his own
thoughts."
-James Allen, British
philosophical writer

Passage Openings Mini-Drill

> In each passage opening below, underline the main idea and write its sidebar summary. Then, diagram the passage, showing contrary opinions, opposing conventional wisdom, or other elements as diagrammed on the previous pages discussing passage openings. Answers begin on page 121.

1:

Question

Where was Olaudah Equiano born? Since 1999, a debate has raged amongst historians about the birthplace of the author, one of very few slaves of African descent to record his autobiography in English in the eighteenth century. In

Line 5 *The Interesting Narrative of the Life of Olaudah Equiano, or Gustavus Vassa, the African*, Equiano himself claims he was born in Africa, describing life in an African village as a free child. He also provides a first-person account of the arduous journey of the Middle Passage, seemingly

10 something only a captured slave could relate in such detail. In 1999, however, professor and author Vincent Caretta asserted that Equiano was actually born a slave in South Carolina. Caretta argued that Equiano's stories of African life and capture came from oral histories of other slaves and

15 information he gathered in books. The professor provided other evidence, such as a baptismal record and a muster roll, showing that the slave was actually born in the English colony. While the question is far from settled, one thing is certain: members of both sides of the debate possess

20 compelling evidence to support their claims.

[sidebar notes: Story; Critics]

2:

When I was a child and not feeling well, my mother would run to the kitchen instead of the medicine cabinet. If I complained of a stomach ache, she concocted a buttermilk and honey elixir to ease my pain. If I had a headache, she

Line 5 made a lemon mayonnaise paste to slather on my forehead to loosen tense muscles. Nothing was too extreme. Once, when I woke up with a sore throat, she sat on my bed and ordered me to open my mouth.

"Why?" I asked apprehensively.

10 "I have a recipe from *Mrs. Winston's Home Remedies* I want to try," she said, stirring a red batter. She was always trying new "miracle cures" from that tattered old book.

"What's in it?"

She looked at me with annoyance. "Don't you worry

15 about that, Charlie. Just open your mouth."

I later learned that the recipe she slathered all over my tongue was a mixture of beets, garlic, and lard. I can still remember its awful taste whenever I get a sore throat.

Now, after nearly fifty years (four of which I spent

20 in medical school and twenty of which I have practiced medicine), I wish I could find that old book. Although I thought those remedies were a sham when I was a child, I have since come to recognize the power of alternative medicine. Practices such as acupuncture, reiki, and even my

25 mom's home remedies deserve more respect and attention from practitioners of Western medicine.

[sidebar notes: Story; Talking about Story; Main Idea]

Pivotal Words

Once the main idea is stated, the remaining paragraphs of the passage will explain, support, or elaborate the main idea. This is most often done by providing examples that prove the thesis, but the author may also add details, compare a similar concept, or quote an authority on the subject. He can also cite opposing viewpoints in order to explain why those opinions are wrong.

Pivotal words include however, thus, *and* in fact, *and are those that indicate the direction that the passage is heading.*

Pivotal words are those that guide a reader through an author's ideas. Spotting these words throughout a passage can help you determine the author's attitude and opinion concerning the main idea, which will ultimately help you when faced with the questions at the end of the passage. Just knowing that the author favors school uniforms or that he disapproves of internet sales tax can help you eliminate wrong answer choices.

The following lists contain the most important pivotal words for which to watch when reading an ACT or SAT passage.

1. U-Turn Words

Authors often use words that signal a "U-turn" in the text to highlight contrasting ideas. These are the most important pivotal words in a passage; if you miss one, you likely miss the author's point and believe in the opposite idea. Consider an example:

> Scholars long believed the painting was completed in 1678, **but** recent evidence indicates that it was not finished until the turn of the century.

Missing a U-Turn Word can result in missing the author's main idea or attitude.

In this sentence, the U-Turn Word *but* contradicts the first idea. Students who fail to notice the U-Turn Word might mistakenly believe that the painting was completed in 1678, when recent evidence indicates that it was completed in 1700 or later.

U-Turn Words may also be subordinating conjunctions at the beginning of a sentence:

> **While** an argument can be made that certain programs on television are harmful to children, not all shows have such negative consequences.

The U-Turn Word *while* indicates that the second part of the sentence is going to oppose the first part. The author believes that some television shows do not have negative consequences. However, if you do not pick up on *while*, you might erroneously determine that the main idea is that programs on television are harmful to children.

The U-Turn Words in Reading passages include all of the following:

but	on the contrary	still
although	on the other hand	nonetheless
yet	instead of	in contrast
despite	conversely	rather than
while	even though	whereas
however	nevertheless	paradoxically
even so	in spite of	not

When U-Turn Words are used in a passage, the author's viewpoint most often lies in the contrasting idea, which is usually the second portion of the sentence.

2. One Way Words (Additional Information)

There are two types of One Way Words. Those that add information to a text are words and phrases that indicate that the author is continuing with or expanding the same idea:

and	besides	in addition
also	further	moreover
as well as	furthermore	too
not only...but also	both...and	

3. One Way Words (Comparable Information)

Another type of One Way Word indicates that the author is making a comparison or recognizing a similarity between two things. Words in this list include the following:

equally important	at the same time	similarly
in like fashion/manner	likewise	analogous to
akin to	comparable to	by the same token
just as	parallels	similar to

4. Cause and Effect Words

When the author is citing reasons that something has occurred, he will likely use Cause and Effect Words to get his point across:

because	since	so
due to	accordingly	thus
therefore	consequently	for this reason
hence	then	as a result
leading to	in order to	resulting in

TIPS and TRICKS
If U-Turn Words are used in the main idea, the author's belief is likely in the second clause of the sentence.

Cause and Effect words are important question indicators because the test makers will likely ask you about either the cause or the effect described.

5. Example Words

The most common type of ACT and SAT passage presents a main idea in the first paragraph followed by paragraphs containing examples. The author may introduce examples with the following words:

for example	for instance	as
such as	like	specifically
a case in point	namely	in particular
including	to illustrate	markedly

6. Opposing Viewpoint Words

If an author acknowledges that there are other viewpoints or beliefs on the topic besides her own, she may set them off with one of the following words or phrases:

granted that	yes	of course
admit	concede	accept

You should expect a U-Turn Word to introduce the author's opinion following a sentence that provides an opposing viewpoint.

7. Emphasis Words

The author can emphasize a point in two ways. He can repeat or rephrase a statement, using specific emphasis words to introduce the reiteration:

again	to repeat	in other words
that is	in essence	in fact

Or he can use emphasis words or phrases to show the importance of the original statement. These words may reveal the main idea or tone of a passage:

above all	indeed	more important
chiefly	especially	singularly
and even	undeniably	undoubtedly
obviously	clearly	certainly
surely	unquestionably	definitely

8. Conclusion Words

If the author offers a conclusion, pay close attention. She is likely summarizing the main idea. Watch for these words to set off a conclusion:

in conclusion	to sum up	in brief
for these reasons	after all	all things considered
in any event	on the whole	finally
in summary	to summarize	to conclude

If the author cites an opposing viewpoint, expect a corresponding question.

⚑ GRATUITOUS VOCAB
reiteration (n): act of repeating

Emphasis Words often provide attitude clues to the author's feelings about the subject.

Now let's examine a passage to see how these pivotal words introduce ideas:

Scientists have long hypothesized that the abundance of species in the Amazon river basin was <u>the result of</u>[1] climatic stability, based on their observations of life in—of all places—the deep sea.
Line 5 <u>Because</u>[2] the abyssal zone, that deepest part of the ocean that is consistently cold and dark, has such a high level of species diversity, scientists concluded that its constant climate and conditions attracted numerous species. <u>Similarly,</u>[3] they noted, the Amazon river basin
10 maintains a relatively unfluctuating tropical rainforest climate, <u>as well as</u>[4] supports a multitude of species.

Recent theories about the Amazon basin, <u>however,</u>[5] dispute this long-standing theory. Some biologists are now suggesting that the rainforest of the Amazon does
15 not, <u>in fact,</u>[6] have a stable climate, <u>but</u>[7] rather one that has seen significant variation over time.

<u>To illustrate</u>[8] their new theory, these biologists point to an oddity among bird species. <u>Although</u>[9] the rainforest is currently constant, with green forest
20 spread throughout, different species of birds inhabit different areas. Scientists studying species distribution wondered why certain parrots lived in specific areas and not elsewhere in the forest. If the conditions were constant, why wouldn't a species spread out? The same
25 mud-dwelling invertebrates can be found in the deepest parts of all the world's oceans, so why couldn't these parrots be found all over the Amazon rain forest?

These biologists proposed that the bird distribution was the result of climactic changes in the Amazon
30 basin during ice ages. They noted that different species of birds were found on low ground than on high ground, and suggested that each of the thirteen ice ages divided the basin in two: the low ground became dry plains, <u>while</u>[10] the high ground retained
35 moisture. This division <u>also</u>[11] separated the resident bird population by <u>both</u>[12] physical location <u>and</u>[12] genetic makeup, forcing each isolated group to adapt to the new climate. With each subsequent ice age, the once continuous population was further divided,
40 <u>thus</u>[13] increasing diversity of species and permanently altering the locality of the birds.

This new theory <u>not only</u>[14] questions the climactic stability of the Amazon River basin, <u>but also</u>[14] provides an alternative argument for the cause of such great
45 species diversity in the rainforest. <u>Granted,</u>[15] there is no conclusive evidence to substantiate this new theory, <u>but</u>[16] its very existence acknowledges that scientists recognize there might be other possible reasons for an abundance of species besides climactic stability.
50 It causes one to wonder if biologists may soon re-examine their beliefs about species diversity in the deep sea.

[1] Cause: climatic stability
Effect: species diversity

[2] Cause: species diversity
Effect: scientists concluded

[3] One-Way Word compares deep sea to river basin

[4] One-Way Word provides additional detail

[5] U-Turn Word indicates contradiction of previous paragraph

[6] Provides emphasis of the main idea

[7] U-Turn Word indicates contradiction of previous paragraph

[8] Introduction of an example

[9] U-Turn Word contrasts reality with expectations

[10] U-Turn Word contrasts two locations

[11] Indicates an additional consequence of division

[12] Gives two equal effects

[13] Cause: Further division
Effect: Increased species diversity and permanent change in locality

[14] Give two equal effects of theory

[15] Acknowledges weakness with theory

[16] U-Turn Word de-emphasizes the weakness and highlights consequences of theory

Did you identify the main idea? The first paragraph contains conventional wisdom, which the main idea opposes in the second sentence of the second paragraph.

Obviously you cannot notate or even read a passage this closely on the real test. But learning to identify Pivotal Words while practicing can be internalized to help you quickly process them on test day.

⋚TIPS and TRICKS⋚
You do, however, have
time to circle U-Turn
Words and Cause and
Effect Words. These
are likely used with ideas
that will be asked about
in the questions.

Learning to spot these pivotal words in ACT and SAT passages can increase your comprehension and even your reading speed. You may consider circling U-Turn Words and Cause and Effect Words, as these most often signal important ideas, especially those that are asked about in the questions following the passage.

Attitude Clues

The tone of a passage is simply the author's attitude toward the subject about which she is writing. Some passages, especially natural science passages like the previous one on the Amazon River basin, are matter-of-fact and impartial, but most ACT and SAT passages have a clear tone. On rare occasion, an author might explicitly state how she feels about a topic:

❧ GRATUITOUS VOCAB
explicitly (adv):
in a clear manner

> I am <u>fascinated</u> by ancient cathedrals. Their architecture
> is <u>worthy of respect and imitation</u>, which I have <u>graciously</u>
> practiced since I started designing buildings twenty years
> ago.

In this passage, the author clearly expresses her fascination and respect, which together constitute the tone or attitude of that paragraph. Tone is not usually that obvious, though, and must be inferred instead. You can do this by identifying key words that hint at the author's feelings. Consider an example:

❧ GRATUITOUS VOCAB
infer (vb): to conclude
based on reasoning or
evidence

> The United States education system <u>must be changed</u>
> if our graduates are to compete for jobs with students
> from other countries. Our school calendars <u>lack</u> hours in
> *Line* a day and days in a year compared to European and Asian
> 5 schedules, resulting in students who are academically
> behind. Part of the <u>blame</u> can be laid on American parents,
> who often value freedom and individuality more than
> discipline and education.

In this passage, the author uses the words *must be changed*, *lack*, and *blame*, which indicate his criticism. The tone of this passage is *critical*.

As you read, be on the lookout for words that reveal the author's true feelings. You may want to underline them as you read in case you have a hard time determining the tone through the passage; you can review all of your underlined words at the end of the passage to easily establish the author's attitude toward the subject.

⋚TIPS and TRICKS⋚
Underline tone words as
you read them. At the
end of the passage, you
can review all underlined
words to determine the
author's attitude.

Pivotal Words and Attitude Clues Mini-Drill

9/1

In each passage below, circle any pivotal words or phrases and underline tone clues. At the end of the passage, note the main idea and the tone of the passage. Answers begin on page 122.

1:   Surprisingly, the argument that graffiti is legitimate art has many proponents in the art world. They point out that a graffiti artist must create an intricate plan before they begin, just as a painter plans on canvas. These artists use a
Line 5 standard medium—spray paint—just as a painter of canvas uses oils or watercolors. And graffiti communicates to its spectators, just as the *Mona Lisa* or *Waterlillies at Giverney* speaks to the beholders of such masterpieces. While these facts are seemingly true, there is one obvious difference
10 between graffiti and other artistic forms that just may revoke graffiti's status as art: graffiti is illegal.
    If creating a work of art is a crime, is it truly art? Advocates for graffiti say that the crime is immaterial, but would they then classify a burglar's ransacking of a home as
15 interior design? Likely not. This example illustrates the fine line between creation and destruction, and gives credence to challengers of graffiti as art. The debate is a murky one, with strong support on each side, but it seems as if the legality of a craft should play a part in determining true art.

Main Idea:

Whether graffiti should be considered
an art or not.

Author's Attitude:

Agrees with graffiti being illegal
Seems to be neutral but leaning towards
"graffiti is illegal" argument

2:   Pregnancy is a hoot. Who knew that I would get such joy out of waddling like a duck and having my ribs stomped by a little boy who is sure to one day be a placekicker in the NFL? Not to mention how much I love shopping these
Line 5 days; maternity clothes are just so darn cute with their elephant-sized waistbands and circus tent tops. Last week I noticed that none of my shoes fit anymore, given my expanding feet. I am happily wearing flip flops, the only shoes that fit, in the middle of January. In Minnesota.
10   The comments that people make are so kind and reassuring, too. Yesterday at my doctor's appointment, an old lady asked "Is there a baby in there, or are you just fat?" Isn't that sweet? My dad recently observed that my face is getting fuller to match my growing belly. He always knows
15 how to make a girl feel better.
    Pregnancy—it's an absolute riot, I tell you. On a serious note, though, I know it will all be worth it when these nine, long, torturous months are over.

Main Idea:

Pregnancy is torturous but it's worth the wait.

Author's Attitude:

She doesn't like pregnancy
Sarcastic

Multiple Viewpoints

As if ACT and SAT reading passages are not difficult enough, the test makers like to select passages that contain multiple viewpoints. The more opinions a passage contains, the more likely students are going to misinterpret the author's viewpoint, which is often the main idea. Consider an example:

> Literary critics have praised author Toni Morrison for her deft handling of female character development in novels that typically feature powerful and troubling themes. While
> Line
> 5 some have called the author a feminist, Morrison has never referred to herself as such, asserting that she seeks to craft viewpoints which embrace equality for all. But one of the strengths of her writing is the uniquely female point of view her characters bring to situations of intolerance and oppression. By their very nature, Morrison's dynamic
> 10 portrayals assert that women deserve equal rights in any forum.

This passage contains the opinions of four different people or groups of people! Were you able to decipher the author's point of view?

> Literary critics have praised author Toni Morrison for her   ------ Literary critics' view
> deft handling of female character development in novels
> that typically feature powerful and troubling themes. While
> some have called the author a feminist, Morrison has never   ------ Some people's view
> Line
> 5 referred to herself as such, asserting that she seeks to craft   ------ Morrison's view
> viewpoints which embrace equality for all. But one of
> the strengths of her writing is the uniquely female point
> of view her characters bring to situations of intolerance
> and oppression. By their very nature, Morrison's dynamic   ------ Author's view
> 10 portrayals assert that women deserve equal rights in any
> forum.

The ACT and SAT are unlikely to include four different viewpoints in one passage, but you should always be on alert for at least two or three different opinions. They may not occur in the same paragraph, but they can still cause confusion when determining the author's main idea and attitude toward the subject. Remember, also, that U-Turn words can separate the viewpoints of two people in a single sentence:

> Some watchdog groups argue that television is harmful to children, but not all programs have negative effects.

This sentence presents the viewpoint of some watchdog groups (*television is harmful to children*) and the opinion of the author (*not all programs have negative effects*).

To help you keep track of different viewpoints throughout a passage, consider notating as you read. Use "VP" to show a viewpoint, being sure to label each one with a word, abbreviation, or symbol to indicate the viewpoint's owner:

> Although the International Astronomical Union has recently downsized Pluto from a planet to a dwarf planet, <u>some scientists still contend that Pluto is a planet</u>, given that it orbits around the sun and has enough gravity to
> *Line*
> 5 be spherically shaped; however, because Pluto has other large objects in its orbit, <u>it is clear that it is merely a dwarf planet</u>. This declaration has caused quite a stir among the astronomical community, but as astrophysicist Richard Conn Henry remarked, "I think that, when the dust settles,
> 10 people will recognize that <u>there really are just eight planets</u>."

VP—Scientists

VP—Author

VP—Expert

⊰TIPS and TRICKS⊱
Identify each viewpoint as you read in order to save time when you have to return to the passage to answer questions.

The test makers purposely select passages with multiple viewpoints in an attempt to confuse you; avoid this pitfall by labeling the viewpoints as you read.

Double Negatives

Another strategy used by the ACT and College Board is to select passages with double negative statements. Although you were likely taught never to use a double negative (such as "I do not have no homework"), there are exceptions to every rule. These expressions are grammatically correct when two negatives make a positive:

Double Negative	Actual Meaning
It is not unlike him to yell.	It is like him to yell.
It is not impossible to win.	It is possible to win.
He is not unfriendly.	He is friendly.

If you come across a double negative in a test passage, slow down and closely read the sentence to make sure you understand its meaning. You can even cross out the double negative so that you do not stumble on the sentence if you have to return to that portion of the passage to answer a question:

> Although the monks from the northwest quadrant have no dietary restrictions, it is ~~not un~~common to find members of the monastery who are practicing vegetarians.

�* CAUTION: TEST TRAP
Double negatives are used to add confusion to the passage. Avoid any issues by crossing out the double negative itself.

By crossing out *not un-*, you remove the double negative and can more clearly see that the meaning is *it is common*. While double negatives are not prevalent in every passage on the ACT or SAT, they are "not uncommon."

Multiple Viewpoints and Double Negatives Mini-Drill

In each passage below, mark the multiple viewpoints using "VP" and notate the owner of the viewpoint. Then answer the question about the double negative statement. Answers begin on page 123.

1:   File sharing, the practice of allowing the electronic exchange of files over a network such as the Internet, has in recent years led to the emergence of a new and complex set of legal issues for intellectual property owners. Identifying offenders is not unfeasible, but the rapid and often *Author VP* undetectable movement of digital copies of copyrighted material makes identification particularly difficult. In addition, prosecuting such offenses is time-consuming and expensive.

Line 5

   Many owners of intellectual property have claimed that enforcement of these violations is necessary in order to send a signal to other possible offenders. For example, in 2000, members of the band *Metallica* filed suit against a music-sharing company to end the free distribution of their copyrighted material. "From a business standpoint, this is about piracy—a.k.a. taking something that doesn't belong to you and that is morally and legally wrong," said drummer Lars Ulrich. The file sharers, however, typically claim that they did not know they were sharing copyrighted material, and that regardless, the widespread use of file sharing networks renders the protection of copyrights impossible. And then there are some copyright holders, like 50 Cent and Moby, who encourage file sharing as a means to promote their music. "What is important for the music industry to understand is that this really doesn't hurt the artists," said Curtis Jackson, the rapper known as 50 Cent, in a 2007 interview. "A young fan may be just as devout and dedicated no matter if he bought it or stole it."

10

15

20

25

How does the author feel about identifying offenders in line 5?

(A) It is possible.
B) It is impossible.
C) It is illegal.
D) It is legal.

2:   Federal rules of evidence have long prohibited the presentation in court of many types of "hearsay," evidence that is recounted second-hand rather than reported directly by a witness. This decision is based on the notion that only the most readily verifiable evidence should be allowed consideration by any court in making its determinations. Much like in a childhood game of "Telephone," the words of the original speaker have a way of becoming altered and warped when passed from person to person. Dr. Kinsley has argued, however, that the rules of evidence as currently written are unacceptably overreaching, defining too many types of evidence as hearsay when the value of that evidence would far outweigh any associated detriment if allowed court admissibility. But modern hearsay rules are not unwarranted.

Line 5

10

15

How does the author feel about modern hearsay rules in lines 14 and 15?

A) They are overextended.
B) They become distorted.
(C) They are needed.
D) They are not needed.

Master Literary Fiction Passages

Literary Fiction passages are excerpts from novels, short stories, and memoirs. While a memoir is technically non-fiction, it is written in a style that mimics fiction, so you should treat it as a Literary Fiction passage when applying reading strategies.

Fiction passages most often appear as single passages, but on occasion they are used in the paired passages.

These passages are always excerpts, so they are a small portion of a long story. For this reason, it is impossible to identify the main idea. In fact, it is difficult and unnecessary to pinpoint any of the elements in MAPS; you cannot gather the main idea and the author's attitude without reading a majority of the story, and the purpose and structure do not apply to narrative fiction.

There is only one element for which to search when reading a fictional passage: the characters' feelings. How do the characters feel about each other or about their situation? In many of the passages, there is tension or disagreement between two characters. These feelings are revealed, sometimes overtly and other times subtly, through the characters' speech, actions, and thoughts. Consider an example:

> I slammed my glass down in anger. "How could you do this to me?"
> "I am so sorry," she cried. Regret was painted all over her face.

In this short passage, the author is straightforward in describing how the characters are feeling. The narrator is angry and the woman is regretful. Their emotions might not always be so blatant, however:

> I slammed my glass down. "How could you do this to me?"
> "I am so sorry," she cried.

In this passage, you have to infer that the narrator is angry (from the slamming of the glass) and the woman is regretful (from her apology and crying).

≡TIPS and TRICKS≡
Do not identify the MAPS of fictional passages. Instead, concentrate on how the characters feel about each other and the situation in which they find themselves.

♦ GRATUITOUS VOCAB
overtly (adj): openly
subtly (adj): in a manner that is difficult to perceive

Most passages on the tests mix blatant statements of feelings with subtle emotional clues. Consider an example:

> "Did you hear about your brother?" my father asked, knowing full well that Mother had already told me about Peter's promotion at the bank. "He's really making something of himself, I tell you. I always knew that boy would go far."
>
> *Line*
> 5
> I drank from my iced tea to avoid having to answer. I had been compared to my twin for nearly twenty-five years and I was still coming up short.
>
> "So, Robert," he began, "when are you going to
> 10 get promoted at the art gallery?" Here it was again. A comparison.
>
> "Dad, I am a painter," I said. "I don't get promoted. I don't even work for the gallery. Just being displayed there is a tremendous honor."
>
> 15 "Hmph," he grunted. He stirred his cocktail with a finger. "Honor doesn't mean the same thing today as it did in my day then, I guess. Being recognized for saving three men on the battlefield, that was an honor."
>
> I could not win. I was never going to please my father
> 20 because I was never going to succeed at what he considered honorable.

In this passage, the narrator feels frustration at being compared to his brother and at being unable to please his father. We learn this through his actions (drinking iced tea to avoid conversation) and his thoughts (recognizing that he *was still coming up short* in line 8 and *could not win* in line 19). You can sense a hint of suppressed anger through phrases like *knowing full well* (line 2) and *I could not win* (line 19).

On the father's part, he feels disappointed in Robert. Since the father is not the narrator, we do not have access to his thoughts, but we can analyze his words and actions. A reader might think that he is innocently talking about Peter at first, but his words later in the passage reveal that he was probably discussing Peter for the reason Robert believes: to make a comparison between his successful son (Peter) and his unsuccessful son (Robert). He grunts (line 15), showing disagreement with Robert's statement about the honor of having artwork displayed, and then compares what he feels is real honor to Robert's lesser accomplishment (lines 16-18). Additionally, he seems unaware of what Robert's job entails, but has some knowledge of Peter's occupation.

These thoughts belong to two fictional characters, not the author. Be careful not to confuse a character's belief with the author's belief. The author's attitude is not revealed, nor is it needed in fictional passages.

On the ACT, Literary Fiction passages are usually pulled from texts written in the last fifty years. The SAT will use these same sources, but they will also select passages from 19th and early 20th century novels.

The majority of passages that were written in the last fifty years come from authors who are members of a minority group. These passages usually involve a character from an oppressed group, frequently of an underrepresented ethnicity (usually written by an author of the same ethnicity), who may or may not be dealing with situations arising from her cultural background. If the character is facing issues due to her ethnicity, expect her to address alienation, assimilation, or cultural differences. Because these passages were written in the relatively recent past, they are easy to read and often considered the least difficult passages on the test.

While we have addressed the most common sources of Literary Fiction passages, you should know that they can come from other sources as well. You may find a novel written by a Caucasian male in the 1940s, which is neither "minority fiction" nor a turn of the century novel. Sometimes, though, these types of passages are set in the 19th or early 20th century or they are still written about a character from an underrepresented group, so reading them is similar to reading the more common sources. Either way, you should read them just like you read all fictional passages, searching for the characters' feelings toward each other or toward their situation.

To prepare for all ACT and SAT fictional passages, but especially those from previous centuries, you should read one or two novels in the weeks preceding the test. Submerging yourself in text that is similar to the passages on the ACT and SAT will not only prepare you for the style of the passages, but will also introduce you to many ACT and SAT vocabulary words that appear in Reading questions.

On the following pages are two lists of sources for previous official Literary Fiction passages on the ACT and SAT. Note the date that each literary work was originally published; the ACT only has one (out of forty-two passages) that was published prior to 1950 while the SAT has twelve published before that date. These passages are marked with an asterisk by the date. You should also note that the SAT uses memoirs more often than does the ACT. As you are looking for novels, memoirs, or short stories to read prior to your test, we highly recommend reading other works by the authors on these lists as they will give you an idea of the style of writing that will appear on the ACT and SAT.

GRATUITOUS VOCAB
alienation (n): the act of becoming indifferent or unfriendly
assimilation (n): the act of absorbing or adapting

You should prepare for literary fiction passages by reading novels or short stories in the days leading up to the test. Consider reading other literary works by the authors listed here.

Previous ACT Literary Fiction Passage Sources

Title	Author	Date	Type
"The Behavior of the Hawkweeds"	Andrea Barrett	1996	Short Story
"Bye Bye Brewster"	Steven Barthelme	2006	Short Story
Agassiz	Sandra Birdsell	1991	Novel
"From Aboard the Night Train"	Kimberly M. Blaeser	1993	Short Story
Monkey Bridge	Lan Cao	1997	Novel
Monkey King	Patricia Chao	1997	Novel
The Alchemist	Paulo Coelho	1993	Novel
"American History"	Judith Ortiz Cofer	1992	Short Story
"My Father's Son"	Steven Corbin	1996	Short Story
Queen of Dreams	Chitra Banerjee Divakaruni	2004	Novel
The Antelope Wife	Louise Eldrich	1998	Novel
Chamber Music	Doris Grumbach	1979	Novel
Mr. Ives' Christmas	Oscar Hijuelos	1995	Novel
Power	Linda Hogan	1998	Novel
Lily Nevada	Cecelia Holland	1999	Novel
Another Heaven, Another Earth	H.M. Hoover	1981	Novel
"Only the Little Bone"	Davide Huddle	1996	Short Story
"Aggi's Last Dance"	Josephine Huntington	1997	Short Story
Homeland	John Jakes	1993	Novel
A Map of My Home	Randa Jarrar	2008	Novel
Toning the Sweep	Angela Johnson	1993	Novel
Against the Flood	Ma Van Khang	2000	Novel
Equal Affections	David Leavitt	1989	Novel
"Mother"	Andrea Lee	1984	Short Story
Aloft	Chang-rae Lee	2004	Novel
China Bay	Gus Lee	1991	Novel
Night Water	Helen Elaine Lee	1996	Novel
"Tattoo"	Rai a Mai	2006	Short Story
"At Schindlers"	David Malouf	2000	Short Story
The Fisher King	Paule Marshall	2000	Novel
The Magic Keys	Albert Murray	2005	Novel
Bel Canto	Ann Patchett	2001	Novel
My Glove	Katherine A. Powers	2008	Memoir
"The Threshold"	Cristina Peri Rossi	1986	Short Story
The Ground Beneath Her Feet	Salman Rushdie	1999	Novel
Homecoming: A Novel	Bernhard Schlink	2006	Novel
The Spirit of the Place	Samuel Shem	2008	Novel
"Elba"	Marly Swick	1991	Short Story
The Bonesetter's Daughter	Amy Tan	2001	Novel
"Golden Glass"	Alma Luz Villanueva	1982	Short Story
Winter Wheat	Mildred Walker	1944*	Novel
The Mozart Season	Virginia Euwer Wolff	1991	Novel
Tropic of Orange: A Novel	Karen Tei Yamashita	1997	Novel

Confidence Quotation
"It is what you read when you don't have to that determines what you will be when you can't help it."
-Oscar Wilde, Irish novelist and playwright

Previous SAT Literary Fiction Passage Sources

Title	Author	Date	Type
Unafraid of the Dark	Rosemary Bray	1999	Memoir
Shirley	Charlotte Bronte	1849*	Novel
The Professor	Charlotte Bronte	1857*	Novel
"Black Ice"	Lorene Cary	1991	Short Story
"Epiphany: The Third Gift"	Lucha Corpi	1992	Memoir
"The Open Boat"	Stephen Crane	1897*	Short Story
Breath, Eyes, Memory	Edwidge Danticant	1994	Novel
Great Expectations	Charles Dickens	1861*	Novel
Deliverance	James Dickey	1970	Novel
Through the Ivory Gate	Rita Dove	1987	Novel
Rebecca	Daphne Du Maurier	1938*	Novel
The Second Life of Samuel Tyne	Edi Edugyan	2004	Novel
The Crimson Petal and the White	Michel Faber	2002	Memoir
The Spirit Catches You and You Fall Down	Anne Fadiman	1997	Memoir
A Room with a View	E.M. Forster	1908*	Novel
Howards End	E.M. Forster	1910*	Novel
"The Overcoat"	Nicolai Gogol	1842*	Short Story
Bloodlines: Odyssey of a Native Daughter	Janet Campbell Hale	1993	Memoir
I Could Tell You Stories	Patricia Hampl	1999	Memoir
Geronimo Rex	Barry Hannah	1972	Novel
The Balloonist	MacDonald Harris	2011	Novel
Lost in Translation: A Life in a New Language	Eva Hoffman	1989	Memoir
Dust Tracks on a Road	Zora Neale Hurston	1942*	Memoir
The Namesake	Jhumpa Lahiri	2003	Novel
Confessions of Summer	Phillip Lopate	1979	Novel
One Hundred Years of Solitude	Gabriel Garcia Marquez	1967	Novel
The Groves of Academe	Mary McCarthy	1952	Novel
The Strangeness of Beauty	Linda Minatoya	1999	Novel
Sula	Toni Morrison	1973	Novel
"The Moons of Jupiter"	Alice Munro	1978	Short Story
The Last Italian: Portrait of a People	William Murray	1992	Memoir
"A Moving Day"	Susan Nunes	1990	Short Story
"The Schartz-Metterklume Method"	Saki	1911*	Short Story
Places Left Unfinished at the Time of Creation	John Philip Santos	1999	Memoir
Preservation Hall	Scott Spencer	1976	Novel
Angel of Repose	Wallace Stegner	1971	Novel
The Joy Luck Club	Amy Tan	1989	Novel
The Little Friend	Donna Tartt	2002	Novel
Angel	Elizabeth Taylor	1957	Novel
"White Lies"	Paul Theroux	1979	Short Story
Invisible Thread: An Autobiography	Yoshiko Uchida	1992	Memoir
Ethan Frome	Edith Wharton	1911*	Novel
Summer	Edith Wharton	1917*	Novel

Titles that were published prior to 1950 are marked with an asterisk (*). As you can see, the SAT uses these "classic" novels much more often than does the ACT.

Chapter Summary

There are several strategies you should employ when reading ACT and SAT passages:

1. Adjust Your Attitude

- Attack the passage as if you are excited to read it.
- Pretend that the topic is interesting.

2. Adjust Your Reading Speed

- Slow down for the Main Idea, difficult topic sentences, and short passages.
- Speed up for supporting paragraphs and easier text.
- Read passages in 2½ minutes or less.
- Do not read every word or move your lips while reading.

3. Practice Active Reading

1. Predict: Make guesses about the outcome and author's reaction.
2. Question: Ask questions as you read.
3. Notate: Summarize each paragraph or section with short notes.
4. Visualize: Picture the setting and the author reacting.
5. Relate: Connect to the passage by comparing it to your personal experience.
6. Paraphrase: Rephrase difficult text using your own words.

4. Identify Non-Fiction Passage MAPS

- Main Idea (the central theme of the passage)
- Author's Attitude (how the author feels about the subject)
- Purpose (the reason the author wrote the piece)
- Structure (how the passage is organized)

5. Recognize Patterns in Non-Fiction

- Passage Openings: Determine if a non-fiction passage opens in a common format to help you determine the main idea.
- Pivotal Words: Watch for words that indicate change, similarity, conclusion, emphasis, or other direction to help pinpoint opinions.
- Attitude Clues: In order to determine the tone, underline words or phrases as you read that indicate an author's feelings towards his subject.
- Multiple Viewpoints: Keep different viewpoints straight by notating them throughout the passage.
- Double Negatives: Cross out double negatives (*Soccer is not unlike football*) in order to reveal a positive message (*Soccer is like football*).

<u>Confidence Quotation</u>
"Desultory reading is delightful, but to be beneficial, our reading must be carefully directed." -Seneca, Roman philosopher

6. Master Literary Fiction Passages

- Do not identify the MAPS of fictional passages. Instead, concentrate on how the characters feel about each other and the situation in which they find themselves.
- The ACT tends to use relatively recent sources for Literary Fiction passages while the SAT uses both these sources and classic novels as passages.
- Read one or two novels or memoirs that mimic the style of Literary Fiction passages in the weeks leading up to your ACT or SAT.

READING STRATEGIES ANSWER KEY

Identify the Maps Mini Drill—Page 98

Main Idea:

Chinese and Italian immigrants brought their cuisine to America, where it became a staple in American cooking and eating. From lines 2-5 and 61-62.

Attitude:

The author could be described as *appreciative, admiring, enthusiastic,* and *respectful* of Chinese and Italian food. He reveals his feelings with the words *supremely important* (Line 5), *imaginatively* (17), *accomplish something extremely significant* (27-28), *exotic allure* (30), *ingenuity* (41), *magnificent* (46), and *triumph* (52).

Purpose:

The author appears to be writing to celebrate Chinese and Italian immigration or to applaud Chinese and Italian cooking. A piece like this might appear as an introduction to an ethnic cookbook or as a sidebar in a textbook about the history of Chinese and Italian immigration.

Structure:

Paragraph 1: Introduction and Main Idea
Paragraph 2: Example: Chinese immigration's effect on American cuisine.
Paragraph 3: Example: Italian immigration's effect on American cuisine.
Paragraph 4: Result/Summary: Italian cuisine became a staple in our diet.

Passage Openings Mini Drill—Page 103

Passage 1:

Where was Olaudah Equiano born? Since 1999, a debate ← Question
has raged amongst historians about the birthplace of the
author, one of very few slaves of African descent to record
Line his autobiography in English in the eighteenth century. In
5 *The Interesting Narrative of the Life of Olaudah Equiano,*
or Gustavus Vassa, the African, Equiano himself claims
he was born in Africa, describing life in an African village
as a free child. He also provides a first-person account
of the arduous journey of the Middle Passage, seemingly
10 something only a captured slave could relate in such detail.
In 1999, however, professor and author Vincent Caretta
asserted that Equiano was actually born a slave in South
Carolina. Caretta argued that Equiano's stories of African
life and capture came from oral histories of other slaves and
15 information he gathered in books. The professor provided
other evidence, such as a baptismal record and a muster
roll, showing that the slave was actually born in the English
colony. While the question is far from settled, one thing
is certain: <u>members of both sides of the debate possess</u> ← Main Idea
20 <u>compelling evidence to support their claims</u>.

Two
Possible
Answers

Sidebar Summary:
Both sides = good evidence

Passage 2:

When I was a child and not feeling well, my mother ←
would run to the kitchen instead of the medicine cabinet. If
I complained of a stomach ache, she concocted a buttermilk
and honey elixir to ease my pain. If I had a headache, she
Line made a lemon mayonnaise paste to slather on my forehead
5 to loosen tense muscles. Nothing was too extreme. Once,
when I woke up with a sore throat, she sat on my bed and
ordered me to open my mouth.
"Why?" I asked apprehensively.
10 "I have a recipe from *Mrs. Winston's Home Remedies* I
want to try," she said, stirring a red batter. She was always
trying new "miracle cures" from that tattered old book.
"What's in it?"
She looked at me with annoyance. "Don't you worry
15 about that, Charlie. Just open your mouth."
I later learned that the recipe she slathered all over my
tongue was a mixture of beets, garlic, and lard. I can still
remember its awful taste whenever I get a sore throat. ←
Now, after nearly fifty years (four of which I spent
20 in medical school and twenty of which I have practiced
medicine), I wish I could find that old book. Although I
thought those remedies were a sham when I was a child,
I have since come to recognize <u>the power of alternative</u>
<u>medicine</u>. <u>Practices</u> such as acupuncture, reiki, and even my ← Main Idea
25 mom's home remedies <u>deserve more respect and attention</u>
<u>from practitioners of Western medicine</u>.

Anecdote

Sidebar Summary:
Alternative medicine works

Pivotal Words and Attitude Clues Mini Drill—Page 109

Circle pivotal words and underline tone clues:

Passage 1:

    Surprisingly, the argument that graffiti is legitimate art has many proponents in the art world. They point out that a graffiti artist must create an intricate plan before they

Line begin, just as a painter plans on canvas. These artists use a

5 standard medium—spray paint—just as a painter of canvas uses oils or watercolors. And graffiti communicates to its spectators just as the *Mona Lisa* or *Waterlillies at Giverney* speaks to the beholders of such masterpieces. While these facts are seemingly true, there is one obvious difference

10 between graffiti and other artistic forms that just may revoke graffiti's status as art: graffiti is illegal.

    If creating a work of art is a crime, is it truly art? Advocates for graffiti say that the crime is immaterial, but would they then classify a burglar's ransacking of a home as

15 interior design? Likely not. This example illustrates the fine line between creation and destruction, and gives credence to challengers of graffiti as art. The debate is a murky one, with strong support on each side, but it seems as if the legality of a craft should play a part in determining true art.

Main Idea:

Graffiti as art is debatable, but the legality of the medium should be considered in determining whether it is art.

Author's Attitude:

Skeptical
Somewhat critical

Passage 2:

    Pregnancy is a hoot. Who knew that I would get such joy out of waddling like a duck and having my ribs stomped by a little boy who is sure to one day be a placekicker in

Line the NFL? Not to mention how much I love shopping these

5 days; maternity clothes are just so darn cute with their elephant sized waistbands and circus tent tops. Last week I noticed that none of my shoes fit anymore, given my expanding feet. I am happily wearing flip flops, the only shoes that fit, in the middle of January. In Minnesota.

10   The comments that people make are so kind and reassuring, too. Yesterday at my doctor's appointment, an old lady asked "Is there a baby in there, or are you just fat?" Isn't that sweet? My dad recently observed that my face is getting fuller to match my growing belly. He always knows

15 how to make a girl feel better.

    Pregnancy—it's an absolute riot, I tell you. On a serious note, though, I know it will all be worth it when these nine, long, torturous months are over.

Main Idea:

Pregnancy is difficult.

Author's Attitude:

Sarcastic
Humorous

Multiple Viewpoints and Double Negatives Mini Drill—Page 112

Passage 1:

File sharing, the practice of allowing the electronic exchange of files over a network such as the Internet, has in recent years led to the emergence of a new and complex set of legal issues for intellectual property owners. <u>Identifying offenders is not unfeasible, but the rapid and often undetectable movement of digital copies of copyrighted material makes identification particularly difficult. In addition, prosecuting such offenses is time-consuming and expensive.</u>   *VP—Author*

Many owners of intellectual property have claimed that <u>enforcement of these violations is necessary in order to send a signal to other possible offenders.</u> For example, in 2000, members of the band *Metallica* filed suit against a music-sharing company to end the free distribution of their copyrighted material. "<u>From a business standpoint, this is about piracy—a.k.a. taking something that doesn't belong to you and that is morally and legally wrong,</u>" said drummer Lars Ulrich. The file sharers, however, typically claim that <u>they did not know they were sharing copyrighted material, and that regardless, the widespread use of file sharing networks renders the protection of copyrights impossible.</u> And then there are some copyright holders, like 50 Cent and Moby, who <u>encourage file sharing as a means to promote their music.</u> "What is important for the music industry to understand is that <u>this really doesn't hurt the artists,</u>" said Curtis Jackson, the rapper known as 50 Cent, in a 2007 interview. "<u>A young fan may be just as devout and dedicated no matter if he bought it or stole it.</u>"

Line 5 (at "Identifying")

VP—Many owners

VP—Ulrich

VP—File sharers

VP—Some holders

VP—50 Cent

How does the author feel about identifying offenders in line 5?

(A) It is possible.
(B) It is impossible.
(C) It is illegal.
(D) It is legal.

The correct answer is (A). The author states:

"Identifying offenders is not unfeasible."

If you cross out the double negative, it becomes:

"Identifying offenders is ~~not un~~feasible."

Or:

"Identifying offenders is feasible."

The author believes it is feasible, or possible, to identify offenders.

Passage 2:

Federal rules of evidence have long prohibited the presentation in court of many types of "hearsay," evidence that is recounted second-hand rather than reported directly by a witness. This decision is based on the notion that only the most readily verifiable evidence should be allowed consideration by any court in making its determinations. Much like in a childhood game of "Telephone," the words of the original speaker have a way of becoming altered and warped when passed from person to person. Dr. Kinsley has argued, however, that <u>the rules of evidence as currently written are unacceptably overreaching,</u> defining too many types of evidence as hearsay when the value of that evidence would far outweigh any associated detriment if allowed court admissibility. <u>But modern hearsay rules are not unwarranted.</u>

Line 5

VP—Kinsley

VP—Author

How does the author feel about modern hearsay rules in lines 14 and 15?

(A) They are overextended.
(B) They become distorted.
(C) They are needed.
(D) They are not needed.

The author states:

"Modern hearsay rules are ~~not un~~warranted."

Or:

"Modern hearsay rules are warranted."

The author believes that hearsay rules are warranted, or needed.

CHAPTER EIGHT:
STRATEGIES FOR SINGLE PASSAGES

There are two different types of passages on the ACT and SAT: single passages and paired passages. In addition to the general reading strategies in the previous chapter, each type has its own specific strategies required for mastery.

On the ACT you can expect three single passage sets, each of which will range between 800 and 900 words. As we discussed previously, the reading level is typically between 8th grade and 12th grade. You have about 2½ minutes to read each of the passages so that you can complete the section in the allotted 35 minutes.

The SAT has four single passage sets—one more than the ACT—but they are only 650 to 750 words long. The reading level starts with 9th grade and progresses to early undergraduate. We recommend that you read each passage in less than 2 minutes and 30 seconds to give you enough time in the 65 minute section.

The remaining passage set on both the ACT and the SAT is the paired passage set, which we will discuss in the following chapter.

It is important to apply the strategies from the previous chapter to all of your reading; the strategies in this chapter, however, are specific to a particular type of passage.

Confidence Quotation
"Reading furnishes the mind only with materials of knowledge; it is thinking that makes what we read ours."
-John Locke, English philosopher & physician

Strategies for Reading the Passages

The previous chapter discussed general strategies to employ while reading. Those strategies are especially helpful on the ACT and SAT, but they can be applied to all of your reading, from school assignments to articles from your favorite magazine.

The strategies in this chapter, however, are meant to help you master reading passages on standardized tests. The first three steps, addressed on the following pages, pertain to reading the passaage:

1. **If necessary, notate line references from questions.**
2. **Read the introduction.**
3. **Read the entire passage.**
4. Read the questions.
5. If necessary, return to the passage.
6. Prephrase an answer.
7. Match an answer choice.

The last four steps will be addressed later in the chapter.

1. If necessary, notate line references from questions.

⸙ GRATUITOUS VOCAB
proficient (adj): competent or skilled

The goal of every ACT and SAT test taker should be to become a proficient reader who actively reads and comprehends a passage with a single reading. Students who have reached this goal should disregard this first step, as they already know how to focus while reading.

Most students, however, have yet to become proficient readers. After all, that's why you are using this book, right? This first strategy is an option for students who find they lose focus through a passage or for those who have a hard time identifying important text.

⸙TIPS and TRICKS⸙
Placing sidebars next to the passage is an optional strategy for students who have difficulty focusing while reading.

Before reading, quickly glance at each question following the passage to see if it has a specific line reference. If so, draw a "sidebar" next to that part of the passage. For example, if the first question refers to lines 4-6, draw a line on the left side of the passage between lines 4 and 6. If the next question cites lines 12-21, draw a line extending from line 12 to line 21. You should not spend any time perfectly placing your sidebars; if the question references lines 34-38, it is okay if you mark line 33 through line 38 because you are in a hurry. The point of this strategy is to highlight portions of text about which you must answer questions later. On the following page, consider an example of a passage in which the line references are marked by a sidebar.

This passage is taken from a novel set in 2014. It presents two characters—Robert, a Mexican American painter in New York, and his father, an immigrant and retiree who achieved success in the banking business. Robert has traveled home to Michigan to visit his parents.

"Did you hear about your brother?" my father asked, knowing full well that Mother had already told me about Peter's promotion at the bank. "He's really making something of himself, I tell you. I always
5 knew that boy would go far."

I drank from my iced tea to avoid having to answer. I had been compared to my twin for nearly twenty-five years and I was still coming up short.

"So, Robert," he began, "when are you going to
10 get promoted at the art gallery?" Here it was again. A comparison.

"Dad, I am a painter," I said. "I don't get promoted. I don't even work for the gallery. Just being displayed there is a tremendous honor."

15 "Hmph," he grunted. He stirred his cocktail with a finger. "Honor doesn't mean the same thing today as it did in my day then, I guess. Being recognized for saving three men on the battlefield, that was an honor."

20 I could not win. I was never going to please my father because I was never going to succeed at what he considered honorable.

My father was a young child when my grandparents came to America. They were migrant
25 workers who only planned on staying the summer at the tomato farm, but when my Uncle Miguel contracted polio, they decided to remain through the winter—a decision that changed the course of my family's history. My grandparents never returned to
30 Mexico after the farmer hired them full time, and my father was raised along with the white children on the farm. Upon graduating high school with honors, he enlisted in the marines and was sent to Vietnam, years he rarely talks about except to define honor, courage,
35 and fear. When he came home from the war, he went to the University of Michigan on a scholarship which led to a job with the largest bank in the county. Within ten years, he was vice president of the bank, and within twenty, he was running it. As he liked to say,
40 "Not bad for a poor immigrant from Mexico."

My brother had taken a similar road. He was valedictorian of his high school class, a Gulf War veteran, and a college graduate. He was a loan officer at the same bank that my father had worked. And I
45 was none of these things. I was an artist, a career that helped free me from my father and imprison me in his judgment at the same time.

1. In line 41, "road" most nearly means:

    A) pavement.
    B) life journey.
    C) thoroughfare.
    D) future.

2. The second paragraph indicates that

    A) Peter is taller than Robert.
    B) Robert's father had a successful career.
    C) Robert's mother does not consider art an honorable pursuit.
    D) Peter's choices have been favored over Robert's decisions by their father.

3. The father responds to Robert's comments in lines 12-14 by doing which of the following?

    A) Challenging Robert's definition of honor
    B) Denying one son the same respect as the other
    C) Recalling the challenges he faced growing up
    D) Agreeing that Robert's successful endeavors are different than Peter's accomplishments

4. The father's comments in lines 1-5 can best be described as

    A) accusatory.
    B) boastful.
    C) disappointed.
    D) deprecating.

5. Peter is similar to his father in all of the following ways EXCEPT:

    A) He is a war veteran.
    B) He works for a bank.
    C) He is an immigrant.
    D) He is a college graduate.

Answers: 1) B 2) D 3) A 4) B 5) C

Notice that the line references in each question do not follow the order of the passage. The first question asks about line 41, near the end of the passage, while the second question is about the second paragraph, near the beginning of the passage. This tends to follow the format of the ACT, while the SAT is more likely to ask about portions of the passage in the order they occur.

Notating the line references should take about 30 seconds, depending on the length of the passage and the number of questions. It is important that you do not read the questions as you do this! There is not enough time to read each question before reading the passage. Simply glance at the question and look for the numbers that represent a line reference. If the question has a line reference, mark it in the passage. If it does not have a line reference, skip it.

The purpose of this strategy is to alert you to important text. If you know that you are going to be asked about a line or paragraph, you should read that sidebar portion more carefully. You can read text without a sidebar more quickly, since specific questions will not be asked about that section.

Again, remember that your ultimate goal should be to eventually read the passage without marking sidebars. This strategy is meant to help students struggling to focus while reading. To determine if you need to employ this strategy, take several timed sections from *The Official ACT Prep Guide* or *The Official SAT Study Guide*; try two without sidebar line references and two with them. Which passages were easier for you? The answer to this question will determine whether you need to complete this optional first step.

2. Read the introduction.

Before reading the passage, be sure to read the introduction that precedes it. The passages are excerpts, often taken from the middle of a long document, so the introductory blurb provides the context you need to understand the passage. If you do not read this introduction, you are not likely to understand what you are reading. It's like starting a movie in the middle and trying to understand the plot; however, if someone gives you a brief synopsis of the parts you have missed, it's much easier to get into the film.

When reading the introduction, pay close attention to two pieces of information: who wrote the passage and the year it was written. Knowing who wrote the passage can help you make predictions about the main idea and the author's attitude. If the topic of the passage is cloning and it is written by a research scientist, you would probably predict that the author supports cloning. But if it is written by a conservative religious figure, you can surmise that the author opposes genetic manipulation. Your prediction may not be correct, but by venturing a guess you will clearly recognize your mistake and find it easier to keep track of the author's beliefs.

The year that the piece was written is important, too. It can also help you predict an author's attitude toward the topic. For example, imagine that the subject of the passage is calculator use in math class. If the author is a teacher from the 1970s, it is likely that he opposes the use of calculators in the classroom. He is probably an advocate of rote memorization and "showing your work." But if the article is by a math teacher from the present time, she will likely approve of students using calculators because they are much more accepted and commonplace these days. These little predictions are important because you will probably pay attention to whether you are right or wrong—and either way, it helps you stay focused on the test.

You should also note the year to help you understand the passage. For example, a former SAT practice test contains a fictional passage published in 1842, in which the main character is a government official who makes copies. If this piece were set in the present day, we could surmise that the character has a job standing in front of a large machine that makes copies of documents. Because it doesn't take much skill to push a "Copy" button, copier jobs probably do not require advanced education. But this story is set in the nineteenth century, before copy machines were invented. Therefore, we cannot assume that this is a job requiring little skill. In fact, copying in 1842 was likely done by hand, so the person doing the copying had to be able to read and write well, skills that were not necessarily common during the time period. While it's unlikely you will miss a question because you make false assumptions about the era in which a story takes place, these false assumptions can negatively affect your visualization of the passage. The more you understand a passage, the better your results.

3. Read the entire passage.

You must read the entire passage on the ACT and SAT before moving to the questions. It does not matter what your English teacher recommends or what your older brother did on the ACT four years ago; while they may be experts in English or other fields, they are not ACT and SAT experts who have dedicated hours, weeks, months, and years of study strictly to standardized tests, and in particular, to the ACT and the SAT. Students who consistently do well in the Reading section of the tests *always* read the entire passage. Our instructors who take the ACT and SAT and score in the 95th percentile or higher *always* read the entire passage. We strongly recommend that you follow their lead.

Confidence Quotation
"The more I practice, the luckier I get."
-Jerry Barber, professional golfer

We emphatically advise that you read the entire passage. We are aware of the myths that exist about skimming, skipping, and sifting the passage, but these are just that—myths. Beware not to heed these myths from previous test takers or misinformed adults:

Myth 1: You should skim the passage.
Skimming works well when reading newspaper and magazine articles, as these sources are written for simplicity and entertainment. The ACT and SAT, on the other hand, are written to confuse and bore. The test makers know that some students employ skimming, so they use text that is difficult to analyze with a cursory glance. The amount of time that you save by skimming will be lost, along with additional time, once you reach the questions.

Myth 2: You should read the questions first.
On an untimed test, this might be an advisable strategy because you have the luxury to go between the questions and the passage as often as you please. But on the SAT and especially on the ACT, you simply do not have time to read the questions, read the passage, and then read the questions again. Plus, given the time constraints and the number of questions, it is highly unlikely you would even remember what to look for when reading; the amount of information you gather from as many as 11 questions will get lost or confused when returning to an 800 word passage. We have had our expert instructors practice this approach in the past and all of them reported running out or nearly running out of time before completing the section. If these 95th percentile scorers (several of whom were English majors in college) struggle with this strategy, we are quite sure it will not benefit a high school test taker.

Myth 3: You should only read the first and last sentence of each paragraph.
This strategy is based on the misconception that the main idea of the passage and of each paragraph is always in the introductory or concluding sentence of a paragraph. We have already studied several examples of passage openings in which the main idea was in the middle of the first paragraph or was the second sentence of the second paragraph. A student who uses this strategy would completely miss the main ideas of these passages!

Efficient and proficient readers read the entire passage before moving to the questions. They do not skim and they do not omit sentences. They know that the passages are designed to sabotage any strategies that involve reading shortcuts. Finally, they practice the general strategies for active reading that we highlighted in the previous chapter. It would be wise to reread that chapter or revisit its summary at the completion of this section.

Remember the strategies from the previous chapter as you read: look for the MAPS of non-fiction passages and the feelings of characters in Literary Fiction passages. We have covered the first three steps of attacking a single passage. After reading the passage, you should follow additional steps when dealing with each question. We will discuss these steps after the following drill.

Strategies for Reading the Passages Drill

In the passage below, create sidebars for the line references in the questions. Then notate the passage as you read, determining the MAPS of the passage. The answers for the questions are meaningless because we want you to concentrate on strategy now. We will return to these questions in the next drill. Notations begin on page 150.

The following passage, written in 1998 by a classical music critic, discusses changes to the genre. [doesn't line change?]

Line
In 1989, Americans and observers all over the
world watched in amazement as the Berlin Wall
crumbled, bringing down along with it an enormous
complex of calcified belief systems. Whether
5 because of synchronicity or simply the deceptive
but irresistible human urge to draw connections, an
observer of the broad spectrum of classical music
in the United States might have detected something
similar happening in that world as well. In the way [some ppl might have guessed change in music]
10 composers operated and the kinds of music they
wrote, in the sorts of performing institutions that
brought that music and music of the past to the
listening public, old models and ways of thinking
that had begun to prove decisively unworkable were
15 being chipped away.

Now, almost a decade later, U.S. classical music [CM coming back]
stands on the verge of an enormous rejuvenation.
The process is far from complete—indeed, in some
areas it has scarcely begun—but the seeds that have
20 been sown over the past years unmistakably are
bearing fruit. The music that is being written today
boasts a combination of vitality and accessibility
that have been missing from American music for too
long. A similar spirit of adventure and innovation
25 can increasingly be found among the country's solo
performers and musical organizations.

Artistic liberation, of course, is a slower and [CM coming back is slow]
more diffuse process than political liberation. In the
absence of a single Promethean figure* on the order
30 of Beethoven or Picasso, old orthodoxies are more
likely to be eroded than exploded. So it is that much
of the musical life in the United States still clings to
the old ways. Some prominent composers continue
to write in the densely impenetrable language forged
35 during the modernist period and clung to in the face
of decades' worth of audience hostility or indifference. Some opera companies and symphony orchestras operate as though the United States was still a
cultural outpost of Europe, uncertain of the value of
40 anything that doesn't derive from the Old World.

But the signs of change are there—among younger
composers struggling to find their own voice in
defiance of old models, among performers eager to

make those voices heard, and among organizations
45 daring enough to give the nation's musical life a
distinctively American profile at last.

Nothing is more important to this process than
the production of new music, and here is where the
picture is at once most heartening and most varied.
50 From the end of World War II until well into the
1970s, the dominant vein in American music
was the arid, intricate style that had grown out of
early modernism and continued to flourish in the
supportive but isolated arena of academia. Much
55 of this music was based on serialism, the system
derived from the works of Schöenberg, Webern, and
Berg in which the key-centered structures of
tonal music were replaced with a systematically
evenhanded treatment of all 12 notes of the
60 chromatic scale. Even composers whose works were
not strictly serialist, such as Elliott Carter and Roger
Sessions, partook of the general preference for
intellectual rigor and dense, craggy surfaces. The
fact that audiences were nonplused by this music, to
65 say the least, was taken merely as an indication that
the composers were ahead of their time.

* A person who is a catalyst to change and advancement.

1. According to the passage, classical music composed
between World War II and the fall of the Berlin Wall
can be characterized as

A) Answer A
B) Answer B
C) Answer C
D) Answer D

2. The statements in lines 4-9 ("Whether . . . as well") suggests that classical music was

A) Answer A
B) Answer B
C) Answer C
D) Answer D

3. In the second paragraph, the author's attitude toward the rejuvenation of classical music can best be described as

A) Answer A
B) Answer B
C) Answer C
D) Answer D

4. In lines 28-31 ("In the . . . exploded"), it can be inferred that Beethoven and Picasso both

A) Answer A
B) Answer B
C) Answer C
D) Answer D

5. In line 29, "order" most nearly means

A) Answer A
B) Answer B
C) Answer C
D) Answer D

6. The author criticizes "some opera companies and orchestras" (lines 37-38) because they

A) Answer A
B) Answer B
C) Answer C
D) Answer D

7. In lines 37-40 ("Some opera...Old World"), the author implies that

A) Answer A
B) Answer B
C) Answer C
D) Answer D

8. Lines 44-46 ("and among . . . at last") suggest that before changes were made

A) Answer A
B) Answer B
C) Answer C
D) Answer D

9. In context, the term "process" (line 47) refers to

(A) Answer A
(B) Answer B
(C) Answer C
(D) Answer D

10. The tone of the statement in lines 47-49 is best described as

A) Answer A
B) Answer B
C) Answer C
D) Answer D

Strategies for Reading the Questions

Now that we have looked at the first three steps that address reading the passage, we will turn our attention to the last four steps for answering the questions:

1. If necessary, notate line references from questions.
2. Read the introduction.
3. Read the entire passage.
4. **Read the questions.**
5. **If necessary, return to the passage.**
6. **Prephrase an answer.**
7. **Match an answer choice.**

Let's examine each more closely.

4. Read the questions.

While this may seem like a patronizing imperative, there is more to this step than you may realize.

Reading questions have two parts: a question stem and four answer choices.

SAT Question

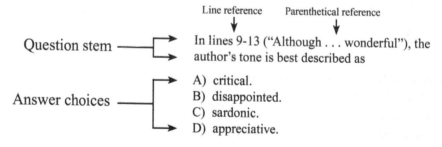

ACT Question

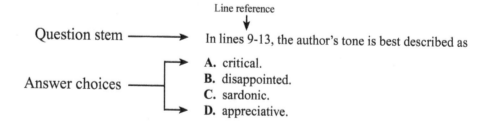

The ACT does not typically use parenthetical references with line references. In this example, you are expected to know that you should start reading the sentence that begins in line 9 and ends in line 13.

The question stem consists of a question or—more often—an incomplete statement. It may also contain a line reference to the passage, as in the examples here, where the text being considered begins in line 9 and ends in line 13. The SAT will usually include parenthetical references to indicate the first word of the reference ("Although") and the last word of the reference ("wonderful"). The ACT does not include this parenthetical reference as the test makers assume you know to start at the beginning of the sentence or paragraph in line 9 and read to the end of the sentence or paragraph in line 13.

Every word counts on the ACT and SAT. This is true for both the questions and the answer choices, but for now, let's look at how this impacts a question. Consider the passage and question below:

> Familiar songs are like cozy blankets. They provide warmth and comfort, never more so than when I feel down and worn out. They wrap around me, assuring me that everything will be okay. My favorite artist is jazz legend Ella Fitzgerald. Her voice is warm honey on a cold day, uplifting my spirits and reminding me how beautiful the world can be.

1. The paragraph establishes a comparison between a woman's

   A) feelings about music and the comfort provided by blankets.
   B) favorite jazz artist and the beauty of life.
   C) familiar music and the arms of a stranger.
   D) melodious voice and the soothing qualities of honey.

Many students will fail to pay attention to the word *woman's* in the question stem. They process the word *comparison* and then completely fail to notice the word *woman's*. The passage does not help you because the comparison between *songs* and *blankets* is a simile, while the comparison between Ella Fitzgerald's *voice* and *honey* is a metaphor. Since similes are much easier to identify than metaphors, most students incorrectly choose choice (A). A closer reading of the question, however, reveals that the test makers are inquiring about the comparison between Ella Fitzgerald's voice and warm honey, and thus the correct answer is (D).

☠ CAUTION: SAT TRAP!
Failing to carefully read every word of the question can lead to disaster.

We should also note that some students miss this question because they assume that the author of the passage is a woman. But where does the passage say this? You should never assume the gender, ethnicity, or age of an author on the ACT or SAT. This information may be provided in the introduction or in the passage itself, but if not, you cannot answer questions based on your hunches and assumptions.

There are some specific words and phrases to watch for in question stems. Many questions will begin with *according to the author* or *according to the passage*, as in the following example:

> According to the author, those who "reject science" (line 61) are

These questions ask you to provide the author's opinion, and here you are asked to provide the author's opinion on those who reject science. This may not necessarily be what you believe, or what others in the passage believe, but what the author himself believes.

Be careful not to confuse others' beliefs with the author's belief:

> The passage indicates that those who "reject science" believe

This question asks about the belief of people who reject science, which is not necessarily the same as the belief held by the author. Pay close attention to whom the question is referring.

There is only one correct answer for every question on the ACT and SAT. The other three answers have a specific reason they are wrong.

Many reading questions use the words *primarily, mostly, mainly,* and *chiefly*. The ACT and College Board claim that these words indicate that more than one answer may be correct, but that one of the answers is best. We know, however, that this is misleading. Three answers are always wrong and there is a specific reason they are wrong. You do not need to worry about choosing one answer that is "more correct" than another. There is only one right answer.

The final word for which you should watch is *except*. While EXCEPT questions used to be prevalent on the SAT, there are no longer any in *The Official SAT Guide*, so it is possible that these will only appear on the ACT from now on. EXCEPT questions contain three answers that satisfy the question and one that does not:

> The author makes use of all of the following EXCEPT
>
> A) imagery.
> B) sarcasm.
> C) rhetorical question.
> D) personal voice.

❧ GRATUITOUS VOCAB
leniency (n): the state of being merciful

☠ CAUTION: SAT TRAP!
"Except" questions are traps with a warning sign.

In a rare display of leniency, the test makers will warn you that the question is tricky by using capital letters for the word EXCEPT. These questions basically ask you to find the wrong answer instead of the right answer, which can make them more complicated for students who do not read the questions closely. The three answer choices that satisfy the question can usually be found by combing through the text, a task which in and of itself is not difficult, but is time consuming. Students who notate each paragraph with a 3 or 4 word summary stand to answer these questions much more quickly than those who do not notate as they read.

The majority of the questions following passages are not really questions—
they are actually incomplete statements:

> The sentence in lines 24-28 primarily serves to

It is much easier to answer a question than it is to finish a sentence (which
is exactly why the ACT and the College Board use incomplete statements).
For this reason, good test takers rephrase the question stem and turn it into an
actual question in their heads:

> *What is the purpose of the sentence?*

Notice that the line reference is not included in the paraphrased question. That
is because line references are not necessary to understand what the question
is asking and the extra information can cause you to forget the question. You
can use the line references to return to the text, but you do not need to include
them in your rephrased question.

Consider a few more examples of turning incomplete statements into
questions:

> In line 34, "spot" most nearly means
>
> *What does "spot" mean?*
>
> The author of Passage 2 would most likely view the
> statement in lines 2-6 ("Once . . . time") of Passage 1 as
>
> *How would the author of Passage 2 view that statement?*
>
> The author cites an expert primarily in order to
>
> *Why does the author cite an expert?*

Rephrasing is a powerful tool on Reading questions, and one that you should
practice regularly.

TIPS and TRICKS
Most ACT and
SAT questions are
actually incomplete
statements, so turn
them into questions
by paraphrasing. It's
much easier to answer
a question than to
complete a sentence.

5. If necessary, return to the passage.

Some questions require an understanding of the entire passage, like the following examples:

> The primary purpose of the passage is to
>
> The tone of the passage can best be characterized as
>
> The passage provides the most information about
>
> The passage is primarily concerned with

These questions (or incomplete statements) assess your knowledge of the passage as a whole. You cannot return to one specific spot in the passage to find the answer or reread for understanding.

But many questions on the SAT and some questions on the ACT are about a specific line, sentence, or paragraph, and you must return to the passage in order to answer the question. The test makers are sometimes even kind enough to refer you back to the specific section with a line reference or paragraph reference.

GRATUITOUS VOCAB
context (n): the parts of text surrounding a word that contribute to its meaning

Most test prep books will instruct you to read a sentence above and below the actual line reference both to gather context and look for the actual answer. This is a good strategy, but only for specific question types. So how do you know what to read when you return to the passage?

If the line reference is a single word or phrase:

Sometimes the line reference is one word or a short phrase, as in the following examples:

> According to the author, the "lost souls" (line 31) can best be described as
>
> As it is used in line 55, the word *sniggle* most nearly means
>
> The description of how Logan "worked the gears of the machine that his father called a distractor" in lines 5-6 primarily serves to

TIPS and TRICKS
If a line reference contains a single word or a short phrase, return to the passage and read a few lines above and below the line reference. The answer is almost always determined by understanding the surrounding text.

When the line reference is anything less than a complete sentence, return to the passage and **read the text surrounding the line reference**. In the first example above, you would want to start a few lines above line 31 and read until a few lines below line 31. The answer is almost always in the text that encompasses the line reference.

If the line reference is a complete sentence or more:

A line reference may also be an entire sentence, group of sentences, or an entire paragraph:

> The four lessons discussed in lines 42-61 serve primarily to

> The tone of the third paragraph (lines 23-46) is best described as

> The sentence in lines 75-77 ("The wish . . . Blake") suggests that Blake was most concerned about

⋮TIPS and TRICKS⋮

If a line reference contains a complete sentence or more, return to the passage and read just that line reference. The answer is almost always determined by understanding the line reference itself.

When the line reference is a complete sentence or more, **read just that specific line reference.** In the first example above, you would begin reading the sentence that starts in line 42 and read until the sentence that ends in line 61. The answer is almost always located within the given line reference when it is a complete sentence or more.

Notice we say "almost always." This is because there is always a first for everything on standardized tests, and we want you to be prepared should the test makers make a change. But in our experience, this helpful strategy has always led us to the correct answer.

Line Reference Reading Guide

If the line reference contains a single word or phrase, read a few lines above through a few lines below the reference.

> Example:
> According to the passage, the "fountains of youth and prosperity" in line 47 primarily refers to...

If the line reference contains a complete sentence or more read just the specified line reference.

> Example:
> According to the passage, the statement in lines 54-59 most nearly means...

---

6. Prephrase an answer.

Prephrasing is a skill employed by the best test takers. It simply means that, whenever possible, you predict an answer to a Reading question before looking at the answer choices.

This is by far the most important strategy on reading passages. It helps you connect with the text and ensures that you understand what the question is asking. When you finally look at answer choices, prephrasing prevents you from falling into common traps, which will be covered in Chapter Ten. Good readers naturally use this strategy, but those who read less frequently may need to practice prephrasing until it becomes a habit.

Some students use their hands to cover up the answer choices while prephrasing. If you find that you are sneaking peeks at the answers, then try this technique until you are more comfortable with the strategy.

Let's examine how prephrasing works by rereading a portion of a passage from a previous exercise:

> "Did you hear about your brother?" my father asked, knowing full well that Mother had already told me about Peter's promotion at the bank. "He's really making something of himself, I tell you. I always
> Line
> 5 knew that boy would go far."
> I drank from my iced tea to avoid having to answer. I had been compared to my twin for nearly twenty-five years and I was still coming up short.
> "So, Robert," he began, "when are you going to
> 10 get promoted at the art gallery?" Here it was again. A comparison.
> "Dad, I am a painter," I said. "I don't get promoted. I don't even work for the gallery. Just being displayed there is a tremendous honor."
> 15 "Hmph," he grunted. He stirred his cocktail with a finger. "Honor doesn't mean the same thing today as it did in my day then, I guess. Being recognized for saving three men on the battlefield, that was an honor."

Now consider a corresponding question:

1. The father's comments in lines 1-5 can best be described as

    A) Answer A
    B) Answer B
    C) Answer C
    D) Answer D

You should rephrase the incomplete statement so that it is an actual question: *How would you describe the father's comments?* Since this question contains a line reference that is a complete sentence or more, go back to lines 1-5 and read the father's comments just in those specific lines: "'Did you hear about your brother?' my father asked, knowing full well that Mother had already told me about Peter's promotion at the bank. 'He's really making something of himself, I tell you. I always knew that boy would go far.'"

So, how would you describe his comments? Some students want to venture that the comments are mean or hurtful, and while the rest of the passage does reveal that the comments bother the narrator, you cannot assign those feelings to them by just reading lines 1-5. In those specific lines, the father is proudly bragging about his son. Good prephrases are *proud*, *pleased*, or *bragging*.

7. Match an answer choice.

Once you prephrase an answer, then look at the real answer choices. Find the one that most closely matches your prephrase and select it as the right answer:

> The father's comments in lines 1-5 can best be described as
>
> A) accusatory.
> B) boastful.
> C) disappointed.
> D) deprecating.

Prephrasing can help you avoid attractive wrong answers like A and C in this question.

The answer that is closest to your prephrase is (B).

Let's try the prephrasing and matching an answer choice for another question from the passage:

> The second paragraph indicates that
>
> A) Answer A
> B) Answer B
> C) Answer C
> D) Answer D

Rephrase the question: *What does the second paragraph indicate?* Then return to the passage to reread the second paragraph: "I drank from my iced tea to avoid having to answer. I had been compared to my twin for nearly twenty-five years and I was still coming up short." This indicates that the narrator feels his father values his brother more than him. Good prephrases include *The narrator feels less important than his brother* or *the father compares his sons and feels Peter has done better than Robert.*

Now match an answer choice:

The second paragraph indicates that

A) Peter is taller than Robert
B) Robert's father had a successful career
C) Robert's mother does not consider art an honorable pursuit
D) Peter's choices have been favored over Robert's decisions by their father

The closest match is answer choice (D).

We cannot overemphasize the importance of prephrasing before matching an answer choice. Students who prephrase report a higher comfort level with the text and the questions, and they ultimately report higher ACT and SAT scores. Active reading creates a running commentary in your head while reading the passage and prephrasing creates a similar mental conversation while working through the questions.

We should note that not all answers can be prephrased. Some questions are worded awkwardly or ask about an inference that is difficult to identify. If you find a question with an answer that is impossible to predict, it is okay; you will just have to work through the answer choices without a prephrase.

♦ GRATUITOUS VOCAB
commentary (n): *series of comments*

<u>**Confidence Quotation**</u>
"But I don't think I have any particular talent for prediction, because when you have three or four elements in hand, you don't have to be a genius to reach certain conclusions.
-Antonio Tabucchi, Italian novelist

THE POWERSCORE ACT AND SAT READING BIBLE

Notes:

Strategies for Reading the Questions Problem Set

Reread the following passage. Rephrase the question stems using your own words and prephrase an answer to that question. Record both your rephrase and prephrase on the lines provided. Then select an answer that most closely matches your prephrase. The first one has been done for you. Answers begin on page 152.

The following passage, written in 1998 by a classical music critic, discusses changes to the genre.

In 1989, Americans and observers all over the world watched in amazement as the Berlin Wall crumbled, bringing down along with it an enormous complex of calcified belief systems. Whether

Line
5   because of synchronicity or simply the deceptive but irresistible human urge to draw connections, an observer of the broad spectrum of classical music in the United States might have detected something similar happening in that world as well. In the way

10 composers operated and the kinds of music they wrote, in the sorts of performing institutions that brought that music and music of the past to the listening public, old models and ways of thinking that had begun to prove decisively unworkable were

15 being chipped away.

Now, almost a decade later, U.S. classical music stands on the verge of an enormous rejuvenation. The process is far from complete—indeed, in some areas it has scarcely begun—but the seeds that have

20 been sown over the past years unmistakably are bearing fruit. The music that is being written today boasts a combination of vitality and accessibility that have been missing from American music for too long. A similar spirit of adventure and innovation

25 can increasingly be found among the country's solo performers and musical organizations.

Artistic liberation, of course, is a slower and more diffuse process than political liberation. In the absence of a single Promethean figure* on the order

30 of Beethoven or Picasso, old orthodoxies are more likely to be eroded than exploded. So it is that much of the musical life in the United States still clings to the old ways. Some prominent composers continue to write in the densely impenetrable language forged

35 during the modernist period and clung to in the face of decades' worth of audience hostility or indifference. Some opera companies and symphony orchestras operate as though the United States was still a cultural outpost of Europe, uncertain of the value of

40 anything that doesn't derive from the Old World.

But the signs of change are there—among younger composers struggling to find their own voice in defiance of old models, among performers eager to

make those voices heard, and among organizations
45 daring enough to give the nation's musical life a distinctively American profile at last.

Nothing is more important to this process than the production of new music, and here is where the picture is at once most heartening and most varied.

50 From the end of World War II until well into the 1970s, the dominant vein in American music was the arid, intricate style that had grown out of early modernism and continued to flourish in the supportive but isolated arena of academia. Much

55 of this music was based on serialism, the system derived from the works of Schöenberg, Webern, and Berg in which the key-centered structures of tonal music were replaced with a systematically evenhanded treatment of all 12 notes of the

60 chromatic scale. Even composers whose works were not strictly serialist, such as Elliott Carter and Roger Sessions, partook of the general preference for intellectual rigor and dense, craggy surfaces. The fact that audiences were nonplused by this music, to say

65 the least, was taken merely as an indication that the composers were ahead of their time.

* A person who is a catalyst to change and advancement.

1. According to the passage, classical music composed between World War II and the fall of the Berlin Wall can be characterized as

Rephrase the question:
How can you characterize classical music composed between WWII and the fall of the Berlin Wall?

Prephrase the answer:
Inflexible and dense

A) accessible and defiant.
B) avant-garde and elaborate.
C) dense and banal.
D) intricate and vivacious.

2. The statement in lines 4-9 ("Whether . . . as well") suggests that classical music was

Rephrase the question: __What does the statement__

__suggest about classical music__

_____

_____

Prephrase the answer: __It was dying & changing__

_____

_____

_____

   A) deemed unpopular and old-fashioned by the general public.
   B) responsible for a rift between contemporary and conventional composers.
   C) held to rigid standards prior to the 1990s.
   D) lacking a creative individual who could bring change to the genre.

3. In the second paragraph, the author's attitude toward the rejuvenation of classical music can best be described as

Rephrase the question: __How can you describe the author's__

__attitude towards the rejuvenation of classical music?__

_____

_____

Prephrase the answer: __Positive__

_____

_____

_____

   A) anxious.
   B) cynical.
   C) ambivalent.
   D) favorable.

4. In lines 28-31 ("In the . . . exploded"), it can be inferred that Beethoven and Picasso both

Rephrase the question: __Infer what Beethoven &__

__Picasso did.__

_____

_____

_____

Prephrase the answer: __big influences__

_____

_____

_____

   A) preserved old, reliable European techniques when mastering their crafts.
   B) disagreed with composers from previous. generations who refused to acknowledge America's influence on classical music.
   C) struggled to gain acceptance among the music and art communities of their times.
   D) brought accelerated changes to the long-standing conventions of their respective disciplines.

5. In line 29, "order" most nearly means

Rephrase the question: _What does "order" mean?_

_____

_____

_____

Prephrase the answer: _____

_____

_____

_____

   A) command.
   B) arrangement.
   C) discipline.
   D) degree.

6. The author criticizes "some opera companies and orchestras" (lines 37-38) because they

Rephrase the question: _Why does the author criticize it?_

_____

_____

_____

Prephrase the answer: _____

_____

_____

_____

   A) only play music that is impenetrable and dense.
   B) do not hire younger composers with new ideas.
   C) align themselves with obsolete political parties.
   D) do not appreciate classical music composed by Americans.

7. In lines 37-40 ("Some opera…Old World"), the author implies that

Rephrase the question: _What does the author imply?_

_____

_____

_____

Prephrase the answer: _____

_____

_____

_____

   A) professional orchestras find American compositions unworthy.
   B) the talent of European composers is unrivaled by American composers.
   C) American composers write symphonies that are much more daring and defiant than the symphonies of European composers.
   D) some professional musicians prefer to play European compositions in concert.

8. Lines 44-46 ("and among . . . at last") suggest that before changes were made

Rephrase the question: ___What do the lines suggest about___ ___the changes made before?___

_____

_____

Prephrase the answer: _____

_____

_____

A) orchestras throughout the world were afraid to request new musical styles.
B) the United States did not have a distinguishable sound to their classical music.
C) older composers were not sympathetic to younger musicians' plights.
D) serialists were partial to certain tones.

9. In context, the term "process" (line 47) refers to

Rephrase the question: ___What does the term "process"___ ___mean?___

_____

_____

Prephrase the answer: _____

_____

_____

A) the eradication of European influence from American classical music.
B) the revitalization of American classical music.
C) the liberation of American composers from public criticism.
D) the incorporation of modernism and serialism into current classical music.

10. The tone of the statement in lines 47-49 is best described as

Rephrase the question: ___Describe the tone___

_____

_____

_____

Prephrase the answer: _____

_____

_____

A) decisive.
B) disappointed.
C) skeptical.
D) scornful.

Chapter Summary

There are several strategies you should employ when reading ACT and SAT passages:

Strategies for Reading the Passages

1. If necessary, notate line references from questions.
   - This is an optional strategy for students who struggle with maintaining focus, but the goal of all test takers should be to avoid this strategy if possible.
   - Skim the questions strictly for line references before reading the passage and make sidebars that correspond to each reference.

2. Read the introduction.
   - The introduction helps you understand the context of the excerpt, as the passage likely came from a much longer source.
   - Pay attention to who wrote the passage and the year it was published.

3. Read the entire passage.
   - Avoid shortcuts or gimmicks such as skimming the passage or reading the questions first.
   - The only way to fully understand an ACT and SAT passage and answer the questions correctly is to read the entire passage.

Strategies for Reading the Questions

4. Read the question.
   - It is important to read every word in the question stem.
   - Turn an incomplete sentence into a question by rephrasing.

5. If necessary, return to the passage.
   - If the line reference is a single word or phrase, return to the passage and read from about three lines above the line reference to about three lines below the line reference.
   - If the line reference is a complete sentence or more, return to the passage and read just the lines in the line reference.

6. Prephrase an answer.
   - If possible, predict an answer to the question before reading the answer choices.
   - Prephrasing an answer to the question is the most important strategy in the Passage-Based Reading sections.

7. Match an answer choice.
   - Once you prephrase an answer, find an answer choice that is closest to your prephrase.

Notes:

STRATEGIES FOR SINGLE PASSAGES ANSWER KEY

Strategies for Reading the Passages Drill—Page 132

Note: CM = Classical Music

Line

    In 1989, Americans and observers all over the world watched in amazement as the Berlin Wall crumbled, bringing down along with it an enormous complex of calcified belief systems. Whether
5 because of synchronicity or simply the deceptive but irresistible human urge to draw connections, an observer of the broad spectrum of classical music in the United States might have detected something similar happening in that world as well. In the way
10 composers operated and the kinds of music they wrote, in the sorts of performing institutions that brought that music and music of the past to the listening public, old models and ways of thinking that had begun to prove decisively unworkable were
15 being chipped away.

CM like Berlin Wall: changing

    Now, almost a decade later, U.S. classical music stands on the verge of an enormous rejuvenation. The process is far from complete—indeed, in some areas it has scarcely begun—but the seeds that have
20 been sown over the past years unmistakably are bearing fruit. The music that is being written today boasts a combination of vitality and accessibility that have been missing from American music for too long. A similar spirit of adventure and innovation
25 can increasingly be found among the country's solo performers and musical organizations.

Changes being made

    Artistic liberation, of course, is a slower and more diffuse process than political liberation. In the absence of a single Promethean figure* on the order
30 of Beethoven or Picasso, old orthodoxies are more likely to be eroded than exploded. So it is that much of the musical life in the United States still clings to the old ways. Some prominent composers continue to write in the densely impenetrable language forged
35 during the modernist period and clung in in the face of decades' worth of audience hostility or indifference. Some opera companies and symphony orchestras operate as though the United States was still a cultural outpost of Europe, uncertain of the value of
40 anything that doesn't derive from the Old World.

Change = slow process

    But the signs of change are there—among younger composers struggling to find their own voice in defiance of old models, among performers eager to make those voices heard, and among organizations
45 daring enough to give the nation's musical life a distinctively American profile at last.

Signs of change

I   Nothing is more important to this process than the production of new music, and here is where the picture is at once most heartening and most varied.
50 From the end of World War II until well into the 1970s, the dominant vein in American music was the arid, intricate style that had grown out of early modernism and continued to flourish in the supportive but isolated arena of academia. Much
55 of this music was based on serialism, the system derived from the works of Schöenberg, Webern, and Berg in which the key-centered structures of tonal music were replaced with a systematically evenhanded treatment of all 12 notes of the
60 chromatic scale. Even composers whose works were not strictly serialist, such as Elliott Carter and Roger Sessions, partook of the general preference for intellectual rigor and dense, craggy surfaces. The fact that audiences were nonplused by this music, to say
65 the least, was taken merely as an indication that the composers were ahead of their time.

* A person who is a catalyst to change and advancement.

New music being written

Main Idea:
Classical music is undergoing major changes.

Author's Attitude:
Appreciative of the changes; positive

Purpose:
To explain and promote changes to classical music

Structure:
Passage Opening: Comparison followed by main idea
Remaining passage explains the main idea by providing examples of changes

Strategies for Reading the Questions Problem Set—Page 144

1. According to the passage, classical music composed between World War II and the fall of the Berlin Wall can be characterized as

Paraphrase the question: How can you characterize classical music composed between World War II and the fall of the Berlin Wall?

Prephrase the answer: Inflexible and dense

Answer: C

2. The statement in lines 4-9 ("Whether . . . as well") suggests that classical music was

Paraphrase the question: What do these lines suggest about classical music?

Prephrase the answer: Classical music was undergoing similar changes, throwing out old ways and accepting new ways

Answer: C

3. In the second paragraph, the author's attitude toward the rejuvenation of classical music can best be described as

Paraphrase the question: In the second paragraph, what is the author's attitude toward the rejuvenation of classical music?

Prephrase the answer: excited, positive, glad, hopeful

Answer: D

4. In lines 28-31 ("In the . . . exploded"), it can be inferred that Beethoven and Picasso both

Paraphrase the question: What can you infer about Beethoven and Picasso in these lines?

Prephrase the answer: They brought enormous change to their genres.

Answer: D

5. In line 29, "order" most nearly means

Paraphrase the question: What does "order" mean in this line?

Prephrase the answer: level, importance

Answer: D

6. The author criticizes "some opera companies and orchestras" (lines 37-38) because they

Paraphrase the question: Why does the author criticize some opera companies and orchestras?

Prephrase the answer: They do not value classical music from the US.

Answer: D

7. In lines 37-40 ("Some opera...Old World"), the author implies that

Paraphrase the question: What does the author imply in these lines?

Prephrase the answer: Note: Difficult to prephrase. Some students might pick up that these orchestras would rather play music by European composers.

Answer: D

8. Lines 44-46 ("and among . . . at last") suggest that before changes were made

Paraphrase the question: What do these lines suggest about the time before changes were made?

Prephrase the answer: Note: Difficult to prephrase. Some students may realize that the nation's musical life did not previously have an American profile.

Answer: B

9. In context, the term "process" (line 47) refers to

Paraphrase the question: What does "process" mean in this line?

Prephrase the answer: change, giving the nation's musical life an American profile

Answer: B

10. The tone of the statement in lines 47-49 is best described as

Paraphrase the question: What is the tone of these lines?

Prephrase the answer: adamant, emphatic, firm

Answer: A

CHAPTER NINE:
STRATEGIES FOR PAIRED PASSAGES

Paired passages share a related theme in which they support, oppose, or complement each other. The subject of paired passages most often comes from Humanities, History, Social Studies, or Science, but Literary Fiction has occasionally been used on past tests.

The paired passages on the ACT have a word count of 400-500 words for each individual passage, meaning a total near 900 words for both passages. Each passage in the SAT paired passage set is 350 to 400 words for a total near 750 words.

If the specific-test formatting were removed, the paired passages of the ACT and SAT would be nearly indistinguishable. It's highly unlikely that you would be able to tell if you were looking at an ACT test or an SAT test. The passages come from similar sources and the questions assess the same reading skills. But the formatting is a bit different on each test, so we want to look at their individual characteristics more closely before discussing the strategies for tackling paired passages.

The ACT labels the passages as "Passage A" and "Passage B," while the SAT titles them "Passage 1" and "Passage 2." The ACT lists the author of each passage in the heading; the SAT does not, but the authors are provided in the introduction. The most striking difference is on the ACT, where the test makers have grouped the questions about each passage together and labeled them as such. For example, boxes above the questions will say something like "Questions 1-4 ask about Passage A," "Questions 5-7 ask about Passage B," and "Questions 8-10 ask about both passages." The SAT does not label the questions as such, but it is relatively easy to determine this information anyway.

For the ease of discussion, we will refer to the passages as "Passage 1" and "Passage 2" throughout this book.

The SAT has long been testing paired passages, but the ACT added them in 2015. For this reason, there is a dearth of ACT paired passages available for practice. If you complete all of the official ACT paired passages, we highly recommend using old SAT tests to continue honing your paired passage reading skills. You can find many of these old SATs in the Free Help Area of the PowerScore website.

On the following pages we examine a paired passage set as it would appear on the ACT and on the SAT so you can more clearly understand the subtle differences. Do not read the passage or answer the questions at this time, but simply study the formatting of paired passages on each test.

We will read and complete the following paired passage set at the end of this chapter.

ACT Paired Passages Format

Natural Science: Passage A is adapted from *Astronomy*, a 2016 book written by Andrew Fraknoi et al. Passage B is adapted from the 1881 book *Zetetic Astronomy: Earth Not a Globe* published by Samuel Rowbotham, who believed that the Earth was not a sphere, but a circular plane.

Passage A by Andrew Fraknoi et al.

Our concept of the cosmos—its basic structure and origin—is called cosmology, a word with Greek roots. Before the invention of telescopes, humans had to depend
Line on the simple evidence of their senses for a picture of
5 the universe. The ancients developed cosmologies that combined their direct view of the heavens with a rich variety of philosophical and religious symbolism.

At least 2000 years before Columbus, educated people in the eastern Mediterranean region knew Earth was round.
10 Belief in a spherical Earth may have stemmed from the time of Pythagoras, a philosopher and mathematician who lived 2500 years ago. He believed circles and spheres to be "perfect forms" and suggested that Earth should therefore be a sphere. As evidence that the gods liked spheres, the
15 Greeks cited the fact that the Moon is a sphere.

The writings of Aristotle (384–322 BCE), the tutor of Alexander the Great, summarize many of the ideas of his day. They describe how the progression of the Moon's phases—its apparent changing shape—results from our
20 seeing different portions of the Moon's sunlit hemisphere as the month goes by. Aristotle also knew that the Sun has to be farther away from Earth than is the Moon because occasionally the Moon passed exactly between Earth and the Sun and hid the Sun temporarily from view. We call
25 this a solar eclipse.

Aristotle cited convincing arguments that Earth must be round. First is the fact that as the Moon enters or emerges from Earth's shadow during a lunar eclipse, the shape of the shadow seen on the Moon is always round. Only a
30 spherical object always produces a round shadow. If Earth were a disk, for example, there would be some occasions when the sunlight would strike it edge-on and its shadow on the Moon would be a line.

As a second argument, Aristotle explained that travelers
35 who go south a significant distance are able to observe stars that are not visible farther north. And the height of the North Star —the star nearest the north celestial pole—decreases as a traveler moves south. On a flat Earth, everyone would see the same stars overhead. The only possible explanation
40 is that the traveler must have moved over a curved surface on Earth, showing stars from a different angle.

Passage B by Samuel Rowbotham

The moon does not shine by reflection, but by a light peculiar to herself—that she is in short self-luminous. The moon is said to be a sphere. If so, its surface could
45 not possibly reflect; a reflector must be concave or plane, so that the rays of light may have an "angle of incidence." If the surface is convex, every ray of light falls upon it in a line direct with radius, or perpendicular to the surface. Hence there cannot be an angle of incidence and therefore
50 none of reflection. But during full moon the whole disc shines intensely, an effect which from a spherical surface is impossible.

As the moon is self-luminous, her surface could not be darkened or "eclipsed" by a shadow of the earth—
55 supposing such a shadow could be thrown upon it. In such a case, the luminosity instead of being diminished, would increase, and would be greater in proportion to the greater density or darkness of the shadow. As the light in a bull's-eye lantern looks brightest in the darkest places, so would
60 the self-shining surface of the moon be most intense in the umbra or deepest part of the earth's shadow.

The moon shining brightly during the whole time of eclipse; and the light of the moon having a different character to that of the sun; the earth not a globe, and not
65 in motion round the sun, but sun and moon always over the earth's plane surface, render the proposition unavoidable as it is clearly undeniable that a lunar eclipse does not and could not in the nature of things arise from a shadow of the earth, but must of sheer logical necessity be referred
70 to some other cause.

We have seen that, during a lunar eclipse, the moon's self-luminous surface is covered by a semi-transparent something; that this "something" is a definite mass, because it has a distinct and circular outline, as seen during its first
75 and last contact with the moon. As a solar eclipse occurs from the moon passing before the sun, so, from the evidence above collected, it is evident that a lunar eclipse arises from a similar cause—a body semi-transparent and well-defined passing before the moon; or between the moon's surface
80 and the observer on the surface of the earth.

That many such bodies exist in the firmament is almost a matter of certainty; and that one such as that which eclipses the moon exists at no great distance above the earth's surface, is a matter admitted by many of the leading
85 astronomers of the day.

Questions 1–3 ask about Passage A.

1. As used in line 4, the word *picture* most nearly means:
   A. appreciation.
   B. photograph.
   C. example.
   D. understanding.

2. According to Passage A, Aristotle cited all of the following as evidence that the Earth was round EXCEPT:
   F. the difference in height of the North Star as an observer moves from north to south.
   G. the intermittent passing of the moon between Earth and the sun.
   H. the shape of the shadow on the moon during a lunar eclipse.
   J. the visibility of some stars in the south that are not visible in the north.

3. It can most reasonably be inferred from the final paragraph of Passage A (lines 34-41) that:
   A. the curvature of the Earth prevents observers from seeing the same stars at a point in the north as at a point in the south.
   B. the North Star rotates around Earth.
   C. a lunar eclipse is evidence that the Earth is round.
   D. a self-luminous moon would be visible to observers in both the Northern Hemisphere and the Southern Hemisphere.

Questions 4–6 ask about Passage B.

4. The primary function of paragraph 1 of Passage B (lines 42-52) is to:
   F. explain why the moon cannot reflect light.
   G. provide an example of self-luminous sources.
   H. illustrate how the moon cannot be darkened by the Earth's shadow.
   J. introduce a new theory about the purpose of full moons.

5. According to Passage B, the author believes that if lunar eclipses were caused by the Earth's shadow, the moon would:
   A. have a shadow in the shape of a straight line.
   B. not be visible.
   C. shine brighter than normal.
   D. have a light that is much different than the light of the sun.

6. According to Passage B, Rowbotham believes that lunar eclipses are caused by:
   F. a full moon reflecting sun rays that occur at a ninety degree angle of incidence.
   G. the self-luminosity of the moon.
   H. the shadow of the Earth when the Earth is directly between the moon and the sun.
   J. a circular, translucent mass passing between the Earth and the moon.

Questions 7-10 ask about both passages.

7. Based on the passages, it can most reasonably be inferred that Aristotle in Passage A and the author of Passage B would agree that:
   A. the Earth does not revolve around the sun.
   B. Pythagoras's theories about the shape of the Earth were incorrect.
   C. the object that causes lunar eclipses is round.
   D. solar eclipses are caused by the sun passing in front of the moon.

8. Compared to the tone of Passage B, the tone of Passage A is more:
   F. whimsical.
   G. ambivalent.
   H. critical.
   J. detached.

9. Another author wrote the following about the shape of the Earth:

   Of course the Earth is a globe, as the gods in the heavens would only use a flawless shape in creating our flawless paradise.

   Based on the passages, this statement most closely echoes the views of which person?
   A. The author of Passage A
   B. The author of Passage B
   C. Pythagoras
   D. Aristotle

10. Which choice best states the relationship between the two passages?
    F. Passage B defends a theory introduced in Passage A.
    G. Passage B challenges an argument in Passage A.
    H. Passage B elaborates on the conclusion of Passage A.
    J. Passage B defends a claim in Passage A.

SAT Paired Passages Format

Passage 1 is adapted from *Astronomy*, a 2016 book written by Andrew Fraknoi et al. Passage 2 is adapted from the 1881 book *Zetetic Astronomy: Earth Not a Globe* published by Samuel Rowbotham, who believed that the Earth was not round, but a circular plane.

Passage 1

Our concept of the cosmos—its basic structure and origin—is called cosmology, a word with Greek roots. Before the invention of telescopes, humans had
Line to depend on the simple evidence of their senses for a
5 picture of the universe. The ancients developed cosmologies that combined their direct view of the heavens with a rich variety of philosophical and religious symbolism.

At least 2000 years before Columbus, educated people in the eastern Mediterranean region knew Earth was
10 round. Belief in a spherical Earth may have stemmed from the time of Pythagoras, a philosopher and mathematician who lived 2500 years ago. He believed circles and spheres to be "perfect forms" and suggested that Earth should therefore be a sphere. As evidence that the
15 gods liked spheres, the Greeks cited the fact that the Moon is a sphere.

The writings of Aristotle (384–322 BCE), the tutor of Alexander the Great, summarize many of the ideas of his day. They describe how the progression of the Moon's
20 phases—its apparent changing shape—results from our seeing different portions of the Moon's sunlit hemisphere as the month goes by. Aristotle also knew that the Sun has to be farther away from Earth than is the Moon because occasionally the Moon passed exactly between
25 Earth and the Sun and hid the Sun temporarily from view. We call this a solar eclipse.

Aristotle cited convincing arguments that Earth must be round. First is the fact that as the Moon enters or emerges from Earth's shadow during a lunar eclipse, the
30 shape of the shadow seen on the Moon is always round. Only a spherical object always produces a round shadow. If Earth were a disk, for example, there would be some occasions when the sunlight would strike it edge-on and its shadow on the Moon would be a line.

35 As a second argument, Aristotle explained that travelers who go south a significant distance are able to observe stars that are not visible farther north. And the height of the North Star—the star nearest the north celestial pole—decreases as a traveler moves south. On a flat
40 Earth, everyone would see the same stars overhead. The only possible explanation is that the traveler must have moved over a curved surface on Earth, showing stars from a different angle.

Passage 2

The moon does not shine by reflection, but by a light
45 peculiar to herself—that she is in short self-luminous. The moon is said to be a sphere. If so, its surface could not possibly reflect; a reflector must be concave or plane, so that the rays of light may have an "angle of incidence." If the surface is convex, every ray of light
50 falls upon it in a line direct with radius, or perpendicular to the surface. Hence there cannot be an angle of incidence and therefore none of reflection. But during full moon the whole disc shines intensely, an effect which from a spherical surface is impossible.

55 As the moon is self-luminous, her surface could not be darkened or "eclipsed" by a shadow of the earth—supposing such a shadow could be thrown upon it. In such a case, the luminosity instead of being diminished, would increase, and would be greater in proportion to
60 the greater density or darkness of the shadow. As the light in a bull's-eye lantern looks brightest in the darkest places, so would the self-shining surface of the moon be most intense in the umbra or deepest part of the earth's shadow.

65 The moon shining brightly during the whole time of eclipse; and the light of the moon having a different character to that of the sun; the earth not a globe, and not in motion round the sun, but sun and moon always over the earth's plane surface, render the proposition unavoid-
70 able as it is clearly undeniable that a lunar eclipse does not and could not in the nature of things arise from a shadow of the earth, but must of sheer logical necessity be referred to some other cause.

We have seen that, during a lunar eclipse, the moon's
75 self-luminous surface is covered by a semi-transparent something; that this "something" is a definite mass, because it has a distinct and circular outline, as seen during its first and last contact with the moon. As a solar eclipse occurs from the moon passing before the sun, so,
80 from the evidence above collected, it is evident that a lunar eclipse arises from a similar cause—a body semi-transparent and well-defined passing before the moon; or between the moon's surface and the observer on the surface of the earth.

85 That many such bodies exist in the firmament is almost a matter of certainty; and that one such as that which eclipses the moon exists at no great distance above the earth's surface, is a matter admitted by many of the leading astronomers of the day.

1

As used in line 5, the word *picture* most nearly means:

A) appreciation.
B) photograph.
C) example.
D) understanding. *(circled)*

2 *(marked X)*

According to Passage 1, Aristotle cited all of the following as evidence that the Earth was round EXCEPT:

A) the difference in height of the North Star as an observer moves from north to south.
B) the intermittent passing of the moon between Earth and the sun.
C) the shape of the shadow on the moon during a lunar eclipse. *(circled)*
D) the visibility of some stars in the south that are not visible in the north.

3

It can most reasonably be inferred from the final paragraph of Passage 1 (lines 35-43) that:

A) the curvature of the Earth prevents observers from seeing the same stars at a point in the north as at a point in the south. *(circled)*
B) the North Star rotates around Earth.
C) a lunar eclipse is evidence that the Earth is round.
D) a self-luminous moon would be visible to observers in both the Northern Hemisphere and the Southern Hemisphere.

4

The primary function of paragraph 1 of Passage 2 (lines 44-54) is to:

A) explain why the moon cannot reflect light. *(circled)*
B) provide an example of self-luminous sources.
C) illustrate how the moon cannot be darkened by the Earth's shadow.
D) introduce a new theory about the purpose of full moons.

5

According to Passage 2, the author believes that if lunar eclipses were caused by the Earth's shadow, the moon would:

A) have a shadow in the shape of a straight line.
B) not be visible.
C) shine brighter than normal. *(circled)*
D) have a light that is much different than the light of the sun.

6

According to Passage 2, Rowbotham believes that lunar eclipses are caused by:

A) a full moon reflecting sun rays that occur at a ninety degree angle of incidence.
B) the self-luminosity of the moon.
C) the shadow of the Earth when the Earth is directly between the moon and the sun.
D) a circular, translucent mass passing between the Earth and the moon. *(circled)*

7

Based on the passages, it can most reasonably be inferred that Aristotle in Passage 1 and the author of Passage 2 would agree that:

A) the Earth does not revolve around the sun.
B) Pythagoras's theories about the shape of the Earth were incorrect.
C) the object that causes lunar eclipses is round. *(circled)*
D) solar eclipses are caused by the sun passing in front of the moon.

8 *(marked X)*

Compared to the tone of Passage 2, the tone of Passage 1 is more:

A) whimsical.
B) ambivalent. *(circled)*
C) critical.
D) detached.

9

Another author wrote the following about the shape of the Earth:

Of course the Earth is a globe, as the gods in the heavens would only use a flawless shape in creating our flawless paradise.

Based on the passages, this statement most closely echoes the views of which person?

A) The author of Passage 1
B) The author of Passage 2
C) Pythagoras *(circled)*
D) Aristotle

10

Which choice best states the relationship between the two passages?

A) Passage 2 defends a theory introduced in Passage 1.
B) Passage 2 challenges an argument in Passage 1. *(circled)*
C) Passage 2 elaborates on the conclusion of Passage 1.
D) Passage 2 defends a claim in Passage 1.

(handwritten notes: 1-3 | P1; 4-6 | P2; 7-10 | P1 & P2)

Strategies for Attacking Paired Passages

You can expect exactly 10 questions about the paired passages on the ACT, and either 10 or 11 questions about the paired passages on the SAT. Roughly one third of the questions are about the first passage, one third are about the second passage, and one third are about both passages, but this may vary from test to test.

Most of these paired sets have passages with opposing viewpoints. One author may support animal cloning while the other opposes it. Or one passage cites obesity as the reason for apathy, while the other blames apathy for the national rise in obesity. Occasionally the authors might agree on a topic, though, so you cannot always expect opposing viewpoints.

There may be some clues to help you predict the authors' points of view. When the passages are about the exact same topic and written during the same era, they will likely disagree with one another. But when the passages are about two slightly different, yet related, topics, such as the American Revolution of 1776 and the Russian Revolution of 1917, expect similar viewpoints.

You should apply the reading strategies previously covered in this book, from active reading to notating line references, as you read each passage. In addition, there are some strategical steps that are specific to paired passages:

1. **Read the introduction.**
2. **Read Passage 1.**
3. **Do not go on to Passage 2. Instead, answer the questions about Passage 1.**
4. **Reread the introduction.**
5. **Read Passage 2.**
6. **Answer the questions about Passage 2.**
7. **Answer the questions about both passages.**

Let's briefly discuss each step on the following pages.

♦ GRATUITOUS VOCAB
apathy (n): lack of emotion or excitement

⋮TIPS and TRICKS⋮
Passages written about the exact same topic in the same era will likely disagree, while passages about two slightly different topics will likely agree.

---

1. Read the introduction.

Just as with single passages, the blurb at the beginning of paired passages will provide background information for each passage. This information can help you understand the passages and make predictions about whether the authors will agree or disagree about the topic. On rare occasion, the introduction may even state that the passages provide different views on a single subject, indicating opposing viewpoints.

≥TIPS and TRICKS≤
After reading the introduction, make a prediction about whether the two authors will agree or disagree about their mutual topic.

2. Read Passage 1.

As you read the first passage, employ all of the strategies that we have previously covered. Be sure to determine the MAPS of the passage. The paired passages are often easier to read than the single passages, so it should not be a difficult task to find the main idea or determine the author's attitude. Be sure to briefly notate the main idea next to the passage; because the two passages likely have opposing viewpoints, notating paired passages helps you keep the information straight.

≥TIPS and TRICKS≤
Writing sidebar summaries is extremely important in paired passages because the questions are designed to confuse the information in Passage 1 with the information in Passage 2.

3. Do not go on to Passage 2. Instead, answer the questions about Passage 1.

The test questions and answer choices are designed to confuse the information in Passage 1 with the information in Passage 2. If you read both passages back-to-back, you are likely to fall into these traps, so it is important to read the first passage and move right to the questions about Passage 1.

About one-third of the questions will be strictly about Passage 1. On the ACT, these are always first and are clearly labeled. The released tests for the current SAT all show that the first 3 to 5 questions, although unlabeled as on the ACT, are about Passage 1. In the recent past, however, the College Board attempted to deter students from using this powerful strategy by mixing Passage 1 and Passage 2 questions throughout the question field. Therefore, SAT test takers should scan each question to see whether it says "Passage 1" or has a line reference to the first passage. If it does, answer the question. If the question is about Passage 2 or both passages, skip it and come back to it later.

⚡ CAUTION: SAT TRAP!
If you read both passages before answering the questions, you will likely fall into question traps that are designed to take advantage of you.

Keep in mind that scanning a question is not the same thing as reading a question. You should not read the questions; simply glance at them specifically looking for the passage number or a line reference.

♦ GRATUITOUS VOCAB
meticulous (adj):
extremely careful and
precise with details

Because you may be skipping some questions on the SAT, you must be meticulous in marking your answers in the answer booklet. Be sure to bubble the correct question number, omitting those that you skip in the test booklet. Remember to employ the strategies for reading the questions that we covered in the previous chapter.

4. Reread the introduction.

Once you complete all of the questions that are only about Passage 1, reread the introduction so that you become reacquainted with the context of the second passage.

5. Read Passage 2.

It is extremely important to practice active reading through Passage 2 so that you find comparisons and contrasts to the first passage. Be sure to notate the main idea and the author's attitude, and note any differences in these two elements with the elements in the first passage.

≣TIPS and TRICKS≣
Look for a point of
agreement as you read
Passage 2.

If the authors of the two passages completely disagree on a topic, you should expect them to agree on some small detail, about which you are guaranteed to be asked in the questions. For example, when one author believes that classrooms should be equipped with video cameras and the other asserts that this technology is a violation of students' rights, they may both agree, however, that crime rates in schools have increased in recent years. If you can find this small case of agreement as you read, you will save yourself many seconds, if not minutes, because you will not have to search through both passages when you come to the agreement question.

≣TIPS and TRICKS≣
Look for outside
opinions in a passage
and consider how the
other author would
react to those opinions.

Also watch for one of the authors to cite a person or group who has an opposite viewpoint of the author himself. Using the previous example in which Author 1 advocates for classroom cameras and Author 2 opposes the technology, imagine that Author 2 quotes the president of a teacher's association who is lobbying for cameras in the classroom (in an attempt to disqualify the president's comments). Therefore, Author 1 and the president have similar viewpoints; expect a question in which you are asked to make a comparison between the two people.

Once you finish reading, consider the MAPS before moving on.

6. Answer the questions about Passage 2.

Now scan the remaining questions, answering only those about the second passage. On the ACT, these are clearly labeled, but on the SAT, you will need to skip any question about both passages. Even though you have now read both passages, you may learn new information about Passage 2 by answering the questions solely about that passage. You can use this information later when attempting the questions about both passages.

◎ SAT ONLY ◎

The SAT has been known to intermix the questions about Passage 1 and Passage 2.

7. Answer the questions about both passages.

The remaining questions should be about both passages. Answer them after completing the questions for Passage 2.

There are some specific question types that occur when inquiring about both passages and we will cover those in detail in later chapters.

By employing the strategies here, you can make quick work of the paired passage set on both the ACT and the SAT. These passages are often the most intimidating of the Reading section, but students who practice the PowerScore techniques know that they are usually the easiest passages to read and complete.

Strategies for Attacking Paired Passages Problem Set

Choose to complete either the ACT-formatted paired passages on pages 156-157 or the SAT-formatted paired passages on pages 158-159. Follow the steps for completing paired passages that we covered in this chapter. After reading Passage 1, consider the MAPS of the passage and then answer all of the questions that are just about Passage 1. Then read Passage 2 and consider its MAPS. Answer all of the questions that are just about Passage 2 before moving on to the questions about both passages. The answers are provided on page 165.

Chapter Summary

There are several strategies you should employ when reading ACT and SAT paired passages:

Strategies for Attacking Paired Passages

1. Read the introduction.
   - The introduction helps you understand the context of the excerpts, as the passage likely came from a much longer source.
   - Pay attention to who wrote the passages and the year it was published.
   - Based on the introduction, make a prediction about whether the authors will agree or disagree on the topic.

2. Read Passage 1.
   - Avoid shortcuts or gimmicks such as skimming the passage or reading the questions first.
   - The only way to fully understand an ACT and SAT passage and answer the questions correctly is to read the entire passage.

3. Do not go on to Passage 2. Instead, answer the questions about Passage 1.
   - It is important to read every word in the question stem.
   - Turn an incomplete sentence into a question by rephrasing.
   - If necessary, return to the passage to read a line reference.
   - Prephrase an answer before reading the answer choices.
   - Match your prephrase to an answer choice.
   - On the SAT, be careful to complete your answer booklet correctly if you are forced to skip questions.

4. Reread the introduction.
   - This will allow you to become reacquainted with the context of the second passage.

5. Read Passage 2.
   - Follow all of the strategies listed above for reading Passage 1.

6. Answer the questions about Passage 2.
   - Follow all of the strategies listed above for answering the questions for Passage 1.

7. Answer the questions about both passages.

STRATEGIES FOR PAIRED PASSAGES ANSWER KEY

Strategies for Attacking Paired Passages Problem Set—Page 163

Note: Odd-numbered questions will have the same answer for both the ACT and the SAT problem set. The even-numbered questions will have two answers listed: F/G/H/J for ACT and A/B/C/D for SAT.

1. (D)   Prephrase: "humans had to depend on the simple evidence of their senses for a [sense/vision/ understanding] of the universe"

    If your prephrase does not lead you to *understanding* in choice (D), plug each answer choice into the sentence to find the one that makes sense:

    (A) appreciation: Before the invention of telescopes, humans had to depend on the simple evidence of their senses for an *appreciation* of the universe
    (B) photograph: Before the invention of telescopes, humans had to depend on the simple evidence of their senses for a *photograph* of the universe
    (C) example: Before the invention of telescopes, humans had to depend on the simple evidence of their senses for an *example* of the universe
    (D) understanding: Before the invention of telescopes, humans had to depend on the simple evidence of their senses for an *understanding* of the universe

    If you are still unsure (and likely have narrowed it to A and D), look for other words in the paragraph that may be synonyms of *picture*. The phrase *direct view of the heavens* in line 6 should help you choose (D).

2. (G or B) Prephrase: It is difficult to prephrase this question and much easier to simply find the three pieces of evidence cited by Aristotle in the last two paragraphs of the first passage.

    (F/A) ACT: lines 36-38 SAT: lines 37-39
    (G/B) This evidence is not cited.
    (H/C) ACT: lines 28-29 SAT: lines 29-30
    (J/D) ACT: lines 34-36 SAT: lines 35-37

3. (A)   Prephrase: While it is possible to prephrase an inference in a single sentence, it is more difficult to find the inference in a complete paragraph. It is easier to read the answer choices and decide if they apply to that paragraph.

    (A) Aristotle cited that the Earth was round because "travelers who go south a significant distance are able to observe stars that are not visible farther north." This infers that the shape of the earth prevents the observer from seeing the stars in both places. There is further evidence of this inference when the authors write "on a flat Earth, everyone would see the same stars overhead."
    (B) There is no discussion of the North Star moving.
    (C) This is a fact from the previous paragraph.
    (D) Only the author of the second passage discusses a self-luminous moon.

4. (F or A) Prephrase: To explain why the moon does not shine by reflection.

    (F/A) The first sentence of the paragraph should easily lead you to this answer. All of the other sentences in the paragraph are explaining why the moon does not shine by reflection.
    (G/B) Sources were never provided in this passage.
    (H/C) This is the main idea of the second paragraph, not the first.
    (J/D) The purpose of full moons is not discussed in the passage.

5. (C) Prephrase: "in such a case, the luminosity instead of being diminished, would increase"

    (A) The first passage discusses a straight line shadow but the second passage does not.
    (B) This is opposite of what the author believes, which is that the moon would shine brighter.
    (C) The second paragraph discusses lunar eclipses and the author asserts that the self-luminous moon would look brighter given the dark shadow.
    (D) The author does believe that the light of the moon is different than the light of the sun (lines 66-67 ACT, lines 66-67 SAT), but this has nothing to do with his thoughts about lunar eclipses in the previous paragraph.

6. (J or D) Prephrase: An object that is round and semi-transparent passing before the moon.

    (F/A) The author discusses the angle of incidence in the first paragraph, but not in relation to eclipses.
    (G/B) The theory of self-luminosity is separate from his theory about lunar eclipses.
    (H/C) This is not discussed.
    (J/D) The author addresses the cause of lunar eclipses in the last two paragraphs: "it has a distinct and circular outline" and "a lunar eclipse arises from...a body semi-transparent and well-defined passing before the moon."

7. (C) Prephrase: It is difficult to prephrase an inference when looking at complete passages.

    (A) Neither Aristotle nor the author of the second passage discuss the Earth revolving around the sun.
    (B) Pythagoras's theory was that the Earth was round; Aristotle would agree with this, while the author of the second passage would disagree with it.
    (C) Aristotle believed that the Earth, which was round, caused lunar eclipses (line 29 ACT, line 30 SAT), while Rowbotham believed that it was a round, semi-transparent object (line 74 ACT, line 77 SAT). So they both believed the cause was a round object.
    (D) The first passage explains that a solar eclipse is when the Moon passes between the Earth and the sun (lines 21-25 ACT, lines 22-26 SAT), which is different than what this answer choice states. The second author does not discuss solar eclipses, only lunar eclipses.

8. (J or D) Prephrase: Analytical, uninvolved, unconcerned

    (F/A) *Whimsical* means *playful*, which does not describe the first passage.
    (G/B) *Ambivalent* means *having mixed feelings*; the authors of the first passage do not reveal their feelings, but rather objectively discuss the beliefs of others.
    (H/C) The opposite could be argued as true; while the authors of the first passage are objective, the author of the second passage is critical of those who believe the Earth is round.
    (J/D) The authors of the first passage are discussing Aristotle's beliefs rather than their own; they are explaining history in an objective manner. Rowbotham, however, is much more adamant in defense of his theories. He is clearly trying to defend himself and persuade others to believe him. Thus, we can say the tone of the first passage is more *detached*.

9. (C) Prephrase: Pythagoras

    In the second paragraph of the first passage, it states that Pythagoras believed the Earth was round because circles and spheres were "perfect forms."

10. (G or B) Prephrase: The first passage explains why Pythagoras and Aristotle thought the Earth was round; the second passage explains why they are wrong.

    (F/A) The second passage defends its own theories, not theories from the first passage.
    (G/B) The second passage challenges Aristotle's argument that a lunar eclipse is evidence that the Earth is round.
    (H/C) In order for this to be true, the authors of the two passages would have to agree.
    (J/D) This is opposite of the correct answer.

THE POWERSCORE ACT AND SAT READING BIBLE

CHAPTER TEN
ANSWER CHOICE ANALYSIS

In this chapter, we will look at the characteristics of right and wrong answers so that you can quickly learn to eliminate the counterfeit answers and select the correct choice.

You are likely wondering why we are "putting the cart before the horse" and discussing the answer choices before covering the specific types of questions. By reviewing answer choices now, you will have more opportunities to practice selecting the right answers and eliminating the wrong ones in the problem sets in the following chapters. We can also point to answers in our explanations for those problem sets and state "this is an Extreme Answer" without explaining that concept over and over because you will know what an Extreme Answer is after reading this chapter. Finally, these strategies are universal to all types of Reading questions, so it is convenient to discuss them here before looking at the specific types of questions.

It is important to understand that right answers share common attributes; selecting the right answer is not simply the process of eliminating the three wrong answers. Knowing that an answer choice has the characteristics of a right answer will help increase your confidence in selecting it, so we will discuss correct answers in the first section of this chapter.

> ✎ GRATUITOUS VOCAB
> *attributes* (n): qualities

Then we will turn our attention to the common answer traps on both tests. We have given these answers specific names to help you remember them while you are testing:

- Opposite Answers
- Extreme Answers
- True But Wrong Answers
- True To A Point Answers
- True To You Answers
- Copycat Answers (SAT only)

> Understanding the construction of wrong answers goes a long way in helping you select the right answers.

Each type of answer trap is intentionally designed to trick you, so it's important you cover this section of the book carefully.

Right Answers

There is a certain comfort in multiple choice questions, knowing that the right answer is there on the page staring up at you. In ACT and SAT Reading questions, the right answer is the only answer that can be proven true.

If the question asks you to interpret a phrase or sentence from the passage, the right answer will often be a paraphrase of the actual passage. Consider an example:

≥TIPS and TRICKS≤
The right answer tends to paraphrase the passage.

> While the United States was fighting the War of 1812 with Britain, a series of violent incidents occurred when <u>authorities entered Seminole territory to recapture</u>
> Line <u>runaway slaves</u>, which aggravated the Seminole and
> 5 increased hostility.

1. According to the passage, the "hostility" (line 5) between the United States and the Seminole was intensified by which of the following?

   A) Wrong answer
   B) Officials invading Native American territory to reclaim escaped slaves.
   C) Wrong answer
   D) Wrong answer

The correct answer, choice (B), is a reworded version of lines 3 and 4. Compare the wording of the passage and the correct answer:

Words from Passage	Words from Correct Answer
authorities	officials
entered	invaded
Seminole	Native American
territory	*territory*
recapture	reclaim
runaway	escaped
slaves	*slaves*

Confidence Quotation
"Two trucks loaded with a thousand copies of Roget's Thesaurus collided as they left a New York publishing house last week, according to the Associated Press. Witnesses were stunned, startled, aghast, taken aback, stupefied, appalled, surprised, shocked and rattled." -Alan Schlein

When adjectives and verbs are used in the original passage, the correct answer will likely use synonyms for these words. Even some of the nouns may be replaced with synonyms, although you should not discount an answer for using the same nouns that were used in the passage. After all, there are only so many ways you can say *spaghetti* or *elephant* or *pants*! If a noun does not have many recognizable synonyms, the test makers will reuse the word in the answer choice. But since adjectives and verbs have many alternatives, they will likely be replaced with different words.

Even questions that ask you to draw conclusions about the passage will have right answer choices that prefer synonyms over the actual words from the text. It's one way that the test makers can actually assess whether you understand the passage or are just regurgitating words you happened to read.

The SAT will almost always use synonyms, while the ACT will use both synonyms and words from the original text.

The right answer will also include all of the important ideas from the cited line reference, unlike some wrong answers that only provide a portion of the information. Study another example:

> Melner attributes the decline in school enrollment to several factors. For one, families are moving out of the area to find work. For another, lackluster test results
> Line cause some existing and most new families to choose
> 5 other districts.

2. According to the passage, enrollment in the school district has decreased because of families'

   A) Wrong answer
   B) Wrong answer
   C) Wrong answer
   D) emphasis on jobs and performance.

⋮TIPS and TRICKS⋮
The correct answer incorporates all of the important ideas from the line reference.

The correct answer includes both *moving out of the area to find work* (emphasis on jobs) and *lackluster test results* (emphasis on performance). As we will discuss in the next section, wrong answers may address only one of those reasons. The right answer includes all of the important ideas.

Another characteristic of right answers is that they tend to be more general than wrong answers:

> The festival allowed us to acknowledge our German heritage after hiding our ancestry the rest of the year. For one weekend, my sisters and I could feast on
> Line mettwurst and maultaschen, dance the landler, and play
> 5 Topfschlagen without worrying about the anti-German sentiments permeating the country after the war. It was our most memorable weekend of 1946.

3. According to the passage, the narrator remembers the "festival" (line 1) with fondness because

   A) he learned a German dance called the landler.
   B) Wrong answer
   C) German sausages were prepared for the first time that year.
   D) it allowed him to celebrate his culture.

⋮TIPS and TRICKS⋮
Right answers tend to be more general than wrong answers.

The correct answer, (D), uses the broad term *culture* to describe the German food, dance, and game that were a part of the festival. The two wrong answers use more specific language. Choice (A) is wrong because it claims the narrator learned a dance; the passage just states that he *danced* the landler, not that he *learned* it. But notice that this answer is quite specific. As is (C). The answer in (C) is wrong because the passage only says that he *ate* mettwurst, not that it was the first time they were *prepared* that year. But again, the use of *German sausages* is quite specific. Sometimes the correct answer is this particular, too, especially if the question asks about a specific event, but when in doubt, select the most general answer choice.

The right answer can be proven using the passage.

The right answer is the only answer that can be defended or proven in the text. While many questions ask you which answer best characterizes or most effectively supports an argument in the passage, there is only one choice that completely and correctly answers the question. As we will see, something makes the other four answer choices wrong. When you select an answer, you should be pretty confident that it is correct because you can point to a specific portion of the text that proves the answer.

☠ CAUTION: TEST TRAP
Test makers often place the "best" wrong answer choice above the right answer choice.

You should note that the test makers often put the most attractive wrong answer choice above the right answer. If they can trick you into selecting an answer before reading the correct one, then they helped colleges weed out students who are careless and inattentive to detail. Always read all four answer choices before making your selection. And steer clear of any answer choice that presents an idea directly opposite of your predicted answer.

Now that you know what to look for in the right answers, let's look more closely at common wrong answers!

Notes:

Wrong Answers

If only one answer can be right, then three others are wrong. The test makers carefully write these wrong answer choices, intentionally using language and ideas that trick unsuspecting test takers. Learning how these incorrect answers are crafted can help you spot them, which is why eliminating wrong answers can sometimes be easier than determining the right answer.

Opposite Answers

Be on the lookout for an answer choice that has a meaning opposite of your prephrase. These Opposite Answers play on students' self-doubt, as many test takers will assume they misunderstood the passage and that it actually said the opposite of what they originally understood. Do not doubt your initial reading unless you reread the text and have a new understanding!

Let's return to the previous question for a good example of an Opposite Answer, where the statement in the answer choice had the opposite meaning as the passage:

> The festival allowed us to acknowledge our German heritage after hiding our ancestry the rest of the year. For one weekend, my sisters and I could feast on
> *Line* mettwurst and maultaschen, dance the landler, and play
> 5 Topfschlagen without worrying about the anti-German sentiments permeating the country after the war. It was our most memorable weekend of 1946.

3. According to the passage, the narrator remembers the "festival" (line 1) with fondness because

   A) he learned a German dance called the landler.
   B) he was able to conceal his German heritage.
   C) German sausages were prepared for the first time that year.
   D) it allowed him to celebrate his culture.

We have already determined that answer choice (D) is correct: he liked the festival because he was able to celebrate his German heritage. But look at choice (B). This presents an idea opposite of the correct answer: that instead of acknowledging his culture, he hid it. Notice that it also uses the phrase *German heritage* from lines 1-2. Sadly, some students will read this answer choice and assume they misread the passage. They select (B) without ever reading the last two answer choices.

Be confident in your prephrase or in your reading of the text and avoid answers with an opposite meaning.

Extreme Answers

In an ACT and SAT answer choice, every word counts, and each of those words should be read literally. Let's analyze the meaning of the following answer choice:

    A) People in the neighborhood think that Mr. Wilson is mean.

Because this answer choice has no modifiers, it states that *ALL* people in the neighborhood think that Mr. Wilson is mean—including Mrs. Wilson, neighboring infants and children, and Mr. Wilson's friends. Because statements like this one are so extreme, the makers of the ACT and SAT are likely to use modifiers to subdue the meaning. Consider some examples:

    B) <u>Most</u> people in the neighborhood think that Mr. Wilson is mean.
    C) <u>Many</u> people in the neighborhood think that Mr. Wilson is mean.
    D) <u>Some</u> people in the neighborhood think that Mr. Wilson is mean.

Each of these answer choices added an adjective modifier to *people*, making them easier to defend than the original answer in (A). However, choices (B) and (C) are still somewhat Extreme Answers; the qualifiers *most* and *many* include a lot of people, making these answers difficult to prove. But answer choice (D) is much more moderate. With the use of *some*, you only need to find two people who think Mr. Wilson is mean in order for this answer choice to be true. Sometimes the right answer will also use *somewhat*:

    D) The neighbor thinks that Mr. Wilson is somewhat mean.

In this answer choice, *somewhat* tempers the meaning of *mean*. Instead of proving that Mr. Wilson is always cruel, you only need to find one instance of meanness to make him *somewhat mean*.

Also watch for Extreme verbs. Consider the difference between these three answer choices:

    A) Henry <u>must go</u> to the wedding.
    B) Henry <u>needs to go</u> to the wedding.
    C) Henry <u>should go</u> to the wedding.

It is difficult to defend *must go* and *needs to go*, and it is quite unlikely that the author was that straightforward in the passage. However, *should go* is much easier to prove.

⬦ GRATUITOUS VOCAB
modifiers (n): a word or phrase that modifies the sense of another word

---

☤ CAUTION: TEST TRAP
Extreme Answers use words that make the answer difficult to defend.

⁼TIPS and TRICKS⁼
An answer that uses *some* or *somewhat* is usually the correct answer.

For most ACT and SAT questions, avoid answers that use *most, many, must, needs,* or these other Extreme words:

- *all, total, only, solely, exclusively, completely, entirely, thoroughly*
- *mainly, chiefly, primarily, largely, mostly*
- *invariably, certainly, absolutely, unquestionably*
- *always, never, not*
- words that end in *-est* (*greatest, largest,* etc.)
- words that end in *-less* (*worthless, useless,* etc.)
- words that are preceded by *most* (*most accurate, most important,* etc.)
- words that are preceded by *least* (*least significant, least truthful,* etc.)

Extreme Words are usually modifiers.

Some Extreme Answers are more difficult to pinpoint. Consider these two answers:

A) Penelope was surprised by her mother's <u>vicious</u> reply.
B) Penelope was surprised by her mother's <u>insensitive</u> reply.

Which answer choice is easiest to defend? The word *vicious* makes answer choice (A) the least likely answer. In order for the reply to be vicious, the mother would have had to have been spiteful, cruel, and severe. But the word *insensitive* is much easier to defend. She simply had to say something that was mildly unkind in order to be called insensitive.

Consider the difference between these moderate and extreme word pairs:

Moderate Word	Extreme Word
unfriendly	hostile
happy	elated
sad	despairing
excited	hysterical
impolite	barbaric
mischievous	sinister
opposition	malice
unrealistic	outrageous
challenge	mock
foolish	ludicrous
anxious	frantic
unlikely	impossible
criticize	chastise

You would be wise to avoid answers with these extreme words and others like them.

One Extreme Word that often avoids detection is *nostalgic*. The definition maintains that a person who is nostalgic desires to return to a happier time in the past. Someone who remembers his childhood is not necessarily nostalgic; he would have to express his longing for the happiness from that childhood in order to be considered nostalgic. So unless an author or narrator plans to build a time machine and return to the past, try to avoid an answer choice with the word *nostalgic* or *nostalgia* on the ACT and SAT.

⋛TIPS and TRICKS⋛

Avoid the answer *nostalgic* on the ACT and SAT because it's likely an Extreme Answer.

Let's look at a previous passage with a question utilizing some Extreme Answers:

> Melner attributes the decline in school enrollment to several factors. For one, families are moving out of the area to find work. For another, lackluster test results
> *Line* cause some existing and most new families to choose
> 5 other districts.

2. According to the passage, enrollment in the school district has decreased because of families'

   (A) complete confidence in standardized tests.
   (B) Wrong answer
   (C) outrage over the lack of employment.
   (D) emphasis on jobs and performance.

We previously determined that the correct answer is (D). But examine choice (A). Aside from being totally inaccurate, it uses the word *complete*. This is an Extreme Word, and so the answer choice should be avoided.

Choice (C) uses the Extreme Word *outrage*. In order to prove this word is justified, the families would have had to have shown powerful feelings of anger and resentment. The passage does not indicate they expressed these feelings, let alone even felt them. Both (A) and (C) are Extreme Answers.

Extreme Answers are almost always incorrect on the ACT and SAT. But notice that we've used the modifier *almost* in the previous sentence. That's because there is a slight chance you may encounter an extreme passage. Perhaps you will find a passage where the author detests snakes or adamantly defends the Constitution. If you have an extreme passage, written by an author who is forceful about her beliefs, you can expect some Extreme Answers. These answer choices should be easy to defend, however. If the author states that snakes are wicked and she wishes a plague would wipe them off the face of the Earth, then answer choices with the words *sinister* and *malice* become attractive and defendable. Given the temperate nature of the ACT and SAT, though, it is unlikely you will encounter such an extreme passage. When in doubt, avoid all answer choices with Extreme Words.

⚲ GRATUITOUS VOCAB
temperate (adj):
moderate; not extreme

True But Wrong Answers

True But Wrong Answers are especially tricky because they provide a true statement or conclusion based on the passage; however, they do not answer the specific question at hand. They pull a fact or inference from an earlier or later portion of text, but have little to do with the line reference in question.

Let's consider an example from a previous passage:

This passage is taken from a novel set in 2001. It presents two characters—Robert, a Mexican American painter in New York, and his father, an immigrant and retiree who achieved success in the banking business. Robert has traveled home to Michigan to visit his parents.

"Did you hear about your brother?" my father asked, knowing full well that Mother had already told me about Peter's promotion at the bank. "He's really making something of himself, I tell you. I always
5 knew that boy would go far."
I drank from my iced tea to avoid having to answer. I had been compared to my twin for nearly twenty-five years and I was still coming up short.
"So, Robert," he began, "when are you going to
10 get promoted at the art gallery?" Here it was again. A comparison.
"Dad, I am a painter," I said. "I don't get promoted. I don't even work for the gallery. Just being displayed there is a tremendous honor."
15 "Hmph," he grunted. He stirred his cocktail with a finger. "Honor doesn't mean the same thing today as it did in my day then, I guess. Being recognized for saving three men on the battlefield, that was an honor."
20 I could not win. I was never going to please my father because I was never going to succeed at what he considered honorable.
My father was a young child when my grandparents came to America. They were migrant
25 workers, who only planned on staying the summer at the tomato farm, but when my Uncle Miguel contracted polio, they decided to remain through the winter—a decision that changed the course of my family's history. My grandparents never returned to
30 Mexico after the farmer hired them full time, and my father was raised along with the white children on the farm. He enlisted in the marines upon graduating high school with honors and was sent to Vietnam, years he rarely talks about except to define honor, courage, and
35 fear. When he came home from the war, he went to the University of Michigan on a scholarship which led

to a job with the largest bank in the county. Within 10
years, he was vice president of the bank, and within
20, he was running it. As he liked to say, "Not bad for
40 a poor immigrant from Mexico."
    My brother had taken a similar road. He was
valedictorian of his high school class, a Gulf War
veteran, and a college graduate. He was a banker at
the same bank that my father had worked. And I was
45 none of these things. I was an artist, a career that
helped free me from my father and imprison me in his
judgment at the same time.

2. The second paragraph indicates that

   A) Peter is taller than Robert.
   B) Robert's father had a successful career.
   C) Robert's mother does not consider art an
      honorable pursuit.
   D) Peter's choices have been favored over Robert's
      decisions by their father.

Confidence Quotation
"What counts is not
necessarily the size of
the dog in the fight—
it's the size of the fight
in the dog."
-Dwight D. Eisenhower,
34th President of the
United States

The correct answer for this question is (D). But notice choice (B). This is a
true statement, as indicated in lines 37-39. However, although it is true, it is
wrong, as it does not answer the specific question about the second paragraph.

The third question also has a True But Wrong Answer in (C):

3. The father responds to Robert's comments in lines
    12-14 by doing which of the following?

   A) Challenging Robert's definition of honor
   B) Asserting his power over Robert
   C) Denying one son the same respect as the other
   D) Agreeing that Robert's successful endeavors are
      different than Peter's accomplishments

The entire passage indicates that Robert is not viewed as favorably as his
brother by their father, thus choice (C) is a true statement. However, only
choice (A) correctly identifies the father's reaction to the comments in lines
12-14. His reaction has nothing to do with the brother.

As you can see, these True But Wrong answer choices are especially attractive
given that they provide a true statement from the passage. But you must be
certain that the answer choice you select corresponds with the line reference in
the question.

True But Wrong Answers are common in paired passage question sets.
The answer might be true about Passage 2, but the question is asking about
Passage 1 or about both passages. This is why it is extremely important to
answer questions about Passage 1 before reading the second passage.

⚑ CAUTION: TEST TRAP
True But Wrong
Answers are especially
common in questions
about paired passages.
The truth is often from
the passage that is not
being addressed in the
question.

True To A Point Answers

True to a Point Answers are very attractive choices because they usually start out seemingly correct. Careless test takers might not notice, though, that at some point in the answer choice they become blatantly wrong.

Sometimes these answer choices add new, irrelevant information causing them to be incorrect. For example, if the passage discusses the feeding habits of monarch butterflies, be wary of any answer choice that details the feeding habits of swallowtail butterflies. This answer will appear to be correct when explaining the feeding habits, but once it cites a different butterfly type, it is clearly incorrect.

Let's study some examples:

> Unlike the Tango, a dance which can trace its roots directly back to Argentina and Uruguay, Ballroom Tango saw significant changes in both structure and technique as the dance traveled to the United States
> Line
> 5 and Europe. Film star Rudolph Valentino first brought Ballroom Tango to Hollywood in the early 1920s, and the famous dance instructor Arthur Murray later helped popularize a standardized version which incorporated steps that were common to the US during that period.
> 10 This incarnation of Ballroom Tango was generally considered somewhat less formal and referred to as the "American Style" by the English, who wished to distinguish this informal approach from their own International Style—a technique that was taught in countries
> 15 throughout Europe and had already become the de facto standard in competitions around the world.

1. The standardized version of the Ballroom Tango features which of the following?

    A) Steps that were common in American film
    B) Wrong answer
    C) Conventional American movements
    D) Wrong answer

Choice (A) is appealing because it is True to a Point: *steps that were common*, the phrase in the answer choice, comes right from line 9. But then the answer makes a wrong turn with the phrase *in American film*. The passage does not mention American film in connection with the Ballroom Tango, other than the fact that a film star was responsible for bringing the dance to Hollywood. It does not state that these steps were common in movies, so choice (A) is incorrect. Choice (C), the right answer, uses synonyms to express the idea in lines 8-9.

The most tempting True to a Point Answers have a single word that sabotages the entire answer choice. Consider an example using the Ballroom Tango passage on the previous page:

> 2. According to the passage, the Ballroom Tango is different from the Tango because the Ballroom Tango
>
> A) Wrong answer
> B) was slightly altered once it became popular in America.
> C) Wrong answer
> D) underwent a transformation upon entering countries in the US and Europe.

Choice (B) is incorrect because of a single word: *slightly*. The passage states that the Ballroom Tango *saw significant changes* (line 3) making *slightly altered* significantly incorrect. Note, too, that the answer only includes America, omitting Europe as stated in the passage (line 5). Remember, the correct answer will include all of the important ideas, as does choice (D).

Every word counts in an ACT and SAT answer choice. You must carefully read each possibility, looking for reasons that the answer choice is incorrect. Be sure to eliminate any answer that is only True to a Point, and cross the letter out in your test booklet.

One word can make an ACT and SAT answer choice incorrect, so it is important to read each answer choice carefully.

True To You Answers

One of the biggest mistakes that a student can make is to bring their experience and expectations into the ACT and SAT. Your opinions are not relevant on the Reading portion of the tests, and you should be careful not to let them influence your understanding of a text.

True to You Answers are designed to take advantage of your personal beliefs and prior knowledge. Let's study an example that plays on a common opinion about slavery:

☠ CAUTION: TEST TRAP
True To You Answers trick you into applying prior knowledge or experience to the passage.

> By 1750, slavery was a legal institution in all of the American colonies, the profits of which amounted to 5% of the British economy at the time of the Industrial Revolution. The Transatlantic slave trade peaked in the
> Line
> 5 late 18th century, when the largest number of slaves was captured on raiding expeditions into the interior of West Africa. The slaves were shipped to the Americas in the hulls of large boats, where they experienced extremely cramped quarters, lack of ventilation, and
> 10 unsanitary conditions; a large percentage of the captives died in transit.

1. The author of the passage implies that

   A) the hazardous conditions in which the slaves were shipped resulted in a high mortality rate
   B) Wrong answer
   C) Wrong answer
   D) slavery is uncivilized and immoral

↳ GRATUITOUS VOCAB
objective (adj): not influenced by feelings

In the 21st century, we know that slavery is uncivilized and immoral. That is part of the reason why the Civil War was fought and why the 13th amendment to the Constitution was passed. But it is never stated or even implied in the passage, so you cannot assume that the author shares this belief. The passage itself is very matter-of-fact, presenting data and information, but not imparting the author's opinions. Even the sentence about the death of slaves in transit is emotionless and objective. So if the author does not state his opinion, any feelings assigned to him are untrue, no matter how you feel about the subject yourself. After all, the passage could have been written in 1850 by a plantation owner in Georgia. Do not apply your personal beliefs to any ACT and SAT passage or answer choice! The correct answer to this question is choice (A), while choice (D) is using your personal beliefs against you.

The test makers might also try to trick you into applying your prior knowledge to a passage:

> In late summer, black bears begin gorging on carbohydrate-rich foods in order to put on significant weight and body fat. They can gain as much as 30
> *Line* pounds in a single week! Once fall arrives, the bear
> 5 prepares its den, lining it with leaves and other plants to form a nest.

1. According to the passage, black bears seek "carbohydrate-rich foods" (line 2) primarily because they

   A) Wrong answer
   B) are preparing to hibernate
   C) need to considerably increase their body mass
   D) Wrong answer

Unless you skipped kindergarten and most of elementary school, it's likely that you know bears hibernate. Answer choice (B) is depending on this knowledge to seduce you into selecting it as the right answer choice. But you would be wrong. The passage never mentions hibernation. The reason the black bears gorge on carbs is *to put on significant weight and body fat*. The correct answer is (C). But many, many test takers would choose (B) because they applied their prior knowledge to the passage and failed to read all four answer choices.

Remember, if the author does not state or imply an idea, it simply is not true.

Copycat Answers

The most common characteristic of wrong answers on the SAT is that they copy words or phrases from the passage. These are Copycat Answers. Consider an example from earlier in the chapter:

> While the United States was fighting the War of 1812 with Britain, a series of violent incidents occurred when <u>authorities entered Seminole territory to recapture runaway slaves</u>, which aggravated the Seminole and
>
> Line
> 5 increased hostility.

1. According to the passage, the "hostility" (line 5) between the United States and the Seminole was intensified by which of the following?

    A) Wrong answer
    B) Officials invading Native American territory to reclaim escaped slaves.
    C) Wrong answer
    D) A violent incident that aggravated the American government.

◎ SAT ONLY ◎
Copycat Answers occur on the SAT frequently, but are not a common answer trap on the ACT.

☠ CAUTION: TEST TRAP
Copycat answers use words and phrases directly from the passage.

We have already looked at how the right answer, choice (B), uses synonyms for words in the text. But consider the choice of words used by answer (D):

Words from Wrong Answer	Words from Passage
violent incident	violent incidents (line 2)
aggravated	aggravated (line 4)

The answer uses two words or phrases directly from the text! Sadly, this simple tactic will trick a lot of test takers into choosing this answer.

This answer is not only a Copycat but also an Opposite Answer. The Seminole were aggravated, not the American government as the answer choice states. Always be leery of answer choices that use several words or phrases from the passage.

Note that the ACT will use the exact language of the passage in both the right and wrong answers, so you cannot employ this strategy on the ACT.

Analyzing the Answer Choices Problem Set

In the following exercise, read the paired passage set. For each question, select the correct answer choice and, if possible, label the wrong answer choices as Opposites, Extremes, True But Wrong, True to a Point, True to You, Copycats, or a combination of answer types. The first one has been done for you. Answers begin on page 189.

The following passages discuss the commemoration of Christopher Columbus' arrival in North America. Passage 1 is from a 2015 article written by Shelly Littlecloud; Passage 2 is from a 2011 political blog by Matthew Kennedy.

Passage 1

In 1492, Columbus sailed the ocean blue, resulting in the annihilation of my people. Upon his "discovery," there were more than 10 million Native Americans populating the continent, but by 1900, that number
Line
5 had diminished to 230,000. Such atrocities might be somewhat less offensive or at least mitigated if he had only inadvertently spread European germs that wiped out so many tribes, but Columbus was a murderous tyrant. He kidnapped and enslaved hundreds of natives,
10 allowed his crew to abuse men, women, and children, and mortally wounded those slaves who could not produce gold and riches fit for Spain. Eventually, his arrival in North America led to further genocide, when the government cleared our lands for the white man's
15 pursuit of manifest destiny. It is deplorable that the American dream of homestead ownership is founded on the slaughter of Native Americans and the larceny of their land.

What makes Columbus' savage crimes more unsettling
20 is the honor that is still being bestowed upon him some 500 years later. Christopher Columbus is a national hero; he is exalted in elementary school text books, glorified in the names of our cities and capitals, and commemorated every year on the second Monday in October. In this
25 era of political correctness, it is baffling how the United States government can continue to ignore the cries of my people who demand the forsaking of Columbus Day in favor of Indigenous Peoples' Day. Can you imagine the repercussions if national holidays were issued for
30 other brutal leaders, such as Adolf Hitler or Nathan Bedford Forrest? Fortunately, these tyrants will never be celebrated because the United States recognizes their atrocities and assisted or at least apologized to their victims. In the meantime, though, hundreds of thousands
35 of Native Americans are ignored, insulted, and expected to "just get over it."

I suppose we shouldn't expect much from our government. To make changes to school textbooks and national holidays demands accepting responsibility and making

40 reparations, two acts that threaten the culture, economy, and status quo of the nation. Plus, the ashes of nineteenth century manifest destiny still smolder, as most Americans believe that their leaders have a right to invade and take any land as long as the goal is the common good of
45 the American people and the betterment of the natives of the that land. Never mind what the culture of those natives dictates; Americans, after all, know best. While it may be pointless to expect change, Native Americans will undoubtedly hold on to hope that one day our
50 leaders will recognize the heinousness that our ancestors endured, and take the necessary steps to reduce a historical figure from national hero to national villain.

Passage 2

Columbus Day is in danger of extinction. In several cities in California, it has been replaced by Indigenous
55 Peoples' Day. Parades in honor of the explorer have not occurred in Columbus, Ohio since the 1990s. And South Dakota has renamed the holiday "Native American Day." Even where the holiday is preserved, many people lack enthusiasm for the celebration in fear of offending
60 descendants of native peoples.

All Americans need to reclaim this national holiday. Honoring the incredible achievement of Columbus is not the same as reveling in the hardship and sorrow of native peoples. In addition, historians have exagger-
65 ated the facts surrounding Columbus' discovery while de-emphasizing the barbarism and poverty into which he stumbled in North America. Columbus was at times brutal and did take hostages to Spain, but in his journal, Columbus reported cannibalism, warfare, and slavery
70 among the natives, and upon his second journey, he learned that the crew members he left behind were slaughtered by local inhabitants. Enslavement, brutality, and conquest were not exclusive to Europeans—these atrocities were rampant all over the world—but the
75 remarkable discovery of two continents was something only Columbus accomplished.

It's also worth noting that Columbus made his quest not for riches or fame but to honor his adopted country and spread its religion. His intentions were pure. Some
80 would argue that he and his men engaged in warfare with some of the natives that they encountered, but this happened rarely and only because it was a "kill or be killed" situation. The victims were so deficient in iron

that they did not have the strength to effectively fight
85 the Europeans. Columbus described most of the people
he encountered as "gentle" and "free from wickedness,"
and his design for them included conversion to Christi-
anity, development of a written language, and freedom
from poverty. These goals were ultimately realized, but
90 historians are hesitant to place value on the results. They
would rather look at the negative impact of Columbus
discovering America than the positive impact of Native
Americans discovering Europe.

Columbus's discovery was the first great chapter in
95 our nation's history. His accomplishment was a catalyst
for excellence; enlightenment, democracy, reason, and
individualism are just a few of the core values that are
a direct result of the voyage of the Nina, Pinta, and
Santa Maria. We are not only entitled, but patriotically
100 obligated, to honor the great explorer.

1. Both authors would most likely agree that

A) Columbus' voyage was sanctioned by the king and queen of Spain.
B) Columbus Day should be abandoned in favor of Indigenous Peoples' Day.
C) Columbus exhibited ruthlessness in the Americas.
D) Columbus is viewed as a villain by most Native Americans.

(A) *True to You?*

(B) *True But Wrong (P1)/Copycat (line 28)*

(C) *CORRECT (lines 8-12 and 67-68)*

(D) *Extreme*

2. The author of Passage 1 mentions Adolf Hitler and Nathan Bedford Forest (lines 30-31) primarily to suggest that

A) savageness was not exclusive to the New World.
B) national holidays honoring other villains would cause an uproar by Europeans.
C) Columbus is the only person responsible for decimating a population of people.
D) Columbus' wrongdoings were as terrible as the crimes of two other historical figures.

(A)

(B)

(C)

(D)

3   The author of Passage 1 does not "expect much" (line 37) because

A) most people do not believe that the United States has a right to invade foreign lands.
B) the government fears the cultural and financial consequences of change.
C) Americans choose to celebrate Columbus' quest to free natives from poverty and illiteracy.
D) home ownership has replaced freedom as the American dream.

(A) _____
(B) _____
(C) _____
(D) _____

4. Line 47 ("Americans . . . best") suggests that Americans

A) believe that their judgment concerning appropriate behavior is better than that of Native Americans.
B) support the government in conducting foreign invasions.
C) acknowledge that their country is the most powerful in the Western hemisphere.
D) refuse to make changes to their national holidays.

(A) _____
(B) _____
(C) _____
(D) _____

5. According to the author of Passage 2, there is a lack of "enthusiasm" (line 59) for Columbus Day because

A) many Americans worry that the celebration is an affront to Native Americans.
B) most people view Columbus as a savage tyrant.
C) few private businesses close for the national holiday.
D) Columbus' voyage is considered a Spanish accomplishment rather than an American one.

(A) _____
(B) _____
(C) _____
(D) _____

6. In lines 64-67 ("In addition . . . America"), the passage implies that

    A) Columbus mistakenly believed that he had landed in the Spice Islands.
    B) Columbus was not as barbaric as other European explorers.
    C) historians are partly responsible for Columbus' villainous reputation.
    D) all European explorers reported that the natives in the new world engaged in cannibalism and warfare.

    (A) _____
    (B) _____
    (C) _____
    (D) _____

7. In response to the claim made in lines 21-24 ("Columbus . . . October"), the author of Passage 2 would most likely assert that

    A) Columbus Day honors a murderous tyrant.
    B) Columbus had the purest of intentions for Native Americans.
    C) Columbus Day celebrations should be continued in elementary schools.
    D) brutality was universal and should not detract from Columbus' accomplishment.

    (A) _____
    (B) _____
    (C) _____
    (D) _____

8. The author of Passage 1 and the "historians" (line 90) in Passage 2 would most likely agree that the voyage of Christopher Columbus

    A) resulted from Spain's devotion to spreading Christianity.
    B) led to the development of a written language for Native Americans.
    C) had detrimental consequences for Native Americans.
    D) was the first great accomplishment in our nation's history.

    (A) _____
    (B) _____
    (C) _____
    (D) _____

Chapter Summary

There are two types of answers on the ACT and SAT: right answers and wrong answers.

Right Answers

- Often use synonyms.
- Include all of the important ideas from the line reference or passage.
- Tend to use more general language or ideas.
- Can be proven by the text.
- Are provided below the question. You simply have to locate them.

Wrong Answers

- Cannot be proven by the referenced portion of the text.
- Tend to use more specific language but often fail to include all important ideas from the line reference or passage.
- Are often easier to determine than the right answer.
- Are often placed above the correct answer when they are especially attractive to fool you into selecting the wrong answer without reading all five answer choices.
- Come in several styles that are designed to trap you:
  - **Opposite Answers**
    - Present an idea that is opposite of the right answer and your prephrase.
  - **Extreme Answers**
    - Use words that are difficult to defend. The words may be qualifiers, like *most* and *always*, or adjectives and verbs, like *malicious* and *mock*.
  - **True But Wrong Answers**
    - Make true statements about a portion of the passage that is not the subject of the question.
  - **True To A Point Answers**
    - Provide an answer that is "half-right."
    - Often introduce new information not discussed in the passage.
    - May have a single word that makes the answer choice wrong.
  - **True to You Answers**
    - Present common beliefs that were not provided in the passage.
    - Use facts that are likely a part of your prior knowledge but were not provided in the passage.
  - **Copycat Answers** (SAT only)
    - Use words and phrases directly from the text.

ANSWER CHOICE ANALYSIS ANSWER KEY

Analyzing the Answer Choices Problem Set—Page 184

2. (D)   Prephrase: Two other tyrants are considered terrible so national holidays in their honor do not exist.

   (A) *True But Wrong, Opposite,* and *Copycat.* The author of Passage 1 makes this point in lines 72-73, but he makes it about exclusivity to Europeans.
   (B) *True to a Point.* This answer is correct until you get to the word *Europeans.* According to lines 28-30, it would cause serious repercussions in America (and likely all over the world).
   (C) *Extreme* and *Opposite.* The author implies that Hitler and Forrest have shown similar brutality, so the idea in the passage is opposite the idea in the answer choice. The extreme word *only* should cause you to avoid it, too.

3. (B)   Prephrase: Government does not want to admit responsibility nor change the status quo.

   (A) *Opposite.* According to lines 42-45, most Americans believe the opposite of this statement.
   (C) *True to a Point.* Columbus did look to free natives from poverty and illiteracy, but this is not the full reason he is celebrated or why the author does not expect much.
   (D) This answer does not fit any of the Wrong Answer categories, but is wrong nonetheless. This idea is not discussed in the passage.

4. (A)   Prephrase: Think they know what is best for Native Americans.

   (B) *True But Wrong.* The author states this in lines 42-45, but it is not suggested in line 47.
   (C) This answer does not fit any of the Wrong Answer categories, but is wrong nonetheless. This idea is not discussed in the passage and presents new information (Western hemisphere).
   (D) *Extreme.* The verb *refuse* is extreme, as it applies to all Americans. The answer also uses *national holidays*, rather than just Columbus Day, and nothing is noted about other national holidays in the passage.

5. (A)   Prephrase: Many people fear offending descendants of native peoples (lines 59-60).

   (B) *Extreme.* The word *most* makes this answer extreme. Even the author of Passage 1 does not go so far as to say this.
   (C) *True to You.* This is not discussed in either passage but may be true given your own experiences.
   (D) This answer does not fit any of the Wrong Answer categories, but is wrong nonetheless. This idea is not discussed in the passage.

6. (C)   Prephrase: This answer is difficult to prephrase.

   (A) *True to You.* It's likely that you know this fact from your history classes, but it is not stated or implied in the passage.
   (B) *True to a Point.* The author is making the point that the New World was no stranger to brutality, where the natives had even resorted to cannibalism. But the use of *other explorers* makes it untrue.
   (D) *Extreme* and *Copycat.* The modifier *all* should be immediately suspect, and again, this answer involves *other explorers*, who were not mentioned in the passage. .

7. (D) Prephrase: Everyone was brutal, including the natives. But he is the only one to sail to the Americas so he should still be celebrated.

(A) *Opposite Answer* and *Copycat Answer*. This is the opinion of the author of Passage 1 and the opposite opinion of the author of Passage 2. It uses text from lines 8-9 to try to trick you.

(B) *Extreme* and *True But Wrong*. The word *purest* makes it extreme. The author of Passage 2 does cite Columbus' pure intentions, though, but this is not the argument he would use to refute the claim in lines 21-24.

(C) *True to a Point*. The author of Passage 2 does believe Columbus Day celebrations should continue, but nowhere in the passage does it say anything about elementary school.

8. (C) Prephrase: Columbus engaged in warfare and brutal behavior

(A) *True to You* and *True to a Point*. This is not discussed in the passage, but may be something you remember from history class. The passage does state that Columbus made the voyage to spread religion, but not that this was Spain's reason for funding the voyage.

(B) *Opposite.* The author of Passage 2 would make this point, not the author of Passage 1 or the historians.

(D) *Opposite.* The author of Passage 2 would make this point, not the author of Passage 1 or the historians.

CHAPTER ELEVEN
WORDS-IN-CONTEXT QUESTIONS

There are three main categories of ACT and SAT Reading questions:

1. **Words-in-Context Questions** (WIC)

   These questions ask you to define a word or interpret a phrase from the passage as it is used in context.

2. **Literal Comprehension Questions** (LC)

   Literal Comprehension questions are usually considered the easiest type of reading comprehension question because the answer is directly stated in the passage.

3. **Extended Reasoning Questions** (ER)

   These questions are typically considered more difficult because the answer is not explicitly stated in the passage; you must draw a conclusion based on part or all of the passage to successfully answer these questions.

Each of these categories has question sub-types, which we will examine in detail in the following chapters. This chapter focuses on the first type of question, Words-in-Context.

Understanding the specific type of question stem can help you determine how to answer the question.

Words and Phrases in Context

Words-in-Context questions ask you to interpret the meaning of a word, phrase, or sentence given the context of the surrounding text. These questions may also be called Vocabulary-in-Context questions or Meaning of Words questions.

Each ACT features roughly four to seven Words-in-Context questions. The SAT has two per passage for a total of ten in the Reading section; these are added to eight Words-in-Context questions on the Writing and Language Test to create a Words-in-Context subscore on your official score report.

The most basic—and most common—Words-in-Context questions ask you to define a single word or short phrase from a passage as it is used in the context of a sentence. Consider the short passage and question below:

> In the summer of 1967, Warhol asked his agent to book him on a tour of Western colleges, including the University of Oregon. He planned to speak to the students about the plot development in his underground films.
>
> 1. As it is used in line 1, the word *book* most nearly means
>
>   **A.** dash.
>   **B.** read.
>   **C.** arrest.
>   **D.** schedule.

⋛TIPS and TRICKS⋛
If possible, prephrase the answer to these questions just as you would any other Reading question.

All four answer choices will be the same part of speech. In this case, they are verbs, so you know that *book* is acting as a verb rather than as a noun. The easiest way to solve these questions is prephrase a synonym for the word in question, but if that does not work, test each answer choice in place of the original word in the sentence:

(A) Warhol asked his agent to *dash* him on a tour.
(B) Warhol asked his agent to *read* him on a tour.
(C) Warhol asked his agent to *arrest* him on a tour.
(D) Warhol asked his agent to *schedule* him on a tour.

⋛TIPS and TRICKS⋛
If you cannot determine the meaning of the referenced word, plug each answer choice into the sentence to find the one that makes sense in the context of the passage.

Which one makes sense in the context of the passage? Only answer (D).

The question above is an example of the most common wording of the most basic Words-in-Context questions on the ACT. The SAT uses similar phrasing:

> 1. As used in line 1, "book" most nearly means
>
>   A) dash.
>   B) read.
>   C) arrest.
>   D) schedule.

While these phrasings seem to be the most common in the current official practice tests, Words-in-Context questions could also be expressed like any of the following:

2.   In context, "book" (line 1) most nearly means

3.   As it is used in line 1, "book" is closest in meaning to

4.   In line 1, "book" is best understood to mean

5.   The word "book" (line 1) most nearly means

No matter how the question is asked, the solution method is the same; try each answer choice in place of the word in the question.

Sometimes the questions will be about a short phrase instead of a single word:

> I thought Eddie would run from the room, shame painted on his face like the glaring red wall in his uncle's kitchen, but instead he broke out in song. He rose from the table, tipping his hat and crooning Sinatra, as if Glenn had not just shared the devastating
> Line
> 5 secret.

6.   As used in line 3, the phrase "broke out" most nearly means to

A) erupt in a rash.
B) burst forth suddenly.
C) prepare for consumption.
D) remove by force.

Work through questions about short phrases in the same manner as questions about a single word—by inserting the answer choice in place of the phrase:

(A)   he *erupted in a rash* in song.
(B)   he *burst forth suddenly* in song.
(C)   he *prepared for consumption* in song.
(D)   he *removed by force* in song.

Only choice (B) makes sense when it is inserted into the original sentence. Rather than act embarrassed, Eddie began to sing Frank Sinatra songs.

Notice, also, that the answers to this question were not single word answers as in the first question. The easiest Words-in-Context questions, which are the most common, will have a single word answer as in question 1, but you should not be surprised to see lengthier answers as in question 6.

In the official tests that we analyzed, Words in Context questions made up roughly 10% of the ACT and 15% of the SAT.

↳ GRATUITOUS VOCAB
consumption (n):
the act of eating

If you are unable to determine the correct answer by substituting the answer choices, read a few lines above and a few lines below the original word. Often the text will use a synonym. Consider an example:

> The most famous psychologists of the 20th century had varying views of insanity. Carl Jung was of the persuasion that every human being had a story; when this story was rejected or denied by others, derangement was the result. This theory was widely contended by others, who instead believed that such mental illness was genetic.
>
> *Line 5*

7. As used in line 3, "persuasion" most nearly means

    A) coercion.
    B) belief.
    C) power.
    D) attraction.

≡TIPS and TRICKS≡
If you cannot define the word using the context of the sentence, look for synonyms in the surrounding sentences.

✦ GRATUITOUS VOCAB
teeming (adj): filled; abundant

This passage is teeming with synonyms for the word *persuasion*: *views* (line 2) and *theory* (line 4) are equivalent nouns, but even the verb *believed* (line 5) indicates that the correct answer is (B), *belief*. If you are unsure of the correct answer for a Words-in-Context question, be sure to search the surrounding sentences for clues.

The easiest Words-in-Context questions use common words, like *book* in the first example. For questions with common words, do not expect the most common definition to be the answer. For example, consider the word *handle*. The most common definition for the noun is *the part designed to be held*. So in the following question, you should avoid an answer with this common definition:

> Members of the CB radio club are required to choose a handle that best describes their interests. Linda is "Lady Luck" and Tony goes by "Fish Bait." I struggled with the task, however, unsure of how to address my fascination with insects and spiders, until.....
>
> *Line 5*

≡TIPS and TRICKS≡
For Words-in-Context questions that ask about a common word, like *book* or *handle*, avoid the most common definition.

8. As used in line 2, "handle" most nearly means

    A) knob.
    B) manager.
    C) nickname.
    D) situation.

Choice (A), *knob*, is the most common definition of *handle*, so it is unlikely to be the correct answer. The best choice is (C), as indicated by the nicknames of Linda and Tony.

While Words-in-Context questions with easy words have unusual definition answers, those questions with hard words will likely be answered with the most common definition. The easiest questions test your ability to decode the meaning of words using context clues; the hardest questions test your ability to define vocabulary words:

> Chad was unlike the other students in class. His quiescence was remarkable for his age, reminding me of the Bhikkhus, the Buddhist monks I saw meditating in the village in Nepal.

> 9.   As used in line 2, "quiescence" most nearly means
>
>   A) stillness.
>   B) wisdom.
>   C) influence.
>   D) generosity.

Your best solution strategy for questions about difficult vocabulary is to read the surrounding text for clues. In this example, the Buddhist monks are meditating, indicating that Chad is tranquil and quiet. Answer (A) is best. But the question becomes much more difficult when the vocabulary words appear in the answer choices:

> Chad was unlike the other students in class. His stillness was remarkable for his age, reminding me of a Bhikkhu, the Buddhist monks I saw meditating in the village in Nepal.

> 9.   In line 2, "stillness" most nearly means
>
>   (A) quiescence.
>   (B) sagacity.
>   (C) prominence.
>   (D) altruism.

↳ GRATUITOUS VOCAB
tranquil (adj): calm

↳ GRATUITOUS VOCAB
quiescence (n): quietness
sagacity (n): wisdom
prominence (n): the state of being noticeable
altruism (n): selflessness

On questions like this one, you may need to make an educated guess using decoding strategies, such as prefix, suffix, and root word knowledge. Thankfully, these Words-in-Context questions with vocabulary in the answer choices are quite rare.

If you are running out of time on a Reading section, scan the questions and answer Words-in-Context questions first. You can answer them quickly without reading the entire passage, and most students consider Words-in-Context questions the easiest in the section.

⌐TIPS and TRICKS⌐
If you are running out of time, tackle Words-in-Context questions first!

Statements in Context

Some Words-in-Context questions, on the ACT particularly, will ask you to interpret the meaning of a clause or complete sentence. Let's examine one of these after reading the following passage:

Don't forget the top 300 commonly-occurring vocabulary words in the appendix of this book!

Despite the fact that child development experts agree that children under age seven learn best through play, there is no play in kindergarten anymore. No costume bins, no building blocks, no shopping carts or play kitchens. Every hour of the school days is
Line
5   accounted for and thus there is no time scheduled for unstructured, exploratory play. Literacy instruction has replaced all free time because of new standards that demand that these young children are reading by the end of the year. Even recesses are in jeopardy. At my daughter's school, there is a single twenty minute recess after lunch
10   which likely winds up closer to fifteen minutes when you factor in transition time. Just eight years ago, when I wore the "hat" of teacher, the school at which I worked allowed three recesses for kindergarten classrooms, as the administration recognized that children needed movement and play. These five-year olds also needed naps with the
15   advent of a full-day program, but napping—a developmental staple— is also absent from today's kindergarten classrooms. On my tour of my daughter's school, I asked the principal how the children adjusted with no naps and little play. "We go through a lot of tissues because of tears that first month and the bus drivers have to wake a lot of kids
20   on the way home from school," she said cheerfully, as if damaging children in the quest to get them to read was commendable instead of reprehensible.
     I spoke with the administrator about my concerns over the lack of play, which she dismissed. She said that the kids don't know any
25   better and they still experience joy at school; I was looking at this from my own perspective so I felt like it was a loss, but she assured me they had "movement time" before the school day began and they exercised next to their desks for a few minutes each afternoon.
     She missed my point, though. I'm not as upset about my
30   daughter's inability to release energy as I am about her not experiencing a play-based curriculum. I want her to waste time with Legos, daydream with dolls, and monkey around on the playground. Play lays the foundation for creativity, critical reasoning, and math and language skills. There is no need to force children to read in
35   kindergarten; it does not lead to higher test scores, better jobs, or happier adults. If anything, it creates a generation of anxiety-ridden people who do not have the ability to think critically. Just because they can does not mean they should.

10. In the context of the passage, the author's statement in lines 31-32 most nearly means that she wants her daughter to

   A) be able to burn off energy through vigorous activities.
   B) make it through a day of kindergarten without displaying an emotional outburst or falling asleep on the bus.
   C) acquire knowledge through objects and activities typically associated with children's play.
   D) delay learning to read until she enters the first grade.

The statement in lines 31-32 is this: "I want her to waste time with Legos, daydream with dolls, and monkey around on the playground."

We need to consider the entire passage because the question states we must consider this statement *in the context of the passage*. Based on what we know about the author, she is upset that play is no longer the central focus of kindergarten. She says that recess is in *jeopardy* (line 8), a word that indicates she fears the loss of recess. She expresses her *concerns over the lack of play* (line 23) and states that she is *upset* (line 29) about her daughter *not experiencing a play-based curriculum* (line 30-31). We also know that she believes children learn through play (line 2, 33-34).

Thus she views activities that cause time wasting, daydreaming, and monkeying around as positive experiences that help children learn. The only possible answer is choice (C).

This question asked about a complete sentence, but other questions may address a clause:

> 11. When the author says "I wore the 'hat' of teacher" (line 11), she most likely means that
>
>   A) she used to be employed as a teacher.
>   B) she viewed one of her roles as her daughter's teacher.
>   C) she dressed in a manner similar to that of her daughter's teacher.
>   D) she volunteered in her child's classroom.

This clause is taken from the sentence in lines 11-14: "Just eight years ago, when I wore the hat of 'teacher,' the school at which I worked allowed three recesses for kindergarten classrooms, as the administration recognized that children needed movement and play."

Notice that "I wore the 'hat' of teacher" could stand alone as a sentence. For this reason, we classify this as a Words-in-Context question about a statement.

This question does not tell us to consider the statement *in the context of the passage,* so clues to the right answer are likely in the lines surrounding the statement. Immediately after this line reference, the author states she worked at a school. She is a former teacher, and thus choice (A) is correct.

The most common type of Words-in-Context question will quiz you about a single word or short phrase, but you should also expect an occasional question about a statement in the passage. As long as the question does not direct you to consider the statement *in the context of the passage,* you can answer these questions quickly and without understanding or reading the entire passage; look for them if you are running out of time in the Reading section.

Words-in-Context Questions Problem Set

Read each passage below and on the following page and then answer the corresponding Words-in-Context question. Answers begin on page 201.

The car manufacturer reports that the new model is not only receiving attention from industry executives, but it is also moving well. Dealerships across the country have reported a 10% increase in sales, largely
Line
5 due to the car's technological advances.

1. In line 3, "moving" is closest in meaning to

A) progressing.
B) selling.
C) relocating.
D) running.

The consequences of Houston's actions did not register until he was denied admittance into the army. Suddenly, the dream he had held his entire life was being crushed by the choices he made in five foolish
Line
5 minutes.

2. As used in line 2, "register" most nearly means

A) weigh on him.
B) punish.
C) enroll.
D) have an effect.

When his therapist suggested that John should listen to Ava's concerns, he reacted with coolness. "Why should I meet with her?" he responded. "She is the one who left the band, not the other way around."

3. The word "coolness" (line 2) most nearly means

A) warmth.
B) confidence.
C) indifference.
D) calm.

Christensen receives rent or mortgage reimbursement, use of a luxury car, and memberships to local country clubs, but not all elected officials receive such perquisites. Taylor reports that she must pay
Line
5 her own bills and provide her own transportation as governor of the territory.

4. In line 4, "perquisites" most nearly means

A) memberships.
B) bribes.
C) salary.
D) benefits.

"At least everyone showed up on time," Allie said. "After all, it's only my wedding." Her sarcasm was not lost on the group and it was clear that her piercing remarks were intended for me.
Line
5 "I really am sorry, Sis," I muttered.

5. In context, "piercing" (line 4) most nearly means

A) caustic.
B) frigid.
C) profound.
D) assaulting.

Jarvis grew up privileged in a wealthy suburb of London. As was the norm with young men of his status, he was lettered, having studied at two prestigious universities and learning four languages.
Line
5 Jarvis's father expected his son to pursue a career in law, but the young man had other aspirations.

6. In line 3, "lettered" is best understood to mean

A) erudite.
B) tenacious.
C) athletic.
D) disenchanted.

As a journalist, I've spent the last three years covering a change in the world of education. Seismic waves are rumbling from the basement of the ivory tower and the
Line
5 schoolhouse down your block. The demand for access to both existing and new models of learning is rising as uncontrollably as the average temperature throughout the globe. Our society faces serious existential threats, and the answers aren't written in books. So there's a
10 growing urgency to shift toward models of learning that foster natural creativity and innovation to produce new knowledge, new answers. Yet the educational ecosystem is edging toward collapse—50 million university students in 2000 will become an estimated 250 million by 2025, even as educational costs rise at two to three
15 times the rate of inflation. An estimated 400 million children around the world have too little access to formal schooling. No government in the world has a plan to fix this.
   Meanwhile, informal learning—the kind we do all
20 day every day, as long as our eyes are open and we're not in school—is going through a Cambrian explosion in hackerspaces, libraries, museums, basements and garages. "How-to" is one of the top searches on Google. An entire generation of web geeks is functioning more or
25 less self-taught, because traditional curricula can't keep up with the skills they need.
   All of which brings me to the second force, now arcing overhead—an invisible mesh of electrical signals that connect the people in this square not only to each
30 other, but the world.
   Twenty-five years ago, computer engineers Tim Berners-Lee and Robert Caillou first introduced their creation: "The World Wide Web was developed to be a pool of human knowledge and human culture, which
35 would allow collaborators in remote sites to share their ideas and all aspects of a common project." Today, the web's open and interoperable standards make it possible for 1.75 billion people around the world to build, access, connect, and alter 240 million unique sites, not to
40 mention for millions of people to create and upload 35 hours of video to YouTube, the most popular video site, every minute. The web allows for the creation of wealth, beauty, and human connection on an unprecedented scale.
45 Yet, as more and more of us live, work, create, socialize, shop, bank, and, yes, learn online, the architects of the web are increasingly drawing the parameters of private and public life, and often for corporate profit or political control rather than public benefit.
50 The very principle that has made the web so vast and so powerful—the open structure, held in common, that allows anyone to access and contribute—is under threat as never before.
   The threat is hydra-headed: zealous enforcement of

55 copyright and intellectual property, governments that stifle dissent by disabling servers or censoring keywords, the increasing trade in personal data, legal and illegal infringements on privacy, and public discourse and private relationships that are increasingly funneled
60 through a very small number of commercial web platforms. The response is to assert freedom.

7. The author uses the statement in lines 2-4 ("Seismic . . . block") most nearly to mean that

A) students in affluent districts have more educational opportunities than students in low-income districts.
B) the invention of the internet has brought change to the way teachers deliver curriculum.
C) changes in the field of education are occurring in both classrooms and policy-making departments.
D) the federal government cannot protect the national education system unless changes are made.

8. As it is used in line 21, the phrase "a Cambrian explosion" most nearly means

A) a fiery detonation.
B) a complete extinction.
C) an unusual event.
D) a rapid emergence.

9. When the author says "the architects of the web are increasingly drawing the parameters of private and public life " (lines 46-48), she most likely means that

A) Berners-Lee and Caillou are continually improving the World Wide Web.
B) the people who manage the internet are progressively setting limits for its use.
C) the number of internet users is increasing at a rate that the infrastructure cannot support.
D) the internet is used more for personal reasons than for reasons related to work.

10. As it is used in line 61, the word "assert" most nearly means

A) defend.
B) demand.
C) denounce.
D) deny.

Chapter Summary

Words and Phrases in Context

- Begin by trying to prephrase the answer before looking at the answer choices.
- If you cannot determine the meaning of the referenced word or phrase, test each answer choice in its place to find the one that makes sense in context.
- Search for synonyms in the surrounding lines of the referenced word.
- For questions that ask about a common word, avoid the most common definition.
- If you are running out of time, scan the questions to find the Words-in-Context questions and answer them first. You do not have to read the entire passage to answer them correctly.

Statements in Context

- Some questions will ask you to interpret an entire sentence, while others will require you to determine the meaning of a clause.
- If the question uses the phrase in the context of the passage, you need to consider the entire passage when interpreting the meaning of a statement.

WORDS-IN-CONTEXT QUESTIONS ANSWER KEY

Words-in-Context Questions Problem Set—Page 198

1. (B)

    The second sentence has a context clue with *sales*.

2. (D)

    Many students want to select (A), *weigh on him*, but you do not know how Houston felt about the consequences. You do know that they did not affect him or register with him until he was unable to enlist.

3. (C)

    John reacts with indifference; he sees no reason to meet with Ava.

4. (D)

    The *rent or mortgage reimbursement, use of a luxury car, and memberships to local country clubs* are all benefits of Christensen's job.

5. (A)

    The passage provides a context clue with *sarcasm* in line 2.

    Vocabulary:
    frigid: very cold
    profound: deep; intense

    assaulting: physically attacking
    caustic: severely sarcastic

6. (A)

    Lettered means well-educated.

    Vocabulary:
    erudite: well-educated
    tenacious: unyielding; stubborn

    disenchanted: freed from illusion

7. (C)

    Many clues exist in the paragraph, including *change* in line 2, *the new demand for access to both existing and new models of learning is rising* in lines 4-5, and *shift* in line 9. All indicate *change*. The *ivory tower* refers to education policy makers who are remote from the practicalities of teaching.

8. (D)

    Some test takers may know that the Cambrian explosion was an evolutionary event in which there was a rapid increase in life on earth. If you don't know this, you can figure out that it refers to *a rapid emergence* because the rest of the paragraph indicates that *"how-to" is one of the top searches on Google* and *an entire generation of web geeks* has emerged.

9. (B)

The answer to this question lies in the last two paragraphs. The author states that the internet is being threatened by enforcement of copyright, stifling governments, and more, all of which indicate that there are limits (i.e. *parameters*) being placed on the internet.

10. (B)

To assert means *to state with force*; the closest in meaning is *demand*, which makes sense: the solution to these limiting behaviors on the internet is to demand freedom.

CHAPTER TWELVE
LITERAL COMPREHENSION QUESTIONS

Literal Comprehension questions ask you to recall facts directly stated in the passage. They play on our human tendencies to make assumptions and draw conclusions, which can cause you to miss these otherwise basic questions. Consider a simplified example:

> After graduating from college, Michelle attended law school in New Mexico.

1. The sentence reveals which of the following about Michelle?

    A) She is intelligent.
    B) She grew up in New Mexico.
    C) She is a lawyer.
    D) She pursued a law degree.

There are two facts in the passage: 1) Michelle graduated from college and 2) Michelle attended law school in New Mexico. Therefore, there is only one correct answer: choice (D). Many students, however, will become confused by the assumptions and conclusions they make about Michelle, and the first three answer choices are designed to trick those students:

Never assume anything that cannot be proven on the ACT and SAT!

(A) *She is intelligent.*
    The passage never indicates that Michelle is smart. Not every person who attends law school is intelligent. In fact, it's even possible she cheated on her entrance exam.

(B) *She grew up in New Mexico.*
    Where does the passage say this? She could have moved to New Mexico for law school. We cannot even be sure that she lived in New Mexico while attending law school there. Maybe she lived in Arizona and commuted over state lines.

(C) *She is a lawyer.*
    The passage does not reveal whether Michelle actually graduated from law school. And even if she did graduate, maybe she decided to become a teacher or painter or doctor instead.

In the official tests that we analyzed, Literal Comprehension questions made up roughly 50% of the ACT and 25% of the SAT.

The right answer, (D), restates the fact that Michelle attended law school. Notice that it paraphrases the original sentence; many correct answers of Literal Comprehension questions will use synonyms or reworded expressions.

Some questions use common phrases that can help you identify them as Literal Comprehension questions:

- According to the author/passage/statement/phrase/line....
- The author/passage/statement/phrase/line indicates....
- The author/passage/statement/phrase/line reveals....
- The author/narrator considers
- The author/narrator argues
- The author/narrator asserts
- Referring to.... or ...refers to....
- Because.... or ...because....

These phrases indicate that the answer is clearly stated right in the passage. You should be excited to find any questions on your test with these phrases because you do not have to draw a conclusion—you simply need to return to the text to find the answer.

For the majority of Literal Comprehension questions with a line reference, you will need to read above and/or below the line reference to find the answer. This is especially true of questions where the line reference is for a single word or phrase, like the following:

1. According to the author, "those who win" (line 5) are people who

2. The passage indicates that the "separation" (line 61) was caused by

3. In lines 22-23, the phrase "rites of passage" refers to

For these questions, the answers will lie in surrounding text, so you should begin one sentence before the line reference and read one sentence below the line reference when searching for the answer.

Some questions should be answered by looking only at the specific text provided by the line reference. These questions usually have a longer line reference, including an entire sentence or group of sentences:

4. In lines 12-16, the author argues that graphic novels are literature because

The answer to this question must be found in the specific line reference. The question does not ask what the author argued in line 11 or in line 17, but specifically in lines 12-16. What does the author argue in that specific section? He may have a different argument in line 10, so reading above the reference can cause you to become confused.

TIPS and TRICKS
For Literal Comprehension questions with a single word or phrase in quotation marks, read above and below the line reference to find the answer.

For questions with a line reference that includes a full sentence or group of sentences, read just that portion of the text to determine the correct answer.

Consider another:

> 5. The customer's comments in lines 45-50 ("When . . sold") indicate that a car is desirable when it

Again, this question asks about the comments in a specific sentence or group of sentences, occurring in lines 45-50; you will not find the answer in line 44 or line 51. If there is a comment in line 52, it might indicate something different, thus leading you to the wrong answer choice.

If you fail to find an answer that matches your prephrase after reading just the specific lines cited, then read the sentence above and the sentence below to see if more information is provided. Sometimes an author will provide an introductory explanation before the line or a clarifying statement after the line. But for most Literal Comprehension questions with a long line reference, the answer will be found in that specific reference.

There are four specific types of Literal Comprehension questions:

1. Main Idea
2. Facts and Details
3. Reasons and Results
4. Comparison and Contrast

Understanding each type of Literal Comprehension question will help you more easily identify and answer questions. Let's look at each of these more closely.

Literal Comprehension questions ask you to recall facts from the passage. Those facts are usually rewritten with synonyms in the correct answer.

Main Idea Questions

Some test prep materials will group main idea questions with Extended Reasoning questions, the question type we will examine in the next chapter, but according to the College Board's website, students must "show their understanding of information directly stated, including the main idea." For this reason, we have chosen to discuss Main Idea questions with Literal Comprehension questions.

Plus, the main idea of the passage is usually directly stated, as we saw in the section on common types of passage openings in Chapter Seven. It is most often in the first paragraph, but may also be located at the beginning of the second paragraph or at the end of the passage.

Questions about the main idea are not as prevalent as some tutors or test prep books make them out to be. In the official tests we analyzed, just 3% of ACT *and* 3% of SAT questions focused on the main idea of the passage or a specific paragraph. Identifying the main point of the passage, however, is integral to understanding the finer points of the text, from Facts and Detail questions to Extended Reasoning questions. So while actual questions about the main idea are not crucial to your success on the test, understanding the main idea is imperative to your mastery of the passage.

Main Idea questions usually do not include a line reference unless they are about a specific paragraph. The most common wording of Main Idea questions is the first one below, but you should expect to see any (or a variation of) these questions:

1. The passage is primarily concerned with

2. The author's main point in the passage is that

3. The passage provides the most information about

4. What is the main idea of the third paragraph?

5. The main idea of the last paragraph is that

The answer to these questions is the one that best summarizes the main idea. Remember, the right answer will be a paraphrased version of the main point, and it must be broad enough to cover the entire passage or the entire paragraph. One or two of the wrong answers will likely be True But Wrong answers, taken directly from the passage, which summarize a specific sentence or paragraph, but not the entire passage or the paragraph in question.

Main Idea Questions ask you to determine the author's main point. They usually do not include line references.

☠ CAUTION: TEST TRAP
Common wrong answers for Main Idea questions about often True But Wrong answers, as explained in Chapter Ten.

Let's study an example:

Most archaeologists believe that Machu Picchu, a pre-Columbian Incan city, was built in the 15th century by the ruler Pachacutec. According to this view, the site was constructed on a mountain ridge as a personal estate for the powerful emperor; he extended his refuge to 1200 of the most elite of Incan aristocracy, who resided in the fortress for at least three generations until the Spanish conquest a century later. Rolf Muller, however, argues that the construction of the city actually started sometime between 2300 and 2100 BC.

Line 5

Muller's theory is based on the alignment of buildings and landmarks in accordance with stars in the sky in the previous millennium. Using advanced mathematical computations, Muller has produced convincing evidence that the most important sites in Machu Picchu were built around the procession of equinoxes that occurred before 2000 BC.

10

Muller also cites architectural anomalies as evidence that the city was built over thousands of years, rather than in a single generation. For example, three of the most famous landmarks—The Hitching Post, The Temple of the Sun, and The Room of Three Windows—were constructed with exacting precision and masterful masonry, skills for which the Incas are well-known. But there are many buildings that were fashioned in a much cruder manner and others that show developing skill, indicating that the city was slowly constructed over long periods of time. A city that was designed by a single architect or even a group of architects working simultaneously would have more architectural consistency.

15

20

Muller, whether right or wrong, has certainly given archaeologists something to think about. I suspect this debate will be discussed in academic papers and in colleges for years to come.

25

≈TIPS and TRICKS≈
If you notate the passage with sidebar summaries as you read, the main idea will be easier to determine.

The main idea is stated in the last sentence of the first paragraph: *Rolf Muller, however, argues that the construction of the city actually started sometime between 2300 and 2100 BC.* Now consider a question about the main idea of the passage:

1. The passage is primarily concerned with

   A) three landmarks that dispute accepted theories about the construction of an Incan city.
   B) the hypothesis that the construction of Machu Picchu began much earlier and took much longer than previously believed.
   C) the Incan ruler Pachacutec's desire to create a sanctuary for elite members of society.
   D) the lack of architectural consistency in Machu Picchu.

The best answer is (B). It paraphrases the stated main idea and covers the subject of every paragraph in the passage.

☠ CAUTION: TEST TRAP
Common wrong answers for Main Idea questions about the entire passage focus on the point of one paragraph, not the entire passage.

Wrong answers for Main Idea questions about a specific paragraph may state the main idea of the previous or next paragraph.

Consider the structure of the passage:

> Paragraph 1: Conventional wisdom followed by opposing main idea
> Paragraph 2: Evidence that the city was built *much earlier than previously believed*
> Paragraph 3: Evidence that the city's construction *took much longer than previously believed*
> Paragraph 4: Acknowledgement that Muller's idea is a *hypothesis*

To review common locations of the main idea in ACT and SAT passages, return to Chapter Seven.

The three supporting paragraphs are incorporated into the main idea.

Let's analyze the wrong answers, too:

(A) *three landmarks that dispute accepted theories about the construction of an Incan city*
True But Wrong: the three landmarks are discussed in lines 17-19, but nowhere else in the passage. The main idea must pervade all paragraphs!

❧ GRATUITOUS VOCAB
sanctuary (n): a safe or holy place

(C) *the Incan ruler Pachacutec's desire to create a sanctuary for elite members of society*
True But Wrong: this view is part of the first paragraph's conventional wisdom that Muller attempts to disprove. It is not mentioned elsewhere in the passage.

(D) *the lack of architectural consistency in Machu Picchu*
Copycat/True But Wrong: the last sentence of the third paragraph contains this idea, but it is not present in any of the other paragraphs. The main idea must be supported by each paragraph.

Once you choose your answer, reread the short summary notations you made next to each paragraph. If each summary supports your answer choice, you have selected the right answer. But if the answer choice does not have anything to do with one or more of the paragraphs, you need to select a new answer.

To further practice determining the Main Idea, return to the section in Chapter Seven on Passage Openings.

Facts and Details Questions

Questions about the facts and details of a passage ask you to interpret a phrase, sentence, or portion of the passage. These are by far the most prevalent Literal Comprehension questions, and the example from the first page of this chapter about Michelle in law school is a simplified version of a Facts and Details question.

These questions often use the phrases we highlighted earlier in this chapter. Consider some specific examples:

Facts and Details questions ask you to interpret a specific portion of a passage. The answer is directly stated in the passage.

1. According to the author, the "last song of the day" was a ballad by

2. The statement in lines 2-3 ("The end . . . supposed") primarily indicates that the author believes

3. In lines 31, the image of "lighthouses" refers to

4. According to the passage, King most consistently supported

5. In lines 59-62 ("There . . . water"), the author asserts that the engineer was

The answers to these questions are directly stated in the passage. Remember, when returning to the passage, read the lines above and below the line reference when it cites only a word or phrase (like questions 1 and 3 above), and read just the specific line reference when the question cites an entire sentence or group of sentences (like questions 2 and 5 above).

As we discussed in the previous section, the correct answer will usually be a paraphrase of the actual passage. This is especially true for Literal Comprehension questions because they are interpreting a portion of the passage. Adjectives and verbs from the text are often replaced with synonyms in the correct answer choice, and even some nouns might be altered.

Confidence Quotation
"I was always looking outside myself for strength and confidence, but it comes from within. It is there all the time."
-Anna Freud, psychoanalyst and daughter of Sigmund Freud

Let's look at an example. The following text is a portion of a longer passage:

> The majority of the board members claimed that if the proposed building was erected, run-off from the parking lot would pollute Lake Homer, situated just a half-mile from the
> *Line* site, so they ferociously opposed its passing. Board member
> 5 Anderson, however, was anxious to agree to the legislation.

1. As indicated in lines 1-4, the proposal was met with

    A) considerable opposition for a water quality study of Lake Homer.
    B) feigned indifference for the erection of the structure.
    C) ferocious support for a new location for the parking lot.
    D) savage resistance for the construction of the building.

♦ GRATUITOUS VOCAB
feigned (vb): faked

Only answer choice (D) restates the idea of the passage: *the proposal was met with savage resistance for the construction of the building*. Notice that *ferociously opposed* was replaced with *savage resistance* and that *erected* was substituted with *construction*. The noun *building* was in both the original text and the correct answer.

Once again, let's examine the wrong answers, too:

(A) *considerable opposition for a water quality study of Lake Homer*
     True to a Point: this answer is wrong because the portion of the passage in question mentioned nothing about a water quality study. Note that this wrong answer used the word *opposition*, a form of the word *opposed* used in line 4 of the original text.
(B) *feigned indifference for the erection of the structure*
     Opposite/Copycat: the board members *ferociously opposed* the erection of the structure, so *feigned indifference* is wrong. This answer uses a form of the word *erected*, from the original passage.
(C) *ferocious support for a new location for the parking lot*
     Copycat/Opposite: the word *support* is an opposite answer, since the word in the passage is *opposed*. Plus, the location of the parking lot was not discussed in this portion of the passage. Notice, however, that the answer used the word *ferocious* to try to trick test takers into selecting it as the right answer.

Remember, the correct answer includes all of the important information from the passage. Wrong answers tend to leave out details.

The correct answer will include all of the basic ideas from the text and will not add any new information, as did answer choices (A) and (C). It will likely use synonyms for adjectives, verbs, and even some nouns from the original text, unlike answer choices (A), (B), and (C).

A specific type of Facts and Details question uses the words *refers to* and asks you to identify what a word or phrase alludes to. These questions are very similar to Words-In-Context questions; although you are not searching for a definition, a synonym in surrounding text is often the answer:

> The committee vetoed the proposal for school uniforms
> because they were afraid of public outcry, but it is impossible to
> predict the reaction of the students and parents. Other districts
> in the state have mandated uniforms and report no backlash.
> In fact, these districts have all reported that their students and
> parents have responded positively to the policy. To defeat
> a proposal out of fear of grievances is not only foolish, but
> also cowardly, and it's astounding that any policies have been
> passed at all.

Line
5

1. In line 4, the term "backlash" refers to

   A) defeat of a new proposal.
   B) opposition to mandatory school uniforms.
   C) efforts needed to pass new policies.
   D) positive reinforcement for school rules.

Questions using refers to can be solved in a similar manner as Words-in-Context questions.

The synonyms *public outcry* (line 2) and *grievances* (line 7) point to the correct answer: *opposition to mandatory school uniforms.*

Sometimes the adjectives *this* and *these* in the text indicate that the answer is in a preceding sentence:

> Proponents of the proposal have gone so far as to petition the
> community and contact the superintendent. But these measures
> are not going to get the proposal passed; only the committee
> members are able to overturn the ruling.

1. The term "measures" in line 2 refers to the

   A) efforts made to pass the proposal.
   B) ranking of school officials.
   C) length of time since the proposal was rejected.
   D) level of importance of specific proposals.

If *this* or *these* are used in the surrounding text, look at the sentence immediately preceding the reference. In this case, the previous sentence is about petitioning the community and contacting the superintendent, both of which can be categorized as efforts being made to pass the proposal in (A).

≡TIPS and TRICKS≡
If the question's line reference includes the pronouns *this* or *these*, the answer is probably in the line immediately preceding the reference.

While you should always read surrounding text for questions with a single word or single phrase reference, it is especially important for questions that ask what a term *refers to.*

≿TIPS and TRICKS≾
Sidebar summaries save time for EXCEPT questions.

We have already discussed EXCEPT questions earlier in this book, but it bears noting that these queries are often Facts and Details questions. The answers, which are usually interpreted facts and details, are provided in the text, but you must search for them. Recording short summaries of each paragraph as you read will save you time should you come across an EXCEPT question.

Literal Comprehension questions about Facts and Details simply ask you to choose an answer that restates the original text while maintaining meaning. Once you understand how to avoid the wrong answer choices and zero in on the right one, these will likely become the easiest Reading questions for you.

Facts and Details Problem Set

Read each short passage below and then answer the corresponding Literal Comprehension questions. Answers begin on page 222.

With access to the Internet suddenly becoming universal, many advertisers have shifted their focus away from traditional mass media and towards online advertising. Recent studies suggest that by 2015, the Internet will attract close to $40 billion from advertisers in the United States alone, five times as much as it did a decade earlier. This projected development, coupled with a shrinking share of advertising revenues, has caused tradi- tional mass media companies to increasingly deploy emerging technologies in television advertising, direct marketing, and billboard advertising that promise to help clients tailor their messages to specific demographic groups. Clearly, technological innovations have created a new, consumer-centered model in advertising that may ultimately redefine the very notion of mass communication.

Line 5
Line 10
Line 15

1. In line 8, the "development" refers to

   A) the recent innovations in technology
   B) the decrease in advertising revenues
   C) the increase in spending for online advertising
   D) the shift from traditional advertising strategies to online advertising

2. The statement in lines 14-17 ("Clearly . . . communication"), indicates that the author believes that

   A) conventional media outlets target specific groups through television and billboards
   B) a new advertising standard based on consumers has resulted from advancements in technology
   C) the advertising industry needs to redefine its definition of mass marketing
   D) revenue from online marketing will significantly increase in the next decade

I could have offered him six or seven reasons why our marriage had failed, but as was his usual tendency with things I had to say, he did not want to hear them. Instead, he stormed off the patio and into the villa, where he loudly packed his single bag of belongings. I had bought everything in our home, of course. I worked double shifts at the bar for three straight years to support us while he "worked" on his music, claiming he would get his break any day, a day that never came. I bought the TV he watched, the couch he lounged on, the food he ate, even the guitar he sometimes played. I suppose I could have gone in and asked him to leave that, too, but I didn't want to engage him another minute. I just wanted him to do what he did best when the pressure got too high—leave.

The irony of our relationship had eroded my toler- ance like waves pounding the coastline. When we first married, he promised to support me while I went to nursing school, but here we were, ten years later, and I was not a nurse, nor was he my advocate. He hadn't been able to keep a job in ten years and he had no concern for what I wanted or required.

Twenty minutes later I heard the cab pull up the drive and the front door slam. While it should have been hard for me to believe that a ten year marriage could be ended with two sentences, it was a perfect ending to a terse, apathetic relationship. I should have uttered those words sooner.

Line 5
Line 15
Line 20
Line 25

3. The narrator indicates that her husband failed to do all of the following EXCEPT

   A) support her needs
   B) land a record contract
   C) listen to what she had to say
   D) flee stressful situations

4. The phrase "irony of our relationship" (line 16) refers to the husband's

   A) failed commitment
   B) unsuccessful music career
   C) unemotional response
   D) silent departure

Reasons and Results Questions

Literal Comprehension questions that fall into this category ask you to provide the reasons for, or the results of, an action, event, or belief.

Reason questions use Cause and Effect words:

because	since	caused by	due to

Consider some examples:

1. The author criticizes those who "defend this belief" (line 18) because

2. The passage characterizes lemurs as "lovable" (line 51) since they are

3. The narrator indicates that the "tension" (line 22) and "disagreement" (line 23) were caused by

The answers to these questions can occur before or after the line reference. Although it seems like the cause should logically come before the effect, an author may introduce a problem before citing the reasons for it.

Result questions, which appear infrequently on the ACT and SAT, require you to state the outcome of a situation. They do not use a common vocabulary, but examples include the following:

4. Shelly responds to the accusation made in line 11 by doing which of the following?

5. The scientist shows that he is unaffected by criticism of his theory by

6. The passage indicates that "those vagabonds" (line 41) will eventually

The answers to Result questions usually occur after the line reference because of the natural sequence of events. These questions occur more frequently in Literary Fiction passages than in Non-Fiction passages because characters often respond to comments and situations.

Both Reasons and Results questions rarely cite an entire sentence, so you must read around the single word or single phrase line reference to determine the cause or outcome. Also, be prepared for the question that does not include any line reference—for these questions you must use your knowledge of the passage as a whole to determine the correct answer.

Recognizing common vocabulary can help you quickly determine a question type and the best solution method.

Results questions, which occur infrequently, are most likely to appear in Literary Fiction passages.

Consider an example passage with questions from this category:

> Many patients are hesitant to seek second opinions when making decisions about their health, even when considering major medical procedures. This hesitation is sometimes based on a lack of familiarity with a relatively new physician, but even where a strong relationship has been developed between doctor and patient, the person being treated often perceives the interest in a second opinion as an affront to the doctor who has provided the first opinion. This tendency is rather unfortunate, given the potential benefits; most patients who seek a second opinion will either receive further confirmation that a particular path represents the proper plan, or a contrary perspective which may suggest alternative methods for treatment.

Line 5

10

1. According to the author, many patients fail to "seek second opinions" (line 1) because they

    A) do not realize the potential benefits of dual diagnoses.
    B) worry about offending their original doctor.
    C) are unable to make decisions when presented with too much information
    D) refuse to acknowledge the original diagnosis

Confidence Quotation
"Today is yesterday's effect and tomorrow's cause." -Phillip Gribble

In this Reasons question, we are asked to provide the reason that many patients fail to seek second opinions. There are two reasons in the passage:

1. *a lack of familiarity with a relatively new physician* (line 4)
2. *the person...often perceives the interest...as an affront to the doctor who has provided the first opinion* (lines 6-8)

So either reason might be the answer, or the answer might contain both reasons. Answer choice (B) matches the second reason.

Answer (A) is incorrect because it contains ideas not discussed in the passage. Answers (C) and (D) also have irrelevant information, but many students are tempted by them because they make assumptions. They reason that the patient probably cannot make a decision given two opinions, or that the patient might be scared to admit she has cancer. Remember, never assume on the ACT and SAT! The patient could be the CEO of a major corporation who is able to make decisions given hundreds of opinions. And when did the passage say the patient had cancer? It didn't! Maybe she's just getting a diagnosis for the common cold. If you found yourself thinking seriously about selecting (C) or (D), you need to work on setting assumptions aside before taking the ACT and SAT.

Now consider a Results question for the same passage:

2. The passage indicates that a second opinion most often results in

    A) more informed decisions about courses of treatment.
    B) patients who are confused about which doctor to trust.
    C) insulted doctors who stop treatment on patients.
    D) less hesitation from primary caregivers.

There are two outcomes of second opinions provided in the last sentence of the passage:

1. *patients receive further confirmation that a particular path represents the proper plan* (lines 9-11)
2. *patients receive a contrary perspective which may suggest alternative methods for treatment* (lines 11-12)

Only answer choice (A) effectively summarizes these outcomes. Second opinions provide the patient with additional information about courses of treatment, thus leading to more-informed decision-making.

Answer choice (B) is never discussed in the passage, but again, students who make assumptions might be tempted to choose it. Answer choice (C) might be tempting for students who answered the first question correctly, but it was the *patients* who worried about offending doctors; the passage never said whether the doctors were actually offended by second opinions. Plus, the passage says nothing about doctors stopping treatment. Choice (D), a True to a Point answer, tries to confuse the hesitation of patients (in the passage) with the hesitation of doctors (in the answer choice).

Remember, the answers to Literal Comprehension questions are directly stated in the passage, and the answers to Reasons and Results questions are no different. You should be able to point to a specific portion of the passage and say "The answer is here." The correct answer choice, then, is usually a paraphrased version of the text.

<u>Confidence Quotation</u>
"Energy and persistence conquer all things."
-Benjamin Franklin, Founding Father of the United States

Reasons and Results Problem Set

Read the passage below and then answer the corresponding Literal Comprehension questions. Answers begin on page 223.

James Joyce, the well known Irish writer and poet, credited by many to have played a major role in developing the modernist novel, has long been the subject of intense literary inquiry. A fascinating
Line
5 character himself, Joyce led a hard life which included financial difficulties throughout all but his last few years. He suffered from alcoholism throughout his adult life, a problem that was compounded by other setbacks. As he got older,
10 his eyesight began to fail him, subjecting him to periods of total blindness, and adding to the trauma he suffered as his daughter's psychoses led to her permanent confinement in an asylum.

Perhaps the interesting story of Joyce's own
15 life helps to explain the ongoing fascination with the writer and his works. The author's significant contemporary following is also likely attributable to the fact that his novels, like his perspective, are not conducive to simple interpretation. In a letter, Joyce
20 once described *Finnegan's Wake*, one of his best known works, as "an engine with one wheel (and) no spokes."

Many of Joyce's phrasings are less than readily decipherable, and as a result his works provide
25 seemingly endless opportunity for speculation about construction and meaning. Consensus among literary scholars is often elusive, which is why outlier academics sometimes gain notoriety in the short term with unsubstantiated but well-publicized claims
30 concerning proper interpretation. For example, Danis Rose, a Joyce scholar in Ireland, recently announced dubious plans to publish "Finn's Hotel," a collection of early notes which he claims to be a previously unknown Joyce work, in spite of the fact that the
35 stories have all been published before, and actually provided the foundation for the later, better known *Finnegan's Wake*.

1. The author asserts that Joyce "led a hard life" (line 5) because of all of the following EXCEPT

   A) poor book sales.
   B) a family member's illness.
   C) monetary hardship.
   D) substance abuse.

2. According to the passage, the "ongoing fascination" (line 15) with James Joyce is due to the

   A) notoriety of *Finnegan's Wake.*
   B) complexity of his life and his works.
   C) achievements he attained despite blindness and alcoholism.
   D) possibility of fame for amateur critics who propose unusual theories about the author.

3. The author indicates that one of the results of Joyce's "less than readily decipherable" phrasings (lines 23-24) is

   A) the mass marketing of previously-published novels as undiscovered works.
   B) attention given to the interpretive theories of lesser-known scholars.
   C) agreement among literary critics about the meaning and purpose of Joyce's novels.
   D) expanded readership of Joyce's early notes and short stories.

Comparison and Contrast Questions

The final type of Literal Comprehension question asks you to find similarities or differences among actions, events, characters, and beliefs. Because of the nature of paired passages, you should expect to find most of the Comparison and Contrast questions following the paired passages, but you still may stumble upon one in a single passage, too.

Questions that ask you to find similarities between ideas or passages tend to use a few common words:

both   agree   parallel   is most like   shared by

The most common term in these questions is *both*, but any of the terms above may be used in a Comparison question. Consider some sample questions:

1. Both passages call attention to which quality of William Shakespeare?

2. The authors of both passages would most likely agree that locomotive technology was

3. What parallel between Mr. Darcy and Miss Bennet does the passage reveal?

As these examples suggest, most Comparison questions do not have a line reference. They sometimes rely on your general understanding of a passage, but more often require you to find a detail in the passage without assistance. Remember, these are Literal Comprehension questions, so the answer can be found in the text. This is why we urged you in Chapter Nine to be on the lookout for a point of agreement between two paired passages, even when the passages seem to completely disagree on the main idea.

Also pay close attention to the viewpoints of experts, advocates, opponents, or other people or groups mentioned in the passage. You will likely be asked how these viewpoints compare or contrast with the ideas of the author or other groups of people. If a Comparison question includes a line reference, the reference is likely citing one of these persons or groups. Look immediately above and below the line reference to find the viewpoint of the expert, advocate, or opponent.

Comparison and Contrast Questions occur most often in paired passages. They ask you to find similarities or differences among actions, events, characters, or beliefs.

⸎TIPS and TRICKS⸎
Remember to look for a point of agreement as you read paired passages. Spotting such an instance will save you valuable time should you encounter a Comparison Question.

⚘ GRATUITOUS VOCAB
advocate (n): a person who defends a cause

Contrast questions—those that ask about differences—are slightly less common than questions about similarities, but they also have their own vocabulary:

unlike   contrast   differ

Let's now look at a couple of examples of Contrast questions:

4. Which of the following qualities of William Shakespeare is discussed in Passage 2, but not in Passage 1?

5. The "experts" (line 13) in Passage 1 and the "advocates" (line 71) in Passage 2 differ primarily about whether

For many Contrast questions about paired passages, you will find one topic discussed—most likely in some depth—in one passage but not mentioned at all in the other. Question 4 above is an example of this type. For other Contrast questions, you will likely be asked how the author or main character disagrees with a person or group mentioned in the passage.

One particular type of paired passage Comparison and Contrast question asks you to summarize the similarities or differences between two passages. Consider an example:

6. Which best describes the relationship between Passage 1 and Passage 2?
    A) Passage 1 describes a phenomenon in music, whereas Passage 2 disputes that phenomenon as a real movement.
    B) Passage 1 praises a musician for artistic courage, whereas Passage 2 criticizes that musician's departure from standards.
    C) Passage 1 discusses the impact of history on music, whereas Passage 2 asserts that music is independent of history.
    D) Passage 1 examines the use of instruments in music, whereas Passage 2 centers on a single instrument.

> **TIPS and TRICKS**
> Cross out the corresponding letters of answers that you eliminate to avoid confusion or needless rereading.

To answer these questions, consider the main idea of each passage when selecting your answer. Be careful not to get hung up on a detail, as the wrong answer choices are sure to highlight details rather than the main idea of each passage.

Comparison and Contrast Problem Set

Read the passage below and then answer the corresponding Literal Comprehension questions. Answers begin on page 224.

Passage 1

Pit bulls are not naturally aggressive, but you would never know that given the attention paid to them by the media. Stories about pit bulls on the news highlight
Line only the negative: bites, attacks, and dog fighting
5   scandals. The reporters usually fail to mention that these "bad" dogs have bad owners, who encourage their animals to engage in combative behavior, usually for illegal reasons, and who choose not to spay or neuter their pets. The media also fails to report the positive
10 contributions of this wonderful breed. Many pit bulls are used as therapy dogs at nursing homes, hospitals, and schools, but these stories lack shock value and public uproar, so they are left out of the evening news.

Also missing are reports of dog bites by other breeds.
15 You never hear about Poco the Chihuahua sending children to the ER for stitches from a dog bite, but according to the Health Department, Chihuahuas were among the most vicious dogs in the city last year. The Shi Tzu was also listed as another tiny terror. It is the
20 nature of *all* dogs—especially those that are not spayed or neutered—to bite when threatened, but the pit bull is larger and stronger, thus inflicting more harm than smaller breeds. The media is not only blatantly wrong when characterizing the pit bull as vicious, but also
25 unfair in singling out the breed as the only "dangerous dog."

Passage 2

Many cities have enacted Dangerous Dog Ordinances to protect their citizens from vicious dog bites and attacks. Because Dobermans, German
30 shepherds, pit bulls, and Rottweilers have been known to inflict serious injuries and even death, they are automatically placed on a list of dangerous dogs, and owners must comply with certain rules in order for these dogs to reside within the limits of cities
35 with these ordinances.

The most important requirement for this law is sterilization. Dogs that are not sterilized—either spayed or neutered—are much more aggressive and likely to attack or fight. This rule also ensures that
40 people who own these breeds are not keeping them for blood sport or breeding.

While on private property, these breeds must be confined in a pen with a sturdy roof. A sign visible from the street must warn passers-by that a vicious
45 dog is on the premises. In public, the dogs must be muzzled and on a leash shorter than 6 feet.

While defenders of pit bulls have argued that these rules are unjust for dogs that do not have a history of aggressive behavior, it's history itself that proves
50 these ordinances must be in place. In a mauling last summer, the owner of a pit bull said in the newspaper that his dog never once showed aggression before he attacked an innocent woman at the park. In a story from television this summer, another pit bull
55 launched an unprovoked attack on a poodle at a pet store. Many owners just do not realize that their dogs are truly aggressive until it is too late. Dangerous Dog Ordinances do not forbid people from owning these breeds, but they help ensure the safety of
60 citizens and of the dogs themselves.

1. The authors of both passages would most likely agree that

    A) Chihuahuas are more aggressive than Rottweilers.
    B) large cities should enact ordinances for certain dog breeds.
    C) a sterilized dog is less likely to bite.
    D) dogs that are on public property should be leashed.

2. The author of Passage 1 and the "defenders" (line 47) in Passage 2 would most likely agree that pit bulls are

    A) not known for being aggressive.
    B) often used for dog fighting.
    C) more harmful than smaller dog breeds.
    D) unfairly judged by society.

3. Which of the following aspects is mentioned in Passage 1 but not in Passage 2?

    A) Dog fighting
    B) Smaller dog breeds
    C) Dog bites
    D) Stories from the media about pit bulls

Chapter Summary

Literal Comprehension Questions ask you to recall facts directly stated in the passage. There are four main types of Literal Comprehension Questions:

Main Idea Questions

- The main idea is directly stated in the passage.
- It applies to every paragraph; wrong answers will likely highlight the main idea of a single paragraph.
- These questions do not usually contain line references and depend on your understanding of the entire passage.
- Common wrong answers are True But Wrong.
- Sidebar summaries help students answer these questions quickly.

Facts and Details Questions

- These are the most common Literal Comprehension question.
- The answer is directly stated in the passage.
- The correct answer uses synonyms for the words in the passage and includes all important details.
- If the line reference uses the words *this* or *these*, the answer is probably in the line immediately preceding the line reference.

Reasons and Results Questions

- These questions ask you to interpret the cause or effect of specific actions.
- Reasons and Results questions frequently use cause and effect words.
- The answer is directly stated in the passage.
- The answer to a Results question is usually found after the line reference.
- They are most common in questions from Literary Fiction passages.

Comparison and Contrast Questions

- Comparison and Contrast Questions require you to note similarities and differences between actions, events, characters, and beliefs.
- The answer is directly stated in the passage.
- They are most common in paired passages.
- Watch for a point of agreement as you read paired passages as you will most certainly be asked to make a comparison.

Confidence Quotation
"Perpetual optimism is a force multiplier."
-Colin Powell, four-star general and statesman

LITERAL COMPREHENSION QUESTIONS ANSWER KEY

Facts and Details Problem Set—Page 213

1. (C)   Prephrase: $40 billion from advertisers in the United States alone

The best context clue is the word *this* in *this projected development*. It indicates that the definition of *development* is in the preceding sentence: "Recent studies suggest that by 2015, the Internet will attract close to $40 billion from advertisers in the United States alone, five times as much as it did a decade earlier." The development, then, is the increase in sales of internet advertising. The answer that most closely matches this prephrase is (C).

2. (B)   Prephrase: Technology has changed advertising

Because this is a Literal Comprehension question with a reference to an entire sentence, read only that sentence when trying to determine the answer. You are interpreting that sentence only, and not the sentences around it.

The sentence states "Clearly, technological innovations have created a new, consumer-centered model in advertising that may ultimately redefine the very notion of mass communication." The answer choice that restates this idea is (B): "a new advertising standard based on consumers has resulted from advancements in technology."

Notice the synonyms in the correct answer: *technological innovations* became *advancements in technology. A new, consumer-centered model* became *a new advertising standard based on consumers*.

True But Wrong: Answer choice (A) paraphrases an idea from the previous sentence. For that reason alone it is wrong, but notice that it leaves out direct marketing, and instead only lists television and billboards. The right answer will include all of the important concepts.

True to a Point/Extreme: Answer choice (C) is incorrect because of the wording of the answer. In the referenced sentence, the author states that the new model *may* redefine mass communication; the answer, however, states that the advertising industry *needs* to redefine mass marketing. There is an enormous difference between *may change* and *needs to change*, let alone who is making those changes.

True But Wrong: Answer choice (D) is a belief held by the author, but it is from the beginning of the passage, and not the specific line referenced. Also notice that the line 5 of the passage points out the increase in sales, which is different from revenue. One can infer that revenue increases when sales increase, but since this is a Literal Comprehension question, the answers must be stated, not implied.

3. (D) Prephrase: Impossible to prephrase

Because these are things the husband failed to do, it is a little trickier to answer. Run through each answer choice and insert it in the following blank: "Did he _____?" If you answer *no*, eliminate that answer. Find the one for which you answer *yes*, which is (D):

Did he support her needs? No (Line 21: *he had no concern for what I wanted or required*)
Did he land a record contract? No (Line 9: *a day that never came*)
Did he listen to what she had to say? No (Lines 2-3: *but as was his usual tendency with things I had to say, he did not want to hear them*)
Did he flee stressful situations? Yes (Lines 13-15: *I just wanted him to do what he did best when the pressure got too high—leave*)

4. (A) Prephrase: The narrator supported the husband when he promised he would support her

The irony lies in the fact that her husband promised to support her, but she has consistently supported him. We learn this in lines 16-22. This is a broken promise, or failed commitment, on the part of the husband.

Reasons and Results Problem Set—Page 217

1. (A) Prephrase: Impossible to prephrase

The components of his "hard life" are all contained in the first paragraph:

1. financial difficulties (line 6): Answer (C)
2. alcoholism (line 7): Answer (D)
3. his daughter's psychoses (line 12): Answer (B)

That leaves (A) as the answer.

2. (B) Prephrase: The interesting story of his life and the fact that his books are not easily interpreted

The author provides two reasons for this "ongoing fascination:"

1. the interesting story of Joyce's own life
2. the fact that his novels, like his perspective, are not conducive to simple interpretation

Note that the first statement is from the sentence immediately following the first paragraph, so it is referencing Joyce's personal troubles as the *interesting story*. The author further comments on this *story* when he says *like his perspective* in the second statement. If his novels and his perspective are not conducive to a simple interpretation, then they are the opposite of simple—they are complex. Answer choice (B) is best.

Copycat: Choice (A) is wrong because the passage does not reveal whether *Finnigan's Wake* was notorious (note that the passage does use the word *notoriety* (line 28), tricking some test takers to select this answer).

True to a Point: Choice (C) is incorrect because it only contains two of the setbacks faced by Joyce. It omits financial difficulties and his daughter's psychosis (not to mention the complexity of his works). Remember, the right answer will include ALL important ideas, not just some of them.

True But Wrong: Finally, choice (D) is wrong. While a portion of this answer rings true elsewhere in the passage, it's not the reason for the fascination for Joyce's works.

3. (B) Prephrase: *outlier academics sometimes gain notoriety*

The answer comes from lines 27-30: *outlier academics sometimes gain notoriety in the short term with unsubstantiated but well-publicized claims concerning proper interpretation*. This is an example of the *endless opportunity for speculation* cited in line 25.

Notice that the correct answer (B), uses many synonyms: *attention* for *notoriety*; *interpretive theories* for *unsubstantiated claims*; and *lesser-known scholars* for *outlier academics*.

Answer choice (A) is incorrect because of the words *mass marketing* (not discussed in the passage) and *novels* (it was *early notes* that the scholar claimed were undiscovered in the passage).

Opposite: Answer choice (C) is wrong because it is an opposite answer. The passage states that *consensus among literary scholars is often elusive* (lines 26-27), meaning scholars do not agree.

Answer choice (D) is incorrect because the author does not discuss the increase or decrease in readership. Notice again the use of *short stories*: short stories are not mentioned in the passage at all.

Comparison and Contrast Problem Set—Page 220

1. (C) Prephrase: Difficult to prephrase.

The author of Passage 1 states "It is the nature of *all* dogs—especially those that are not spayed or neutered—to bite when threatened" (lines 19-21) and the author of Passage 2 asserts "Dogs that are not sterilized—either spayed or neutered—are much more aggressive and more likely to attack or fight" (lines 37-39).

Choice (A): Chihuahuas are only discussed in Passage 1, and the author never says they are more aggressive than the bigger dogs, just that they can be aggressive.

True But Wrong/True to a Point: Choice (B): Only the author of Passage 2 believes in these ordinances, and he never specifies that they should only be for *large* cities.

True But Wrong: Choice (D): Only the author of Passage 2 states this.

2. (D) Prephrase: The rules are unfair for non-aggressive dogs.

The author of Passage 1 is pro-pit bull throughout the passage. The defenders "have argued that these rules are unjust for dogs that do not have a history of aggressive behavior." These defenders believe that pit bulls are viewed unfairly, which the author of Passage 1 would agree with given the first paragraph and last sentence of his passage. The best answer is (D).

Opposite: Choice (A): The author of Passage 1 states that pit bulls are not naturally aggressive (line 1), but cites media using stories in which they are highlighted as being aggressive. So while he acknowledges they are known for being aggressive, he disagrees with this.

Opposite: Choice (B): The line about the defenders does not indicate they think this, and the word *often* makes the answer difficult to defend.

Opposite: Choice (C): Since the author and the defenders like pit bulls, they would not (and did not) say this.

3.   (B)   Prephrase: Difficult to prephrase.

Smaller dog breeds are discussed in lines 14-23 of Passage 1, but nowhere in Passage 2.

Choice (A): Dog fighting
Passage 1 line 4; Passage 2 line 41 ("blood sport")

Choice (C): Dog bites
Passage 1 line 4; Passage 2 line 29

Choice (D): Stories from the media about pit bulls
Passage 1 lines 1-26; Passage 2 lines 50-56

CHAPTER THIRTEEN
EXTENDED REASONING QUESTIONS

Extended Reasoning questions make up a substantial portion of both the ACT and SAT Reading sections. These questions usually cause students the most difficulty because unlike Literal Comprehension questions, the answers to Extended Reasoning questions are not directly stated in the passage. You must draw a conclusion based on information in all or part of the passage.

Let's study a simplified example before looking at specific question types:

> After graduating from law school, Michelle was recruited by the best law firm in the city. She turned them down, however, preferring to work for a non-profit organization where the underprivileged were able to retain lawyers. The charity was located a block from where she grew up, so it was a true homecoming and success story for one of the neighborhood's own.

Line
5

1. The paragraph suggests which of the following about "the best law firm in the city?"

    A) It recruited the most talented graduates.
    B) Its job offers were not often turned down.
    C) Its lawyers were considered the most intelligent in the city.
    D) It did not typically represent disadvantaged clients.

The inference occurs in lines 2-5: *She turned them down, however, preferring to work for a non-profit organization where the underprivileged were able to retain lawyers.* This sentence implies that if Michelle had gone to work for the law firm, she would not be representing underprivileged people because they could not retain lawyers there. The best answer is (D). Notice that it uses the word *typically*, making your argument even more sound. It is easier to defend "It *did not typically represent* disadvantaged clients" than "It *did not represent* disadvantaged clients."

Extended Reading questions composed roughly 40% of the ACT Reading questions and 30% of the SAT Reading questions in the released tests that we analyzed.

🔖 GRATUITOUS VOCAB
inference (n):
a conclusion based on reasoning or evidence

The other three answers are not suggested or stated in the passage. In order for (A) to be correct, the passage would have had to state that Michelle was one of the most talented graduates. Then you could conclude that this is why she was recruited. But without that information, (A) is wrong.

Beware of inferences that are True to You, but not actually implied in the passage.

While students might be tempted to assume that answer choice (B) is right given what they know about the best law firms from watching TV law shows (such as high salaries, important cases, etc.), the passage does not discuss any other offer besides the one to Michelle. You cannot assume anything on the ACT or SAT without evidence to support the assumption.

Finally, choice (C) is incorrect because of the word *intelligent*. While a case may be made that they are the best lawyers (because they work for the best law firm), you do not have enough information to know *why* they are best. Maybe the lawyers win cases because they bribe judges. Or maybe they are the most persistent, refusing to give up on cases. Intelligence was not mentioned in the paragraph, nor was any other reason for the law firm's success.

✦ *GRATUITOUS VOCAB*
meticulousness (adj): *careful precision*

This example, while simple, demonstrates the difficulty of Extended Reasoning questions and the meticulousness with which you must read each question and answer choice.

There are three main types of Extended Reasoning Questions, but each type can further be broken down into subtypes:

1. Style Questions
   - Purpose
   - Author's Attitude
   - Rhetorical Devices
   - Passage Organization
2. Inference Questions
   - General Inferences
   - Hypothetical Points of View
3. Advanced Questions
   - Parallel Reasoning
   - Strengthen and Weaken

On the following pages we will explore each type and subtype in more depth. Understanding the question types can help you avoid wrong answers and select the right ones.

Style Questions

Style questions assess your knowledge about the choices made by the author of a passage. They may ask you why the author uses a particular sentence, or require you to identify a metaphor or simile in the text. There are three types of style questions, all of which we explore on the following pages.

Purpose

Purpose Questions ask you to explain the function of a particular section of text. Why did the author use this particular word or phrase? Why did the author write this passage? You might be asked about the purpose of a term, phrase, sentence, group of sentences, paragraph, or the entire passage itself.

Many Purpose Questions use common terms in the question:

purpose   functions   serves   because

The word *because* may be used in other types of questions (like Literal Comprehension Reasons and Results questions), but the terms *purpose*, *function*, and *serve* are most often used in Purpose Questions.

Questions about the passage as a whole are called Primary Purpose Questions and they resemble the following:

1. The main purpose of the passage is to

2. The passage primarily serves to

3. The major purpose of the passage is to

These questions should be easy for you to answer because you will determine the purpose of the passage when identifying the MAPS after reading. Answer choices for purpose questions, including Primary Purpose questions, tend to use verbs as the first word of the answer choice. Study an example in which the verbs are underlined:

1. The primary purpose of the passage is to

    A) <u>define</u> the relationship between employee and supervisor.
    B) <u>challenge</u> a management strategy.
    C) <u>illustrate</u> acceptable office behavior.
    D) <u>compare</u> work ethic today to that of the 1950s.

Understanding these verbs can help you eliminate wrong answers and select the right one. For example, the verb *challenge* indicates that the author disputes a current theory, and the passage must be written to prove this theory wrong. If the author is not questioning a theory, then you can confidently

Purpose questions require you to explain the function of a word, phrase, sentence, paragraph, or passage.

Purpose questions use verbs in their answers. Understanding these verbs is important to your success on these questions.

eliminate this answer in (B). The same goes for *compare*: if two items are not being analyzed for their similarities or differences throughout the entire passage, then answer choice (D) is wrong.

There are three common primary purposes on the SAT—*to argue against*, *to argue for*, and *to explain*—and each has a set of verbs that may be commonly used in the correct answer of a Primary Purpose Question. Be sure you understand the meaning of each one and read any accompanying notes about their use on the ACT and SAT.

Verbs That Argue Against:

argue: to present reasons for or against a thing. If an author is arguing throughout a passage, each paragraph will provide a reason for or against the topic.

assert: to maintain or defend. Note that this can also be to *argue for*.

call into question: to question or dispute.

challenge: to question or dispute. If an author is challenging a topic, each paragraph will present a reason for that challenge.

condemn: to indicate strong disapproval

confront: to challenge.

counter: to oppose.

criticize: to find fault with. If an author is criticizing a topic or theory, he will present reasons why that topic or theory is wrong throughout the passage.

*denounce: to openly condemn. One of the most Extreme of the verbs that argue against something.

dispute: to argue. See *argue*, above.

invalidate: to discredit.

lament: to express sorrow or regret.

object: to argue. See *argue*, above.

oppose: to argue against. If the author argues against a topic, it should be quite clear.

question: to challenge. See *challenge*, above.

raise doubt: to challenge. See *challenge*, above.

raise a question: to challenge. See *challenge*, above.

rebut: to disprove. If the author rebuts a claim, she will provide evidence to show that claim is wrong.

refute: to disprove. See *rebut*, above.

undermine: to weaken or attack.

An author's primary purpose is to argue for, argue against, or explain an idea.

*Any of these verbs could be used in the correct answer choice, but some are more common than others. Verbs in **bold** are more likely to be used in correct answers; verbs with an asterisk (*) are more likely to be used in wrong answers.*

Verbs That Argue For:

acknowledge: to recognize the truth of

advocate: to support. An author who supports a subject will provide reasons for that support.

assert: to maintain or defend. Note that this can also be to *argue against*.

confirm: to verify

defend: to support in the face of criticism. Expect an author who is defending a topic to cite reasons the criticism is wrong.

encourage: to support. See *advocate*, above.

endorse: to support. See *advocate*, above.

promote: to support. See *advocate*, above.

substantiate: to establish as true.

support: to uphold or maintain. See *advocate*, above.

reinforce: to support. See *advocate*, above.

validate: to confirm.

Confidence Quotation
"They can conquer who believe they can."
-Virgil, Roman poet

Verbs That Explain:

advance: to suggest.

*analyze: to investigate closely. See *examine*, below.

address: to discuss. Because all authors discuss their topics on the ACT and SAT, this answer is easy to defend.

articulate: to make clear.

characterize: to describe the qualities of.

clarify: to make clear or easy to understand.

compare: to find similarities and differences. Note that *compare* can also mean finding differences between two things.

consider: to reflect on.

contrast: to find differences. If the author finds similarities between two items, you cannot select *contrast* as an answer.

convey: to make known.

define: to explain the meaning of. An author may define a term in a sentence or paragraph, but it's unlikely he will spend an entire passage defining something.

demonstrate: to explain.

describe: to tell in words. Because all authors describe their topics on the ACT and SAT, this answer is easy to defend.

develop: to elaborate or expand in detail.

Verbs That Explain, continued:

discuss: to consider. See *address*, above.

emphasize: to stress a point. Most authors stress their points, so this is another easy answer to defend.

establish: to prove.

*evaluate: to judge the significance of. Similar to *examine*.

evoke: to suggest or produce.

*examine: to investigate closely. A possible answer, but not as likely as *address*, *discuss*, *show*, and other less benign answers that do not have *closely* in their definition.

explain: to provide causes or reasons for. An author who explains a topic will discuss reasons for it.

explore: to look into. See *address*, above.

expose: to present or make known

highlight: to emphasize. See *emphasize*, above.

illustrate: to make clear by use of examples. If an author provides examples of a topic, they are illustrating their point.

inform: to give knowledge of a fact.

introduce: to present.

note: to mention. See *address*, above.

point out: to indicate. See *address*, above.

present: to introduce. Pay close attention to what the answer choice is presenting; the author may present evidence or theories, but he is unlikely to present an aside or a case study.

*probe: to examine closely. See *examine*, above.

propose: to suggest.

provide: to give. See *present*, above.

put forth: to present. See *present*, above.

reflect: to express.

reveal: to make known.

show: to indicate. See *address*, above.

showcase: to present.

*speculate: to propose a conjecture without facts. This answer is always a possibility, but make sure the author is proposing a new idea, not just writing about one that has already been provided.

stress: to emphasize. See *emphasize*, above.

summarize: to express in brief form.

Confidence Quotation
"Some things have to be believed to be seen."
-Ralph Hodgson, English poet

Verbs That Explain, continued:

    suggest: to introduce for consideration. See *address*, above.

    underscore: to emphasize. See *emphasize*, above.

    urge: to persuade. Most ACT and SAT passages are written to persuade, so this answer is possible. Just make sure the author is trying to convince people to act in support of or opposition to the topic.

The purpose verbs can be used in any purpose question and not just in Primary Purpose questions.

Some Purpose Questions ask you to explain the function of a paragraph or a group of paragraphs. Other purpose questions will be about specific portions of the text. Again, these should not be too difficult to answer if you notate the MAPS of each passage, as the structure of a passage will reveal the function of each of its parts.

Consider some example questions:

    4.   The quotation in lines 51-53 primarily serves to

    5.   The author compares "fundamentalists" and "survivors" in order to

    6.   The primary purpose of the second paragraph is to

    7.   In line 21, the "winds of change" serve as an example of an action that is

When you rephrase these questions, the first word of your paraphrase should almost always be *why*:

    4.   Why did the author use a quotation?

    5.   Why does the author compare "fundamentalists" and "survivors"?

    6.   Why did the author write the second paragraph?

    7.   Why does the author use the "winds of change"?

∃TIPS and TRICKS∃
Rephrased purpose questions should always start with *why*.

Remember, you should always prephrase an answer to each question before looking at the answer choices. Your internal conversation never stops during an ACT or SAT passage! *Why did the author use a quotation? Well, it was provided by a dog trainer and it supports his belief that dangerous dogs should be leashed in the city. So he used an expert's opinion to support his thesis. Which answer choice is closest to my prephrase?* Never underestimate the power of the prephrase! Your prephrased answer will lead you to the correct answer choice and steer you away from the wrong ones.

The majority of purpose questions ask you to explain the function of a single term, short phrase, or sentence. The answers to these questions are in the lines immediately preceding and following the referenced word or phrase. Consider an example:

> From birth, dolphins are able to squeak, click, whistle, and squawk, all of which serve as a means of communicating with other members of the pod. They also have several methods of non-verbal expression. Jaw claps express
> *Line 5* aggression; fin-rubbing shows friendship.

1. The author mentions "jaw claps" (lines 4-5) and "fin-rubbing" (line 5) in order to

   A) illustrate forms of non-verbal communication in dolphins.
   B) clarify that dolphin communication is different than human communication.
   C) suggest that dolphins are similar to humans.
   D) explain how verbal cues are misinterpreted.

If we were to outline this paragraph, the purpose of those two terms becomes quite clear:

I. Dolphin Communication
   A. Verbal Communication
      1. Squeak
      2. Click
      3. Whistle
      4. Squawk
   B. Non-Verbal Communication
      1. Jaw claps
      2. Fin-rubbing

The jaw claps and fin-rubbing are provided as examples of *several methods of non-verbal expression*, just as the squeaks, clicks, whistles, and squawks are examples of verbal communication. Answer choice (A) is correct. Obviously, you do not need to outline every paragraph on the ACT or SAT (nor do you have the time to do so), but we do it here to illustrate how the paragraph is organized, since the organization of the paragraph explains the purpose of those two terms.

The purpose of a term, phrase, or sentence has a wide range of possibilities, from providing an example to defining a term to disproving a theory. Your best strategy for answering questions about the purpose of a passage element is to rephrase the question (*why did the author use this word? this phrase? this sentence?*), reread the portion of the passage that is referenced, and then prephrase an answer to your rephrased question.

↟ GRATUITOUS VOCAB
cue (n): a sensory signal for response

≡TIPS and TRICKS≡
If you are struggling with a Purpose Question, mentally outline the paragraph to see if the structure reveals the answer.

Author's Attitude

Questions about the Author's Attitude ask you to interpret the author's feelings toward the subject, often employing one of the following words:

attitude   tone   feeling

Questions from non-fiction passages ask for the *author's* attitude; questions from literary fiction passages require you to determine the *narrator's* or *character's* attitude.

Questions from nonfiction focus on the author's attitude, while those from literary fiction will concern a character's attitude.

Attitude questions about the general tone of the entire passage may look like the following examples:

1. The tone of the passage can best be described as

2. Compared to the tone of Passage 1, the tone of Passage 2 is more

3. Passage 1 and Passage 2 share a general tone of

4. The author's attitude toward school uniforms might best be described as

We have already discussed the author's attitude toward the main idea of a passage in detail in Chapter 6 when we explained how to find the MAPS of a passage. After you finish reading, you should always briefly consider the Main Idea, Author's Attitude, Purpose, and Structure. This will not only help you understand all of the questions, but also help you directly predict answers to questions about the tone or author's attitude toward the main idea. To review this strategy, return to pages 95-98.

You can review our introduction to the Author's Attitude in Chapter Seven.

Remember, attitude clues are scattered throughout a passage. By underlining these clues as you read, the overall tone is easy to determine at the completion of the passage.

In addition to questions about the tone of the entire passage, you should expect questions about the author's attitude toward people or ideas in the passage. This attitude may be similar to the overall tone; for example, if the author is *critical* of stem cell research, he is likely to be *critical*, *scornful*, or *contemptuous* of the scientists who are conducting that research. He is also likely to be *accepting*, *admiring*, or *respectful* of an expert who speaks out against stem cell research. Consider some examples of these questions:

↳ GRATUITOUS VOCAB
scornful (adj): regarding something as unworthy
contemptuous (adj): regarding something as unworthy

5. The author's attitude toward the "invention of necessity" (line 22) is primarily one of

6. The author's attitude toward the educators in the passage is best characterized as one of

If the question includes a line reference, like question 5 on the previous page, then the answer is likely in the surrounding text. You may need to read a line or two above and below the reference, but the answer is often in the same sentence.

Consider an example:

> Although the characters are well-developed and multi-faceted, the plot is stale. The movie drones on for two hours and twenty minutes, dragging us through scenes that are reminiscent of dozens of other, better movies.

> 1. The author's attitude toward the "characters" (line 1) might best be described as one of
>
>   A) appreciation.
>   B) criticism.
>   C) disappointment.
>   D) ambivalence.

The overall tone of this short passage is one of criticism, as indicated by *stale*, *drones*, *dragging*, and *better*, but the author states the characters are *well-developed and multi-faceted*. This indicates her appreciation of the characters, so answer choice (A) is correct. Be careful not to confuse an author's tone throughout the passage with her attitude about a specific topic in the passage.

Another common attitude question asks you to identify the tone of a sentence or group of sentences:

> 7. The tone of the statement in lines 13-14 ("Living . . . by then") is one of

> 8. The author's tone in the final two sentences is best described as

For these questions, you should only read the line reference to determine the tone of that portion of the passage; the surrounding text will only confuse you.

Let's study an example:

> The ending of the film is debatable, as it reveals that the main character may or may not have been dreaming the entire story. This ambiguity has been a point of contention
> *Line* for many critics. Personally, I can find evidence for both
> 5 scenarios, and constantly waver on the meaning of the ending. But one thing is clear: the character can only move into the future once he accepts the past.

> 1. The tone of lines 6-7 ("But . . . past") is best described as
>
>   A) curious.
>   B) cynical.
>   C) uncertain.
>   D) decisive.

Focus only on the referenced sentence:

But one thing is clear: the character can only move into the future once he accepts the past.

This sentence is firm, definite, and without controversy. The best answer is (D), *decisive*, meaning *indisputable and conclusive*. But if you were to read the sentence above the line reference, you might choose a different answer:

Personally, I can find evidence for both scenarios, and constantly waver on the meaning of the ending.

This sentence is doubtful and unsure, so if you included it, you might be tempted to choose answer choice (C), *uncertain*. For questions about the tone of a specific line reference, you should only read the sentence or sentences in that line reference.

For most passages, the author's tone will either be positive, negative, or neutral, depending on whether he is arguing for the topic, arguing against the topic, or just explaining the topic. Recognizing common attitude words and their related word forms can make these questions easier to answer, so you should familiarize yourself with any of the following words you do not know. The bold words are commonly used in the right answer, while words with asterisks are Extreme Answers that are rarely a part of the correct choice on the ACT or SAT.

Positive Attitude Words:

accepting: open

admiring: feeling approval

advocating: showing support

affectionate: showing attachment or devotion

amusing: humorously entertaining

appreciative: holding in high regards

awed: overwhelmed with admiration

cheerful: pleasant

compassionate: showing deep sympathy

confident: sure

deferent: respectful

delightful: highly pleasing

earnest: having a serious purpose

*ebullient: overflowing with enthusiasm

≥TIPS and TRICKS≤
By knowing the actual definition of each of these words (and not what you think each one means), you can quickly eliminate wrong answer choices.

Positive Attitude Words, continued:

*ecstatic: overflowing with delight

empathetic: understanding

encouraging: favorable or supportive

*euphoric: intensely happy

excited: emotionally charged

fascinated: extremely interested

humorous: funny

intrigued: having a raised curiosity

jocular: joking

open-minded: receptive to new ideas

optimistic: hopeful

*nostalgic: showing desire to return to a happier time

proud: feeling satisfaction with one's achievements

respectful: showing esteem

sympathetic: showing agreement in feeling

*whimsical: fanciful or playful

Attitude words in bold are commonly used in right answers on the ACT and SAT; words with asterisks are common in wrong answer choices.

Negative Attitude Words:

admonishing: cautioning against something

alarmed: fearful

angry: showing a strong feeling of displeasure

annoyed: slightly irritated

apprehensive: anxious or fearful

concerned: troubled

contemptuous: regarding something as unworthy

contentious: tending to argue

critical: finding fault

cynical: distrustful

defiant: boldly resisting

*derisive: showing derision (ridicule)

disappointed: let down

disapproving: expressing that something is wrong

disbelieving: refuting or rejecting

disdainful: regarding something as unworthy

Negative Attitude Words, continued:

dismayed: alarmed, fearful

*disparaging: belittling

dissatisfied: not pleased

doubtful: showing doubt and uncertainty

facetious: not meant to be taken seriously

*fearful: feeling dread

foreboding: predicting evil

frustrated: disappointed

*hostile: antagonistic; characteristic of an enemy

impatient: not accepting delay

incredulous: showing doubt and uncertainty

indignant: showing displeasure for unfairness

*irate: highly angry

lamenting: showing sorrow and regret

*mocking: showing ridicule

mournful: showing sorrow and regret

ominous: predicting evil

*outraged: feeling strongly offended

regretful: showing sorrow and regret

reproachful: full of blame or belittlement

*resentful: showing displeasure at something that caused injury or insult

resigned: yielding; giving in

*sad: showing sorrow

sarcastic: bitter, but not meant to be taken seriously

sardonic: bitter, but not meant to be taken seriously

scornful: regarding something as unworthy

skeptical: showing doubt and uncertainty

*somber: gloomy and dark

*sullen: gloomy and ill-humored

uncertain: showing doubt

wistful: longing

Confidence Quotation
"In the province of the mind, what one believes to be true either is true or becomes true."
-John C. Lilly, physician and writer

Neutral Attitude Words:

*ambivalent: having mixed feelings

analytical: breaking down into parts for closer study

*apathetic: not interested

*astonished: filled with wonder

detached: impartial and objective

didactic: instructive

impartial: neutral and objective

*indifferent: not interested

inquisitive: intellectually curious

*nonchalant: coolly uninterested

objective: unbiased

Be wary of any of the words with asterisks in these lists, as they are common in answer traps on the ACT and SAT. Any word from the Neutral Attitude Words list that means *indifferent* is likely wrong, because if an author is indifferent to a topic, why bother writing about it? And words like *euphoric* (intensely happy) and *outraged* (strongly offended) have modifiers—*intensely* and *strongly*—in their definitions that make them Extreme Answers.

Modifiers can also be included in SAT answer choices themselves, and sometimes point to right and wrong answers. Consider the following question:

1. The tone of the third paragraph ("Because . . . wonder") might best be described as

    A) utterly disdainful.
    B) somewhat critical.
    C) openly resentful.
    D) unshakably confident.

The modifiers of choices (A) and (D) make these answer choices Extreme. *Utterly* and *unshakably* turn benign answers into powerful ones that are much harder to prove. On the other hand, *somewhat* in choice (B) makes this answer more easy to defend. You do not have to prove that the author was completely critical through the entire paragraph; you just have to show that he was a little critical.

Choices that contain the words *somewhat* or *qualified* (meaning *limited*) are often the correct answer for Author's Attitude questions.

An author is unlikely to have mixed feelings, especially in such a short passage.

🔖 GRATUITOUS VOCAB
disdainful (adj): regarding something as unworthy

≡TIPS and TRICKS≡
Answers that use the adjectives *somewhat* or *qualified* are likely correct because these modifiers lessen the significance of the word.

Extreme words are almost always wrong when used as answer choices; however, if they are the correct answer, they should be easy to defend. For example, if an author is *mocking* or *derisive*, he will clearly be making fun of the topic in a manner that is almost cruel. The chances of finding a passage like this on the ACT or SAT are pretty low, though, which is why we are confident in declaring these tones as Extreme.

You should also avoid answers that indicate the author is confused. After all, how could he write this detailed passage if he did not understand what he was writing about? Words in this list include *baffled*, *bewildered*, *confused*, and *puzzled*. They are not likely the correct answer.

Finally, be careful when selecting an answer with two words to describe the tone. Consider two similar examples:

1. The tone of the passage is primarily one of

   A) playful confidence.
   B) worried bewilderment.
   C) begrudging skepticism.
   D) humorous sarcasm.

2. The tone of the passage is best characterized as

   A) playful and confident.
   B) worried and bewildered.
   C) begrudging and skeptical.
   D) humorous and sarcastic.

When selecting an answer choice for this type of question, be sure that the tone is described by both words. For example, if the author's attitude is sarcastic but not humorous, avoid answer choice (D). Both words must clearly be supported by the passage.

Understanding the general tone of a passage is integral to your ability to answer subsequent questions. Knowing how the author feels about a topic can help you predict other outcomes in the passage. You should always find the author's attitude while determining the MAPS of a passage, and then apply this knowledge to other questions in the section.

⸙ GRATUITOUS VOCAB
derisive (adj): mocking

⸙TIPS and TRICKS⸙
Avoid attitude words that indicate the author is confused.

For answers with two attitude words, make sure that both words apply to the passage.

Rhetorical Devices

Rhetorical devices, such as similes and understatements, are techniques that an author uses to enhance his writing, making the language more interesting for the reader.

Questions about rhetorical devices may actually use the words *rhetorical* or *device*, cite an actual rhetorical device (like *simile*), or use one of two phrases:

uses   makes use of

Consider some examples:

1. The author uses which of the following devices in the third paragraph?

2. Both passages make use of which of the following?

3. The metaphor in lines 14-17 ("A butterfly . . . lands") supports the main idea by

4. The last sentence of the first paragraph is an example of the author's rhetorical technique of:

The test makers expect you to recognize about two dozen true rhetorical devices, which we have included in the following list. Familiarize yourself with these techniques before looking at a sample passage. As with the tone words, devices likely used in correct answers or question topics are in bold, while techniques typical in wrong answers include an asterisk:

True Rhetorical Devices:

abstract language: words that refer to ideas or concepts, like *love* and *freedom.*

alliteration: the use of the same letter at the beginning of each work in a phrase. Example: *"Lily likes licking lollipops."*

allusion: a reference to a famous person, event, or work of art. Example: *"She wrote in sonnets, much like Shakespeare."*

analogy: a comparison of two things. Example: *"Oil is to your car's engine like blood is to your body."*

cliché: an overused phrase. Example: *"I am busy as a bee."*

*euphemism: a mild substitution for a word or phrase thought to be harsh or offensive. Examples of euphemisms for *stupid* include *"Not the sharpest tool in the shed"* and *"A few peas short of a casserole."*

figurative language: words that are not meant to be taken literally. Figurative language includes analogies, similes, clichés, metaphors, and other rhetorical devices.

Rhetorical devices are common ACT question matter and they used to be common fodder for SAT questions on previous forms of the test. It seems, however, that questions about rhetorical devices have decreased significantly on the current form of the SAT. We hesitate to declare this an "ACT ONLY" topic, though, as there is a question about "anecdotes" in the Official SAT Study Guide. If you are only taking the SAT, we recommend reviewing this section but not focusing on it if time is an issue in your preparation.

Rhetorical devices in **bold** font are more likely to be correct answers on the ACT and SAT. Devices with asterisks (*) are unlikely right answers.

True Rhetorical Devices, continued:

hyperbole: a deliberate exaggeration. Example: *"I would walk a thousand miles just to get an ice cream cone right now."*

idiomatic expression: an accepted phrase that has a meaning different from the literal meaning of the words. Example: *Hold your horses* (meaning "slow down" versus "picking up your horses in your hand") and *raining cats and dogs* (meaning "raining heavily" rather than "cats and dogs falling from the sky").

imagery: words that appeal to the senses, usually by vivid description. Example: *"When I walked into the kitchen, bacon was sizzling in the pan, permeating the room with its smoky scent. I watched the beads of grease pop and snap in the pan, dancing like a feverish crowd until they vanished in thin air."*

irony: words that convey a meaning opposite of their original meaning. Example: *"The largest dog in the county, a Mastiff weighing in at nearly 200 pounds, is named Tiny."*

metaphor: a comparison of two things in which one of the things is the other thing. A metaphor often uses the word *is*. Example: *"Tim is a scared puppy, waiting for his master with his tail between his legs. He knows he may get fired today, and that it is likely too late to make amends."*

oxymoron: a combination of contradictory terms. Examples of an oxymoron include *"Jumbo shrimp"* and *"doubting believers."*

parenthetical reference: a remark in parenthesis, which usually does not follow the theme or flow of the text. Example: *"I cannot stand the taste of grape flavoring in candy (although I do like grapes) or the smell of sauerkraut."*

*parody: a work that imitates the style of another work for comic effect. Examples include many of the sketches on *Saturday Night Live* and the children's book *The True Story of the Three Little Pigs*, told from the point of view of the wolf. It is unlikely that you will find a parody on the ACT or SAT, so this is probably a wrong answer choice.

personal voice: on the ACT and SAT, personal voice refers to the use of the word "I" in a passage. An author uses personal voice if she writes from her point of view, using personal pronouns.

personification: giving human qualities to animals or inanimate objects. Example: "The car began to complain and moan just an hour into the trip, before deciding to take a rest on the side of the road."

point of view: the narrator's position in the story. You may be asked to identify the narrator of a literary fiction passage on the ACT or SAT, who likely will be an unidentified observer who knows everything taking place, including a character's thoughts.

Expect to identify a rhetorical device or explain its function.

True Rhetorical Devices, continued:

rhetorical question: a question posed by the author for effect and to which she does not expect an answer. Example: *"It is not practical to expect businesses to return overseas jobs to Americans. After all, how can they compete with the price of labor?"*

sarcasm: ironic language intended to convey scorn or insult. For example, sarcasm occurs when an author states "I love deer hunting" when she is clearly an animal activist opposed to hunting.

simile: a comparison of two things using *like* or *as*. Example: *"Tim is like a scared puppy, waiting for his master with his tail between his legs. He knows he may get fired today, and that it is likely too late to make amends."*

*symbolism: when an item stands for an idea. For example, the Brooklyn Bridge might represent freedom in a novel about New York City. Because symbolism is prevalent throughout an entire novel, it will probably not be included in a short excerpt on the ACT or SAT.

understatement: expressing an idea as less important than it really is. Example: *"You could say it's a little warm today. The thermometer is reading 110 degrees in the shade."*

*wordplay: clever use of words, such as puns and double entendres. Example: *"When a clock is hungry it goes back four seconds."* Since ACT and SAT passages are anything but fun, it's unlikely they will use such fun wordplay.

If the author employs one of the preceding rhetorical devices, expect a question about it. You may be asked to simply identify the technique used:

1. In the last paragraph, the author uses which of the following?

   A) Personification
   B) Symbolism
   C) Metaphor
   D) Understatement

Or you may be required to explain the purpose of a rhetorical device:

2. The author's parenthetical reference in line 6 primarily serves to

   A) illustrate a point about cotton fields.
   B) define a term used earlier in the passage.
   C) highlight the author's work experience.
   D) express skepticism about the appropriate use of a term.

Knowing the definitions of these terms is the key to finding the correct answers to both types of questions. When selecting an answer, be sure that you can point to a particular portion of the passage and say "This is a metaphor" or "Here the author uses personification."

This point is especially true for questions in which the test makers cite techniques that are not true examples of rhetorical devices. They are platforms that an author can use, but they are not typically provided on accepted lists of literary rhetorical devices. Examples include writing forms such as *case studies*, *rebuttals*, and *summaries*. The test makers use these terms freely, often intermixed with true rhetorical devices, and your success on these questions depends on your understanding of their definitions.

The test makers use the term "rhetorical devices" to describe all writing techniques and literary devices.

Let's look at an example:

> Many scientists believe that the Roman inhabitants of Pompeii died from suffocation when the volcano Vesuvius erupted in 79 AD, but they actually died instantly from exposure to extremely high temperatures. Tests on nearly
> *Line*
> 5 100 skeletal casts have revealed that the victims did not suffocate on ash flows as originally thought, but rather faced heat as high as 480 degrees Fahrenheit in a pyroclastic cloud that shrouded a 20 kilometer radius of the volcano. Given that a healthy adult can not survive in temperatures of 104
> 10 degrees for more than a few hours without water, it is clear that the level of heat generated by Vesuvius was lethal. Current residents of Naples should take heed: scientists predict another massive eruption in the near future, an event which will bring mass destruction given the high population
> 15 density around the volcano.

1. This passage makes use of which of the following?

    A) A historical case study
    B) An extended simile
    C) An earnest warning
    D) A scientific inquiry

↳ GRATUITOUS VOCAB
earnest (adj): sincere

Once again, modifying words are used to make answer choices more attractive. Because this passage discusses an event from history, choice (A) may trick many test takers with the adjective *historical*. But a *case study* is a detailed research project, usually centered on a person or group in relation to the development of a medical, psychological, or social phenomenon, which is studied over time. Examples include projects on cancer or depression, which can be studied long-term. The eruption of Mt. Vesuvius was a single event and while scientists might study its consequences, it is impossible to conduct a case study on the deceased. Answer choice (A) is incorrect.

Choice (B) is clearly incorrect, as there is no *simile* in the passage.

Choice (D) is also wrong, though many students are tempted to select it given the adjective *scientific*. While the passage does discuss a scientific topic, there is no *inquiry*. An *inquiry* demands a question and an investigation of that question. The author is not wondering how the ancient Romans died; he knows the answer: *they actually died instantly from exposure to extremely high temperatures* (lines 3-4).

The correct answer is (C), *an earnest warning*. The author makes a seriously important plea for the residents of Naples to take heed, warning them that the volcano is due to erupt again (lines 12-15).

The following terms have been used on past ACTs or SATs so you should clearly understand what each one means in case they are used again on future exams.

Other Literary Devices:

As with previous lists, words in bold are common in right answers, while those with an asterisk are common in wrong answers.

authority: an authority is an expert on a subject. If a question asks whether the passage *quotes an authority*, make sure that there is a quotation from a person who has extensive knowledge on the topic.

analysis: breaking down a topic into its basic elements. A passage that discusses the components of a William Faulkner novel is an analysis. Modifiers, like *scientific* analysis or *detailed* analysis, usually make this device hard to defend.

anecdote: a short, amusing story. A passage in which the author recounts a funny incident with his 5 year-old uses an anecdote.

*apology: an expression of regret for wrongdoing. It's unlikely that an ACT or SAT author is going to issue an apology, but you can recognize one by the use of the words *"I'm sorry"* or *"I regret."*

*aside: a temporary departure from the main idea. An aside occurs when a passage about the process of growing oranges diverts to a short discussion of how the author grew strawberries with his grandparents as a child. Asides are unlikely to occur on the ACT or SAT because there is not enough time to include them in a passage.

assertion: a statement of belief with or without proof. *"Graphic novels are educational"* is an assertion. Because most statements in passages are assertions by the author, this is a common device used on the ACT and SAT, and one that should give you pause when evaluating answer choices.

*case study: a detailed research project, usually centered on a person or group in relation to the development of a medical, psychological, or social phenomenon, which is studied over time.

citation: the act of citing an authority or their work. If a passage quotes an authority, it has made a citation.

Other Literary Devices, continued:

commentary: a series of comments or explanations about a topic. Most ACT and SAT passages are commentaries, making answer choices about commentaries easy to defend.

concession: the act of yielding, or giving in, on an argument. The authors of ACT and SAT passages are unlikely to give in on their arguments, but they might make small concessions. For example, if an author is against cosmetic testing on animals, he might concede that the practice in the past has saved human lives. However, he is still against the practice.

confession: acknowledgement of fault. Example: *"I admit that I failed to consider your feelings."* It's unlikely that an ACT or SAT author will confess to being wrong about the main idea, but like a small concession, she may admit that she was wrong about a small detail.

conjecture: an opinion or theory without proof. Example: *"I think that your personality is developed as much by outside influences as it is by genetics."* Like an assertion, this device is easy to defend, as authors make many statements about their beliefs, often without evidence to support them.

criticism: a comment expressing the fault of another idea. Example: *"Investors in the new building are wrong to ignore the pleas of those attempting to restore the original structure."* Authors often criticize people or groups who do not share their beliefs, so this device is commonly used on ACT and SAT passages.

data: a set of facts or statistics, often in numerical form. Example: *"There are over 308 million people in the United States, an increase of 9.7% since the last census."* Data is easily recognizable by its use of numbers, and while it may be used in scientific or historical passages on the ACT and SAT, it is not a very common answer on the test.

*decision: a judgment or conclusion. In order for a decision to be made, an uncertainty has to be present. Since the authors of the ACT and SAT passage are writing about things they already believe in, it's unlikely that they will make a decision in a passage on the ACT or SAT.

definition: the act of defining a word or term. Example: *"A blog is an online journal filled with a writer's observations."* Because ACT and SAT passages often introduce new terms, a definition is quite possible.

description: a description is a statement that describes something or someone. Example: *"Fyodor Dostoevsky was a passionate person, thriving in situations that were dramatic and exciting. He was excessively proud and sometimes domineering."* Many passages on the ACT and SAT, especially literary fiction passages, contain descriptions.

Other Literary Devices, continued:

disclaimer: a denial of responsibility. An example of a disclaimer is the statement *"Smoking cigarettes causes lung cancer"* written on the side of a carton of cigarettes. On the ACT and SAT, disclaimers are less obvious. *"I am not an expert on dogs"* is a disclaimer that may be used by someone who is about to write about canines; the author wants you to understand that her opinion is one of an amateur.

*documentation: written evidence. A birth certificate and driver's license are documentation proving your identity. Unlike evidence, written documentation is not likely to be used on the ACT or SAT.

evidence: proof. Example: *"A study by the University of Arizona revealed that an office desk has hundreds of times more bacteria per square inch than an office toilet seat."* This statement is evidence of the bacteria on office desks. Evidence is often provided on the ACT and SAT, but before selecting this as the answer, make sure you can pinpoint the existence of evidence in the passage.

fact: statement of truth. Example: *"There are 88 keys on a piano."* While most essays contain multiple facts, the passages on the tests also contain opinion, so facts are not a typical answer. If it were the correct answer, the referenced section would need to contain only facts and no opinions.

flashback: a return to an earlier scene. Non-fiction passages are not likely to include flashbacks, but they may occur in literary fiction.

generalization: a statement that is applied to an entire group based on the actions of a few of its members. Example: *"Dogs are friendlier than cats."* This is a generalization because there are certainly some cats that are friendlier than some dogs.

hypothesis: an explanation for a phenomenon. A hypothesis is often associated with science, so *conjecture* and *theory* are more likely to be used as correct answers.

*inquiry: a question or investigation for truth. Inquiries are not common on the ACT or SAT.

*invocation: a prayer to a god or spirits. Example: *"We ask the spirits to protect us from harm."* Because the ACT and SAT strive to remain bias-free, it is unlikely you will find an author making use of an invocation on the tests. However, it is possible—unlikely but possible—that a character in a literary fiction passage would invoke a god or spirits.

list: a series of items. Example: *"Here is a list of the parts of speech: noun, pronoun, verb, adverb, adjective, preposition, conjunction, and interjection."*

observation: something noticed. Example: *"The child chose the blue bowl."* Observations are common in everyday life and on the tests. Plus, they are easy to defend as an answer choice.

Confidence Quotation
"Observation is a passive science, experimentation an active science."
-Claude Bernard, French physiologist

Other Literary Devices, continued:

personal account: a description of an event witnessed or performed by the author. Similar to an anecdote, but without the amusing quality. Personal accounts are told using the personal pronoun "I."

phenomenon: an observable fact or occurrence. A phenomenon can be extraordinary, such as the Northern Lights, or quite simple, such as always putting your left shoe on first. People tend to associate the word with extraordinary events, so they tend to discard it as an answer choice when it is often the correct answer.

position: belief or stand. A person takes a position when they choose a side in an argument; their position is their belief.

rebuttal: a reply intended to disprove an opponent's argument. Unless one of the dual passages was written to directly oppose the other passage, it is unlikely to find a rebuttal used on the ACT or SAT.

reevaluation: a second assessment. Example: *"After finishing the book, I returned to the chapter on dog behavior to analyze it once more."* In order for a reevaluation to appear on the ACT or SAT, the author must admit that this is not his first attempt at analysis.

repetition: restatement of a word or idea. Example: *"One million books had sold. One million people were reading my words. One million opinions about my story."* If repetition is used on the ACT or SAT, it should be quite easy to identify.

*research: diligent investigation to gather facts. An author conducts research before writing a passage, and then uses the facts he finds to compose the passage. It is highly unlikely that this would be a correct answer on the ACT or SAT.

scenario: a predicted sequence of events. Example: *"In one scenario, Bobby keeps the money he finds and feels guilty. In another, he turns the money in and is rewarded for his honesty."*

solution: the act of solving a problem. Example: *"The answer to the water quality problem lies in better education for boaters."* In order for a solution to be present in the passage, there must be an issue that the author is trying to resolve.

speculation: a conjecture arrived at by consideration. Example: *"After serious contemplation, I tend to believe that there are aliens among us."*

*study: a detailed examination of a subject. Studies are so thorough that they are unlikely to appear on the ACT or SAT.

summary: a brief account of something that provides the main points. You may see summaries at the end of a passage. You may also encounter a biographical summary, in which the author provides the main events of someone's life.

Quotation marks are commonly used to express skepticism about the appropriateness of a term.

Other Literary Devices, continued:

theory: a proposed explanation that may or may not be tested. Example: *"I think that mushrooms grow in the field because of the fertilizer used there several years ago."* Theories are common in ACT and SAT passages.

*thesis: the main idea. All ACT and SAT passages contain a thesis, but the term is only the answer if the question is asking about the line containing the main idea. This is not a probable scenario, since the test makers are not likely to point out a passage's main idea. Plus, *thesis* can also mean *an original research project*; the dual definition makes this an answer that is likely to be wrong.

warning: a statement that cautions the reader. Example: *"Dogs should not be left unattended around children as serious consequences can result."* Warnings have appeared on previous tests, especially in passages about the environment.

Remember, when these words are joined by a modifier, both the modifier and the device must accurately describe the passage. While *theory* is a common device used on the tests, a *comprehensive theory* and *amusing theory* are likely wrong answers because the modifiers make them extreme or illogical.

The final literary device of which you should be aware is the use of quotation marks in a passage. This is a common test question concept used in both the current ACT and SAT. Consider an example from a previous passage:

> I could have offered him six or seven reasons why our
> marriage had failed, but as was his usual tendency with
> things I had to say, he did not want to hear them. Instead,
> he stormed off the patio and into the villa, where he loudly
> *Line 5* packed his single bag of belongings. I had bought everything
> in our home, of course. I worked double shifts at the bar
> for three straight years to support us while he "worked" on
> his music, claiming he would get his break any day, a day
> that never came. I bought the TV he watched, the couch he
> *10* lounged on, the food he ate, even the guitar he sometimes
> played. I supposed I could have gone in and asked him to
> leave that, too, but I didn't want to engage him another
> minute. I just wanted him to do what he did best when the
> pressure got too high—leave.

   1.   The quotation marks used in line 7 serve to

      A) define a common term.
      B) introduce a specialized vocabulary.
      C) express doubt about the appropriateness of a word.
      D) cite an authority.

Although the word in quotations indicates that the husband worked, the rest of the passage makes it clear that he clearly did not work. He lounged on the couch and sometimes played music. The wife feels frustrated with his lack of work, and thus uses the quotation marks to express her skepticism surrounding this word. Answer choice (C) is correct.

Quotations used in this manner are like the "air quotes" you might have seen people make when talking; you know, when they say something like "Tony called in sick today" and bend the first two fingers of both hands up and down while saying "sick." It indicates that the speaker clearly does not believe Tony is sick, just as the narrator of this passage does not believe her husband worked.

This is a common reason why quotation marks are used on the ACT and SAT. Answers might use phrases like *show skepticism* or *disagree with the characterization*, but the meaning is the same: the author does not believe that the term applies to the person or situation.

A common purpose of quotation marks is to express doubt about a term.

Quotation marks can also be used to introduce an unknown word or phrase. Consider this example:

> Students divided the city into sections and then proceeded to "warchalk" every neighborhood. Warchalking is the marking of outdoor surfaces such as sidewalks and signposts
> *Line* with chalk symbols that indicate a wireless network is
> 5 available at that location.

2. In line 2, the quotation marks are used to

    A) mock a specific group of people.
    B) introduce a specialized word.
    C) reveal skepticism about a definition.
    D) illustrate a proven theory.

When quotation marks are only used around the first instance of a word, their purpose is usually to introduce an unknown term.

In this passage, the quotation marks are used to introduce *warchalk*. Notice that the next use of the word, *warchalking*, does *not* use quotation marks. When a passage uses quotation marks with only the first instance of an unfamiliar word, it is usually an indication that the term is not commonly known. Answer choice (B) is correct.

The final possible purpose of quotation marks in an ACT or SAT passage is to set off dialogue. If quotation marks are used around a complete sentence, then the answer to a quotation mark question lies in why the author chose to include that dialogue:

> My patients worry about the cost of their prescriptions. "Doc," they begin, "I hate to give up my meds, but I just cannot afford them anymore." It's devastating to hear this
> *Line* because it undermines the weeks, months, and sometimes
> 5 years I have invested in treating their illnesses.

2. In lines 2-3, the author uses quotation marks to demonstrate

    A) the devastation experienced by the narrator.
    B) the prolonged length of time spent treating patients.
    C) that the high cost of medications causes some patients to stop taking them.
    D) that the doctor's office is also affected by the price changes of medications.

If a question asks about quotation marks in dialogue, you must interpret why that dialogue is used.

The quotation itself indicates that the patients are going to stop purchasing their medications, so only answer choice (C) makes sense.

Passage Organization

The final type of question about an author's choices are those questions that ask about the organization of the passage. These questions may use phrases such as the following:

organized   shifts   develops   pattern

Let's look at how these phrases are used in questions:

1. Over the course of the passage, the focus shifts from

2. Which of the following choices best describes the way the passage is organized?

3. Which answer best describes the developmental pattern of the passage?

With these questions, it helps to look at the answer choices to understand what is expected from you when determining the organization of the passage:

4. Over the course of the passage, the main focus shifts from

    A) a summary of a phenomenon to its probable cause.
    B) an explanation of theory to an analysis of its weaknesses.
    C) a discussion of a scientific model to a conversation with an expert.
    D) a warning about a global event to a personal account.

> ✎ GRATUITOUS VOCAB
> *phenomenon* (n):
> an observable fact
> or occurrence

Consider a similar question:

5. Which of the following choices best describes the way the passage is organized?

    A) It summarizes the phenomenon of El Niño and then explains its probable cause.
    B) It explains a theory behind El Niño prediction, then analyzes the theory's weaknesses.
    C) It discusses the most common model of El Niño and then cites an expert's opinion about that model.
    D) It warns about the long term effects of El Niño before sharing the author's personal experiences with El Niño.

Students who note the MAPS of a passage should have no problem answering these questions, as the Structure of the passage is the same as its organization. If you complete sidebar summaries for each paragraph, you will have a written record of the passage's organization to which you can quickly refer back.

> The organization of a passage is simply its structure. Test takers who notate the MAPS of the passage should have no trouble with organization questions.

Roughly 20% of ACT and 15% of SAT Reading questions concern Style. Understanding the Purpose, Author's Attitude, Rhetorical Devices, and Passage Organization are important to your success on the ACT and SAT.

Style Questions Problem Set

Read the passage below and then answer the corresponding Style questions. Answers begin on page 274.

While emerging information technologies have changed the media landscape in recent years, one of the oldest forms of online advertising—the web banner—
Line continues to be a staple of the Internet age. Banner
5 ads are clearly superior to traditional mass media. Embedded as a small image into a web page, banners allow advertisers to reach millions of customers instantaneously without the geographic limitations inherent in traditional newspaper-based advertising. And unlike
10 television commercials, banner ads can be deployed in association with user input from search engines, which significantly increases their potential for impact.

Perhaps the most attractive feature of banner ads, however, is the transparency with which advertisers can
15 allegedly measure their success. Every time a viewer displays a banner in her web browser, she generates what is commonly known as an "impression." An impression turns into a "click-through event" whenever the viewer clicks on the banner. By dividing the number
20 of click-through events by the total number of impressions generated, advertisers can easily measure the click-through rates of their banner ads and tailor their strategies accordingly.

Some experts have recently argued, however, that
25 the media's focus on click-through rates can be detrimental to the success of their campaigns. For instance, if a banner displayed simultaneously on two different websites generates markedly different click-through rates, many advertisers would be tempted to increase
30 the number of banner ad impressions on the website with the higher click-through rate. Such a strategy does not always work, as click-through events can sometimes increase without generating a higher sales volume. Clearly, click-through rate variability provides
35 an imperfect measure of affinity between the website's audience and the ad campaign's target demographic, and should be used with great deliberation.

1. The primary purpose of the passage is to

   A) note the benefits and a potential drawback of using a common advertising strategy.
   B) emphasize the importance of using web banners for small businesses.
   C) explore a new information technology.
   D) refute a theory about targeting a demographic.

2. The author's remark in lines 4-5 ("Banner . . . media") can best be characterized as

   A) an elaborate apology.
   B) a scientific conjecture.
   C) a humorous aside.
   D) a confident assertion.

3. The author compares "television commercials" (line 10) with "banner ads (line 10) primarily in order to

   A) urge television viewers to patronize advertisers.
   B) challenge a common belief among advertising executives.
   C) point out the limitations of another popular advertising strategy.
   D) explain how one media outlet will eventually replace another.

4. Lines 13-15 ("Perhaps . . . success") function primarily to

   A) speculate about why a doomed technology is so commonly used.
   B) provide support for a claim made earlier in the passage.
   C) dispute evidence previously presented in the passage.
   D) explain how a complicated process works.

5. In lines 17 and 18, quotation marks are used to

   A) cite an authority's previous work.
   B) defend the author's choice of words.
   C) highlight specialized terms.
   D) imply skepticism about the characterization of a term.

6. The author's tone in the final sentence is best described as

   A) admiring.
   B) resigned.
   C) cautionary.
   D) scornful.

7. The final paragraph primarily serves to

   A) summarize the reasons for a particular theory.
   B) criticize the beliefs of members of the advertising profession.
   C) acknowledge a shortcoming of a preferred method of advertising.
   D) oppose the use of an accepted advertising strategy.

8. The author's attitude toward the web banner is best described as one of

   A) appreciation.
   B) criticism.
   C) incredulity.
   D) apathy.

9. Over the course of the passage, the main focus shifts from

   A) a discussion about the benefits of a strategy to a warning about over-analyzing one of those benefits.
   B) a study of a media phenomenon to a criticism of the researchers of the phenomenon.
   C) an evaluation of the largest advantage of a business plan to a list of other advantages of the same plan.
   D) an assessment of a particular business practice to an examination of the background of the experts who have studied the practice.

Inference Questions

There are two types of questions that we consider Inference Questions: General Inferences and Hypothetical Points of View.

General Inferences

Most students find inference questions to be the most challenging Reading questions because it is easy to confuse everyday inferences with inferences on the ACT and SAT. The test makers take advantage of this confusion by designing answer choices to further confound you.

An inference is a conclusion made by analyzing specific evidence. It's an educated guess, the kind we make every day in our real lives. Consider some common inferences made from a general statement:

Statement: Scarlett went to the nurse's office.

Fahim's Inference: Scarlett is sick.

Gray's Inference: Scarlett is taking her medication.

Hannah's Inference: Scarlett is going home.

All of these inferences are great guesses, and one or all of them may be correct. Other students with more specific experience or knowledge might draw different conclusions that are less common:

Izzy's Inference: Scarlett works for the nurse.

Jian's Inference: Scarlett went to check on a sick friend.

Klint's Inference: Scarlett steals from the nurse when this nurse is on his lunch break.

There are many possible conclusions, including some that are more probable than others, when making inferences in our daily lives. On the ACT and SAT, however, there is only one right answer. These are standardized tests, so all test takers—including Fahim, Gray, Hannah, Izzy, Jian, and Klint—must be able to draw the exact same conclusion. Understanding this difference between real world inferences and ACT and SAT inferences can help you avoid selecting the wrong answers on the test.

An inference is a conclusion made by analyzing specific evidence.

The correct inference on the ACT or SAT is the one that must be reached by EVERY test taker.

On the ACT and SAT, you should not make regular inferences about a statement. There will be only one conclusion that you can draw—the same conclusion that all other test takers can draw—about a section of text. Consider another general statement and consider how it would be interpreted on the two tests:

Statement: Today was the first time Scarlett visited the nurse's office.

There is only a single inference here that can be proven, and thus only one inference that is correct on the ACT or SAT:

Correct Inference: Scarlett had never been to the nurse's office before today.

You cannot prove any of the following, so these inferences are wrong:

Incorrect Inference: Scarlett has never been sick at school.
Maybe she was sick and went straight home.

Incorrect Inference: Scarlett is a new student.
Maybe she's been at the school for years, but just never got sick.

Incorrect Inference: Scarlett has never met the nurse.
Maybe they met in the hallway.

Inferences are not direct statements on the tests, but they can be proven, so avoid drawing any conclusions for which you cannot find any proof.

General inference questions are revealed by common word usage:

suggests   implies   it can be inferred   assumption

While students of formal logic may have very different definitions for these first three words, on the ACT and SAT they are used interchangeably. What the author suggests is the same as what he implies which is the same as what can be inferred. The term *suggest* is by far the most common inference term on the tests. Let's look at some examples of inference questions:

1. The discussion of werewolves in the second paragraph primarily suggests that

2. The author implies that a child's curiosity "might be hindered" (line 22) because

3. It can be inferred that the narrator considers "formal invitations" (line 54) to be

4. The author's assumption in the first paragraph is that

It is difficult--and even impossible--to prephrase some inference questions.

As with Literal Comprehension questions, plan to read above and below the provided line reference if it only includes a word or phrase. But if the line reference is for a complete sentence, group of sentences, or paragraph, you only need to read that specific text. Let's examine an inference example:

> In August, NASA released the first complete map of ice floes in Antarctica. Researchers can now examine the outward flow of the continent's ice sheets to better help them predict rises in sea level.

1. The first sentence suggests that

   A) researchers were unable to predict changes in sea level with early maps.
   B) the technology to delineate the ice floes was not available until recently.
   C) previously published charts were comparably deficient.
   D) the treacherous terrain of Antarctica made it too difficult for researchers to navigate.

Isolate the sentence about which you are to make an inference:

> *In August, NASA released the first complete map of the ice floes in Antarctica.*

The implication lies in the phrase *first complete map*. What does this suggest about earlier maps? That they were incomplete. Armed with the prephrase *earlier maps were incomplete*, can you match an answer choice? Choice (C) is best.

Understanding why inference answers are wrong can go a long way to helping you understand why the correct one is right. Look at choice (A): for one thing, the first sentence does not discuss changes in sea level. The next sentence does, and the test makers are hoping you read more than just the line reference provided. Remember, when the test asks about a complete sentence, read only that sentence. But even if the line reference included the second sentence, this answer would still be wrong. The answer choice uses *unable to predict changes*, while the passage says the new maps *better help them*, indicating that they are already predicting changes in sea level, just not as well as they will be from now on.

If you chose choice (B), you read too much into the passage. This might be an inference you would make in your real life, like Scarlett going to the nurse's office because she is sick, but it is not one you can make on the ACT and SAT. There is no proof in the passage that technology was unavailable until recently.

Choice (D) is a similar assumption that is made without proof. Even if you know that this statement in (D) is True to You, you cannot select it as an answer choice because the passage does not suggest this is so.

Let's try one more, this time with a longer passage and a shorter line reference:

> As excited as I was to start my new job, my first day was disappointing. I had hoped that Jeremiah would begin my training with intellectual discussions about the history of each painting in the museum, but instead I sat in an office
> *Line 5* stuffing envelopes. I didn't earn a master's degree in art history to mail newsletters about the Ladies' Afternoon Tea series. I suppressed my displeasure, but resolved to speak to Jeremiah about finding interns from the university as soon as possible.

2. In the passage, the narrator implies that the reason her first day at her new job was "disappointing" (line 2) was

   A) she was unable to express her true feelings.
   B) the museum did not employ any students.
   C) she was given a task that she felt was not worthy of her education.
   D) a scheduled monthly event interrupted her training with Jeremiah.

Because the line reference is for a single word (*disappointing* from line 2), you must read around the line reference to find the implication. Since that is a daunting process, it might be easier to eliminate wrong answers than find the inference and prephrase it.

≡TIPS and TRICKS≡
Sometimes it is easier to eliminate wrong inferences than find the correct inference.

Start with choice (A). It's True to a Point: the narrator said she *suppressed her displeasure* (line 7), but it was a personal choice. She could have told her co-workers how she felt, but decided not to. Plus, her true feelings were a result of her disappointment; they did not cause the disappointment.

For choice (B), the narrator states that she will talk to Jeremiah about finding interns. It is possible that students already work at the museum in positions other than internships. And even if there were no interns working at the museum, is this the source of the narrator's disappointment? No.

The narrator is disappointed because she sat in an office stuffing envelopes. In the next sentence, she states *I didn't earn a master's degree in art history to mail newsletters about the Ladies' Afternoon Tea series*. She implies that she is too educated to be completing such a menial task. The best answer is (C).

Choice (D) is wrong for two reasons. For one, her training was not interrupted; it never happened at all, so how could it have been interrupted? For another, what scheduled monthly event was occurring? Yes, she was sending a newsletter about a Ladies' Afternoon Tea series, but nowhere in the passage does it state that this event is monthly or that it was occurring on her first day of work.

This is the thought process you must practice when weeding out wrong answers and securing the right one for an inference question. Remember, the right answer can be proven, while the other four cannot. One or two attractive wrong answer choices will infer too much from the passage.

Hypothetical Point of View

The SAT calls these Hypothetical Point of View questions "Synthesis" questions.

Questions that ask you to predict a person's response to a hypothetical situation are Hypothetical Point of View questions. You are most often asked about how an author would respond, so these questions are similar to Author's Attitude questions; however, the answer is not stated in the passage, so you must make an inference to answer them.

You may also be asked to predict the response of an expert, group, or critic mentioned in the text. In Literary Fiction passages, hypothetical questions ask you to forecast the reactions of the narrator or characters. You can quickly pinpoint some of these questions by the use of *would most likely*:

the author would most likely....
the historians would most likely....
the teacher would most likely....

Let's look at some specific questions:

1. The author of Passage 2 would most likely regard the "downpour" (line 14) mentioned in Passage 1 as

2. The author of Passage A would most likely respond to the third paragraph of Passage B by arguing that

3. The designers in Passage 1 would probably contend that the "fabulous architecture" (line 51) is primarily

4. The gardener and Henry would most likely agree on which of the following points?

Hypothetical Point of View questions occur most often in paired passages. Be prepared to predict what one author would say about an idea in the other passage.

An overwhelming majority of hypothetical questions occur with paired passages, as you can see in the first three examples above. You may occasionally see them in single passages, too, as the last example demonstrates.

The best strategy for answering these questions is prephrasing. Let's practice with the following example:

Passage 1

Antarctica is a pristine, undeveloped continent that has a global impact on the world's environment. It should remain undisturbed, so as not to disrupt the studies of such vital issues as climate change, ozone depletion, and long-range weather forecasting.

Line
5

Passage 2

The Antarctic Protocol of 1991 should be amended to allow for mineral prospecting with strict environmental regulations. All mining expeditions would be underground, so the environment and current research projects would not be affected. Scientists around the globe agree that the untapped resources of the Antarctic may hold secrets that are too valuable to ignore.

10

1. The author of Passage 2 would most likely assert which of the following about the "studies" (line 3) in Passage 1?

    A) Researchers believe their results are less valuable than the discoveries to be made from mining.
    B) Mineral prospecting would allow them to continue without interruption.
    C) Their global impact is over emphasized.
    D) The studies themselves are polluting the continent just as much as economic exploration would.

Begin by summarizing the main ideas: the author of Passage 1 asserts that Antarctica should remain undisturbed so that the study of environmental conditions can continue. The author of Passage 2 believes that mineral prospecting on Antarctica should be allowed as long as strict environmental regulations are in place.

Then rephrase the question:

What would the author of Passage 2 say about the "studies" in line 3?

In Passage 2, the author states that *current research projects would not be affected* by mining (lines 9-10). So he would likely tell the author of Passage 1 that her concern for further study is not an issue; mining would not stop those studies. Armed with this prephrase, match an answer choice: (B).

If you do not hold a conversation with yourself (like this one) while answering Hypothetical Point of View questions, you will become confused when looking at the answer choices. It is extremely important to prephrase the answer to these questions by asking yourself how the author (or narrator or character) would likely respond.

Inference Questions Problem Set

Read the passage below and then answer the corresponding Inference questions. Answers begin on page 274.

Passage 1 is adapted from Maria Donovan, "Spare the Rod" in *Parent Monthly*, 2015. Passage 2 was adapted from Dr. Melissa Rawl, *Parenting Hints, Hacks and Help*, 2008.

Passage 1

"Spare the rod and spoil the child," quote many parents today, unaware that they are citing not the Christian Bible, but rather a poem from 1664.

Line 5 Punishments that were also considered acceptable in the 17th century included stoning, drawing and quartering, and drowning, but spanking is the only one still in use in America today. It is an archaic form of punishment that is never acceptable, and research from childhood and parenting experts indicates that spanking is not only
10 ineffective, but also dangerous to the health and welfare of the child.

Spanking leads to lying, claims James Spencer, a child development specialist. "Spanking teaches a child to fear and avoid his parents," he says. "When faced
15 with such a harsh punishment, the child learns to either falsely deny responsibility or become so manipulative as to avoid discipline. It is a habit that many will carry into adulthood." Parents who are working to create healthy, affectionate bonds with their children should be
20 warned that spanking undermines their efforts. Once a child learns to lie to avoid punishment, he may continue to be dishonest with his parents to avoid serious discussions or uncomfortable situations—those times that most parents hope their child will seek parental support.
25 Worse still is the emotional toll of spanking on children. Depression and antisocial behavior have been linked to spanking in many clinical studies, and children who are spanked are more likely to show aggression or be violent later in life. The more a child is
30 whipped, the less he understands proper social interactions. He believes that it is okay to hit someone who doesn't listen to him or who is rude. After all, isn't that why Mommy spanks him? The true source of spanking is anger; a frustrated parent merely reacts out of rage at
35 her disobedient and disrespectful child. But if the same mother is not allowed to physically lash out at disobedient employees or disrespectful strangers, why is she allowed to do so to her own child?

Spencer cites an archaic poem as the reason. "Parents
40 believe the old adage," he says. "It's difficult to convince them that *using* the rod is what actually spoils the child." Hopefully the current perceptions can be changed by educating parents and sharing the evidence that spanking is harmful. Parents need to understand
45 that spanking leads to confused children, depressed adolescents, and violent adults.

Passage 2

Moderate spanking—that which is neither too forceful nor too frequently meted out—has no adverse effects on a child's well-being. Research studies that
50 conclude anything to the contrary have been made using sweeping generalizations and meager evidence.

Many experts claim that spanking children leads to depressed adults who lack self-control and are violently aggressive. None of their studies, however, account for
55 the fact that these "symptoms" might have actually led to the spanking. Children who are naturally aggressive and violent are more likely to be disciplined and more likely to suffer from depression. To attribute such behavior to spanking without researching whether the
60 behavior already existed in the children is negligent and cause for review.

Additionally, most of these studies are all-inclusive, lumping all parents who spank into the same broad category without consideration of why they spank or
65 how aggressive they may be. Studies of children who are only spanked when their disobedience could result in physical harm might show vastly different results than studies of children who are spanked daily. Furthermore, research on children who are swatted with an
70 open hand will show fewer, if any, long-term effects than research on children who are violently struck with a belt or switch. To conduct studies without qualifying the data is not only irresponsible, but unprofessional.

In our research, we studied 200 subjects who
75 received moderate spanking as a punishment as children. Nearly all of the interviewed subjects were well-adjusted adults—none of them expressed resentment toward their parents or indignation at their parents' choice of punishment—and those who were
80 maladjusted had other, more attributable causes for their dysfunction. It was clear that the long-term effects asserted by other studies were not a factor in children who received moderate spankings as a punishment. We surmise that other research projects on corporal punish-
85 ment with more narrow, focused parameters would yield very different results than the current, all-encompassing studies.

1. The first paragraph of Passage 1 suggests that parents who quote the adage in line 1 believe that

   A) they are citing a Biblical reference.
   B) stoning and drowning are still acceptable forms of punishment.
   C) spanking is an unacceptable form of discipline.
   D) spanking is more effective than positive reinforcement.

2. The author of Passage 1 cites "stoning, drawing and quartering, and drowning" to suggest that

   A) spanking is the only acceptable form of punishment from the 1600s.
   B) spanking is equally as primitive.
   C) the emotional toll of spanking on children is worse than experts originally predicted.
   D) moderate spanking was a preferred method of discipline for parents in the 17th century.

3. By citing the "true source" (line 33) of spanking, the author of Passage 1 implies that

   A) anger frequently results in violence.
   B) workplace abuse is common among parents who spank their children.
   C) parents are dishonest about the reason they spank their children.
   D) the parents themselves were spanked as children.

4. In line 70, the phrase "if any" suggests that the author

   A) found few parents who spank with a closed fist.
   B) prefers spanking with belts over an open hand.
   C) conducted a study with more focused specifications.
   D) believes an open-handed swat is not likely to affect the welfare of a child.

5. In Passage 2, it can be inferred that one indication of an adult being "maladjusted" (line 80) is

   A) not believing in any form of discipline.
   B) using spanking as the primary discipline method on one's own children.
   C) lying to avoid consequences.
   D) harboring a grudge against one's parents.

6. The author of Passage 2 would most likely characterize the "clinical studies" (line 27) in Passage 1 as

   A) accurate.
   B) unscientific.
   C) too broad.
   D) out-of-date.

7. The "specialist" (line 13) in Passage 1 and the "experts" (line 52) in Passage 2 would most likely agree on which of the following statements?

   A) Spanking leads to dishonesty.
   B) Spanking with an open hand is an acceptable punishment.
   C) Children who are only spanked in moderation become well-adjusted adults
   D) Spanking has lasting consequences.

8. Passage 2 as a whole suggests that its author would react to Passage 1 with

   A) ambivalence.
   B) objection.
   C) whimsy.
   D) compliance.

Advanced Questions

Advanced questions require you to apply information from the passage to statements or evidence not presented in the passage. They are extremely rare on the current versions of the ACT and SAT. We would be remiss, however, if we didn't cover them and suddenly a single question popped up on your test. But given their rarity, we recommend skipping this portion of the chapter if you have limited time to prepare for your test.

Parallel Reasoning Questions

Parallel Reasoning Questions ask you to determine which of five situations is most like a scenario in the passage.

Expect to see some of the following phrases in Parallel Reasoning Questions:

situation   most similar to   most analogous to   additional example

Consider some question examples:

1. Which of the following situations is most analogous to the "relationship" cited in the fourth paragraph?

2. The approach to cooking described in lines 54-60 is most similar to which of the following?

3. Which hypothetical situation involves the same "education" (line 61) discussed by the author?

Now consider a passage and question in more detail:

> The Bowl Championship Series (BCS) was a ranking system in place from 1998 until 2013 that determined the top ten teams in college football and then matched those teams in head-to-head games
> *Line* to determine the season's champion. The two top-ranked teams met
> 5 in a championship game, and thus were the only teams to have a shot at the title; the other eight ranked teams participated in "bowl games" that were inconsequential in determining a national champion.
> Critics of the system contended that it was inherently unfair because the rankings were partly determined by polls of sportswriters,
> 10 broadcasters, and coaches. This method was subjective, they said, allowing human opinion to have as much or more weight than factual data, namely a team's win-loss record. Many proposed that the NCAA develop a play-off system, much like college basketball's 64-team tournament, to definitively crown a national champion.
> 15 In 2014, the College Football Playoff debuted, which included a four-team play-off. Ironically, the four teams are now entirely determined by members of a committee, many of whom have never even played football, and thus many pundits are still critical of the system.

If you have a limited time to study prior to your test date, consider skipping this section. These question types appear infrequently.

Parallel Reasoning questions require you to choose a situation that is most similar to a situation in the passage.

1. Which of the following situations is most analogous to the "system" (line 8) in the passage?

    A) A girl is crowned Homecoming Queen because her parents bribed the person who counted votes.
    B) A president of the recycling club is elected by club members.
    C) The importance of each sports teams in a high school is ranked by the revenue it generates.
    D) A valedictorian is chosen based in part on a survey of teachers.

It is impossible to prephrase Parallel Reasoning questions.

To begin, review the argument from the passage about the *system.* You must understand it before you move on to the answer choices:

The Bowl Championship Series (BCS) was a ranking system in place from 1998 until 2013 that determined the top ten teams in college football and then matched those teams in head-to-head games to determine the season's champion.... Critics of the system contended that it was inherently unfair because the rankings were partly determined by polls of sportswriters, broadcasters, and coaches. This method was subjective, they said, allowing human opinion to have as much or more weight than factual data, namely a team's win-loss record.

Now, consider what you know.

The system is:
- for ranking the top teams (line 2)
- partly determined by polls of people in sports (lines 9-10)
- subjective, using opinion rather than just win-loss data (lines 10-12)

Now work through each answer choice and look for one that uses similar logic. You will find the correct answer is choice (D).

In choice (D), the situation presented is:
- for ranking the top student
- partly determined by polls of teachers
- subjective, using opinion rather than just GPA

Choice (D) presents a situation that is similar to the BCS system in the passage.

Choice (A) is incorrect because of the bribe. While you might wonder if some of the people polled for the BCS were bribed, the passage does not state or imply this.

Choice (B) is the most attractive wrong answer. However, an election of a president is not a ranking system nor does it involve any factual data.

Finally, answer choice (C) tricks many people because it is a ranking of sports teams. However, revenue is not mentioned in the passage. Be careful not to apply your personal knowledge of the BCS system (where revenue did play a part in non-BCS bowl games). If it's not stated or implied in the passage, it is irrelevant.

Parallel Reasoning questions require you to process four situations, searching for one that is similar to the scenario in the passage. To solve these questions, break each one down the way that we did here when determining which of the four answers presents an analogous situation.

Strengthen and Weaken Questions

On the SAT, Strengthen and Weaken Questions seem to have morphed into Command of Evidence Questions, which are covered in depth in the next chapter. This is not to say that they could never appear again in the form discussed on the following pages, so SAT test takers would be wise to review both sections. ACT test takers only need to cover them here.

Strengthen Questions ask you to select an answer choice that best supports an argument in a passage; Weaken Questions require you to choose an answer that challenges a position in the passage.

Both types of questions often use hypothetical situations with the phrase *if true*. But there is specialized vocabulary for each type of question as well.

Strengthen Questions most often use the following words:

supports　　　　substantiates　　　　strengthens

Examples of these questions include the following:

1. Which of the following, if true, would best support the "original idea" (line 25)?

2. The information in Passage 2 supports which assumption about the biologists in Passage 1?

3. Which statement about the Revolutionary War, if true, would most directly support the view described in the last paragraph?

Weaken Questions also have their own terms to indicate the question type:

refutes　　　　undermines　　　　disproves
detracts　　　　challenges　　　　weakens

Strengthen Questions require you to choose an example that bolsters the main idea of the passage or paragraph.

Weaken Questions ask you to choose an example that disproves the author's argument.

It is impossible to prephrase an answer to Strengthen and Weaken questions.

Consider several examples:

♦ GRATUITOUS VOCAB
undermine (vb):
to weaken or attack
detract (vb):
to take away from

4. Which of the following, if true, would most effectively undermine the "original idea" (line 25)?

5. Which of the following assertions detracts LEAST from the author's argument in the fourth paragraph?

6. Which statement about the Revolutionary War, if true, would most directly refute the view described in the last paragraph?

As you can see, the questions are very similar except for the word designating whether you are to strengthen or weaken an argument.

Let's examine these questions more closely:

In January, Smith Brothers Books released their new e-reader, the Novello. While it is an inexpensive option, the Novello is limited in its capabilities compared to other machines on the market. Its
Line biggest shortcoming is that it is only compatible with e-books sold
5 by the Smith Brothers, so owners are restricted in their choices of reading material. Works purchased from Amazon, Google, or other online retailers cannot be viewed on the Novello. Another issue involves display problems: the glare projected from the screen can affect readability, unlike the more expensive models available.
10 Finally, the Novello's screen only projects black and white images, which detracts from children's books, illustrated guides, and most novel covers. If given the option between one of the more expensive e-readers and the new Novello, we highly suggest selecting one of the better-known models.

1. Which of the following statements, if true, would best support the main idea of the passage?

A) Other e-readers have the potential need for technical support.
B) The Novello e-reader has the shortest battery life of all e-readers.
C) More expensive e-readers use more electricity than the Novello e-reader.
D) Smith Brothers Books is the third largest book distributor in the United States.

⹃TIPS and TRICKS⹃
To succeed on these questions, first determine the idea or argument that you are strengthening or weakening.

This Strengthen Question asks you to find the statement that adds the most support to the main idea. So you must determine the main idea before you continue. It occurs in lines 2-3: *the Novello is limited in its capabilities compared to other machines on the market.* So the correct answer will likely show how the Novello is limited compared to other e-readers. Can you find the answer that reveals another Novello weakness? Choice (B) is best.

Choice (A) actually weakens the main idea. If the Novello is worse than other e-readers, a statement about how those other e-readers are also limited chips away at the author's main idea.

Choice (C) is similar to (A) in that it reveals a weakness of the other e-readers, thus weakening the author's argument, not strengthening it.

Finally, Choice (D) is incorrect because that statement is irrelevant. It does not prove that Novello is more limited than other e-readers.

Consider the same passage, this time with a Weaken Question:

> In January, Smith Brothers Books released their new e-reader, the Novello. While it is an inexpensive option, the Novello is limited in its capabilities compared to other machines on the market. Its
> *Line* biggest shortcoming is that it is only compatible with e-books sold
> 5 by the Smith Brothers, so owners are restricted in their choices of reading material. Works purchased from Amazon, Google, or other online retailers cannot be viewed on the Novello. Another issue involves display problems: the glare projected from the screen can affect readability, unlike the more expensive models available.
> 10 Finally, the Novello's screen only projects black and white images, which detracts from children's books, illustrated guides, and most novel covers. If given the option between one of the more expensive e-readers and the new Novello, we highly suggest selecting one of the better-known models.

2. Which of the following statements, if true, would most directly undermine the author's argument about the Novello's "biggest shortcoming" (line 4)?

A) Many publishers have not made their books available in electronic form.
B) The Novello comes with an accessory shade to decrease glare.
C) Smith Brothers Books offers a greater selection of e-books than any other retailer.
D) The majority of e-reader owners prefer the Novello to other brands.

≡TIPS and TRICKS≡
It may help you to think of Weaken Questions as counterpoints in a debate. If you faced the author in a debate, which of the answer choices would you use to disprove his point?

Since the question asks you to weaken the argument about the "biggest shortcoming," you must first determine what that shortcoming is: *[the Novello] is only compatible with e-books sold by the Smith Brothers, so owners are restricted in their choices of reading material* (lines 4-6). Now analyze each answer, and ask yourself if it disproves the fact that people who own the Novello are limited in their choices of books.

Choice (A) applies to all e-readers, not just the Novello, so it does not weaken the argument about the biggest shortcoming.

Answer choice (B) does weaken the argument about the glare affecting readability, but this is not the *biggest shortcoming* of the Novello, so it is not the correct answer.

Choice (C) is the answer. If the Smith Brothers offer more e-books than anyone else, then the Novello owners are not limited in their choice of books. In fact, they have as many or more choices than owners of other e-readers. This statement most definitely weakens the argument about the biggest shortcoming of the Novello.

Choice (D) cites owner preferences. Preferences, however, have nothing to do with whether or not the owner has a limited selection of books.

To solve these questions, you must first determine the position of the argument or statement in the question stem. Once you understand what the author is asserting, you can then look at each answer choice and determine whether that answer choice strengthens, weakens, or is irrelevant to the author's argument.

Remember, the answer choices of Advanced Questions usually present information that is not in the passage, including in the correct answer. Whereas Literal Comprehension and other Extended Reasoning answer choices are wrong if new information is added to the answer choices, Advanced Questions ask you to determine which piece of new information strengthens, weakens, or parallels a statement in question.

Weaken Questions are among the most difficult on the ACT and SAT because they require our brains to work "backwards."

Advanced Questions Problem Set

Read the passage below and then answer the corresponding Strengthen, Weaken, and Parallel Reasoning questions. Answers begin on page 277.

The following passage is adapted from Angela Somma, "The Environmental Consequences and Economic Costs of Depleting the Oceans." 2003.

Over the past decade, it became increasingly clear that fisheries resources that were once thought of as nearly inexhaustible had been severely overfished as
Line one fishery after another experienced serious decline.
5 The once-abundant fisheries of bottom-dwelling fish such as cod in New England and eastern Canada were decimated, giant tuna species in the Atlantic were depressed to levels that jeopardized rebuilding, and several species of Pacific and Atlantic salmon were
10 placed on the U.S. endangered species list. And the problem persists. In October 2002, an international scientific advisory commission recommended that all fisheries targeting cod in the North Sea, Irish Sea and waters west of Scotland be closed. Overfishing
15 has obvious detrimental effects on the stocks being overharvested, but it can also harm the ecosystem in which those stocks live and cause economic hardship to fishermen and their communities.

The environmental consequences of overfishing are
20 many and include reduced harvests of the targeted fish, excessive unintentional harvest of non-targeted, under-sized or protected species, and ecosystems changes.

Persistent overfishing can lead to the elimination of the largest and oldest individuals from a population
25 or stock. Overfished populations are characterized by less-productive fish that eventually lead to a decline in stocks. In the United States, recent average yields of all U.S. fisheries resources are roughly 60 percent of the best estimate of long-term potential yield from these
30 resources.

Harvest of non-targeted animals, or bycatch, is estimated to constitute about one-quarter of the global fish catch. Bycatch comprises all of the animals that are caught but not wanted or used, or are required to be
35 discarded by management regulation. It may include specially protected species such as marine mammals or endangered species, juvenile individuals too small to be marketed, or other species of fish without commercial or recreational value to the fisher. The unwanted species
40 are usually discarded, often dead, either at sea or on shore. Various types of fishing gear are non-selective and can ensnare unwanted catch. Purse seine nets can catch juvenile fish and marine mammals such as

dolphins. Longlines catch seabirds, sea turtles, and
45 non-targeted fish along with the targeted catch. Gillnets can also catch seabirds, and lost or discarded gillnets can continue to catch and kill marine animals through what is known as "ghost fishing." Trawls are a particularly non-selective type of gear and can take consider-
50 able bycatch of many different species. In addition, concern is also growing about the changes trawls can make to fish habitat. They are often dragged along the bottom of the seabed and may damage habitat.

Overfishing can have broader adverse effects on
55 the ecosystem as well. As noted above, in the 1990s total world catch reached a plateau. In some cases, this plateau in production was maintained by changes in species composition and by "fishing down the food chain." Top predatory species tend to be fished for first.
60 Once depleted, fishing moves down the food chain and can simplify the marine ecosystem. This, along with environmental changes to important habitat areas, can affect future fish production levels.

Overfishing can cause changes in marine food
65 webs, adversely affecting other species. For example, the decline of Steller sea lions in Alaska has been attributed in part to overfishing of the Stellers' main food sources: pollock, cod, and mackerel. Overfishing
70 also has the potential to indirectly change ecosystems such as coral reef ecosystems. When plant-eating fish are removed from coral reef ecosystems, grazing is reduced, allowing the algae that coexist with corals to flourish and potentially take over, especially if the water
75 contains high levels of nitrogen. Because they often reduce light that enters the water, these algae contribute to the loss of corals, which depend upon light.

1. Which of the following, if true, most effectively undermines the author's argument in the first sentence of the passage?

   A) The grouper and snapper fisheries were closed in Florida.
   B) Scientists discovered that bottom-dwelling, giant tuna, and salmon populations were decimated by disease.
   C) Australia's Great Coral Reef is home to over 1500 species of tropical fish.
   D) The world's population of bottlenose dolphins has decreased slightly since the 1970s.

2. Which of the following, if true, would most directly disprove one of the author's arguments in lines 14-18 ("Overfishing . . . communities")?

   A) Fisherman can target other lucrative species still in abundance if their current target species becomes overfished.
   B) Fishing communities have suffered major financial hardships in the last ten years.
   C) The North Sea cod fishery was reopened shortly after it closed in 2002.
   D) Algae is eaten by many species of fish.

3. Which of the following, if true, best substantiates the claim in the second paragraph?

   A) Fisherman report that their yields of the coveted halibut have decreased by 80% in ten years.
   B) Marine ecosystems are resilient and can withstand changes to the fisheries.
   C) Technological innovations have decreased bycatch by as much as 50%.
   D) Populations of bottom-dwelling fish have been known to recover when a fishery is closed.

4. Which of the following situations is most similar to the "harvest of non-targeted animals" (line 31)?

   A) A hair stylist takes on a new client who then recommends the salon to three friends.
   B) A teacher selects an underachieving student to represent the class in the spelling bee.
   C) A deer hunter intentionally targets a small doe rather than a larger buck.
   D) A farmer accidentally culls part of her immature soybean crop when reaping her wheat crop.

5. Which of the following, if true, would most directly support the view described in lines 69-71 ("Overfishing . . . ecosystems")?

   A) Bycatch yields increase by 25%.
   B) A species that eats coral quickly destroys a reef when the species' only natural predator is overfished.
   C) The wakes from boat traffic erodes coral reefs in shallow waters.
   D) Fisheries around coral reefs are closed to allow populations to rebound.

6. The result of "the loss of corals" (line 77) is most similar to a potential issue caused by which of the following types of "fishing gear" (line 41)?

   A) Purse seine nets
   B) Longlines
   C) Gillnets
   D) Trawls

Chapter Summary

Extended Reasoning Questions require you to draw conclusions based on information in the passage. There are three types of Extended Reasoning Questions:

Style Questions

★ Purpose Questions
- You must determine the function of a word, phrase, sentence, paragraph, or passage.
- Understanding purpose verbs can help you eliminate answer choices.
- An author's primary purpose is to argue against, to argue for, or to explain an idea.

★ Author's Attitude Questions
- The tone of a sentence, paragraph, or passage is the author's attitude toward his subject.
- Noting attitude clues as you read can help you identify the attitude at the end of the passage.
- Understanding attitude words can help you eliminate wrong answers.

★ Rhetorical Devices
- You may be asked to identify or describe the function of a rhetorical device.
- Understanding the different types of rhetorical devices is essential to your success on these questions.

Inference Questions

★ General Inference Questions
- These are the most common Extended Reasoning questions.
- You must draw a conclusion based on a portion of the passage. There is only a single conclusion you can draw on ACT and SAT inferences, unlike in real life conversations.
- It may be easier to eliminate wrong inferences than to select the correct one.

★ Hypothetical Point of View Questions
- These questions ask you to predict a person's response to a specific idea.
- Hypothetical questions are most common in paired passages.
- Prephrasing is key to answering these questions correctly.

Advanced Questions

★ <u>Parallel Reasoning Questions</u>
  - These questions are extremely rare on the current ACT and SAT.
  - You are required to choose a situation that is most similar to a situation in the passage.
  - It is impossible to prephrase Parallel Reasoning Questions.

★ <u>Strengthen and Weaken Questions</u>
  - This type of question is rare on the ACT and appears more often as a Command of Evidence question on the SAT.
  - You are required to choose an example that supports or detracts from an author's argument.
  - It is important that you understand the argument before trying to determine that which supports or undermines it.
  - It is nearly impossible to prephrase Strengthen and Weaken Questions.

<u>Confidence Quotation</u>
"Thinking is the hardest work there is, which is probably the reason why so few engage in it."
-Henry Ford

EXTENDED REASONING QUESTIONS ANSWER KEY

Style Questions Problem Set—Page 254

1. (A) Prephrase: to show the advantages and disadvantages of web banners

    Primary Purpose Question: The first two paragraphs are about the benefits of using web banners. The last paragraph presents a potential problem with the technology, however. Only answer choice (A) addresses both ideas. Note that the correct answer is very broad. It uses *common advertising strategy* rather than *web banner*. Most primary purpose questions tend to have correct answer choices that are general, avoiding specifics from the passage.

    Answer choice (B) is incorrect because it adds information about small businesses and it does not emphasize the importance of these banners.

    Choice (C) is the most attractive wrong answer. But it is incorrect because the passage states *web banners are one of the oldest forms of online advertising* (lines 2-3). Notice that it uses the phrase *information technology* from line 1.

    Choice (D) should be suspicious immediately because of *refute*. The author is not arguing against anything.

2. (D) Prephrase: Difficult to prephrase, but one might say *statement* or *opinion*

    Literary Devices Question: Read only the line reference provided! The use of the phrase *clearly superior* is key. The author is confident in his opinion, so answer choice (D) is correct.

    It is not an *apology* (A) or an *aside* (C). And while a case can be made for the statement being a *conjecture*, it is not *scientific* (B).

3. (C) Prephrase: Show why web banners are better than television commercials

    Purpose Question: The author is listing reasons why the web banner is superior to traditional mass media. The first reason is that web banners reach millions instantly (lines 7-8). The second is that it involves user input (line 11), unlike television. This shows the limitation of television commercials.

    The author does not *urge* (A) or *challenge* (B). He does not say that web banners will replace television or vice versa (D).

4. (B) Prephrase: Show another reason web banners are superior

    Purpose Question: The claim made earlier in the passage is *banner ads are clearly superior to traditional mass media* (lines 4-5). This sentence is providing support for that claim.

    Choice (A) is the most commonly chosen wrong answer, but the word *doomed* makes it wrong. Choice (C) is an Opposite Answer. A process is described later in the second paragraph (D), but whether it is a *difficult* process is a matter of opinion, and it has nothing to do with the topic sentence.

5. (C) Prephrase: introduce new terms

    Literary Devices Question: While *impression* is a common word, it is being used in a new way. A *click-through event* is specialized to online advertising and likely unknown by most readers.

6. (C) Prephrase: somewhat negative; issuing a warning

    Author's Attitude Question: The final sentence is a warning, so the tone is cautionary.

7. (C) Prephrase: Show a drawback of advertising with web banners

    Purpose Question: The final paragraph explains a problem that can occur with web banners if advertisers are not careful. Therefore, choice (C) is correct.

    (A) is incorrect because no summary is provided. Choice (B) is wildly off-base; the author never criticizes the beliefs of a profession in the passage. And choice (D) is wrong because the author supports the use of web banners in the first two paragraphs.

8. (A) Prephrase: respect, positive, approval

    Author's Attitude Question: The author indicates that web banners are *clearly superior* (line 5) and that they have *attractive feature(s)* (line 14). Even when he discusses the issue with click-through events, he places responsibility on the user, not the web banner itself.

9. (A) Prephrase: a discussion about the reason people use web banners to a discussion about how click-through rates should be used with deliberation.

    Passage Organization Question: The first paragraph describes several reasons that web banners are effective advertising tools. The second paragraph describes the best reason—click-through rates. And the third paragraph cautions users to not read too much into click-through rates without deliberate analysis. The best answer is (A).

    Choice (B) is incorrect because there is no *study* and the "experts" in line 24 are not criticized (plus, we do not know if these *experts* are *researchers*). Choice (C) is tricky because the second paragraph does present *an evaluation of the largest advantage of a business* <u>strategy</u> (not necessarily a *plan*), but the other advantages are listed before the second paragraph, not after. The correct answer will include all three paragraphs and show the shift from beginning to end, not from the middle to the beginning. Choice (D) is wrong because the background of the *experts* in line 24 is not discussed.

Inference Questions Problem Set—Page 262

1. (A) Prephrase: They are citing the Christian Bible

    General Inference: The inference comes from *unaware that they are citing not the Christian Bible, but rather a poem*. This infers that people believe the quote is from the Bible. Notice that (B) leaves out *drawing and quartering*, although it is incorrect based on what it says anyway. No one in the passage believes those punishments are acceptable, which is why they are no longer in use. While the author of Passage 1 believes (C), the parents he discusses in the first paragraph use spanking, so they do not believe (C). Choice (D) introduces positive reinforcement, which is not mentioned in the passage.

2. (B)   Prephrase: This is difficult to prephrase, as many inference questions are.

General Inference: The author notes that these punishments are no longer in use, but that spanking, another form of punishment in the 17th century, still is. He is suggesting that it is equally archaic and barbaric. The best answer is (B). Choice (A) is attractive, but wrong, because the author believes spanking is not acceptable. Don't let your personal beliefs or the beliefs of others influence your choice, or you fall into a True To You trap. Choice (C) uses wording from later in the passage (*the emotional toll of spanking on children*), but no predictions were made in the passage. Finally, (D) is wrong because it brings in moderate spanking from Passage 2, an idea not discussed in Passage 1.

3. (C)   Prephrase: The mother provides a different reason for spanking.

General Inference: In the rhetorical question in lines 33-34, the author reveals the reason that "Mommy" gives for spanking. Then he provides the *true source*, which is different than Mommy's reason. Therefore, the parent is dishonest about her reason for spanking. In choice (A), the word *frequently* is Extreme and the author does not make this blanket statement for the world's population (not everyone becomes violent when angry). Choice (B) takes a workplace reference in line 37 and exaggerates it. Choice (D) is never mentioned or inferred in the passage.

4. (D)   Prephrase: There rarely are long-term effects from swatting with an open hand.

General Inference: The phrase *if any* expresses the author's skepticism by suggesting there are no cases of people who were affected long-term by open hand swatting. Choice (A) tries to trick you with the word *few*, but the author does not discuss looking for parents or closed fists. Choice (B) is an Opposite Answer. The author never quite reveals how he feels about spanking with belts and switches, but you can infer that he believes it is a worse punishment than moderate spanking. Choice (C) is True but Wrong. The author did conduct a more focused study, but that is discussed in the final paragraph, and *if any* has nothing to do with it.

5. (D)   Prephrase: Having resentment or indignation

General Inference: The inference occurs in the portion separated by dashes: *none of them expressed resentment toward their parents or indignation at their parents' choice of punishment*. The passage infers that these two facts were signs of the subjects' well-being, so if they had expressed either resentment or indignation, that would have been a sign of maladjustment. The best answer is (D), as harboring a grudge means holding on to resentment. Answers (A) and (B) were not discussed in the passage and choice (C) was only discussed in Passage 1 (and then it was listed as an indication of maladjustment for adults).

6. (C)   Prephrase: Being all-inclusive/not studying if the "symptoms" occurred before spanking

Hypothetical Point of View: The author of Passage 2 thinks that most studies on spanking have included too many subjects without narrowing the focus. He also believes that the researchers failed to determine whether children who were spanked experienced depression and aggression before they were spanked. So he is not going to approve of a study unless it is narrowly focused. Therefore, answer choice (C) is correct. Choice (A) is an Opposite Answer. Choice (B) uses the term *unscientific* to try to get you to mentally connect it to *clinical studies*. While *scientific* and *clinical* may be related vocabulary words, they have nothing to do with each other in this passage. Choice (D) mirrors *archaic* in Passage 1 to try to trick you, but this is not how the author of Passage 2 feels about the clinical studies.

7.   (D)   Prephrase: The effects of spanking continue into adulthood

Hypothetical Point of View: The specialist states that spanking leads to lying, which *is a habit that many will carry into adulthood*. The experts in Passage 2 *claim that spanking children leads to depressed adults who lack self-control and are violently aggressive*. So they both agree that the effects of spanking continue into adulthood. Choice (D) most closely matches this prephrase. Choice (A) is true for the specialist, but not for the experts. Choices (B) and (C) are true for the author of Passage 2, but he is not the topic of this question.

8.   (B)   Prephrase: disapproval, rejection, scorn.

Hypothetical Point of View: This question is difficult because of the vocabulary, not the content. The author of Passage 2 would find the main idea of Passage 1 as wrong given the broad studies conducted to come to that conclusion. He would reject the ideas in Passage 1 as untrue.

Objection means *disagreement or opposition.*

Vocabulary:
ambivalence: mixed feelings
whimsy: carefree humor

compliance: the act of cooperating or yielding

Advanced Questions Problem Set—Page 270

1.   (B)   Prephrase: It is impossible to prephrase this question.

Weaken Question: Consider the argument in the first sentence: *fisheries that were once thought of as nearly inexhaustible had been severely overfished*. Which answer choice weakens this argument? The answer is (B). If the fish that the author cited as having been overfished actually died of disease, then they are not good examples to support her claim.

Choices (A) and (D) support her claim, although (D) is a weak example. Choice (C) is the most commonly selected wrong answer because it seems to portray that fish are thriving in the Great Barrier reef. But you cannot assume this. Maybe all 1500 species are endangered, or maybe none of the species are targeted in fishing.

2.   (A)   Prephrase: It is impossible to prephrase this question.

Weaken Question: The question indicates that there is more than one argument in the line reference, so determine the different arguments:
   1. Overfishing has detrimental effects on stocks.
   2. Overfishing can also harm the ecosystem.
   3. Overfishing can cause economic hardship to fishermen and their communities.

Now work through each answer choice to find the one that weakens one of these arguments. The answer is (A). If fishermen can target other species and make money, then it is unlikely that they or their communities will suffer economic hardship.

None of the other answer choices prove any of the assertions wrong. Choice (B) actually supports the third argument. The remaining two choices are irrelevant to the three arguments in the statement.

3. (A)   Prephrase: It is impossible to prephrase this question.

    Strengthen Question: The second paragraph is a single sentence, which is the entire claim: the consequences of overfishing include reduced harvests of the targeted fish, unintentional harvest of non-targeted fish, and ecosystem changes. The answer choice that provides an example of one of these consequences is answer choice (A): *Fisherman report that their yields of the coveted halibut have decreased by 80% in ten years.* It is a perfect example of *reduced harvests of the targeted fish.*

    Choices (B) and (C) weaken specific points of the author's argument. If these things are true, then overfishing is not as serious as she says it is. Choice (D) is an irrelevant statement, that neither supports nor undermines her argument.

4. (D)   Prephrase: It is impossible to prephrase this question.

    Parallel Reasoning Question: Analyze the lines around line 31 to determine what you know about the harvest of non-targeted species.

    Bycatch:
    * constitutes about 1/4 of the global catch.
    * comprises all of the animals that are caught but not wanted or used.
    * may include protected species, juvenile individuals, or those without value.
    * is discarded.

    Now, which answer is most similar? Answer choice (D).

    The soybeans:
    * were accidentally culled so they are not wanted
    * are immature, so they are discarded like juvenile individuals of fish species

5. (B)   Prephrase: It is impossible to prephrase this question.

    Strengthen Question: Consider the view: *Overfishing also has the potential to indirectly change ecosystems such as coral reef ecosystems.* Which of the answer choices provides proof that overfishing has changed a ecosystem? Answer choice (D). If a species destroys a reef, that ecosystem has changed. If the species was able to destroy this reef because its natural predator was overfished, then it's an indirect change.

    Choice (A) is not about ecosystems. Choice (C) does indicate a changing ecosystem, but the direct cause is boat traffic; we need an answer where the indirect cause is overfishing. Choice (D) does not indicate any change in an ecosystem.

6. (D)   Prephrase: It is impossible to prephrase this question.

    Parallel Reasoning Question: What is the result of the loss of corals? The loss or destruction of habitat or ecosystems.

    Which type of fishing gear from the fourth paragraph causes the loss or destruction of habitat or ecosystems? The trawls *may damage habitat* (line 53). The other three answer choices only threaten birds or marine life.

CHAPTER FOURTEEN
EXCLUSIVE SAT CONTENT

With the redesign of the SAT in 2016, the test makers added two new question types that are not currently included on the ACT Reading test: Command of Evidence Reading questions and Command of Evidence Charts and Graphs questions. So if you are only planning on taking the ACT, you can skip this chapter unless you want to read the Charts and Graphs portion beginning on page 296. This section will provide ACT test takers with strategy suggestions and additional practice for the ACT Science test.

Although new to the SAT, the Command of Evidence Reading questions are not unprecedented on standardized tests. The GRE General Test, which is required for admission to graduate school, asks test takers to select portions of the text that provide evidence for specific questions. The GRE is administered by Educational Testing Services (ETS), who previously created content for the SAT and now serves in a consulting role for the College Board, so it's no surprise that there are similarities between the two tests.

The addition of Charts and Graphs questions to the Reading, Writing and Language, and Math sections of the SAT was an attempt by the College Board to bring the SAT more in line with the ACT, which has a dedicated Science section that uses tables, charts, graphs, and figures. This way the SAT now has a Science score based on infographics about Science passages from across the three subject areas, so the test is better able to compete with the ACT when state departments of education or colleges express a need for science scores. Ironically, your knowledge of Science has little to do with mastery of these questions on either test, as they are more about your ability to analyze data—a math skill—and to connect data to passages—a reading skill. Your SAT Social Studies score is also an assessment of these abilities more so than your knowledge of history or social science.

Both Command of Evidence Reading questions and Command of Evidence Charts and Graphs questions make up a substantial portion of your Reading score, so it's important to review this chapter carefully if you are taking the SAT. Let's get started.

◎ SAT ONLY ◎
This chapter pertains only to SAT question types.

Confidence Quotation
"Science is simply common sense at its best."
-Thomas Huxley, English biologist

Command of Evidence: Reading

Having a "Command of Evidence" in Reading is the College Board's grandiose way of describing whether a test taker is able to pinpoint which line of text answers a specific question. These questions may be intimidating to the untrained student, but we have several tips and tricks to help you.

Best Evidence Paired Questions (Literal Comprehension)

The majority of Command of Evidence Questions are paired with the question immediately preceding it. Let's consider a simplified example:

Best Evidence Paired Questions are extremely common on the SAT. You can expect 8 to 10 question pairs (for a total of 16 to 20 questions) per test.

> Mary had a little lamb, whose fleece was white as snow. And everywhere that Mary went, the lamb was sure to go.
>
> *Line*
> 5   It followed her to school one day which was against the rule. It made the children laugh and play, to see a lamb at school.
>
> And so the teacher turned it out, but still it lingered near, and waited patiently about, till Mary did appear.
>
> "Why does the lamb love Mary so?" the eager
> 10 children cry. "Why, Mary loves the lamb, you know," the teacher did reply.

1. According to the passage, where did the lamb pursue Mary?

    A) To a tract of wooded land.
    B) To a building housing livestock.
    C) To her place of employment.
    D) To an academic institution.

2. Which choice provides the best evidence for the answer to the previous question?

    A) Lines 1-2 ("Mary . . . snow")
    B) Lines 2-3 ("And . . . go")
    C) Lines 4-5 ("It . . . rule")
    D) Lines 7-8 ("And so . . . appear")

Literal Comprehension questions are those that ask you about a fact or detail stated in the passage.

The first question is a Literal Comprehension Facts and Details question, and the second question is a Command of Evidence question, which wants to know *where* you found the answer to the first question. The right answer to the second question is basically a rephrasing of the right answer to the first question:

Question 1: Correct answer (D)
Where did the lamb pursue Mary? To her academic institution.

Question 2: Correct answer (C)
"It followed her to school one day which was against the rule."

The question and the correct answer in number 1 use synonyms for the words in the correct answer for question 2:

Question 1: Correct answer (D)
Where did the lamb <u>pursue</u> Mary? To her <u>academic institution</u>.

Question 2: Correct answer (C)
"It <u>followed</u> her to <u>school</u> one day which was against the rule."

Followed is the word in the text, but it's replaced by *pursue* in the question; similarly, *school* is the word in the text but it's replaced by *academic institution* in the correct answer. The answers to Best Evidence Paired Questions will always say the exact same thing, but usually with synonyms and rephrasings.

Paired Command of Evidence questions are a 2-for-1 special; if you answer the first question correctly, it's likely that you will also correctly answer the second question. Of course, the reverse is true, too: if you miss the first question, you are apt to miss the second one. Luckily, though, you can use the second question to help you find or confirm the correct answer for the first question, so they are actually a welcome addition to the SAT for knowledgeable test takers.

Best Evidence questions can follow both Literal Comprehension questions or Extended Reasoning Inference questions. We will focus on Literal Comprehension as we begin to discuss strategy options and then show how they accompany Extended Reasoning Inference questions later in this section.

Best Evidence questions can occur with both Literal Comprehension and Extended Reasoning questions.

When you finish reading an SAT passage, you should quickly note any Best Evidence Paired Questions before answering the first question. This is easy to do with a quick glance at the questions, as they all look like question 2 on the previous page: the answers are four line references with the first and last word of the reference in quotation marks. It's rare for a passage and all 10 or 11 of its questions to fit on a two-page spread of the test booklet, so you need to flip a page or two to look for all instances of paired questions. On average, there are two per passage.

Mark the first question in each paired set with "PQ" for "paired question" so that when you come to one while working, you know to use the strategies you are about to learn on the following pages. By doing so, you can save yourself some time and potential redundancy when you begin to answer them.

There are three possible solution strategies for answering the first Literal Comprehension question in a set of Best Evidence Paired Questions:

Strategy 1: Know the answer to the question.

≑TIPS and TRICKS≑
Strategy 1: Know and locate the answer based on your initial reading of the passage.

In an ideal world, you will read a question and know the answer just based on your first reading of the passage. You will also likely know where the answer is located in the passage, even without a line reference, because your sidebar summaries make the answer easy to locate. If you don't know where the answer is, you quickly check the four line references in the second question and easily answer this question as well.

Again, this is an ideal strategy and it's probably best suited for advanced students or highly skilled readers. But even if you consider yourself an astute reader, you will likely want to combine this strategy with the next one. Our instructors are top scorers on the SAT Reading section and most of them use a combination of Strategy 1 and Strategy 2.

Strategy 2: Use the 2nd question to locate the answer to the 1st question.

≑TIPS and TRICKS≑
Strategy 2: Use the line references in the second question to locate the answer to the first question.

If you do not immediately know the answer to the first question, you can use the second question to find it. Let's look at an example to see how this strategy works in an 1815 Literary Fiction passage from Jane Austen:

♦ GRATUITOUS VOCAB
vex (vb): irritate
indulgent (adj): lenient; granting desires
nominal (adj): in name only
esteeming (vb): regarding with respect
alloy (n): mixture

Emma Woodhouse, handsome, clever, and rich, with a comfortable home and happy disposition, seemed to unite some of the best blessings of existence; and had lived nearly twenty-one years in the
Line world with very little to distress or vex her.
5   She was the youngest of the two daughters of a most affectionate, indulgent father; and had, in consequence of her sister's marriage, been mistress of his house from a very early period. Her mother had died too long ago for her to have more than an indistinct remembrance of her caresses; and her place had been supplied by an
10   excellent woman as governess, who had fallen little short of a mother in affection.
        Sixteen years had Miss Taylor been in Mr. Woodhouse's family, less as a governess than a friend, very fond of both daughters, but particularly of Emma. Between them it was more the intimacy of
15   sisters. Even before Miss Taylor had ceased to hold the nominal office of governess, the mildness of her temper had hardly allowed her to impose any restraint; and the shadow of authority being now long passed away, they had been living together as friend and friend very mutually attached, and Emma doing just what she liked; highly
20   esteeming Miss Taylor's judgment, but directed chiefly by her own.
        The real evils, indeed, of Emma's situation were the power of having rather too much her own way, and a disposition to think a little too well of herself; these were the disadvantages which threatened alloy to her many enjoyments. The danger, however, was
25   at present so unperceived, that they did not by any means rank as misfortunes with her.

Sorrow came—a gentle sorrow—but not at all in the shape of any disagreeable consciousness.—Miss Taylor married. It was Miss Taylor's loss which first brought grief. It was on the wedding-day
30 of this beloved friend that Emma first sat in mournful thought of any continuance. The wedding over, and the bride-people gone, her father and herself were left to dine together, with no prospect of a third to cheer a long evening. Her father composed himself to sleep after dinner, as usual, and she had then only to sit and think of what
35 she had lost.

The event had every promise of happiness for her friend. Mr. Weston was a man of unexceptionable character, easy fortune, suitable age, and pleasant manners; and there was some satisfaction in considering with what self-denying, generous friendship she
40 had always wished and promoted the match; but it was a black morning's work for her. The want of Miss Taylor would be felt every hour of every day. She recalled her past kindness—the kindness, the affection of sixteen years—how she had taught and how she had played with her from five years old—how she had devoted all
45 her powers to attach and amuse her in health—and how nursed her through the various illnesses of childhood. A large debt of gratitude was owing here; but the intercourse of the last seven years, the equal footing and perfect unreserve which had soon followed Isabella's marriage, on their being left to each other, was yet a dearer, tenderer
50 recollection. She had been a friend and companion such as few possessed: intelligent, well-informed, useful, gentle, knowing all the ways of the family, interested in all its concerns, and peculiarly interested in herself, in every pleasure, every scheme of hers—one to whom she could speak every thought as it arose, and who had such
55 an affection for her as could never find fault.

How was she to bear the change? —It was true that her friend was going only half a mile from them; but Emma was aware that great must be the difference between a Mrs. Weston, only half a mile from them, and a Miss Taylor in the house; and with all her advantages,
60 natural and domestic, she was now in great danger of suffering from intellectual solitude. She dearly loved her father, but he was no companion for her. He could not meet her in conversation, rational or playful.

↳ GRATUITOUS VOCAB

intercourse (n): discussion
unreserve (adj): openness; candor
domestic (adj): pertaining to the household

1. According to the passage, which event initially brought Emma sadness?

   A) Her governess's marriage
   B) Her sister's departure
   C) Her mother's death
   D) Her father's retirement

2. Which choice provides the best evidence for the answer to the previous question?

   A) Lines 5-7 ("She . . . period")
   B) Lines 7-11 ("Her . . . affection")
   C) Lines 28-29 ("It . . . grief")
   D) Lines 33-35 ("Her . . . lost")

Paraphrase the first question: *What first made Emma sad?* This is a Literal Comprehension question, and like most questions paired with a Best Evidence question, it is very specific. It asks not just what made Emma sad, but what FIRST made her sad.

TIPS and TRICKS

If you do not know the answer to the first question in a Best Evidence paired set, skip to the line references in the second question. Return to the passage to read each one and look for the one that answers your paraphrase to the first question.

Let's say you have no idea what the answer is (even though we're betting you do, because you're an intelligent student who has almost completed *The PowerScore ACT and SAT Reading Bible*). It's time to use Solution Strategy 2: skip to the line references in the second question and look for the one that answers your paraphrase to the first question: *What first made Emma sad?*

A) Lines 5-7: *What first made Emma sad?* "She was the youngest of the two daughters of a most affectionate, indulgent father; and had, in consequence of her sister's marriage, been mistress of his house from a very early period."

This statement does not express anything about sadness, and is thus the wrong answer. Note, however, that it does indirectly mention Emma's sister's departure—her sister left when she got married, leaving Emma the mistress of the house. This answer is provided to trick you into selecting choice (B), "Her sister's departure," in the first question.

B) Lines 7-11: *What first made Emma sad?* "Her mother had died too long ago for her to have more than an indistinct remembrance of her caresses; and her place had been supplied by an excellent woman as governess, who had fallen little short of a mother in affection."

Beware of a True to You answer trap! It seems only natural that the loss of her mother would make Emma sad, but there is nothing about sadness in this statement. If anything, it seems that Emma is indifferent to her mother's death since she cannot remember it clearly and she had an excellent governess take her mother's place. Note again how this answer is designed to partially align with answer choice (C), "Her mother's death," in the first question.

C) Lines 28-29: *What first made Emma sad?* "It was Miss Taylor's loss which first brought grief."

Aha! *What first made Emma sad?* Miss Taylor's loss. And how did she lose her? She got married. The correct answer to the first question is choice (A), Her governess's marriage. And the correct answer to the second question is (C), Lines 28-29.

Notice that the first question and its correct answer choice use synonyms for the words in the actual text. Compare the two:

Question 1: Correct answer (A)
Which event <u>initially</u> brought Emma <u>sadness</u>? <u>Her governess's</u> marriage.

Question 2: Correct answer (C)
"It was <u>Miss Taylor's</u> loss which <u>first</u> brought <u>grief</u>."

Initially is substituted for *first*, *sadness* is in place for *grief*, and *her governess's* is used for *Miss Taylor's*.

The SAT relies heavily on synonyms in the correct answer and uses words from the text in incorrect Copycat Answers.

☙ CAUTION: TEST TRAP
Watch Best Evidence questions for incorrect Copycat Answers!

D) Lines 33-35: *What first made Emma sad?* "Her father composed himself to sleep after dinner, as usual, and she had then only to sit and think of what she had lost."

We know from the end of the passage that Emma's father was not a good companion, which compounded the loss of Miss Taylor. But the passage does not mention his retirement from a place of employment which is what you would assume was meant by answer choice (D), "Her father's retirement," in the first question. In this context, it can be interpreted as his *retirement* to bed, but nothing is mentioned in this particular line reference about Emma's sadness.

The correct answer to the second question—Choice (C)—so clearly answers the first question that we could choose it as the correct answer and move on without searching out the line reference in answer choice (D). But for the sake of fully understanding these types of questions and their common traps, we examined it in detail here. On your test, however, confidently select your answer choice as soon as you find one that answers the first question and then move on.

⊰TIPS and TRICKS⊱
When using Strategy 2 to answer the first question in a paired Best Evidence set, move on without reading the remaining choices once you are confident you have found the answer.

Solution Strategy 3: Use the surrounding line references to guess.

Unlike the ACT, the SAT has the habit of presenting questions that progress chronologically with the passage. For example, the first question may be about lines 3-5, the second question about lines 5-15, the third question about lines 23-24, the fourth question about lines 39-44, and so on. Questions about the passage as a whole, such as main idea or primary purpose questions, may occur as the first couple of questions, but questions about specific portions of the passage tend to progress in the manner indicated above. As with most of the patterns on the SAT, there are exceptions to every rule, but for the most part, you can expect the first few questions to be about the beginning of a passage, the intermediate questions to be about the middle of the passage, and the final questions to be about the end of the passage.

⊰TIPS and TRICKS⊱
Strategy 3: When Strategy 1 and 2 fail and you do not know the answer, use the line references in the surrounding questions to make an educated guess.

So when you are completely stumped on a Best Evidence Paired question (or have less than a minute to complete the section), you have a third last-ditch strategy at your disposal; predict where an answer is located based on the line references in previous and subsequent questions.

Let's take a look at the first six questions from a passage on an officially released test to see how this works. We've paraphrased the questions below but have excluded the passage because it's not needed for this "if-all-else-fails" strategy.

1. The main issue that the author describes in the passage is that   ⟵ Entire passage

TIPS and TRICKS
When guessing on the second question of a Best Evidence paired set, pick the answer choice that has a line reference between a previous question's line reference and a subsequent question's line reference.

2. The author uses the phrase "high carnival" (**line 15**) primarily to   ⟵ Line 15

3. The author claims that which of the following was a recent advancement?

4. Which choice provides the best evidence for the answer to the previous question?

    A) Lines 3-7 ("The man . . . sleep")
    B) **Lines 15-22** ("The man . . . decade")
    C) Lines 22-25 ("Public . . . house")
    D) Lines 48-52 ("The male . . . oppression")

    Lines 15-22 (Answers for #4)

5. As used in **line 24**, the word "rule" most nearly means   ⟵ Line 24

6. It can most reasonably be inferred that "the strong-minded" (**line 32**) was   ⟵ Line 32

As you can see, the first question is about the entire passage and thus is not helpful for this particular strategy, but look at questions 2, 5, and 6: the line references are progressing in order, from line 15 to line 24 to line 32. The remaining four questions with this passage (not included here) also progress by line reference, so you can apply Solution Strategy 3 with a high likelihood of answering the paired questions correctly.

So how does that work exactly? Pick the answer choice that has a line reference between a previous question's line reference and a subsequent question's line reference. If forced to make an educated guess on question 4, we would pick answer choice (B) as the line reference in that answer, lines 15-22, is between Line 15 in question 2 and line 24 in question 5.

Once we guess (B) for question 4, we can return to the passage, read the line reference in lines 15-22, and then answer question 3.

Remember, this strategy is not a surefire guarantee that you will answer the question correctly, and it should only be used when Solution Strategies 1 and 2 fail, or when you have less than a minute left in the section and you are scurrying to fill in your bubble sheet with guesses.

In our analysis of released tests, this strategy works with most Best Evidence Paired Questions that are like the one presented on the previous page. One time it is unlikely to work is when the first paired question itself has a line reference in it, such as question 2 (which is paired with question 3) below:

1. As it is used in **line 27**, "synthesize" most nearly means   ←——— Line 27

2. The author indicates that the statement made in by the critics in **lines 36-39** may be

3. Which choice provides the best evidence for the answer to the previous question?   Lines 36-39 (Question for #2)

    A) Lines 10-11 ("The . . . walk")
    B) Line 29 ("When . . . hostility")
    C) Lines 41-44 ("It . . . lost")
    D) Lines 67-71 ("Anthropologists . . . site")

4. The fifth paragraph (**lines 48-59**) functions primarily to   ←——— Lines 48-59

> When a line reference is in the first question in a Best Evidence paired set, you cannot use surrounding questions to answer the second question in the paired set.

In this case, the line reference in question 2 (lines 36-39) is what occurs between the line reference in question 1 (line 27) and the line reference in question 4 (lines 48-59), so you cannot use the information to guess an answer for question 3.

This is an invaluable guessing strategy for Command of Evidence questions, but it can also be applied to other SAT Reading questions to help you locate an answer in the passage when a line reference is not provided. Consider these three questions:

1. As used in **line 21**, "soul" most nearly means   ←——— Line 21

2. According to Bishop, the new theory of solar system formation is significant because   ←——— The answer is probably located between line 21 and line 37

3. After the scientists reported their "discovery" (**line 37**), the university responded by   ←——— Line 37

> **≷TIPS and TRICKS≷**
> You can use the line references of previous and subsequent questions to help you locate the answer to questions that do not provide a line reference.

An astute test taker would begin looking for the answer to question 2 between line 21 and line 37; the surrounding questions reveal where the previous and subsequent answers are found, and since the questions typically follow the order of the passage, question 2 is probably answered somewhere in between.

Best Evidence Paired Questions (Extended Reasoning)

Best Evidence questions are most often paired with Literal Comprehension questions, which is what we have been examining thus far in this chapter. But you should be aware that Best Evidence questions also occur with Extended Reasoning questions, which makes them a little more difficult. Consider one of these based on the passage from Jane Austen's *Emma* on pages 282–283:

1. Based on information in the passage, it can reasonably be inferred that what Emma will miss most about Miss Taylor is her governess'

    A) challenging lessons.
    B) lenient authority.
    C) stimulating conversation.
    D) interest in the adventures Emma planned.

2. Which choice provides the best evidence for the answer to the previous question?

    A) Lines 15-20 ("Even . . . own")
    B) Lines 42-46 ("She . . . childhood")
    C) Lines 50-55 ("She . . . fault")
    D) Lines 56-64 ("How . . . playful")

As we discussed in the previous chapter, Extended Reasoning questions are more difficult because the answer is not explicitly stated in the passage; instead, you have to draw a conclusion based on the text. Sometimes these questions are impossible to prephrase because there can be many inferences in a passage or because you did not pick up on the inference in your first reading. This question, however, is pretty specific, so it may be possible to have a good idea what Emma missed the most about Miss Taylor before looking at the answer choices.

Some advanced readers may be able to use Strategy 1 with Extended Reasoning paired questions, but an overwhelming majority of students will need to use Strategy 2: skip to the line references in the second question and look for the one that answers your paraphrase to the first question: *What will Emma miss most about Miss Taylor?*

A) Lines 15-20: *What will Emma miss most about Miss Taylor?*
"Even before Miss Taylor had ceased to hold the nominal office of governess, the mildness of her temper had hardly allowed her to impose any restraint; and the shadow of authority being now long passed away, they had been living together as friend and friend very mutually attached, and Emma doing just what she liked; highly esteeming Miss Taylor's judgment, but directed chiefly by her own."

Extended Reasoning questions are those that require you to draw a conclusion based on the information in the passage.

≡TIPS and TRICKS≡
Use the same three strategies discussed in the Best Evidence Literal Comprehension section on Best Evidence Extended Reasoning questions.

There is nothing about Miss Taylor leaving or Emma missing her in this passage. It discusses their relationship evolving from governess/charge to friends. While you may assume that Emma misses Miss Taylor's qualities described here (making "lenient authority" in answer choice (B) attractive), you need more evidence to infer that this is what Emma most missed.

B) Lines 42-46: *What will Emma miss most about Miss Taylor?* "She recalled her past kindness—the kindness, the affection of sixteen years—how she had taught and how she had played with her from five years old—how she had devoted all her powers to attach and amuse her in health—and how nursed her through the various illnesses of childhood."

If the previous sentence (line 41-42) had been included, there could be a case for this answer. But it wasn't, and thus there is no reference to missing Miss Taylor. These lines are about how good Miss Taylor was to Emma when Emma was a girl, and is included to entice you into picking answer choice (A), "challenging lessons," in the first question. While the line reference included mention of Miss Taylor teaching Emma, there is nothing about those lessons being *challenging*.

C) Lines 50-55: *What will Emma miss most about Miss Taylor?* "She had been a friend and companion such as few possessed: intelligent, well-informed, useful, gentle, knowing all the ways of the family, interested in all its concerns, and peculiarly interested in herself, in every pleasure, every scheme of hers—one to whom she could speak every thought as it arose, and who had such an affection for her as could never find fault."

Again, this reference lists Miss Taylor's wonderful qualities— certainly qualities that are worthy of being missed by Emma— but the text does not mention Emma's loss. Some could loosely tie this to "interest in the adventures Emma planned" in answer choice (D), as Miss Taylor was *interested in all [the family's] concerns*, but there was no mention of *adventures* planned by Emma.

D) Lines 56-64: *What will Emma miss most about Miss Taylor?* "How was she to bear the change? —It was true that her friend was going only half a mile from them; but Emma was aware that great must be the difference between a Mrs. Weston, only half a mile from them, and a Miss Taylor in the house; and with all her advantages, natural and domestic, she was now in great danger of suffering from intellectual solitude. She dearly loved her father, but he was no companion for her. He could not meet her in conversation, rational or playful."

Here is our correct answer. *How was she to bear the change?* The passage has previously mentioned a *gentle sorrow* (line 27) at Miss Taylor's marriage, but here we have a dramatic question that expresses how hard Miss Taylor's loss will be on Emma. The line reference goes on to say that Emma was *in great danger of suffering from intellectual solitude. She dearly loved her father, but he was no companion for her. He could not meet her in conversation, rational or playful.* This implies that Miss Taylor's presence meant Emma did not suffer from intellectual solitude and that Miss Taylor met Emma in rational and playful conversation. Thus, Emma most missed Miss Taylor's stimulating conversation, choice (D), which means choice (C) is correct in question 1.

Again, these questions are often more difficult because you have to draw a conclusion, but they can be solved in much the same manner as Literal Comprehension questions. And you can even use Strategy 3 if you need to make an educated guess.

Best Evidence Support and Contradict Questions

The remaining types of Command of Evidence reading questions are not as common as the paired questions, but you should still expect to see one or two on your SAT.

These questions are extremely similar to the Strengthen and Weaken questions we covered in the previous chapter. In most Strengthen and Weaken questions, you are asked which statement with new information would strengthen (support) or weaken (contradict) the author's argument. In Support and Contradict questions, you are required to find a line of text from the passage that supports (strengthen) or contradicts (weaken) the author's argument.

These questions are similar to Strengthen and Weaken questions in Chapter Thirteen.

Support Questions heavily outnumber Contradict Questions, so let's start with the more common question type. Support Questions most often use the following words:

> best supports   claim   conclusion

Examples of these questions include the following:

1. Which choice best supports the author's claim that funding for art museums should be subsidized by local, state, and national government?

2. Which choice best supports the conclusion that literary works in the public domain should not be reproduced for commercial purposes?

Most Support Questions will state the claim or conclusion right in the question, as the two previous questions did. For example, in the second one, the claim is that *literary works in the public domain should not be reproduced for commercial purposes*.

Most Support and Contradict questions will provide the claim from the passage in the question itself.

Let's look at a Support Question in more detail using a passage from a Sociology textbook:

You might be wondering: if sociologists and psychologists are both interested in people and their behavior, how are these two disciplines different? What do they agree on, and where do their ideas diverge? The answers are complicated, but the distinction is

Line
5 important to scholars in both fields.

As a general difference, we might say that while both disciplines are interested in human behavior, psychologists are focused on how the mind influences that behavior, while sociologists study the role of society in shaping behavior. Psychologists are interested in
10 people's mental development and how their minds process their world. Sociologists are more likely to focus on how different aspects of society contribute to an individual's relationship with his world. Another way to think of the difference is that in order to understand human behavior, psychologists tend to look inward at areas such
15 as mental health and emotional processes, while sociologists tend to look outward at fields such as social institutions, cultural norms, interactions with others.

Émile Durkheim (1858–1917) was the first to make this distinction in research, when he attributed differences in suicide
20 rates to social causes, such as religious differences, rather than to psychological causes, such as mental well-being. Today, we see this same distinction. For example, a sociologist studying how a couple gets to the point of their first kiss on a date might focus her research on cultural norms for dating or how this process is different
25 for seniors than for teens. A psychologist would more likely be interested in the person's earliest awareness of amorous feelings or the mental processing of desire.

Sometimes sociologists and psychologists have collaborated to increase knowledge. In recent decades, however, their fields have
30 become more clearly separated as sociologists increasingly focus on large societal issues and patterns, while psychologists remain honed in on the human mind. Both disciplines make valuable contributions through different approaches that provide us with different types of useful insights.

1. Which choice best supports the author's claim that psychologists focus on a person's mental development in understanding human behavior?

   A) Lines 1-3 ("You . . . different")
   B) Lines 18-21 ("Émile . . . well-being")
   C) Lines 25-27 ("A psychologist . . . desire")
   D) Lines 32-34 ("Both . . . insights")

Remember to rephrase
question statements
into actual questions!

To solve these questions, rephrase the question: start with the words "*Which choice proves that...*" and fill in the claim or conclusion from the question:

Which choice proves that psychologists focus on mental development?

Then read each choice and evaluate them to find the one that answers your prephrase.

A) Lines 1-3: *Which choice proves that psychologists focus on mental development?* "You might be wondering: if sociologists and psychologists are both interested in people and their behavior, how are these two disciplines different?"

This choice discusses both sociology and psychology; we are likely looking for one that mentions psychology only. Plus, it does not mention a focus on mental development or prove that this is the area on which psychologists focus.

B) Lines 18-21: *Which choice proves that psychologists focus on mental development?* "Émile Durkheim (1858–1917) was the first to make this distinction in research, when he attributed differences in suicide rates to social causes, such as religious differences, rather than to psychological causes, such as mental well-being."

In this line reference, Émile Durkheim is provided as an example of a sociologist, since he is looking at social causes of suicide. We need an example of or information about a psychologist instead.

C) Lines 25-27: *Which choice proves that psychologists focus on mental development?* "A psychologist would more likely be interested in the person's earliest awareness of amorous feelings or the mental processing of desire."

Bingo. This line reference mentions a psychologist examining a person's mental development concerning desire. This choice provides evidence that psychologists focus on mental development and is thus the correct answer.

D) Lines 32-34: *Which choice proves that psychologists focus on mental development?* "Both disciplines make valuable contributions through different approaches that provide us with different types of useful insights."

Like answer choice (A), choice (D) mentions both sociology and psychology and does not prove that psychologists focus on mental development.

While most Support Questions will provide you with the claim or conclusion, a few will ask you to find the claim or conclusion using a line reference:

1. Which choice best supports the author's view of the "psychologists" (line 9)?

   A) Lines 1-3 ("You . . . different")
   B) Lines 18-21 ("Émile . . . well-being")
   C) Lines 25-27 ("A psychologist . . . desire")
   D) Lines 32-34 ("Both . . . insights")

This question is nearly identical to the previous question, but the test makers are requiring you to locate the author's claim in line 9: *Psychologists are interested in people's mental development and how their minds process their world.* Once you find the claim or conclusion, solve it the same way we solved the previous question.

Contradict Questions are much more rare than Support Questions. It's a good thing, too, because they are a little more difficult. It's easy to find evidence to prove something, but your mind has to "work backwards" to find evidence that weakens a conclusion.

Contradict Questions will most likely use the following words:

contradicts   claim   conclusion

We would caution you that words like *undermines*, *detracts*, *refutes*, *challenges*, *disproves*, and *weakens* could be used in place of *contradicts*.

Since the author is not going to contradict herself, the question will likely present a view of a critic, expert, or participant that contradicts with something the author says in the passage. Here are two examples:

1. A critic of free play claims that the lack of recess in kindergarten is beneficial to students. Which statement in the passage contradicts the critic's claim?

2. A scientist concludes that the largest moon of Neptune has a posigrade orbit. Which statement in the passage contradicts the scientist's conclusion?

But just as with Support Questions, there is always a chance that the test makers will cite a contradiction mentioned in the passage by someone besides the author, which means you have to track down the claim or conclusion:

3. Which of the following statements in the passage contradicts the claim of "critics" (line 33) ?

Contradict Questions are not as common as Support Questions.

Let's attempt a Contradict Question using the psychology and sociology passage:

2. A student claims that sociologists focus on the mind of the individual. Which statement in the passage contradicts the student's claim?

   A) Lines 3-4 ("What . . . diverge")
   B) Lines 4-5 ("The answers . . . fields")
   C) Lines 11-12 ("Sociologists . . . world")
   D) Lines 28-29 ("Sometimes . . . knowledge")

To answer these questions, you have to get a little bit more creative with your prephrase, using some form of *Which choice proves that __ DOES NOT ___?*:

*Which choice proves that sociologists
DO NOT focus on the mind of the individual?*

Once again, read each choice and evaluate them to find the one that answers your prephrase:

A) Lines 3-4: *Which choice proves that sociologists DO NOT focus on the mind of the individual?* "What do they agree on, and where do their ideas diverge?"

   This choice does not specifically discuss sociology at all. It is a question, not a statement.

B) Lines 4-5: *Which choice proves that sociologists DO NOT focus on the mind of the individual?* "The answers are complicated, but the distinction is important to scholars in both fields."

   Again, this line reference does not mention sociology specifically.

C) Lines 11-12: *Which choice proves that sociologists DO NOT focus on the mind of the individual?* "Sociologists are more likely to focus on how different aspects of society contribute to an individual's relationship with his world."

   Choice (C) is the correct answer once again. This statement says that sociologists focus on society, not the mind of the individual. It contradicts the student's claim.

D) Lines 28-29: *Which choice proves that sociologists DO NOT focus on the mind of the individual?* "Sometimes sociologists and psychologists have collaborated to increase knowledge."

   The collaboration between the two specialists does not discuss what sociologists focus on.

As you can see, Support and Contradict questions are closely related to the Strengthen and Weaken questions we discussed in Chapter Thirteen. They are actually a welcome change on the SAT, as the claim or conclusion is usually provided, making them easier to answer.

Command of Evidence Questions make up a substantial portion of an SAT Reading section, which is why we have covered them in such detail. Best Evidence Paired Questions may appear with a Literal Comprehension question or an Extended Reasoning question, but there are many strategies to help you answer them correctly. Support and Contradict questions have fewer strategy options, but they are more straightforward and thus often easier to answer.

The test makers use the Command of Evidence umbrella to also cover the Charts and Graphs questions that accompany Reading passages, and we will examine them next.

There are usually two Command of Evidence Reading Questions per passage so it would be wise to review this section carefully!

Command of Evidence: Charts & Graphs

At the end of two of your SAT Reading passages you will find one or two related charts, graphs, tables, or diagrams. These figures will accompany one Science passage and either the Social Studies or History passage. They will not follow the Literary Fiction passage.

The informational graphic (or "infographic") appears at the end of the passage but before the questions. Although the charts and graphs will be related to a topic in the passage, they are not typically created by the author of the passage; instead, they are a figure that the test makers found that relates to the passage. Thus your understanding of the chart, table, graph, or figure will not affect your understanding of the passage. For this reason, we want you to complete the section in the following order:

1. **Read the passage.**
2. **Do not read or study the chart, graph, table, or diagram. Skip it and instead answer the questions that are only about the passage.**
3. **Return to the figure and scan it for basic information.**
4. **Answer the questions concerning the figure.**

It is important to answer the questions about the passage while the passage is fresh in your mind. Much like our suggested strategy for the paired passages, moving on to the charts or tables may confuse you, especially if the infographic contradicts a point made in the passage.

The questions about the charts and tables will be the last two or three questions in the section; once you reach the first one, you know it is time to return to the infographic for a quick analysis.

So what do you look for when scanning a figure? Start with the title as it will usually be descriptive enough to explain what the data is showing. Sometimes a chart or graph will have an explanatory note below the infographic, and you should read this after the title if it is present. Next move to the figure itself, and briefly examine it to get a broad sense of what the data is measuring. Do not worry about specifics yet—the questions will direct your attention to the specifics that need to be studied. Instead, try to get a general sense of trends, patterns, or outliers.

Let's take a few minutes to examine some common types of diagrams used on the SAT: bar graphs, line graphs, scatter plots, pictographs, pie charts, Venn diagrams, and tables. This is not an exhaustive list, and you may see an unusual graph or a diagram on the test, but these are the most common infographics on the SAT.

Bar Graphs

A bar graph uses horizontal or vertical bars to represent data. The horizontal axis is called the *x*-axis and the vertical axis is called the *y*-axis, but these terms are unimportant; what matters is that you know how to use the labels on each axis to identify the information being presented.

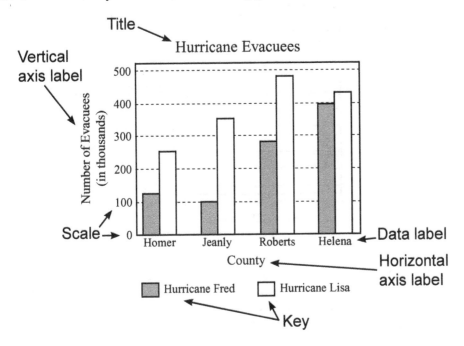

This bar graph is called a two-column bar graph because it's providing data for two different events in two different columns. The vertical axis shows the number of people evacuated during a hurricane using a scale that increases in increments of one hundred thousand. Note that the label shows us this increase is "in thousands" and that the actual scale only shows an increase in hundreds. Graph makers do this to save room and make the graph easier to read.

The horizontal axis is labeled "County," so each set of columns represents one of four counties. These counties are labeled Homer, Jeanly, Roberts, and Helena. Underneath this axis is a key identifying the gray columns as the number of evacuees during Hurricane Fred and the white columns as the number of evacuees during Hurricane Lisa.

It is impossible to use this graph to name the exact number of evacuees in any given month for either hurricane. Take the evacuees from Jeanly County during Hurricane Lisa as an example. The white column on Jeanly County seems to extend about halfway between 300,000 and 400,000. We could estimate that 350,000 people evacuated from Jeanly County during Hurricane Lisa. Questions about a graph like this would ask for an estimate instead of an exact answer.

⚥ CAUTION: TEST TRAP
Pay close attention to the units and scale used on the axes!

Note that bar graphs can be "flipped" so that the bars are horizontal instead of vertical. This graph conveys the same exact data as the previous bar graph:

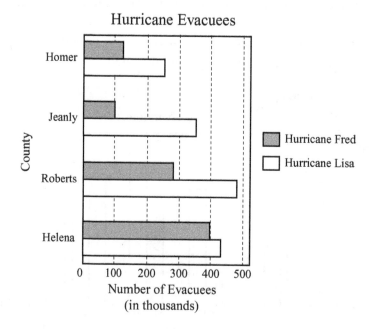

Bar graphs can be horizontally or vertically oriented.

Bar graphs can also have stacked columns to convey additional data:

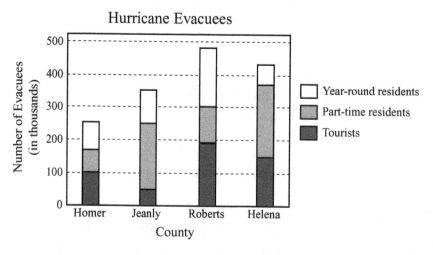

Graph keys always contain important information to help you interpret the figure.

This graph illustrates not only how many total people evacuated a county, but how many of these people were year-round residents, part-time residents, or tourists. For example, of the roughly 480,000 people who evacuated from Roberts County, about 110,000 of them were part-time residents. We know this because the Roberts County part-time residents bar (which is light gray) starts at around 190,000 and ends at 300,000.

$$300,000 - 190,000 = 110,000$$

Bar graphs are common on the SAT so you would be wise to familiarize yourself with their characteristics.

Line Graphs

A line graph also uses horizontal and vertical axes but it plots data as points on a graph and connects the points to form a line:

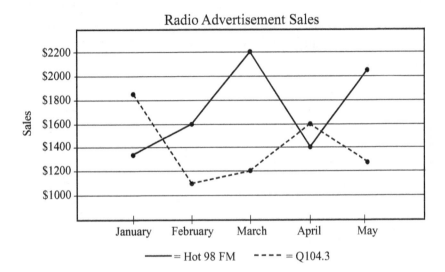

Bar graphs and line graphs both appear frequently on the SAT.

This line graph represents the dollar amount of radio ads sold for two radio stations over the course of five months, from January to May. Like a bar graph, it is often impossible to find the exact amount of a data point, but once again you can make fairly accurate estimates. For example, in February, Q104.3 sold roughly $1100 in radio ads.

Consider another line graph comparing the temperatures in Phoenix in June and December. Note that the horizontal labels are at the top of the graph.

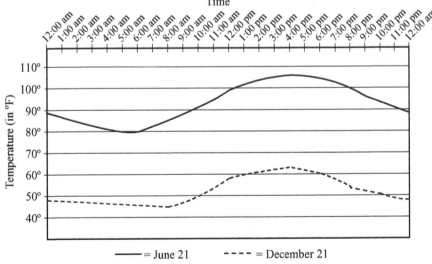

At noon the temperature averages about 100° in June and 58° in December.

Scatter Plots

A scatter plot also illustrates data as points on the graph with horizontal and vertical axes, but the data is *not* connected by a line. The points may show a trend in the data, in which case we can draw a line of "best fit" that captures the trend. This straight line is drawn as close as possible to the points in the trend, placing a similar number of points above and below the line, and it ignores any outliers:

A line of best fit shows a trend in data. It is not typically shown on the scatter plot, but is instead left for the test taker to draw.

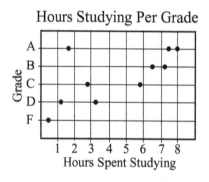

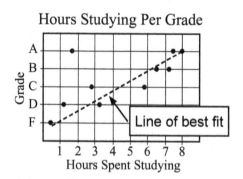

In this scatter plot, there is a clear trend that shows the more hours a student spent studying, the higher the grade. The only exception is the student who received an A after studying for approximately an hour and forty-five minutes. This is an outlier and is thus not included in the line of best fit.

Occasionally a scatter plot will not reveal any trends, therefore making a line of best fit unnecessary:

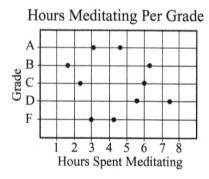

It is clear from this graph that the number of hours spent meditating does not influence a student's grade.

Pictographs

A pictograph—somewhat rare on the SAT—uses pictures to represent data:

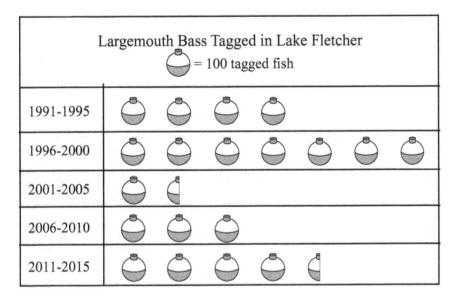

This pictograph depicts the number of largemouth bass tagged in a particular lake during five year increments. For example, between 2011 and 2015 there were 450 fish tagged in Lake Fletcher. We know this because each "bobber" represents 100 fish, and there are four and a half bobbers for that time period.

Pie Charts and Venn Diagrams

A pie chart, often used to represent percentages, uses a circle to display data. A Venn diagram uses two circles to represent data:

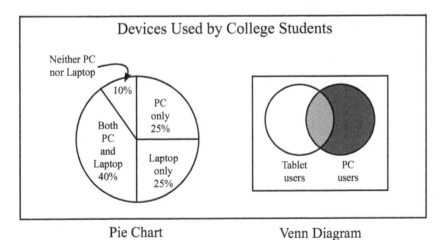

Pie Chart   Venn Diagram

This pie chart represents the percentage of college students who use a PC only (25%), a laptop only (25%), both a PC and a laptop (40%), or neither a PC nor a laptop (10%).

The Venn diagram is more vague, simply showing that some college students use a tablet only, others use a PC only, and some use both a tablet and a PC. Actual data is not provided so there is no way to determine an exact number of students or an exact percentage of students.

Tables

Tables organize information in an easy-to-read format:

EMPLOYEE BENEFITS		
Years Worked	Vacation Days	Commission Percentage
1 to 5	10	4%
5 to 9	14	9%
10 to 20	17	16%
20 or more	21	25%

In this table, we can see that an employee who has worked 10 to 20 years receives 17 vacation days and a 16% commission. Doesn't it make you want to stay in school where there are at least 80 vacation days a year?

The test makers like to use scientific terms in tables to make them seem more difficult, but the terms are either explained in the diagram or passage or the definitions of the terms are not required to solve the Charts and Graphs question. For example, in the following table, you may be asked to find the percentage of time an onion root cell is in the anaphase stage of mitosis:

Onion Root Cell Mitosis by Stage

Cell stage	Number of cells	Time in stage (hours)	Percent time in stage
Interphase	20	13.2	55%
Prophase	10	6.6	27%
Metaphase	3	2	8%
Anaphase	2	1.3	5%
Telophase	1	.48	2%

You can determine that the answer is 5% without having any knowledge of what *anaphase* means. If you come to a table with scientific terms, do not let the terms intimidate you—you do not need any scientific knowledge to do well on these questions.

Bar graphs, line graphs, and tables are the most common infographics to appear on the SAT Reading section.

≡TIPS and TRICKS≡
Do not let scientific or unfamiliar terms intimidate you! The definitions will either be provided or not needed.

Charts and Graphs: Common Answer Traps

Before we to examine how charts and graphs are tested on the SAT, let's revisit the common answer traps for regular Reading questions, which we discussed in Chapter Ten, as these are some of the same traps laid by test makers for the Charts and Graphs questions.

Opposite Answers

Some wrong answers to Charts and Graphs questions will offer information that is the opposite of the correct answer or opposite of data presented in the figure. For example, if a pie chart shows that 25% of Civil War soldiers who served in the Union Army were born in a country other than America, there may be an Opposite Answer that states 25% of soldiers who served in the Union Army were born in the United States.

Extreme Answers

Be suspicious of any answers that use Extreme words such as *always*, *only*, *never*, *mainly*, and *absolutely*. The correct answer is more likely to use moderate words like *roughly*, *about*, or *somewhat*.

True But Wrong Answers

True But Wrong Answers are those that are factually correct but do not answer the specific question. In Charts and Graphs questions, True But Wrong Answers may cite factual data from somewhere else in the figure, from a second accompanying figure that is not referenced in the question, or from the passage itself, but they do not answer the question being asked.

True to a Point Answers

Just as in regular Reading questions, True to a Point Answers are often the most attractive wrong answers because they appear correct on your initial reading. On closer inspection, however, you will realize that the test makers slipped new information into the answer. For example, if a line graph shows that the correct dosage of *acetaminophen* for a 40 pound child is 7.5 mL, a wrong answer choice may state that a 40 pound child should receive 7.5 mL of *ibuprofen*. Correct dosage, wrong medicine!

True to You Answers

Finally, be on the lookout for any answer choices that play on your prior knowledge or experience. If a bar graph rates the popularity of five social media platforms, do not let your opinion or your experience influence your answers. You may know that the most popular site made $3 billion *last* year, but the graph might be showing projected revenue for *next* year. Pay careful attention to titles, headings, labels, and keys to avoid falling into a True to You trap.

☠ CAUTION: TEST TRAP
Common reading answer traps will appear in Charts and Graphs questions.

Charts and Graphs Example Passage

To begin our discussion of question types, read the following passage and consider its infographics. We will return to them throughout the chapter.

Remember to practice active reading, including notating the passage as you read, as discussed in Chapter Seven.

Since it is not possible to go back in time to directly observe and measure climate, scientists use indirect evidence, such as tree rings, ice cores, and ocean sediments, to determine the drivers, or factors, that
Line may be responsible for climate change. The data shows a correlation
5 between the timing of temperature changes and drivers of climate change.

Prior to 1780 and the birth of the Industrial Era, there were three drivers of climate change that were not related to human activity or atmospheric gases. The first of these is the Milankovitch cycles, which
10 describe the effects of slight changes in the Earth's orbit on Earth's climate. These cycles have ranges in length between 19,000 and 100,000 years, so one could expect to see some predictable changes in the Earth's climate associated with changes in the Earth's orbit at a minimum of every 19,000 years.

15 The second natural factor responsible for climate change is the variation in the sun's intensity, which is the amount of solar energy the sun emits in a given amount of time. There is a direct relationship between solar intensity and temperature: as solar intensity increases, the Earth's temperature correspondingly increases. Some scientists believe
20 that changes in solar intensity actually caused the Little Ice Age.

Finally, a third natural driver of climate change are volcanic eruptions. Although eruptions may last for only a matter of days, the solids and gases released during an eruption can influence the climate for years, generally cooling the Earth's temperatures. For example,
25 volcanoes in Iceland erupted in 1783 for eight months, causing haze-effect cooling, a global phenomenon that occurs when dust, ash, or other suspended particles block out sunlight. These eruptions produced some of the lowest average temperatures on record in Europe and North America during the winters of 1783 and 1784. It stands to reason then
30 that the eruptions that last for a year or more can affect the temperature even more drastically.

The most significant drivers of climate, however, are directly caused by humans rather than nature: greenhouse gases such as carbon dioxide and methane. These greenhouse gases trap the heat from the sun in
35 our atmosphere, much like the glass panes of a greenhouse prevent heat from escaping through the ceiling. The result of this "greenhouse effect" is steadily increasing temperatures, frequently referred to as "global warming." Human activity releases carbon dioxide into the atmosphere through the burning of fossil fuels, deforestation, cement
40 manufacture, and animal agriculture. Methane is released from rice paddies, natural gas fields, and landfills. These greenhouse gases cause the Earth's temperature to rise, which in turn increases the oceans' water temperature. Clathrates, frozen chunks of ice and methane found at the bottom of the ocean, begin to melt and release more methane
45 into the atmosphere. It is a vicious cycle: the more greenhouse gases there are in the atmosphere, the more thermal energy is reflected back to Earth, increasing temperatures and releasing additional greenhouse gases.

Evidence supports the fact that humans are directly responsible for
50 these increases in carbon dioxide and methane. Data for atmospheric
carbon dioxide concentration levels reveal a historical pattern of the
gas increasing and decreasing, cycling between a low of 180 parts
per million (ppm) and a high of 300 ppm. Scientists have concluded
that it previously took around 50,000 years for the atmospheric
55 carbon dioxide level to increase from its low minimum concentration
to its higher maximum concentration. More recently, however,
atmospheric carbon dioxide concentrations have increased from 280
ppm in 1950 to over 400 ppm in 2016. This increase has happened
very quickly, in a matter of seventy years rather than over thousands
60 of years. What is the reason for this difference in the rate of change
and the increase in carbon dioxide? The only plausible answer when
comparing the historical data and the current data is modern human
society. No other driver of climate change has yielded variations in
atmospheric carbon dioxide levels at this rate or to this magnitude.

*Our example here
and on the following
pages comes from a
science passage, but
remember that one of
the infographics on your
test will follow a social
studies passage.*

Figure 1

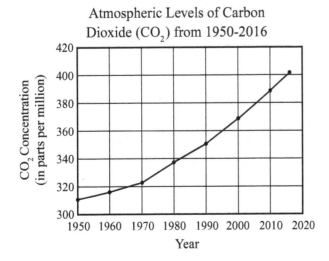

Atmospheric Levels of Carbon
Dioxide (CO_2) from 1950-2016

Figure 2

Greenhouse Gas Levels

*Most passages have a
single infographic, but
some, like this one, will
have two.*

Gas	Pre-1750 atmospheric levels	Recent atmospheric levels	Atmospheric lifetime[1]	GWP[2]
Carbon dioxide (CO_2)	280 ppm*	398 ppm	100-300 years	1
Methane (CH_4)	722 ppb**	1834 ppb	12.4 years	28
Nitrous oxide (N_2O)	270 ppb	328 ppb	121 years	265
Ozone (O_3)	237 ppb	337 ppb	hours to days	n/a[3]

* parts per million   ** parts per billion
[1] The amount of time the gas stays in the atmosphere.
[2] Global warming potential: The amount of energy the emissions of one ton of a gas will
absorb over 100 years relative to the emissions of one ton of CO_2. The larger the GWP,
the more that a gas warms the Earth compared to CO_2 in the same time period.
[3] The short lifetime of ozone precludes meaningful calculation of its GWP.

Charts and Graphs: Location Questions

This question type is the easiest of the Charts and Graphs questions, as you simply have to locate the answer using the figure. These questions depend only on your understanding of the infographic and can be answered without even reading the passage. You can expect one to three per test.

Location Questions are a type of Literal Comprehension question; the answer is in the test booklet and you simply have to find it. For this reason, Location Questions use phrases much like Literal Comprehension passage questions that indicate the figure contains the answer:

Location Questions are the Literal Comprehension questions of the Charts and Graphs world. The answer is stated in the figure-- you just have to find it.

- According to the figure/chart/graph/table....
- According to the data in the figure/chart/graph/table....
- Based on the figure/chart/graph/table....
- Based on the data in the figure/chart/graph/table....
- In the figure/chart/graph/table....
- The data in the figure/chart/graph/table indicates....

Most SAT passages with Charts and Graphs questions have a single figure accompanying the passage, but some will have two figures. The two infographics may be similar and closely related, such as two pie charts showing identical data from two different years. Or the figures may be completely different with distinct data, like the line graph and the table following our climate change passage.

Let's look at some example questions from the climate change passage:

1. According to figure 1, between 1970 and 1980 the concentration of carbon dioxide

    A) decreased by over 20 parts per million.
    B) decreased at the same rate as the levels decreased between 2000 and 2010.
    C) increased by about 13 parts per million.
    D) increased at the same rate as the levels increased between 1950 and 1960.

Location Questions will always direct you to the figure or figures containing the data that answers the question. For example, in the question above, note that it refers only to figure 1; thus, you can ignore both the passage and figure 2. The phrase *According to figure 1* indicates that the answer will be found in figure 1 and nowhere else.

So return to figure 1, the line graph of atmospheric levels of carbon dioxide:

Figure 1

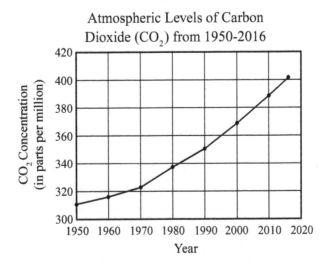

Atmospheric Levels of Carbon Dioxide (CO_2) from 1950-2016

To begin answering Location Questions, analyze any information mentioned in the question before reading the answer choices. In this question, we are directed to study the CO_2 concentration between the years 1970 and 1980. Looking at the line graph, we can see that during this decade the levels of CO_2 increased from about 324 ppm to 338 ppm. These numbers are not exact data points, but rather estimates from the graph. Now turn your attention to the answer choices and figure out which one answers our rephrased question: *What happened to the concentration of CO_2 between 1970 and 1980? It...*

(A) *decreased by over 20 parts per million.*
We have already determined that the levels increased between 1970 and 1980, so this answer can be dismissed. It's an Opposite Answer.
(B) *decreased at the same rate as the levels decreased between 2000 and 2010.*
Again, the levels increased in this time period, so this answer is wrong.
(C) *increased by about 13 parts per million.*
We determined that the levels increased from about 324 ppm to 338 ppm which is 14 ppm, or *about 13 parts per million.* This is likely the correct answer.
(D) *increased at the same rate as the levels increased between 1950 and 1960.*
Look at the year 1950 to 1960 on the graph. There is an increase from about 312 ppm to about 317 ppm, which is an increase of 5 ppm. This rate is not the same rate increase of 14 ppm between 1970 and 1980.

Choice (C) is the correct answer.

Consider another Location Question:

2. Based on the data in figure 2, which gas has the highest global warming potential?

    A) CO_2
    B) CH_4
    C) N_2O
    D) O_3

This time the question directs us to the second figure, so the answer will not be found in the passage nor in figure 1. Look only at figure 2:

Figure 2

Greenhouse Gas Levels

Gas	Pre-1750 atmospheric levels	Recent atmospheric levels	Atmospheric lifetime[1]	GWP[2]
Carbon dioxide (CO_2)	280 ppm*	398 ppm	100-300 years	1
Methane (CH_4)	722 ppb**	1834 ppb	12.4 years	28
Nitrous oxide (N_2O)	270 ppb	328 ppb	121 years	265
Ozone (O_3)	237 ppb	337 ppb	hours to days	n/a[3]

* parts per million   ** parts per billion
[1] The amount of time the gas stays in the atmosphere.
[2] Global Warming Potential: The amount of energy the emissions of one ton of a gas will absorb over 100 years relative to the emissions of one ton of CO_2. The larger the GWP, the more that a gas warms the Earth compared to CO_2 in the same time period.
[3] The short lifetime of ozone precludes meaningful calculation of its GWP.

Never overlook a footnote or explanation below the figure. It may be essential in helping you understand the information presented.

Based on the question, we need to find information about global warming potential. This term is not used in any of the columns or rows, but GWP is the heading of the last column. According to the second footnote, GWP stands for global warming potential, and "the larger the GWP, the more that a gas warms the Earth compared to CO_2 in the same time period."

The gas with the highest GWP number is nitrous oxide, or N_2O, at 265, so choice (C) is correct again. It would be wise to read the third footnote, however, to make sure that Ozone (O_3) is not in contention. According to the footnote, Ozone lives so briefly that it cannot be a factor in GWP.

Note that the test makers try to make the question more difficult by using chemical symbols instead of the names of the gasses in the answer choices. These symbols are provided directly after the gases' names in the first column so there is no reason to be intimidated. All information for Location Questions will be provided in the figure and no outside science knowledge is required.

This table has a lot of data and three footnotes, but we only needed to look at the first and last columns (and two of the three footnotes) to answer it correctly. When attempting a Location Question, ignore any extraneous information as it may confuse you or take time away from the question at hand.

♦ GRATUITOUS VOCAB
extraneous (adj):
irrelevant; unnecessary

Nearly all Location Questions will refer to a single figure. But you should be prepared for the occasional question that requires you to locate data in both figures. Here's an example:

3. According to the data in figure 1, in which of the following years was the measurement for "recent atmospheric levels" of carbon dioxide in figure 2 most likely taken?

    A) 2009
    B) 2010
    C) 2015
    D) 2016

The question informs us that we need to consider both figures in order to solve this question:

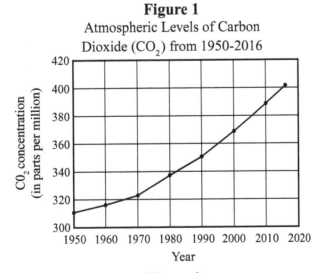

Figure 1
Atmospheric Levels of Carbon Dioxide (CO_2) from 1950-2016

Figure 2
Greenhouse Gas Levels

Gas	Pre-1750 atmospheric levels	Recent atmospheric levels	Atmospheric lifetime[1]	GWP[2]
Carbon dioxide (CO_2)	280 ppm*	398 ppm	100-300 years	1
Methane (CH_4)	722 ppb**	1834 ppb	12.4 years	28
Nitrous oxide (N_2O)	270 ppb	328 ppb	121 years	265
Ozone (O_3)	237 ppb	337 ppb	hours to days	n/a[3]

First we must direct our attention to figure 2, and specifically to the column heading "*recent atmospheric levels.*" According to the table, the recent atmospheric levels of carbon dioxide were 398 ppm.

Now turn your attention to figure 1 and find the point on the graph that the atmospheric levels of carbon dioxide were 398 ppm. In 2016, the levels were over 400 ppm but it appears that in 2015 the levels were around 398 ppm. In 2010, the levels were roughly 388 ppm and they were even lower still in 2009. Choice (C) is the answer.

Because Location Questions do not require you to understand or even read the passage, you may want to jump to them if time is running out and you still have unread passages. For example, if you have read and completed the first four passages but only have one or two minutes left in the section to complete the fifth and final passage (which happens to include an infographic), skip to the last two or three questions, or those concerning the figure. You should be able to pick up points by answering the Location Questions (and the Conclusion Questions, discussed next) without reading the passage.

:TIPS and TRICKS:
If you only have one or two minutes left in a section and haven't started reading a passage yet, skip to its Charts and Graphs questions: you can answer most of them without reading the passage.

Notes:

Charts and Graphs: Conclusion Questions

Like Location Questions, Conclusion Questions can be answered without reading the passage. These questions ask you to draw a conclusion based solely on the data in a graph, chart, table, or other figure. Of the three types of questions accompanying Charts and Graphs, Conclusion Questions are the least commonly occurring. You can expect one to two per test.

While Location Questions are a form of Literal Comprehension, Conclusion Questions are a type of Extended Reasoning and thus use similar verbiage to Reading questions about inferences:

- Which statement/choice/claim is best supported by data in the figure....
- Data in the figure/chart/graph/table most strongly supports....
- The figure/chart/graph/table suggests that....

As with other Extended Reasoning questions, the word *suggests* will always alert you to the fact that the answer is inferred and not stated. You will be drawing a conclusion instead of locating the exact answer.

Let's return to our climate change theme, but this time with a new figure showing carbon dioxide emissions due to the burning of fossil fuels. A question follows on the next page:

Conclusion Questions are the Extended Reasoning questions of the Charts and Graphs section. The answer is not explicitly stated in the infographic, but a conclusion about the information can be drawn.

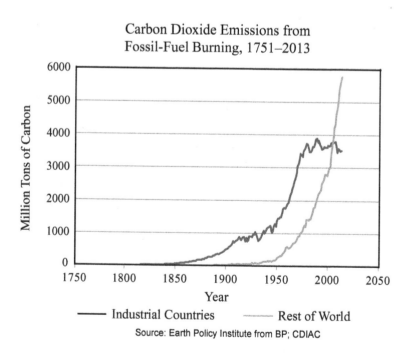

Carbon Dioxide Emissions from Fossil-Fuel Burning, 1751–2013

Source: Earth Policy Institute from BP; CDIAC

1. Which of the following statements is supported by the information presented in the figure?

   A) Non-industrial countries did not begin manufacturing goods until the 1820s.
   B) Industrial countries reduced the rate of carbon dioxide emissions in the last quarter of the twentieth century.
   C) Developing countries are directly responsible for the vast majority of historical carbon emissions.
   D) Industrial countries agreed to reduce their greenhouse emissions following the United Nations Convention on Climate Change in 1997.

Three of the answer choices will be proven false, and only one will be true based on the information in the graph. Let's evaluate each answer choice:

(A) *Non-industrial countries did not begin manufacturing goods until the 1820s.*
There are two problems with this answer. The first is that it assumes that manufacturing is the cause of fossil fuel burning, but the graph does not state this. Remember, the answers to Location and Conclusion questions must be found in the referenced figure or figures. The second problem with this answer is the 1820s reference. It appears that non-industrial countries did not begin burning fossil fuels until closer to 1900.

(B) *Industrial countries reduced the rate of carbon dioxide emissions in the last quarter of the twentieth century.*
This is true. The peak of the Industrial Countries line occurs near 1980 and there are several drop-offs in the last quarter of the century.

(C) *Developing countries are directly responsible for the vast majority of historical carbon emissions.*
This answer has two Extreme phrases: *directly* and *vast majority*. For that reason alone, you should be suspicious. But it's incorrect because industrial countries have a longer history of carbon emissions, starting near 1820 while the rest of the world did not begin until closer to 1900. Non-industrial countries did not pass industrial countries for carbon emissions until close to 2010.

(D) *Industrial countries agreed to reduce their greenhouse emissions following the United Nations Convention on Climate Change in 1997.*
This may be a True to You answer, as many countries did agree to the Kyoto Protocol in 1997. But the graph does not mention this convention, so the answer is wrong.

Choice (B) is the right answer. To solve these questions, analyze each answer choice in the context of the figure, eliminating those that make erroneous assumptions or cite incorrect data.

> **≡TIPS and TRICKS≡**
> To answer Conclusion Questions, evaluate each answer choice to determine whether it is true or false.

Conclusion Questions might require you to make an inference based on two figures:

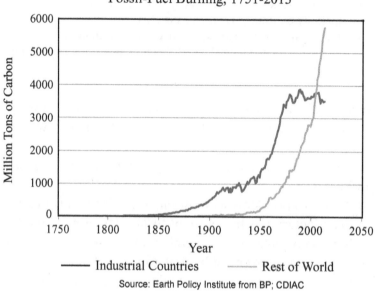

Figure 1

Carbon Dioxide Emissions from
Fossil-Fuel Burning, 1751-2013

Source: Earth Policy Institute from BP; CDIAC

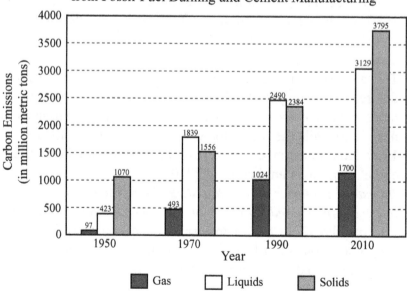

Figure 2

Global Carbon Dioxide Emissions
from Fossil-Fuel Burning and Cement Manufacturing

2. Taken together, the two figures suggest that the global carbon dioxide emissions

  A) decreased after 1950 because of regulations put in place by industrial countries.
  B) are produced more by cement manufacturing than by fossil-fuel burning.
  C) are at the highest levels when there is more carbon dioxide solid emissions than carbon dioxide liquid emissions in a given year.
  D) increased between 1990 and 2010 due in part to increased fossil-fuel burning in non-industrial countries.

Remember, to answer Conclusion Questions, you must evaluate each answer choice to determine if it is true or false:

(A) *decreased after 1950 because of regulations put in place by industrial countries.*
Start with figure 1 and look at the two curves at 1950. The industrial countries' emissions continue to increase until about 1975. Non-industrial countries continued to increase through the entire graph. Taken together, these are global emissions. Thus we cannot deduce that emissions decreased after 1950. Figure 2 supports this as well, as the emissions are shown to increase every twenty years.

(B) *are produced more by cement manufacturing than by fossil-fuel burning.*
Figure 2 is the only infographic that mentions cement manufacturing, and there is no way to tell in that bar graph whether fossil fuel burning or cement manufacturing makes up a greater portion of carbon dioxide emissions. Figure 1 does not clarify this, as it shows only emissions from industrial countries compared to the rest of the world.

(C) *are at the highest levels when there is more carbon dioxide solid emissions than carbon dioxide liquid emissions in a given year.*
Use figure 2 to determine what years had higher solid emissions than liquid emissions: 1950 and 2010. While 2010 is close to the highest level of global emissions levels (it actually occurs in 2013 per figure 1), 1950 is relatively low for emissions. It's the lowest level in figure 2 and near the bottom of the curves in figure 1. If we took the estimated emissions for 1950, we would have roughly 1400 million tons of carbon for industrial countries and 300 million tons for the rest of the world, for a global total of 1700 million tons. In the year 2013, however, there are about 3600 million tons in industrial countries and 5800 million tons in non-industrial countries, for a global total approaching 10,000.

(D) *increased between 1990 and 2010 due in part to increased fossil-fuel burning in non-industrial countries.*
This is true. Figure 2 shows us that global emissions increased

between 1990 and 2010. But figure 1 indicates that fossil fuel burning in industrial nations during these years actually decreased. In this same figure, though, we can see that emissions due to fossil fuel burning increased significantly between 1990 and 2010 in non-industrial countries, thus, their actions are at least partly (if not entirely) responsible for the increase in carbon dioxide emissions.

Choice (D) is the correct answer.

Conclusion Questions are usually slightly more difficult than Location Questions, but they can still be solved without reading the passage. The same cannot be said for the final type of Charts and Graphs questions: Connection Questions.

Charts and Graphs: Connection Questions

Connection Questions require you to connect information from a figure to information in the passage, so you must read the passage before tackling these questions. They are easy to identify because they will mention both the figure and either the passage or the author of the passage. Consider some example questions:

- The data in the figure most directly supports which idea from the passage?
- How does the table support the author's claim that...?
- The author of the passage would most likely claim that the data in the figure are....

Connection Questions are common on the SAT, and based on released practice tests, you can expect one to five per test.

There are two main types of Connection Questions. The first asks you to use the data in a figure to support or contradict a claim in the passage. These are similar to the Support and Contradict questions for Command of Evidence Reading questions that we covered earlier in this chapter:

1. How does the figure support the author's claim that hurricanes are more likely to impact Texas during La Niña?

2. Data in the table provide the most direct support for which of the following ideas in the passage?

The author's claim is stated in the first question (*hurricanes are more likely to impact Texas during La Niña*), but will be listed as the correct answer choice in the second question.

The second type of question resembles the Hypothetical Point of View Questions from the previous chapter. They ask how an author would likely respond to the information in the figure:

1. The author of the passage would most likely consider the data in figure 1 to be

2. The author of the passage would likely respond to the data in the table by arguing that

We will look closely at how to solve both of these question types, but first reacquaint yourself with the passage and scan the new figures on the following pages.

Connection Questions appear frequently on the SAT.

There are two types of Connection Questions: those that ask you to support or contradict a claim from the passage and those that require you to predict how the author would react to the data in a figure.

Because many readers will not complete this chapter all in one sitting, we have reprinted the climate passage here. It is important to read it again as your success on Connection Questions will depend on your understanding of the passage.

Since it is not possible to go back in time to directly observe and measure climate, scientists use indirect evidence, such as tree rings, ice cores, and ocean sediments, to determine the drivers, or factors, that
Line may be responsible for climate change. The data shows a correlation
5 between the timing of temperature changes and drivers of climate change.

Prior to 1780 and the birth of the Industrial Era, there were three drivers of climate change that were not related to human activity or atmospheric gases. The first of these is the Milankovitch cycles, which
10 describe the effects of slight changes in the Earth's orbit on Earth's climate. These cycles have ranges in length between 19,000 and 100,000 years, so one could expect to see some predictable changes in the Earth's climate associated with changes in the Earth's orbit at a minimum of every 19,000 years.

15 The second natural factor responsible for climate change is the variation in the sun's intensity, which is the amount of solar energy the sun emits in a given amount of time. There is a direct relationship between solar intensity and temperature: as solar intensity increases, the Earth's temperature correspondingly increases. Some scientists believe
20 that changes in solar intensity actually caused the Little Ice Age.

Finally, a third natural driver of climate change are volcanic eruptions. Although eruptions may last for only a matter of days, the solids and gases released during an eruption can influence the climate for years, generally cooling the Earth's temperatures. For example,
25 volcanoes in Iceland erupted in 1783 for eight months, causing haze-effect cooling, a global phenomenon that occurs when dust, ash, or other suspended particles block out sunlight. These eruptions produced some of the lowest average temperatures on record in Europe and North America during the winters of 1783 and 1784. It stands to reason then
30 that the eruptions that last for a year or more can affect the temperature even more drastically.

The most significant drivers of climate, however, are directly caused by humans rather than nature: greenhouse gases such as carbon dioxide and methane. These greenhouse gases trap the heat from the sun in
35 our atmosphere, much like the glass panes of a greenhouse prevent heat from escaping through the ceiling. The result of this "greenhouse effect" is steadily increasing temperatures, frequently referred to as "global warming." Human activity releases carbon dioxide into the atmosphere through the burning of fossil fuels, deforestation, cement
40 manufacture, and animal agriculture. Methane is released from rice paddies, natural gas fields, and landfills. These greenhouse gases cause the Earth's temperature to rise, which in turn increases the oceans' water temperature. Clathrates, frozen chunks of ice and methane found at the bottom of the ocean, begin to melt and release more methane
45 into the atmosphere. It is a vicious cycle: the more greenhouse gases there are in the atmosphere, the more thermal energy is reflected back to Earth, increasing temperatures and releasing additional greenhouse gases.

Evidence supports the fact that humans are directly responsible for
50 these increases in carbon dioxide and methane. Data for atmospheric carbon dioxide concentration levels reveal a historical pattern of the gas increasing and decreasing, cycling between a low of 180 parts per million (ppm) and a high of 300 ppm. Scientists have concluded that it previously took around 50,000 years for the atmospheric carbon

55 dioxide level to increase from its low minimum concentration
to its higher maximum concentration. More recently, however,
atmospheric carbon dioxide concentrations have increased from 280
ppm in 1950 to over 400 ppm in 2016. This increase has happened
very quickly, in a matter of seventy years rather than over thousands
60 of years. What is the reason for this difference in the rate of change
and the increase in carbon dioxide? The only plausible answer when
comparing the historical data and the current data is modern human
society. No other driver of climate change has yielded variations in
atmospheric carbon dioxide levels at this rate or to this magnitude.

Figure 1

Impact of Historic Volcanic Eruptions

Year	Eruption	Eruption Duration	SO₂ Released (million tons)	(°C) Temp. Decrease	Cooling Duration
1783	Laki	8 months	122	1.0	2-5 years
1815	Tambora	6 months	55	0.7	2-5 years
1883	Krakatau	2 days	38	0.3	1-3 years
1902	Santa Maria	2 days	45	0.4	1-3 years
1912	Katmai	3 days	30	0.2	1-3 years
1963	Agung	1 year	15	0.3	1-3 years
1980	St. Helens	1 day	2	0.1	1-3 years
1982	El Chichon	6 months	13	0.6	1-3 years
1991	Pinatubo	1 day	20	0.5	2-5 years

The table above shows the amount of sulfur dioxide (SO_2) released from major volcanic
eruptions as well as the resulting global temperature decrease and the estimated
duration of that decrease. Sulfur dioxide combines with water in the stratosphere to
form sulfuric acid, which creates a haze and leads to global cooling.

Figure 2

Solar Cycle Length versus Temperature

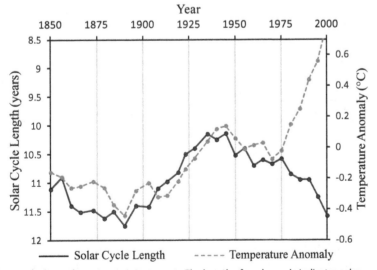

The graph above shows two measurements. The length of a solar cycle indicates solar
intensity; the hotter the sun, the shorter the cycle. The temperature anomaly shows the
departure from long-term average global temperatures; a positive value reveals that
the temperature was warmer than average while a negative anomaly indicates that the
temperature was cooler than normal.

These are new
infographics related to
the climate passage.

♦ GRATUITOUS VOCAB
anomaly (adj): a
deviation from normal;
irregularity

Let's start with a basic question asking you to support a claim from the passage:

1. Do the data in the table in figure 1 provide support for the authors' claim that volcanoes were responsible for global cooling during the winters of 1783 and 1784?

   A) Yes, because Laki decreased the average temperature by 1° C for 2 to 5 years.

   B) Yes, because for each volcanic eruption listed, the average temperature was affected by more than 0.5°C for at least a year.

   C) No, because the table does not indicate that Laki is in Iceland.

   D) No, because Agung erupted for a longer period of time than did Laki but Agung did not affect the average temperature as severely as Laki.

Notice that the claim is given to you: *volcanoes influenced climate during the winters of 1783 and 1784*. This claim was made in the passage in lines 24-29: "For example, volcanoes in Iceland erupted in 1783 for eight months, causing...some of the lowest average temperatures on record in Europe and North America during the winters of 1783 and 1784." Questions like this one are the easiest of Connection Questions because you do not have to find any information from the passage; instead, you simply need to evaluate each answer choice using the figure:

Figure 1

Impact of Historic Volcanic Eruptions

Year	Eruption	Eruption Duration	SO_2 Released (million tons)	(°C) Temp. Decrease	Cooling Duration
1783	Laki	8 months	122	1.0	2-5 years
1815	Tambora	6 months	55	0.7	2-5 years
1883	Krakatau	2 days	38	0.3	1-3 years
1902	Santa Maria	2 days	45	0.4	1-3 years
1912	Katmai	3 days	30	0.2	1-3 years
1963	Agung	1 year	15	0.3	1-3 years
1980	St. Helens	1 day	2	0.1	1-3 years
1982	El Chichon	6 months	13	0.6	1-3 years
1991	Pinatubo	1 day	20	0.5	2-5 years

The table above shows the amount of sulfur dioxide (SO_2) released from major volcanic eruptions as well as the resulting global temperature decrease and the estimated duration of that decrease. Sulfur dioxide combines with water in the stratosphere to form sulfuric acid, which creates a haze and leads to global cooling.

Tables like this one present a lot of data. Questions on the SAT will likely look only at a few pieces of data, meaning that most of the information presented is an extraneous distraction.

Your task is to evaluate each answer choice statement by locating information in the table. You must first prove whether the statement is true; if it is false, you can eliminate the answer choice. If the statement is true, however, then you must determine whether the statement supports the claim for the "Yes" answers in (A) and (B) or disputes the claim for the "No" answers in (C) and (D).

Let's now analyze each answer choice:

(A) *Yes, because Laki decreased the average temperature by 1° C for 2 to 5 years.*

First, determine if this statement is indeed true. According to the second row of the table, Laki erupted in 1783 and decreased the global temperature by 1° C for 2-5 years. This is a true statement. But does it support the claim that *volcanoes influenced climate during the winters of 1783 and 1784*? Yes. The temperature was lowered for 2 to 5 years, so the winters of 1783 and 1784 fall into that time period. This is the correct answer and confident test takers will select it and move on without wasting time evaluating the other three choices (or at the very least, they will mark it for review should there be remaining time at the end of the section). To help you fully understand this question type, though, it is important to read the explanations below for the other three answers.

(B) *Yes, because for each volcanic eruption listed, the average temperature was affected by more than 0.5°C for at least a year.*

Is this statement true? No. Krakatau's eruption only decreased temperatures by 0.3°C. Santa Maria, Katmai, Agung, and St. Helens also disprove this statement.

(C) *No, because the table does not indicate that Laki is in Iceland.*

Is this statement true? Yes. There is nothing in the table about the location of the listed volcanoes. But does it dispute the claim that *volcanoes influenced climate during the winters of 1783 and 1784*? No. The question does not mention Iceland, and the location of the volcanoes has nothing to do with the climate during the winters of 1783 and 1784.

(D) *No, because Agung erupted for a longer period of time than did Laki but Agung did not affect the average temperature as severely as Laki.*

Is this statement true? Yes. Agung erupted for a year but only decreased the temperature by 0.3° C, while Laki only erupted 8 months but affected temperature by 1.0° C. But does it dispute the claim that *volcanoes influenced climate during the winters of 1783 and 1784*? No—it actually supports the claim, since it shows that Laki affected temperature. But this answer says "No," meaning it does not support the claim, which is not true.

Connect Questions like these are considered the easiest because they state the claim right in the question—you simply have to analyze the figure to determine which section of data supports the claim.

Evaluate each answer choice to determine its validity and then decide whether it supports or disputes the claim in the question.

As we have already demonstrated in previous chapters, whenever you are asked to strengthen or support an idea on the Reading section of the SAT, you should also be prepared to weaken or undermine a viewpoint. This goes for Connection Questions, too:

2. Based on the data in figure 1, which pair of eruptions undermines the authors' claim that volcanoes that erupt for less than twelve months influence the climate less significantly than do the eruptions that last for longer periods of time?

    A) Laki and Santa Maria
    B) Laki and St. Helens
    C) Santa Maria and Agung
    D) Agung and St. Helens

Again, the claim is provided for you: *volcanoes that erupt for less than twelve months influence the climate less significantly than do the eruptions that last for longer periods of time*. This is a paraphrased version of lines 29-31 in the passage: "It stands to reason then that the eruptions that last for a year or more can affect the temperature even more drastically."

Your task will be to analyze the climate changes caused by each volcano pair, searching for the two volcanoes that together disprove that longer-lasting eruptions have greater impact on climate. You can predict that the answer will have one volcano that erupted for a year or more with a lower temperature decrease than that of a volcano that erupted for less than a year.

Consider figure 1 again:

Figure 1

Impact of Historic Volcanic Eruptions

Year	Eruption	Eruption Duration	SO_2 Released (million tons)	(°C) Temp. Decrease	Cooling Duration
1783	Laki	8 months	122	1.0	2-5 years
1815	Tambora	6 months	55	0.7	2-5 years
1883	Krakatau	2 days	38	0.3	1-3 years
1902	Santa Maria	2 days	45	0.4	1-3 years
1912	Katmai	3 days	30	0.2	1-3 years
1963	Agung	1 year	15	0.3	1-3 years
1980	St. Helens	1 day	2	0.1	1-3 years
1982	El Chichon	6 months	13	0.6	1-3 years
1991	Pinatubo	1 day	20	0.5	2-5 years

The table above shows the amount of sulfur dioxide (SO_2) released from major volcanic eruptions as well as the resulting global temperature decrease and the estimated duration of that decrease. Sulfur dioxide combines with water in the stratosphere to form sulfuric acid, which creates a haze and leads to global cooling.

Astute students will automatically notice that Agung is the only volcano to have erupted for a year or more, and thus it must be included in the right answer. If neither volcano erupted for a year or more, the answer cannot support nor undermine the authors' claim, since the authors are comparing a long-lasting (year or more) volcanic eruption to a shorter (less than a year) eruption.

These students can jump right to answer choices (C) and (D) because they are the only two that include Agung. We've included analysis of (A) and (B), though, to help you see the pattern among wrong answer choices:

Connection Questions are usually difficult-- if not impossible-- to prephrase, but in questions like these you can often predict what the answer choice will prove or disprove.

(A) *Laki and Santa Maria*
Start with Laki. It erupted for 8 months and decreased temperatures by 1° C. Santa Maria erupted for 2 days and decreased temperatures by 0.4° C. This pair supports the authors claim because the longer-lasting eruption had greater impact.

(B) *Laki and St. Helens*
Laki erupted for 8 months and decreased temperatures by 1° C. St. Helens erupted for 1 day and decreased temperatures by 0.1° C. This pair supports the authors claim because the longer-lasting eruption had greater impact.

(C) *Santa Maria and Agung*
Santa Maria erupted for 2 days and decreased temperatures by 0.4° C. Agung erupted for 1 year and decreased temperatures by 0.3° C. This undermines the author's claim because the longer-lasting eruption had less impact than the shorter eruption. Choice (C) is the answer.

(D) *Agung and Laki*
Agung erupted for 1 year and decreased temperatures by 0.3° C. Laki erupted for 8 months and decreased temperatures by 1° C. This pair supports the authors claim because the longer-lasting eruption had greater impact.

Weaken questions are more difficult than strengthen questions because of the way they require you to think about the data, but they will almost always be presented in a question that provides the author's claim.

The most common type of Connection Question, however, will ask you to select the claim that is supported by the data in the figure:

The most common type of Connection Question tasks you with selecting a claim from the passage that is supported by the data in a figure.

3. Data in the table in figure 1 most directly support which of the following claims in the passage?

A) Modern industrialization is the most significant influence on climate.
B) Volcanic eruptions can have long-term effects on global temperatures.
C) Solar intensity is one of four factors that determine weather changes.
D) Due to the Earth's orbit, there are predictable changes to the Earth's climate over time.

If there are two figures present, you will need to watch for claims that are supported by the other, unreferenced figure in an attempt by the test makers to catch those students who do not read carefully. Make sure you analyze the correct figure, in this case figure 1 again:

Figure 1

Impact of Historic Volcanic Eruptions

Year	Eruption	Eruption Duration	SO_2 Released (million tons)	(°C) Temp. Decrease	Cooling Duration
1783	Laki	8 months	122	1.0	2-5 years
1815	Tambora	6 months	55	0.7	2-5 years
1883	Krakatau	2 days	38	0.3	1-3 years
1902	Santa Maria	2 days	45	0.4	1-3 years
1912	Katmai	3 days	30	0.2	1-3 years
1963	Agung	1 year	15	0.3	1-3 years
1980	St. Helens	1 day	2	0.1	1-3 years
1982	El Chichon	6 months	13	0.6	1-3 years
1991	Pinatubo	1 day	20	0.5	2-5 years

The table above shows the amount of sulfur dioxide (SO_2) released from major volcanic eruptions as well as the resulting global temperature decrease and the estimated duration of that decrease. Sulfur dioxide combines with water in the stratosphere to form sulfuric acid, which creates a haze and leads to global cooling.

We have reprinted the figure here, but you may need to return to the passage on page 318 as you work through each answer choice.

CAUTION: TEST TRAP
Watch out for True But Wrong answers in questions like these. The claim might be asserted in the passage, but the data does not support it.

In these types of questions, the wrong answers are actual claims from the passage but they are not connected to the figure, making them attractive True But Wrong answers. The answer you choose must be an actual claim from the passage AND describe the data in the figure.

Consider each answer choice and compare it to figure 1:

(A) *Modern industrialization is the most significant influence on climate.*
In lines 60-64 of the passage, the authors state, "What is the reason for this difference in the rate of change and the increase in carbon dioxide? The only plausible answer when comparing the historical data and the current data is modern human society. No other driver of climate change has yielded variations in atmospheric carbon dioxide levels at this rate or to this magnitude." So this is a true claim, as the passage also indicates that the increase in carbon dioxide has resulted from the Industrial Era. But is it supported by figure 1? No. This table is about volcanoes' influence on climate, not industrialization.

(B) *Volcanic eruptions can have long-term effects on global temperatures.*
The authors state in lines 22-24, "Although eruptions may last for only a matter of days, the solids and gases released during an eruption can influence the climate for years, generally cooling the Earth's temperatures." So this statement is true. But is it supported by figure 1? Yes. The table shows major volcanic eruptions and their cooling of global temperatures for 1 to 5 years.

(C) *Solar intensity is one of four factors that determine weather changes.*
Is this claim true? Yes. In lines 17-19, the authors write, "There is a direct relationship between solar intensity and temperature: as solar intensity increases, the Earth's temperature correspondingly increases." But is it supported by figure 1? No. Figure 1 is about volcanoes, not solar activity. Be careful, though! Figure 2 is about solar intensity and thus this question will trap test takers who do not read carefully!

(D) *Due to the Earth's orbit, there are predictable changes to the Earth's climate over time.*
This claim is stated in lines 12-14, but look at the table: it does not mention Earth's orbit nor provide any predictable data over time.

These questions are a bit more difficult—and more common—than the Connection Questions that provide the author's claim in the question, but they can be solved by carefully evaluating each choice.

Remember, when you confidently find the answer, move on! You can come back to the question to double check your answer if time remains at the end of the section.

Let's look at another:

4. The data from years 1850 to 1975 in figure 2 supports which of the following ideas in the passage?

 A) Milankovitch cycles can occur every 19,000 years.
 B) A short solar cycle is likely responsible for the Little Ice Age between the years 1300 and 1870.
 C) Humans have had significant influence on the climate.
 D) There is a correlation between global temperatures and the sun's magnitude.

Note that not only are we directed to figure 2, but to a specific range of years: from 1850 to 1975. We have marked that period in the figure and must disregard data after 1975:

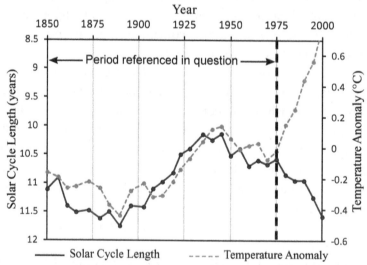

Figure 2

Solar Cycle Length versus Temperature

The graph above shows two measurements. The length of a solar cycle indicates solar intensity; the hotter the sun, the shorter the cycle. The temperature anomaly shows the departure from long-term average global temperatures; a positive value reveals that the temperature was warmer than average while a negative anomaly indicates that the temperature was cooler than normal.

This line graph is a bit tricky because it displays two measurements on its y-axis. The first, on the left, is the solar cycle length. The footnote explains that the solar cycle length determines the intensity of the sun; cooler periods have long solar cycles and hotter periods have short solar cycles. The solid black line on the graph represents solar cycle length.

The second measurement on the y-axis is temperature anomaly, labeled on the right. Again, the footnote provides a definition: a departure from long-term average global temperatures. The greater the anomaly, the warmer the temperature. The dashed gray line represents the data for temperature anomaly.

So what does the data from 1850 to 1975 reveal? The solar cycle length and the temperature anomaly seem to nearly match during that time period, indicating a direct relationship. But let's look at the answer choices to see if we are correct:

(A) *Milankovitch cycles can occur every 19,000 years.*
In lines 11-12, the authors proclaim that Milankovitch cycles "have ranges in length between 19,000 and 100,000 years." So this claim, while true, isn't exactly accurate; they don't occur every 19,000 years, but every 19,000 *to* 100,000 years. The graph also does not document Milankovitch cycles, so this answer is incorrect.

(B) *A short solar cycle is likely responsible for the Little Ice Age between the years 1300 and 1870.*
The authors state in lines 19-20, "Some scientists believe that changes in solar intensity actually caused the Little Ice Age." The graph does not show the Little Ice Age, nor does it suggest its causes. The graph begins in 1850, whereas the Little Ice Age began in 1300 according to the answer choice.

(C) *Humans have had significant influence on the climate.*
This answer is True But Wrong. The authors do believe that humans "are the most significant drivers of climate" (line 32), and while a case may be made that the data between 1970 and 2000 supports this, the data between 1850 and 1970 shows a relationship between temperature and the sun, not between temperature and humans.

(D) *There is a correlation between global temperatures and the sun's magnitude.*
Bingo. We prephrased the answer before we even read the answer choices. The solid line of solar cycle length has a similar path to the dashed line of temperature anomaly, indicating that "There is a direct relationship between solar intensity and temperature: as solar intensity increases, the Earth's temperature correspondingly increases" (lines 17-19).

Now we will turn our attention to the final–and likely the most difficult—type of Connection Question: those that ask you how an author would interpret a figure. Similar to Hypothetical Point-of-View questions in the Extended Reasoning chapter, you are tasked with predicting an author's reaction to someone else's data based on the author's stated views.

⚲ GRATUITOUS VOCAB

divergence (adj): movement in different directions

5. In figure 2, the data shows a direct relationship between solar cycle length and temperature anomaly until around 1975, at which point there is a sudden divergence of data between the two measurements. The authors of the passage would most likely attribute this divergence to

A) a volcanic eruption in the 1970s that caused global temperatures to increase considerably.
B) an extended period of longer-than-average solar cycles resulting from increased sunspot activity.
C) a substantial increase in carbon dioxide due to human enterprise.
D) scientists' ability to harness the methane released from clathrates on the ocean floor.

Rephrase the question: *Why is there a sudden difference after 1975?* Looking at the graph we see that the solar cycle length (the solid line) from 1975 to 2000 stays within the ranges it previously reached from 1850 to 1975. But the temperature anomaly increases drastically, literally going "off the chart" around 1995, meaning that the planet is much warmer than expected.

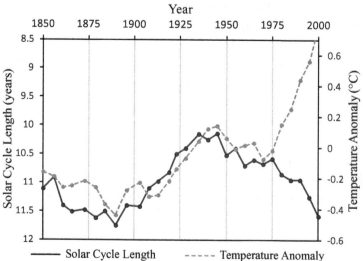

Figure 2
Solar Cycle Length versus Temperature

The graph above shows two measurements. The length of a solar cycle indicates solar intensity; the hotter the sun, the shorter the cycle. The temperature anomaly shows the departure from long-term average global temperatures; a positive value reveals that the temperature was warmer than average while a negative anomaly indicates that the temperature was cooler than normal.

We can prephrase the answer to this question by considering what the authors wrote about recent changes in climate. In lines 56-63 they state, "More recently, however, atmospheric carbon dioxide concentrations have increased from 280 ppm in 1950 to over 400 ppm in 2016. This increase has happened very quickly, in a matter of seventy years rather than over thousands of years. What is the reason for this difference in the rate of change and the increase in carbon dioxide? The only plausible answer when comparing the historical data and the current data is modern human society." They believe *the only possible reason* for the sudden, drastic increase in carbon dioxide, which "cause[s] the earth's temperature to rise" (line 41-42), is humans, and more specifically "human activity" (lines 38-40).

Now match an answer choice:

(A) *a volcanic eruption in the 1970s that caused global temperatures to increase considerably.*
This does not match the prephrase. Plus, we know from our work with figure 1 that volcanoes can affect global temperatures long term, but volcanoes generally lower temperatures, not raise them.

(B) *an extended period of longer-than-average solar cycles resulting from increased sunspot activity.*
Again, this answer is not in agreement with our prephrase. And according to the explanation below the line graph, longer solar cycles bring cooler temperatures, not warmer ones.

(C) *a substantial increase in carbon dioxide due to human enterprise.*
Here is our match! Choice (C) is the correct answer.

(D) *scientists' ability to harness the methane released from clathrates on the ocean floor.*
This answer does not correspond to the prephrase and is not discussed in the passage. Clathrates are actually melting and contributing to the increase in methane in the atmosphere, but nothing is mentioned about scientists harnessing that methane.

Although they are usually more difficult than the Connection Questions that ask you to support a claim, hypothetical questions are less common and may not appear on every single SAT. But when faced with one, attack it as you would a Hypothetical Point of View question: prephrase an answer that predicts how the author would respond.

The best way to solve any hypothetical question--whether about the passage or about the passage and graphic--is to predict what the author would say when presented with the new information.

SAT Command of Evidence Problem Set

Read the passage below and then answer the corresponding Command of Evidence Reading and Command of Evidence Charts and Graphs questions. Answers begin on page 336.

The following passage is adapted from the 2016 OpenStax textbook, *Principles of Economics*.

The formal study of economics began in 1776 when Adam Smith, a Scottish philosopher, published *The Wealth of Nations*, his classic tome on commerce and capitalist systems. Many authors had written on economics in the centuries before Smith, but he was the first to address the subject in a comprehensive way, addressing topics such as productivity, free trade, and the division of labor. It was this division of labor—assigning the various tasks performed in order to produce a good or service to different workers rather than a single worker completing all of the production steps—that Smith believed was responsible for economic growth. When the tasks involved with producing a good or service are divided and subdivided, workers and businesses can produce a greater quantity of output.

To illustrate the benefits of division of labor, Smith analyzed the production of a pin. From his observations in pin factories, he noted that there were several tasks required in the creation of a pin, including drawing out a piece of wire, cutting it to the right length, straightening it, putting a head on one end and a point on the other, and packaging it for sale. Smith counted eighteen distinct tasks that could be completed by different people in the creation of a single pin. In factories that divided this labor among employees, ten workers were able to make 48,000 pins per day. Outside of the factory, however, where laborers produced pins entirely on their own, ten people might generate only 200 pins per day.

How does the division of labor create such a considerable difference in yield? Smith offered three reasons. First, specialization in a particular small job allows workers to focus on the parts of the production process where they have an advantage. People have different skills, talents, and interests, so they will be better at some jobs than at others. The particular advantages may be based on educational choices, which are in turn shaped by interests and talents. For example, only those with medical degrees qualify to become doctors. For some goods, specialization may be affected by geography—it is easier to be a wheat farmer in North Dakota than in Florida, just as it is easier to be a salt

water fishing captain in Florida than in North Dakota. Whether because of interests, education, or location, when people specialize in the creation of what they do best, they will be more productive than if they produce a combination of goods and services.

Another reason that division of labor leads to increased output is that workers who specialize in certain tasks—such as assembly line workers, hair stylists, and heart surgeons—often learn to produce goods and services more efficiently and with higher quality. These employees are not only valued for their skilled labor but also for their keen insight into improvement. Specialized employees often understand their job so well that they are able to suggest innovative ways to complete their tasks with more speed and less cost. Businesses often benefit from this specialization model, too; in many cases, businesses that focus on only a few products are more successful than corporations that make a wide range of products.

Finally, Smith asserted that specialization allows businesses to take advantage of economies of scale, which is the idea that as the level of production increases for a good or service, the average cost of producing each individual unit declines. For example, if a factory produces only 100 cars per year, the average production cost of each car is quite high. Yet if the same factory produces 50,000 cars a year, assembly lines with specialized workers and huge machines will significantly decrease the average cost of production per car. Plus, the price of raw materials needed to make a product will be discounted when the manufacturer purchases larger quantities. The costs of production are spread out over a greater number of goods.

When employees can focus on jobs that benefit from their preferences and talents, learn to perform their tasks better, and work in larger organizations, the ultimate result is that society as a whole can produce and consume far more than if each person tried to produce all of their own goods and services. The division and specialization of labor has been a force against the problem of scarcity.

Figure 1

Clock Company Production Statistics

Year	Total Employees	Division of Labor*	Total Units Produced	Units per Employee	Cost per Unit
1	5	1	1,000	200	$100
2	15	1	3,000	200	$60
3	15	15	30,000	2000	$60
4	30	15	60,000	2000	$30
5	40	20	70,000	1750	$32
6	50	25	80,000	1600	$35
7	60	15	120,000	2200	$20
8	90	15	180,000	2000	$20

* The number of employees tasked with completing one unit.

The table above shows employment and clock unit statistics from a clock factory for a single model of clock over eight years of production.

Figure 2

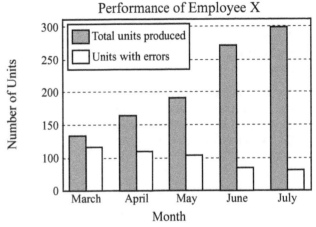

Performance of Employee X

The chart above shows the performance of a new worker, Employee X, at a jewelry-making factory. The employee works on an assembly line, where he hand paints intricate designs on beads for necklaces. Each unit equals one bead completed.

1. The passage indicates that Adam Smith maintained that the division of labor led to

   A) the production of fewer goods and services.
   B) forced geographic specialization.
   C) more educational choices.
   D) economic development.

2. Which choice provides the best evidence for the answer to the previous question?

   A) Lines 1-4 ("The . . . systems")
   B) Lines 8-13 ("It . . . growth")
   C) Lines 37-39 ("The . . . talents")
   D) Lines 41-42 ("For some . . . geography")

3. Based on the information in the passage about the ten employees in the pin factory observed by Smith, it can most reasonably be inferred that

   A) the employees took pride in their jobs.
   B) some of the workers had to complete more than one task.
   C) each of the workers could complete 4800 pins per day on their own.
   D) the pin factory employed only the most skilled laborers.

4. Which choice provides the best evidence for the answer to the previous question?

   A) Lines 17-18 ("To . . . pin")
   B) Lines 18-23 ("From . . . sale")
   C) Lines 23-27 ("Smith . . . day")
   D) Lines 27-30 ("Outside . . . day")

SAT Command of Evidence Problem Set

5. According to the passage, which of the following might be a factor in a person's choice of specialized career?

   A) A former teacher
   B) The person's physical location
   C) The book *The Wealth of Nations*
   D) A factory's management team

6. Which choice provides the best evidence for the answer to the previous question?

   A) Lines 4-8 ("Many . . . labor")
   B) Lines 35-37 ("People . . . others")
   C) Lines 41-44 ("For some . . . Dakota")
   D) Lines 54-56 ("These . . . improvement")

7. Which of the following choices best supports the passage's claim that specialized employees are appreciated for their knowledge about their jobs?

   A) Lines 26-28 ("In factories . . . day")
   B) Lines 37-39 ("The . . . talents")
   C) Lines 45-48 ("Whether . . . services")
   D) Lines 56-59 ("Specialized . . . cost")

8. A factory worker at a computer company claims that the cost per unit in manufacturing computers is the same, whether the company produces one computer or one million computers. Which statement in the passage contradicts the employee's claim?

   A) Lines 13-16 ("When . . . output")
   B) Lines 33-35 ("First . . . advantage")
   C) Lines 56-59 ("Specialized . . . cost")
   D) Lines 74-76 ("Plus . . . quantities")

9. The passage asserts that mass production is more cost-effective than the production of small quantities because

   A) manufacturing expenses are distributed over a more sizeable quantity of products.
   B) employees are able to suggest cost-reducing measures to improve efficiency.
   C) free trade policies allow businesses to enter international markets.
   D) employers can offer lower wages for workers who specialize in a single skill.

10. Which choice provides the best evidence for the answer to the previous question?

    A) Lines 13-16 ("When . . . output")
    B) Lines 17-18 ("To . . . pin")
    C) Lines 49-54 ("Another . . . quality")
    D) Lines 76-77 ("The . . . goods")

SAT Command of Evidence Problem Set

11. Based on the data in the table in figure 1, the clock company produced the most units per employee when there were how many total employees?

    A) 30
    B) 40
    C) 60
    D) 90

12. The data from Year 2 and Year 3 in figure 1 most directly support which of the following claims from the passage?

    A) Lines 13-16 ("When . . . output")
    B) Lines 33-35 ("First . . . advantage")
    C) Lines 59-62 ("Businesses . . . products")
    D) Lines 64-68 ("Finally . . . declines")

13. Based on the data in figure 1, which two years undermine the authors' claim that as the level of production increases, the average cost of producing a single unit decreases?

    A) Year 1 and Year 2
    B) Year 3 and Year 4
    C) Year 5 and Year 6
    D) Year 7 and Year 8

14. According to the graph in figure 2, Employee X exhibited which of the following sets of trends during the first five months of his employment?

    A) His productivity and accuracy decreased.
    B) His productivity and accuracy increased.
    C) His productivity decreased while his accuracy increased.
    D) His productivity increased while his accuracy decreased.

15. Do the data in figure 2 support Adam Smith's claim that a division of labor leads to increased output?

    A) Yes, because the data provide evidence of a steady increase in the number of units completed each month.
    B) Yes, because the data reveal a decrease in the percentage of errors each month.
    C) No, because the data do not compare the employees' output on an assembly line to the employees' output working as individuals.
    D) No, because the data do not indicate how many workers are on the assembly line.

16. The authors' of the passage would most likely consider the data in figure 2 to be evidence of

    A) an employee learning to generate goods more proficiently due to specialization.
    B) the benefits of economies of scale resulting from a division of labor.
    C) employees having different interests and skill sets.
    D) educational experiences influencing a person's career choice.

Chapter Summary

There are two types of Command of Evidence Questions: those Reading questions that require students to find evidential text from the passage and those Charts and Graphs questions that ask students to analyze an infographic.

Command of Evidence: Reading Questions

★ Best Evidence Paired Questions
- The majority of Command of Evidence questions are paired with the prior question.
- You must choose the line reference that best supports the answer to the previous question.
- Best Evidence questions can be paired with Literal Comprehension or Extended Reasoning questions.
- The correct answer for the first question will be a rephrasing of the correct answer to the second question.
- You should mark the first question of each Best Evidence pair so you can answer them together when you come to them; this will help you avoid redundancy and wasted time.
- There are three strategies for Best Evidence questions:
  1. Know the answer.
  2. Use the second question to answer the first question.
  3. Use the line references in surrounding questions to make an educated guess.

★ Best Evidence Support and Contradict Questions
- These questions are similar to regular Strengthen and Weaken questions.
- You are asked to find the line of text that would best support or contradict an author's claim.
- Most questions will state the claim directly in the question; others may require you to locate the claim in the passage.

Command of Evidence: Charts and Graphs Questions

Strategies for Passages with a Chart or Graph

1. Read the passage.
2. Do not read or study the chart, graph, table, or diagram. Skip it and instead answer the questions that are only about the passage.
3. Return to the figure and scan it for basic information.
4. Answer the questions concerning the figure.

- Watch for common answer traps: Opposite Answers, Extreme Answers, True But Wrong Answers, True to a Point Answers, and True to You Answers.
- Do not let scientific or unfamiliar terms intimidate you; the definitions will be provided or are unnecessary to answer the questions correctly.
- If time is running out and you have an entire passage left, skip to the Charts and Graphs questions; you do not need to read the passage to correctly answer some of them.

Common Types of Charts and Graphs

- Bar Graphs
- Line Graphs
- Pie Charts
- Tables
- Pictographs
- Venn Diagrams
- Scatter Plots

Types of Charts and Graphs Questions

★ Location Questions
- Similar to Literal Comprehension questions, the answers to Location Questions are located in the figure.
- You can answer these without reading the passage.
- These questions usually only refer to a single figure, but on occasion will ask you to consider two figures.

★ Conclusion Questions
- Similar to Extended Reasoning questions, the answers to Conclusion Questions are inferred based on information in the figure.
- You can answer these without reading the passage.
- To answer these, find the only answer that is true.
- Conclusion Questions are the rarest of the Charts and Graphs questions.

★ Connection Questions
- Connection Questions require you to connect information from a figure to information in the passage.
- These questions occur frequently on the SAT.
- There are two types of Connection Questions: 1) Use data to support or contradict a claim in the passage and 2) Determine how an author would react to specific data.

EXCLUSIVE SAT CONTENT ANSWER KEY

SAT Command of Evidence Problem Set—Page 330

1. (D)
2. (B)

Prephrase: Several options, including *economic growth, increased output,* and *specialized workers.*

Best Evidence Paired Question (Literal Comprehension): The entire passage is about the benefits of the division of labor according to Adam Smith, so there may be several places where a correct answer can be found. But only one of the answer choices in question 1 will be correct. In lines 8-13, the author states: "It was this division of labor...that Smith believed was responsible for economic growth," making choice (B) correct in question 2.

In question 1, choice (A) is an Opposite Answer because Smith believed that the division of labor increased output (lines 13-16). Choice (B) is Extreme with the use of *forced.* The passage states that location *may* affect specialization (line 41), but does not indicate that these are forced decisions. And choice (C) is a Copycat answer from line 38. People may specialize based on *educational choices,* but nowhere does the passage state that the division of labor will result in more educational choices.

3. (B)
4. (C)

Prephrase: It is difficult to prephrase Inference questions.

Best Evidence Paired Question (Extended Reasoning): For question 3, it is difficult to make an inference without analyzing the answer choices, so start with (A). Nothing in the paragraph indicates or infers that the employees took pride in their jobs. For all we know, they were humiliated working in a pin factory and could have an output of 100,000 pins per day if they cared more about their jobs.

Choice (B) is the answer, though. In lines 23-27, the passage states: "Smith counted eighteen distinct tasks that could be completed by different people in the creation of a single pin. In factories that divided this labor among employees, ten workers were able to make 48,000 pins per day." How did these 10 workers do 18 tasks? Some of them must have completed more than one task. Thus, choice (C) is correct in question 4.

Back to question 3: choice (C) is incorrect. Smith noticed that workers who did not have a division of labor could only make 20 pins per day. And choice (D) is wrong for the same reason that (A) is wrong. The employees could be the least skilled laborers in town, and the factory could produce a million pins per day with different workers. We have no idea about the skill level of the employees even though Smith believes that specialization improves skill. Maybe these were ten brand new employees so they had no time to improve.

5. (B)
6. (C)

Prephrase: *Interests, skills, talents, educational choices,* and *geography*

Best Evidence Paired Question (Literal Comprehension): In the third paragraph, the author explains what may make a person pick one career over another. For question 5, the only answer in the answer choices from this paragraph is (B), the person's physical location, as explained in lines 41-44: "For some goods, specialization may be affected by geography—it is easier to be a wheat farmer in North Dakota than in Florida, just as it is easier to be a salt water fishing captain in Florida than in North Dakota."

In question 5, choice (A) may be attractive because of the use of *educational choices* in the paragraph. But teachers are not mentioned. Neither (C) nor (D) is mentioned as an influence in the choice of career.

7. (D)   Prephrase: Impossible to prephrase

Best Evidence Support Question: The paraphrased claim in the question comes from lines 54-56: "These employees are not only valued for their skilled labor but also for their keen insight into improvement." And the supporting sentence follows immediately after in lines 56-59: "Specialized employees often understand their job so well that they are able to suggest innovative ways to complete their tasks with more speed and less cost.

8. (D)   Prephrase: Impossible to prephrase, but looking for an answer that proves mass producing is cheaper.

Best Evidence Contradict Question: The correct answer is (D), lines 74-76: "Plus, the price of raw materials needed to make a product will be discounted when the manufacturer purchases larger quantities." If the prices of materials are less expensive, then the cost per unit will be less expensive.

9. (A)
10. (D)

Prephrase: Several options, including *economies of scale, discounted materials, assembly lines,* and *the cost of production is spread out over more goods.*

Best Evidence Paired Question (Literal Comprehension): The answer to question 9 comes from the second to last paragraph, which discusses the cost advantages of mass production. The only answer in question 10 from this paragraph is (D), lines 76-77: "The costs of production are spread out over a greater number of goods."

In question 9, choice (B) is True But Wrong. We know from lines 56-58 that this answer choice is true, but it's not a reason that mass production is more cost effective; this would hold true whether the group of employees produced 10 goods or 10 million goods. Choice (C) may be True to You, but it uses business jargon to try to trick you into selecting it. Free trade is mentioned in the first paragraph as a topic of *The Wealth of Nations* but it is not explained nor discussed as a reason that mass production is cost-effective. Finally, answer choice (D) is untrue and not discussed in the passage.

11. (C) Location Question

Year	Total Employees	Division of Labor*	Total Units Produced	Units per Employee	Cost per Unit
	30			2000	
	40			1750	
	60			2200	
	90			2000	

12. (A) Connection Question

Year	Total Employees	Division of Labor*	Total Units Produced	Units per Employee	Cost per Unit
2	15	1	3,000	200	$60
3	15	15	30,000	2000	$60

In Year 2 and Year 3, the company had the same number of employees. However, they went from having one worker assemble a complete clock to a division of labor, where each of the fifteen employees completed a task, and they increased the output by 900%. Thus, lines 13-16 are supported by this statistic: "When the tasks involved with producing a good or service are divided and subdivided, workers and businesses can produce a greater quantity of output."

Choice (D) is the most commonly selected wrong answer, but the cost per unit did not decrease, despite the large increase in total units produced.

13. (C) Connection Question

Year	Total Units Produced	Cost per Unit
1	1,000	$100
2	3,000	$60
3	30,000	$60
4	60,000	$30
5	70,000	$32
6	80,000	$35
7	120,000	$20
8	180,000	$20

In the other three pairs of years, the cost per unit *decreases* or *stays the same* as the total units produced increases, which supports the claim in the question. Only in Year 5 and Year 6 does the cost per unit *increase* while the total units produced increases. This undermines the author's claim.

14. (B)   Conclusion Question

It's easy to see that the employee's productivity increased; he started at around 170 units in March and completed 300 units in July. This eliminates choices (A) and (C).

The tough part is in understanding the reciprocal relationship between errors and accuracy. His number of errors decreased, meaning that his accuracy increased. Thus choice (B) is correct.

15. (C)   Connection Question

In order to see if division of labor leads to increased output, we would need to see evidence like that observed by Smith in a pin factory: how many units are produced by people who complete an entire unit vs. how many units are produced by the same number of people on an assembly line? This bar graph shows only a single employee, and while it is true that her output has increased, it does not show the output of the other people on her team nor does it show how many units she could produce without help.

16. (A)   Connection Question

Remember, this graph represents a single employee, so it does not reveal any information about the division of labor. It only shows that the one employee has improved over time, which the authors will likely attribute to the fact that "workers who specialize in certain tasks...often learn to produce goods and services more efficiently and with higher quality" (lines 50-54).

CHAPTER FIFTEEN
PROBLEM SETS AND REVIEW

Now that you have read about reading strategies, passage formats, and question and answer analysis, it is time to test your knowledge with passage problem sets. But before you begin, take a few minutes to review the most important points from the previous chapters.

ACT Reading Test Format

- There are four "sets" of passages: three that contain single passages and one that contains paired passages about a related topic.
- There are 10 questions per passage set for a total of 40 questions.
- Passages are 500 to 900 words, from 8th grade to 12th grade reading level.
- Passages are pulled from four main subject areas: Literary Fiction, Science, Social Studies, and Humanities.

SAT Reading Test Format

- There are five "sets" of passages: four that contain single passages and one that contains paired passages about a related topic.
- There are 10 or 11 questions per passage set for a total of 52 questions.
- Passages are 500 to 750 words, from 9th grade to early undergraduate reading level.
- Two of the passages will have an accompanying table, graph, or figure.
- Passages are pulled from four main subject areas: Literary Fiction, Science, Social Studies, and History.

Time Management

- Aim to read passages in 2½ minutes or less.
- On the ACT, you have 35 minutes to complete the Reading Test. Budget 10 minutes for the four passage sets and 25 minutes for questions. This gives you 37.5 seconds per question.
- On the SAT, you have 65 minutes to complete the Reading Test. Budget 12½ minutes for the four passage sets and 52½ minutes for questions. This gives you just over a minute per question.
- Practice timed sections using a timer so you get the feel for how long you have worked on a question.
- Always guess when you do not know the answer before moving on to the next question. There is no penalty for wrong answers.
- If you finish a section before time is called, review your answers. Never finish early on the ACT or SAT.

General Reading Strategies

1. **Adjust your attitude.**
   - Attack the passage as if you are excited to read it.
   - Pretend that the topic is interesting.

2. **Adjust your reading speed.**
   - Slow down for the Main Idea, difficult topic sentences, and short passages.
   - Speed up for supporting paragraphs and easier text.

3. **Practice active reading.**
   - Predict: Make guesses about the outcome and author's reaction.
   - Question: Ask questions as you read.
   - Notate: Summarize each paragraph or section with short notes.
   - Visualize: Picture the setting and the author reacting.
   - Relate: Connect to the passage by comparing it to your personal experience.
   - Paraphrase: Rephrase difficult text using your own words.

4. **Identify non-fiction passage MAPS.**
   - Main Idea (the central theme of the passage)
   - Author's Attitude (how the author feels about the subject)
   - Purpose (the reason the author wrote the piece)
   - Structure (how the passage is organized)

5. **Recognize patterns on the ACT and SAT.**
   - Determine if a non-fiction, long passage opens in a common format to help you determine the main idea.
   - Watch for common patterns, such as pivotal words, attitude clues, multiple viewpoints, and double negatives.

6. **Master Literary Fiction Passages.**
   - Identify the characters' feelings about each other and the situation in which they find themselves.
   - Do not worry about finding the MAPS in fictional passages.

Single Passage Strategies

Passage Strategies

1. If necessary, notate line references from questions.
   - This is an optional strategy and is not optimal.
   - Skim the questions strictly for line references before reading the passage and make sidebars that correspond to each reference.

2. Read the introduction.
   - The introduction helps you understand the context of the excerpt.
   - Pay attention to who wrote the passage and the year it was published.

3. Read the entire passage.
   - Avoid shortcuts or gimmicks.
   - You must read the entire passage to understand it.

Question Strategies

4. Read the question.
   - Read every word in the question stem.
   - Turn an incomplete sentence into a question by rephrasing.

5. If necessary, return to the passage.
   - If the line reference is a single word or phrase, return to the passage and read from about three lines above the line reference to about three lines below the line reference.
   - If the line reference is a complete sentence or more, return to the passage and read just the lines in the line reference.

6. Prephrase an answer.
   - Prephrase an answer to the question before reading the answer choices.

7. Match an answer choice.
   - Find an answer choice that is closest to your prephrase.

Confidence Quotation
"Natural ability is important, but you can go far without it if you have the focus, drive, desire and positive attitude."
-Kristen Sweetland, Canadian Triathlete

Paired Passage Strategies

1. Read the introduction.
   - The introduction helps you understand the context of the excerpts, as the passage likely came from a much longer source.
   - Pay attention to who wrote the passages and the year they were published.
   - Based on the introduction, make a prediction about whether the authors will agree or disagree on the topic.

2. Read Passage 1.
   - Avoid shortcuts or gimmicks such as skimming the passage or reading the questions first.
   - The only way to fully understand an ACT and SAT passage and answer the questions correctly is to read the entire passage.

3. Do not go on to Passage 2. Instead, answer the questions about Passage 1.
   - It is important to read every word in the question stem.
   - Turn an incomplete sentence into a question by rephrasing.
   - If necessary, return to the passage to read a line reference.
   - Prephrase an answer before reading the answer choices.
   - Match your prephrase to an answer choice.
   - On the SAT, be careful to complete your answer booklet correctly if you are forced to skip questions.

4. Reread the introduction.
   - This will allow you to become reacquainted with the context of the second passage.

5. Read Passage 2.
   - Follow all of the strategies listed above for reading Passage 1.

6. Answer the questions about Passage 2.
   - Follow all of the strategies listed above for answering the questions for Passage 1.

7. Answer the questions about both passages.

Question Types

Words-In-Context Questions
- These questions require you to interpret a word, phrase, an entire sentence, or a clause in the passage.

Literary Comprehension Questions
- These questions ask you to recall facts directly stated in the passage.
- The most common question type simply asks for Facts and Details, but you will also encounter Main Idea, Reason and Results, and Comparison and Contrast questions.

Confidence Quotation

"There are admirable potentialities in every human being. Believe in your strength and your youth. Learn to repeat endlessly to yourself, 'It all depends on me.'"
-André Gide, Nobel Prize-winning French author

Extended Reasoning Questions
- These questions require you to draw conclusions based on information in the passage.
- There are three types of Extended Reasoning questions: 1) Style Questions (which may address an author's purpose, attitude, or use of rhetorical devices), 2) Inference Questions (which may be about a general inference or a hypothetical point of view), and 3) Advanced Questions (which may ask you to find parallel reasoning or a way to strengthen or weaken an argument).

Answer Choice Traps

☠ Opposite Answers
- Present an idea that is opposite of the right answer and your prephrase.

☠ Extreme Answers
- Use words that are difficult to defend.

☠ True But Wrong Answers
- Make true statements about a portion of the passage that is not the subject of the question.

☠ True To A Point Answers
- Provide an answer that is "half-right."

☠ True to You Answers
- Use facts that are likely a part of your prior knowledge but were not provided in the passage.

☠ Copycat Answers (SAT only)
- Use words and phrases directly from the text.

Exclusive SAT Content

Command of Evidence Reading Questions
- These questions test your ability to pinpoint where in the text an answer is located.
- Most questions will be Best Evidence Paired Questions, but you can also expect some Best Evidence Support and Contradict Questions.

Command of Evidence Charts and Graphs Questions
- These questions ask you to interpret data from line graphs, bar graphs, scatter plots, pie charts, or other infographics.
- Location Questions simply ask you to locate the information in the figure, while Conclusion Questions require you to draw a conclusion based on the data. Connection Questions connect the information in the passage to the data in a figure.

Some of the questions on the following problem sets are SAT-only type questions. In the directions for each set, we explain that you can skip these questions if you are focusing only on the ACT. We would, however, recommend that you complete them anyway, as the skills needed to tackle these questions are tested in other ways on the ACT.

Single Passages Problem Set 1 (Literary Fiction)

Read the following passage and then answer the corresponding questions. Questions 8 and 11 are types of questions that appear only on the SAT. If you are taking the ACT, you may choose to skip these. Answers begin on page 366.

This passage is from the 1911 novel, *Ethan Frome*, by Edith Wharton. As it opens, Ethan Frome has been sent to pick up his wife's cousin, Mattie, who is serving as a live-in house-keeper and caretaker for the ailing wife. He watches Mattie through the window as the town dance ends.

As he stood in the darkness outside the church these memories came back with the poignancy of vanished things. Watching Mattie whirl down the floor from hand
Line to hand he wondered how he could ever have thought
5 that his dull talk interested her. To him, who was never gay but in her presence, her gaiety seemed plain proof of indifference. The face she lifted to her dancers was the same which, when she saw him, always looked like a window that has caught the sunset. He even noticed two
10 or three gestures which, in his fatuity, he had thought she kept for him: a way of throwing her head back when she was amused, as if to taste her laugh before she let it out, and a trick of sinking her lids slowly when anything charmed or moved her.
15 The sight made him unhappy, and his unhappiness roused his latent fears. His wife had never shown any jealousy of Mattie, but of late she had grumbled increas-ingly over the house-work and found oblique ways of attracting attention to the girl's inefficiency. Zeena had
20 always been what Starkfield called "sickly," and Frome had to admit that, if she were as ailing as she believed, she needed the help of a stronger arm than the one which lay so lightly in his during the night walks to the farm. Mattie had no natural turn for housekeeping, and her
25 training had done nothing to remedy the defect. She was quick to learn, but forgetful and dreamy, and not disposed to take the matter seriously. Ethan had an idea that if she were to marry a man she was fond of the dormant instinct would wake, and her pies and biscuits
30 become the pride of the county; but domesticity in the abstract did not interest her. At first she was so awkward that he could not help laughing at her; but she laughed with him and that made them better friends. He did his best to supplement her unskilled efforts, getting up
35 earlier than usual to light the kitchen fire, carrying in the wood overnight, and neglecting the mill for the farm that he might help her about the house during the day. He even crept down on Saturday nights to scrub the kitchen floor after the women had gone to bed; and Zeena, one
40 day, had surprised him at the churn and had turned away silently, with one of her queer looks.
Of late there had been other signs of her disfavour, as intangible but more disquieting. One cold winter morning, as he dressed in the dark, his candle flickering
45 in the draught of the ill-fitting window, he had heard her speak from the bed behind him.

"The doctor don't want I should be left without anybody to do for me," she said in her flat whine.
He had supposed her to be asleep, and the sound of her
50 voice had startled him, though she was given to abrupt explosions of speech after long intervals of secretive silence.
He turned and looked at her where she lay indistinctly outlined under the dark calico quilt, her high-boned face
55 taking a grayish tinge from the whiteness of the pillow.
"Nobody to do for you?" he repeated.
"If you say you can't afford a hired girl when Mattie goes."
Frome turned away again, and taking up his razor
60 stooped to catch the reflection of his stretched cheek in the blotched looking-glass above the wash-stand.
"Why on earth should Mattie go?"
"Well, when she gets married, I mean," his wife's drawl came from behind him.
65 "Oh, she'd never leave us as long as you needed her," he returned, scraping hard at his chin.
"I wouldn't ever have it said that I stood in the way of a poor girl like Mattie marrying a smart fellow like Denis Eady," Zeena answered in a tone of plaintive
70 self-effacement.
Ethan, glaring at his face in the glass, threw his head back to draw the razor from ear to chin. His hand was steady, but the attitude was an excuse for not making an immediate reply.
75 "And the doctor don't want I should be left without anybody," Zeena continued. "He wanted I should speak to you about a girl he's heard about, that might come—"
Ethan laid down the razor and straightened himself with a laugh.
80 "Denis Eady! If that's all, I guess there's no such hurry to look round for a girl."
"Well, I'd like to talk to you about it," said Zeena obstinately.
He was getting into his clothes in fumbling haste. "All
85 right. But I haven't got the time now; I'm late as it is," he returned, holding his old silver turnip-watch to the candle.
Zeena, apparently accepting this as final, lay watching him in silence while he pulled his suspenders over his
90 shoulders and jerked his arms into his coat; but as he went toward the door she said, suddenly and incisively: "I guess you're always late, now you shave every morning."

1. The sentence in lines 7-9 ("The. . . sunset" is best described as

   A) an understatement.
   B) an allusion.
   C) a simile.
   D) a cliché.

2. The "gestures" referred to in line 10 might best be characterized as

   A) flirtatious behavior.
   B) offensive symbols.
   C) symptoms of illness.
   D) a secret code.

3. The phrase "latent fears" (line 16) refers to Ethan's worry that

   A) Zeena suspected his feelings for Mattie.
   B) Mattie found him dull.
   C) Mattie would marry Denis Eady.
   D) Mattie's departure would leave Zeena without a caretaker.

4. In context, "turn" (line 24) most nearly means

   A) excursion.
   B) opportunity.
   C) inclination.
   D) revolution.

5. The sentence in lines 19-23 ("Zeena . . . farm") suggests that

   A) the townspeople did not believe Zeena was ill.
   B) Zeena and Ethan walked together each evening.
   C) Mattie was not physically capable of helping Zeena.
   D) Ethan felt guilty about his inability to care for his wife.

6. The "defect" in line 25 refers to Mattie's

   A) intellectual shortcomings.
   B) lack of strength.
   C) poor domestic skills.
   D) inability to find a husband.

7. Ethan believes Mattie will become more serious about domestic chores when

   A) she has a husband for whom she cares.
   B) Zeena grumbles about the housework.
   C) the Fromes replace her with a new caretaker.
   D) he is caught completing her chores.

8. Which choice provides the best evidence for the answer to the previous question?

   A) Lines 27-31 ("Ethan . . . her")
   B) Lines 37-41 ("He even . . . looks")
   C) Lines 53-55 ("He . . . pillow")
   D) Lines 80-81 ("'Denis . . . girl'")

9. In the context of the passage, the narrative in lines 33-41 ("He did . . . looks") suggests that

   A) Zeena did not approve of Mattie dating any of the men in town.
   B) Ethan is compulsively neat and organized.
   C) Zeena expects her husband to contribute to the household chores.
   D) Ethan is worried that Zeena will replace their incapable housekeeper.

10. The passage suggests that Zeena believes Denis Eady

    A) belongs to a higher social class than Mattie.
    B) fears she will not approve of him as a husband for her cousin.
    C) has already proposed to Mattie.
    D) will reside with the Fromes when he marries Mattie.

11. Which choice provides the best evidence for the answer to the previous question?

    A) Lines 16-19 ("His . . . inefficiency")
    B) Lines 37-41 ("He . . . looks")
    C) Lines 67-70 ("'I wouldn't . . . self-effacement'")
    D) Lines 88-93 ("Zeena . . . morning'")

12. Ethan responds to his wife's concerns about Mattie leaving after marriage with

    A) tender reassurance.
    B) feigned composure.
    C) immediate denial.
    D) weak excuses.

13. In the context of the entire passage, it can be inferred that

    A) Ethan deeply respects the vows of marriage.
    B) Zeena's illness is progressing more rapidly than originally predicted.
    C) Ethan is in danger of losing his job at the mill.
    D) Zeena is suspicious of her husband's feelings for Mattie.

Single Passage Problem Set 2 (Social Studies/Humanities)

Read the following passage and then answer the corresponding questions. Question 6 is a type of question that appears only on the SAT. If you are taking the ACT, you may choose to skip the question. Answers begin on page 368.

The following passage is from Noel Polk, "Faulkner at 100." Published in *Humanities* in 1997.

Faulkner lived a good deal of his life in opposition to many of the things Mississippi has come to represent; his life and a good deal of his work are frontal assaults on its
Line middle-class pretensions, its cultural backwardness, and
5 its racist politics.

Mississippians, of course, resented their collective portrayal in his works, and returned his implicit criticism with a combination of indifference and calumny. It swallowed hard and reacted negatively when he analyzed
10 its racist traditions in *Light in August* (1932), *Absalom, Absalom!* (1936), *Go Down, Moses* (1942), and *Intruder in the Dust* (1948); but when in the mid fifties he carried his criticism to the public arena, "official" Mississippi began to return the antagonism with all the power
15 its newspapers and pulpits, bully and religious, could muster. During his lifetime and for some years beyond, official Mississippi was hard put indeed to find anything nice to say about him either publicly or privately, and there were times when a public ceremony in his home
20 state connected with him and his work would have more likely been an assembly to burn his books than to have his portrait hung or his books discussed. Faulkner has long since had the last laugh, and it may be too easy, this side of the tumultuous days of the Civil Rights
25 movement, to undervalue his personal struggle in taking the public stands he took. If we do, though, we will miss a good deal of the significance of his life and work as it grew out of the complex combination of powerful emotions that Mississippi evoked in him and, thanks to
30 him, in us. Indeed, Faulkner scholars and readers in other countries tell me that part of his continuing appeal to them lies precisely in his love of and his commitment to his own country, so that part of what makes him international seems to be his very localness in Mississippi.
35 In a 1933 essay, Faulkner suggested that a writer in Mississippi had two alternatives: to escape or to indict. He tried the former by simply leaving as frequently as he could: to Canada, where he enlisted in the Royal Air Force, in an unsuccessful effort to get into World War
40 I; to New Haven and New York in the early twenties; to New Orleans and Europe in the mid twenties; to Hollywood sporadically to try to make a living when his novels weren't selling. He often indicted his home region in several novels and stories, which frequently depicted
45 the South's and Mississippi's people as backward, violent, oppressive, and ignorant.

Yet escape Mississippi he could not, either in his fiction or in his personal life—drawn to it as he was because it was home and because it provided the specific
50 energy for much of his fiction. The conflicts that Mississippi caused in him were so terrific that readers and critics have surely been right to assume that Quentin Compson's torment at the end of *Absalom, Absalom!* is also Faulkner's: Asked by his Harvard roommate why
55 he hates the South, Quentin responds "I dont. I dont! I dont hate it! I dont hate it!" His most famous character describes a state of mind that cannot admit that it loves what it hates or that it hates what it loves.

But Faulkner knew, or learned, that to escape or to
60 indict is not to engage or to understand, and it seems to me that one of the most important threads running through his work is the gradual expansion of his willingness to engage rather than simply to repudiate his home region. All of his fiction, but especially his late work,
65 is marked by an unrelenting insistence that his fictional characters face their own and their culture's powerful complexities and deal with them rather than try to escape them.

1. The passage is primarily concerned with Faulkner's

    A) criticism of the middle class in the South.
    B) relationship with the state of Mississippi.
    C) attempts to move away from his homeland.
    D) acceptance of his heritage.

2. The author's remark in lines 8-12 ("It . . . *Dust*") can best be described as

    A) personification.
    B) an analogy.
    C) symbolism.
    D) a parody.

3. In lines 16-22 ("During . . . discussed"), the author suggests that during Faulkner's lifetime the government of Mississippi

    A) profited from the success of Faulkner's books.
    B) was embroiled in the Civil Rights debate.
    C) contemplated burning the author's works.
    D) was unlikely to recognize the author's accomplishments.

4. Lines 22-26 ("Faulkner . . . took") suggest that

    A) Mississippi acknowledged its racist politics after the Civil Rights movement.
    B) Faulkner was amused by the public reaction to his books.
    C) the perceived difficulty for Faulkner in criticizing Mississippi has been tempered by time.
    D) the emotional toll on the people of Mississippi and on Faulkner was a consequence of exposing racism.

5. According to the author, one reason that international readers continue to appreciate Faulkner's works is the author's

    A) attempts to escape his heritage.
    B) protest of Southern racism.
    C) devout patriotism to the United States.
    D) provincial depictions of Mississippi.

6. Which choice provides the best evidence for the answer to the previous question?

    A) Lines 6-8 ("Mississippians . . . calumny")
    B) Lines 30-34 ("Indeed . . . Mississippi")
    C) Lines 37-43 ("He . . . selling")
    D) Lines 59-64 ("But . . . region")

7. In line 43, "indicted" most nearly means

    A) endorsed.
    B) referenced.
    C) traveled to.
    D) criticized.

8. In line 50, the "conflicts" refer to

    A) racial tensions in Mississippi before the Civil Rights movement.
    B) Faulkner's internal struggle with his feelings about his home state.
    C) the veiled antagonism that existed between Mississippi and Faulkner.
    D) disagreements between Quentin Compson and his roommate.

9. In line 51, "terrific" most nearly means

    A) outstanding.
    B) frightening.
    C) premium.
    D) intense.

10. The reference to "Quentin Compson" (lines 52-53) primarily serves to

    A) demonstrate that all of Faulkner's characters object to Southern ways of life.
    B) introduce Faulkner's most famous novel
    C) draw a parallel between the character's and Faulkner's feelings.
    D) argue that political changes are needed in Mississippi.

11. The last paragraph suggests that Faulkner eventually realized that he

    A) had to come to terms with his culture.
    B) affected innocent citizens by criticizing Mississippi.
    C) could help alleviate some of Mississippi's racial tensions by working with the government.
    D) created characters that echoed his personal feelings.

Single Passage Problem Set 3 (Science)

Read the following passage and then answer the questions. Questions 4, 6, 13, and 14 are types of questions that appear only on the SAT. If you are taking the ACT, you may choose to skip these. Answers begin on page 369.

The following passage is from Bob Silbert, "The Big Question: The Reason for the Genesis Mission." Published for NASA in 2011.

Where did the world come from? According to Iroquois legend, a pregnant woman fell from the clouds and needed a place to land, so a muskrat brought mud
Line from the bottom of the sea and laid it onto the back
5 of a turtle, where it grew into the Earth. The Vikings, meanwhile, had it that the Earth was built from the body parts of a giant frost ogre.

Modern science offers a much stranger story:

An immense gas cloud, peppered with atoms made by
10 stars, squeezed itself together so tightly that its center ignited into a nuclear furnace and became our sun. The remaining bits and pieces of the cloud, known as the solar nebula, clumped together and formed the planets, moons, asteroids, and comets.

15 Scientists have plenty of evidence that this is correct, but an important chunk of the story is missing. According to Don Burnett, principal investigator for the Genesis mission[1], scientists think they understand how collisions of kilometer-size asteroids can ultimately build a
20 planet. "But," he said, "how you go from a dust grain to a kilometer is pretty much an open issue at the present time."

Gravity alone doesn't seem to do the trick. "People have tried to do the theories," Burnett explained. "There
25 are gravitational instabilities that apparently happen in a thin disk of gas (that, under the right circumstances, could lead to dust and gas accreting into larger bodies), but it is widely accepted that the amount of turbulence under the conditions of the solar nebula would prevent
30 these gravitational instabilities from working. We don't know—it's a wide-open question—how you go from a micron to a kilometer."

Another puzzle, which has been perplexing cosmochemists for decades, may help to point the way to an
35 explanation of how the planets began to form. In most ways, the ingredients that make up the solar system appear to have been very well-mixed, so that the proportions of isotopes of most elements look the same everywhere. But scientists have found surprising differences
40 in the isotopes of certain elements. And this anomaly is particularly striking with regard to isotopes of the most abundant element of the planets in the inner solar system: oxygen.

Scientists have proposed various chemical processes
45 to help explain these differences, and identifying the right ones could lead to a good theory of how those first dust grains began to stick together and form the seeds of today's planets. But one vital piece of information has
50 been missing: a thorough analysis of the composition of the solar nebula. Learn how the solar system started out,

and you can attempt to explain how it evolved to what we see today. How can anyone analyze a cloud of gas and dust that existed some 4.6 billion years ago? The key,
55 scientists believe, is the Sun.

"The composition of the Sun is the starting composition for everything in the solar system," Burnett said. That's because nearly all of the original solar nebula exists today as the Sun, which has more than 99% of the
60 solar system's mass. And while the Sun's core undergoes great changes as it turns hydrogen into helium and, in the process, liberates the energy that makes our lives possible, the atoms that make up the outer portion of the Sun are thought to be virtually unchanged since the birth
65 of the solar system. Analyze the Sun's surface, and you produce a picture of the original cloud of gas and dust from which the solar system formed.

But a mission to fly to the Sun, scoop up a sample of its surface, and return it to Earth is well beyond
70 today's capabilities. How then to put the Sun under the microscope?

[1]A space mission in which the Genesis probe collected solar wind from the sun.

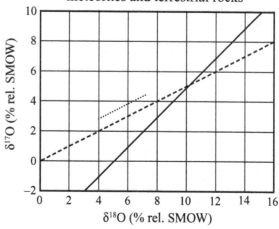

Oxygen isotope ratios of meteorites and terrestrial rocks

- - - - Earth and moon
·········· Meteorites from Mars
——— Carbonaceous Chondrite Meteorites

The graph above compares the ratio of oxygen isotopes on the Earth, moon, Mars, and carbonaceous chondrite meteorites. The lower case delta (δ) that precedes the isotope name indicates how much the ratio of these isotopes to ^{16}O differs from that same ratio in a reference standard (the Standard Mean Ocean Water or SMOW), expressed in per mil, or parts-per-thousand.

Cosmologists believe that planetary objects with ratios resulting in parallel slopes were created in a similar manner.

1. The primary purpose of the passage is to

    A) explain difficulties with examining solar nebula.
    B) dispute gravitational forces as the cause of Earth's creation.
    C) compare the legendary origins of the Earth with the factual explanation.
    D) defend the Genesis space mission.

2. In line 9, "peppered" most nearly means

    A) seasoned.
    B) pelted.
    C) interspersed.
    D) invigorated.

3. The prevailing mystery about planet formation that eludes scientists is understanding how

    A) to safely explore the surface of the sun.
    B) gravity becomes unstable in turbulent environments.
    C) large masses are created from small particles.
    D) an immense gas cloud was pressed tightly.

4. Which choice provides the best evidence for the answer to the previous question?

    A) Lines 11-14 ("The remaining . . . comets")
    B) Lines 20-22 ("'But . . . time'")
    C) Lines 35-39 ("In most . . . everywhere")
    D) Lines 49-51 ("But . . . nebula'")

5. According to the passage, gravity by itself does not explain the origin of planets because

    A) the composition of the sun cannot be confirmed.
    B) the laws of gravity cannot be adapted to larger celestial bodies.
    C) the isotopes of some elements are not proportional to others in soil samples.
    D) the volatile environment of solar nebula prevent expected gravitational behaviors from occurring.

6. Which choice provides the best evidence for the answer to the previous question?

    A) Lines 24-30 ("'There. . . working'")
    B) Lines 30-32 ("'We . . . kilometer'")
    C) Lines 33-35 ("Another . . . form")
    D) Lines 40-43 ("And this . . . oxygen")

7. In line 45, "differences" refer to

    A) the varying elements in solar nebula and planets.
    B) the disproportion of isotopes of some elements in planetary composition.
    C) chemical processes that may indicate the origin of Earth.
    D) the two leading theories of how large celestial bodies were created.

8. The statement in lines 60-65 ("And while . . . system") indicates that

    A) life on Earth is sustained by vast transformations occurring in the sun's core.
    B) the sun accounts for an overwhelming majority of the solar system's mass.
    C) the outer portion of the sun has little effect on Earth's atmosphere.
    D) the sun is relatively unchanged from its creation 4.6 billion years ago.

Continue this passage on the next page.
⟶

9. In context, "picture" (line 66) most nearly means

   A) conception.
   B) reminiscence.
   C) photograph.
   D) development.

10. Lines 68-70 ("But a . . . capabilities") suggests that

    A) it is too dangerous to fly near the sun.
    B) studying the Earth's composition will reveal information about the make-up of the sun.
    C) it may one day be possible to travel to the sun to retrieve a sample of its outer layer.
    D) the ingredients that make up the sun may never be known.

11. The passage demonstrates use of all of the following EXCEPT

    A) direct quotation.
    B) parenthetical reference.
    C) personal anecdote.
    D) rhetorical questions.

12. The tone of this passage can be described as both

    A) nostalgic and respectful.
    B) baffled and sullen.
    C) skeptical and emphatic.
    D) curious and appreciative.

13. According to the data in the figure, when the ratio of $\delta^{17}O$ of carbonaceous chondrite meteorites is 5, what is the approximate ratio of $\delta^{18}O$?

    A) 0
    B) 4
    C) 6
    D) 10

14. Which statement is best supported by the data presented in the figure?

    A) Rocks from Mars have lighter isotopes in proportion to ^{16}O than do rocks from Earth.
    B) The moon likely broke from the Earth due to a cosmic collision.
    C) The discovery of the oxygen isotopes in carbonaceous chondrite meteorites offered scientists alternative theories about the origins of planets.
    D) Scientists believe that Earth and Mars have comparable origins.

Notes:

Single Passage Problem Set 4 (Social Studies/History)

Read the following passage and then answer the corresponding questions. Questions 5 and 6 are types of questions that appear only on the SAT. If you are taking the ACT, you may choose to skip these. Answers begin on page 371.

The following passage is adapted from Joseph P. Reidy, "Black Me in Navy Blue During the Civil War." Published in *Prologue* magazine, 2001.

Given the wealth of available information about Civil War soldiers, the comparative poverty of such knowledge about Civil War sailors borders on the astonishing.
Line Two explanations account for this imbalance. First, the
5 broad narrative of presidential leadership and the clash of armies in Virginia that Ken Burns's *The Civil War* told so powerfully all but excludes naval forces from the tale. Second, existing accounts of the naval Civil War have focused on the strategic role of naval forces in
10 the contest, the governmental architects of naval policy, the naval officers who masterminded operations, and the innovations in technology and weaponry to the near exclusion of the enlisted sailors' war. No image of "Jack Tar"[1] comparable to Bell I. Wiley's classic portraits of
15 "Billy Yank" and "Johnny Reb"[2] fills the popular imagination or the works of Civil War historians.

Because the navy, unlike the army, was racially integrated, understanding the history of black sailors requires some effort but even more interpretive caution to
20 unravel it from that of all Civil War sailors. Exploring the similarities and differences in the experiences of black and white enlisted men must avoid viewing the racial groups in strictly monolithic terms that do not allow for internal complexity and diversity and shifting, if not
25 altogether porous, borders. The work must also beware currently popular understandings of the black soldiers' experience. Often framed around the Fifty-fourth Massachusetts Volunteer Infantry, that tale depicts stoic sacrifice and daunting perseverance in pursuit of freedom
30 and equality that in the end was crowned with "Glory," the impression conveyed by the popular feature film. The black sailors' story fits awkwardly, if at all, within that image.

The black enlistees who had been slaves—in many
35 instances down to the time of enlistment—stood apart from the freemen of all colors and nations. Often accepted into service on a supposition of inferiority, stigmatized as "contrabands," and rated and paid at the lowest levels of the rating and pay scales, these men
40 often could not escape the stereotypes cast upon them no matter how creditably they performed their assigned duties. In, but not necessarily of, the crews with which they served, the contrabands performed the manual labor necessary to keep a steam vessel functioning and the
45 busywork that officers considered the foundation of good order and discipline on warships: holystoning[3], scrubbing, scraping, painting, and polishing. Although black men routinely served on gun crews at general quarters, they stood a far greater chance of serving with small-
50 arms crews, armed with swords, rifles, and pistols, for repelling boarders, and with damage control units, armed

with water hoses for dousing fires and battle-axes for cutting away damaged spars and rigging. Small-arms
55 crews consisting of contrabands generally exercised separately from those consisting of white sailors.

Although the Navy Department did not establish a formal system of racial separation during the Civil War, Secretary Welles's guidelines for recruiting and rating
60 black sailors nearly accomplished exactly that. For wittingly or not, the policy reinforced the prejudices of recruiters, naval officers, and white enlisted men to the effect that black enlistees would contribute to the war effort as laborers and servants rather than as skilled
65 seamen. Of the approximately 17,600 men whose base rating is recorded, more than 14,400 (or 82 percent) were rated as boy or landsman[4]. This discounting of black men's seafaring skill at times plagued even the most experienced of men. For several of his many enlistments,
70 James Forten Dunbar, nephew of the prominent Philadelphia sailmaker and abolitionist James Forten, was rated a landsman rather than seaman, to which his three decades of naval service more than entitled him.

[1]Term used to refer to Navy seamen.
[2]Terms used to refer to Union and Confederate army soldiers, respectively, later depicted by Wiley in mid-20th century books
[3]Scrubbing ship decks with soft sandstone.
[4]The lowest rank in the Navy was boy, followed by landsman. The rank of seaman was higher than both.

1. The tone in the first sentence is best described as

A) somewhat perplexed.
B) cautiously hopeful.
C) hopelessly distressed.
D) boldly emphatic.

2. In line 2, "poverty" is best understood to mean

A) difficulty.
B) scarcity.
C) contingency.
D) bankruptcy.

3. The author suggests which of the following about the "image" (line 13) of Jack Tar?

    A) It was not popular until several years after the Civil War.
    B) It is not as glorified as the representations of Civil War soldiers.
    C) It was reserved for black sailors instead of white sailors.
    D) It was not created by a famous author.

4. The author of the passage most strongly suggests that

    A) the Navy was considered more elite than the army.
    B) the public mistakenly assumes that all black enlistees fought for the Union.
    C) few black sailors enlisted to pursue freedom and equality.
    D) accounts of black soldiers in the Civil War are often romanticized.

5. Which choice provides the best evidence for the answer to the previous question?

    A) Lines 4-8 ("First . . . tale")
    B) Lines 17-20 ("Because . . . sailors")
    C) Lines 27-33 ("'Often . . . image'")
    D) Lines 60-65 ("For . . . seamen'")

6. Which choice best supports the author's claim that many black enlistees were not freed from slavery until they joined the Navy?

    A) Lines 13-16 ("No image . . . historians")
    B) Lines 34-36 ("The . . . nations")
    C) Lines 42-47 ("'In . . . polishing'")
    D) Lines 57-60 ("Although . . . that'")

7. In line 38, the quotation marks around the word "contrabands" serve to

    A) deny the power of a label.
    B) quote a military authority.
    C) introduce unfamiliar jargon.
    D) highlight the use of sarcasm.

8. The duties listed in lines 46-47 serve as examples of

    A) inferior assignments reserved for black enlistees.
    B) basic jobs performed by new recruits.
    C) daily chores assigned to small-arms crews.
    D) orders issued by the admiral of a ship.

9. The author of the passage suggests that black sailors most often were assigned to small arms crews because

    A) white sailors assigned to gun crews refused to work with black crew members.
    B) the Navy declined to give black enlistees any weapons.
    C) small-arms crews were considered inferior to gun crews.
    D) the Navy made an effort to adequately utilize the individual skills of each sailor.

10. Which of the following examples, if true, would most effectively undermine the author's argument in the last paragraph?

    A) A black enlistee with ten year's experience on a riverboat was ranked as seaman.
    B) A white sailor served on a small-arms crew.
    C) A white enlistee became a commissioned officer after four year's service.
    D) A black sailor was not allowed to eat at the officer's table in the galley.

11. In context, "rating" (line 66) most nearly means

    A) reprimand.
    B) classification.
    C) appraisal.
    D) limit.

12. According to the passage, James Forten Dunbar is an example of someone who

    A) enlisted to pursue freedom and equality.
    B) attained the rank of seaman.
    C) was not effectively employed because of his race.
    D) disagreed with the Navy Department's system of racial separation.

Single Passage Problem Set 5 (Science)

Read the following passage and then answer the questions. Questions 5 and 10 are types of questions that appear only on the SAT. If you are taking the ACT, you may choose to skip these. Answers begin on page 373.

The following passage is adapted from the 2016 OpenStax textbook, *Biology*, by Yael Avissar, Jung Choi, Jean DeSaix, et. al.

Viruses are diverse entities. They vary in their structure, their replication methods, and in their target hosts.
Nearly all forms of life—from bacteria and archaea to
Line eukaryotes such as plants, animals, and fungi—have
5 viruses that infect them. While most biological diversity
can be understood through evolutionary history, such
as how species have adapted to conditions and environments, much about virus origins and evolution remains
unknown.
10   Viruses were first named in 1898, but a series of
important events around the globe led to their discovery.
In 1884, French microbiologist Charles Chamberland
invented the Chamberland Pasteur filter, a porcelain
filter with pores smaller than bacteria, which could
15 remove from any liquid sample all bacteria visible in a
microscope. Then in 1886, German agricultural chemist
Adolph Mayer demonstrated that tobacco mosaic
disease, a non-fungal disease of tobacco plants, could
be transferred from a diseased plant to a healthy one via
20 plant sap despite the fact that bacteria were not visible in
the sap extracts. Dmitri Ivanowski, a Russian botanist,
connected Chamberland's and Meyer's research in
1892; he showed that tobacco mosaic disease could be
transmitted via plant sap even after the Chamberland-
25 Pasteur filter had removed all microscopically visible
bacteria from the extract. He suggested that an undetectable infectious agent was the cause, but it wasn't until
Dutch microbiologist Martinus Beijerinck replicated the
experiments and confirmed Ivanowski's results that the
30 term *virus* was applied to the tiny organisms. Still, it was
many years before it was proven that these "unfilterable"
infectious agents were not simply very small bacteria but
were a new type of very small, disease-causing particle.
     Virions, single virus particles, are very small, about
35 20–250 nanometers in diameter. Unlike bacteria (which
are about 100 times larger), we cannot see viruses with a
compound light microscope, which was the only microscope available to the scientists of the 19th century. It
was not until the development of the electron microscope
40 in the late 1930s that scientists got their first good view
of the structure of the tobacco mosaic virus and other
viruses. The surface structure of virions can be observed
by both scanning and transmission electron microscopy,
whereas the internal structures of the virus can only be
45 observed in images from a transmission electron microscope. The use of these technologies has allowed for the
discovery of many viruses of all types of living organisms. They were initially grouped by shared morphology.
50 Later, groups of viruses were classified by the type of

nucleic acid they contained, DNA or RNA, and whether
their nucleic acid was single- or double-stranded. More
recently, molecular analysis of viral replicative cycles
has further refined their classification.
55   Although biologists have accumulated a significant
amount of knowledge about how present-day viruses
evolve, much less is known about how viruses originated in the first place. When exploring the evolutionary
history of most organisms, scientists can look at fossil
60 records and similar historic evidence. However, viruses
do not fossilize, so researchers must conjecture by
investigating how today's viruses evolve and by using
biochemical and genetic information to create speculative virus histories.
65   While most findings agree that viruses don't have
a single common ancestor, scholars have yet to find
a single hypothesis about virus origins that is fully
accepted in the field. One such hypothesis, called devolu-
tion or the regressive hypothesis, proposes to explain
70 the origin of viruses by suggesting that viruses evolved
from free-living cells. However, many components of
how this process might have occurred are a mystery. A
second hypothesis (called escapist or the progressive
hypothesis) accounts for viruses having either an RNA
75 or a DNA genome and suggests that viruses originated
from RNA and DNA molecules that escaped from a host
cell. A third hypothesis posits a system of self-replication
similar to that of other self-replicating molecules, likely
evolving alongside the cells they rely on as hosts; studies
80 of some plant pathogens support this hypothesis.
     As technology advances, scientists may develop and
refine further hypotheses to explain the origin of viruses.
The emerging field called virus molecular system-
atics attempts to do just that through comparisons of
85 sequenced genetic material. These researchers hope
to one day better understand the origin of viruses, a
discovery that could lead to advances in the treatments
for the ailments they produce.

1. The main purpose of the passage is to

    A) examine the technological inventions that allowed
       scientists to view microscopic particles.
    B) describe the experiments that led to the discovery
       of viruses.
    C) discuss the origin and history of viruses.
    D) evaluate the common hypotheses about the
       evolution of viruses.

2. Which of the following statements can most reasonably be inferred from the passage?

    A) Scientists do not have access to as much historical evidence about viruses as they do about most other organisms.
    B) The Chamberland Pasteur filter was invented to cure tobacco plants of disease.
    C) Bacteria cannot be viewed under a compound light microscope.
    D) Scientists have rejected all previous theories about the origin of viruses.

3. According to the passage, which scientist initially determined that filtered sap could transmit disease?

    A) Charles Chamberland
    B) Adoph Mayer
    C) Dmitri Ivanowski
    D) Martinus Beirjerinck

4. The authors suggest that little was known about viruses for so long because

    A) scientists were unsure how viruses should be classified.
    B) fungal diseases were often erroneously cited for causing illnesses.
    C) viruses do not fossilize.
    D) they were undetectable with compound light microscopes.

5. Which choice provides the best evidence for the answer to the previous question?

    A) Lines 16-21 ("Then . . . extracts")
    B) Lines 35-41 ("Unlike . . . viruses")
    C) Lines 49-54 ("'Later . . . classification'")
    D) Lines 60-64 ("However . . . histories'")

6. As it is used in line 46, "allowed" most nearly means

    A) permitted
    B) assigned
    C) considered
    D) made possible

7. The primary function of the fourth paragraph (lines 55-64) is to

    A) highlight the classification system for viruses.
    B) identify current hypotheses about the evolution of viruses.
    C) explain why the origin of viruses is still unknown today.
    D) compare the fossil records of viruses to those of other organisms.

8. As it is used in line 68, "field" most nearly means

    A) expanse of cleared land.
    B) a branch of study.
    C) a remote job location.
    D) the visible area.

9. According to the passage, some scientists propose that viruses originated

    A) from escaped bacteria.
    B) by duplicating themselves.
    C) from free-living DNA and RNA molecules.
    D) by imitating plant pathogens.

10. Which choice provides the best evidence for the answer to the previous question?

    A) Lines 55-58 ("Although . . . place")
    B) Lines 56-60 ("When . . . evidence")
    C) Lines 72-77 ("'A second . . . cell'")
    D) Lines 77-79 ("A third . . . hosts'")

11. The passage indicates that compared to bacteria, virions

    A) are much smaller.
    B) are more likely to be filtered.
    C) contain fewer DNA and RNA molecules.
    D) spend more time in host organisms.

12. Which of the following events in the passage occurred last chronologically?

    A) The electron microscope was invented.
    B) Viruses were filtered from plant sap.
    C) Martinus Beijerinck replicated Dmitri Ivanowski's experiments with tobacco plants.
    D) Viruses were classified by the number of strands in their nucleic acid.

Single Passage Problem Set 6 (Social Studies/Great Global Conversation)

> Read the following passage and then answer the corresponding questions. Questions 4, 11, 13, 14, and 15 are questions that appear only on the SAT. If you are taking the ACT, you may choose to skip these. Answers begin on page 375.

The following passage is adapted from U.S. Secretary of State Hillary Clinton's address to the United Nations Commission on the Status of Women, 2010.

Fifteen years ago, delegates from 189 countries met in Beijing for the Fourth World Conference on Women. It was a call to action—a call to the global community to
Line work for the laws, reforms, and social changes neces-
5 sary to ensure that women and girls everywhere finally have the opportunities they deserve to fulfill their own God-given potentials and contribute fully to the progress and prosperity of their societies.

For many of us in this room today, that was a call to
10 action that we have heeded. You have worked tirelessly, day in and day out, to translate those words into realities. And we have seen the evidence of such efforts everywhere.

In South Africa, women living in shanty towns came
15 together to build a housing development outside Cape Town all on their own, brick by brick. And today, their community has grown to more than 50,000 homes for low income families, most of them female-headed.

In Liberia, a group of church women began a prayer
20 movement to stop their country's brutal civil war. It grew to include thousands of women who helped force the two sides to negotiate a peace agreement. And then, those women helped elect Ellen Johnson Sirleaf president, the first woman to lead an African nation.

25 In the United States, a young woman had an idea for a website where anyone could help a small business on the other side of the world get off the ground. And today, the organization she co-founded, Kiva, has given more than $120 million in microloans to entrepreneurs in
30 developing.

Now these are just a few of the stories of what women around the world do every day to confront injustice, to solve crises, propel economies, improve living conditions, and promote peace. Women have shown time and
35 again that they will seize opportunities to improve their own and their families' lives. And even when it seems that no opportunity exists, they still find a way. And thanks to the hard work and persistence of women and men, we have made real gains toward meeting the goals
40 set in Beijing.

But the progress we have made in the past 15 years is by no means the end of the story. It is, maybe, if we're really lucky, the end of the beginning. There is still so much more to be done. We have to write the next
45 chapter to fully realize the dreams and potential that we set forth in Beijing. Because for too many millions and millions of girls and women, opportunity remains out of reach. Women are still the majority of the world's poor,
50 the uneducated, the unhealthy, the unfed. In too many places, women are treated not as full and equal human

beings with their own rights and aspirations, but as lesser creatures undeserving of the treatment and respect accorded to their husbands, their fathers, and their sons.

55 Women are the majority of the world's farmers, but are often forbidden from owning the land they tend to every day, or accessing the credit they need to invest in those farms and make them more productive.

Women care for the world's sick, but women and girls
60 are less likely to get treatment when they are sick.

Women raise the world's children, but too often receive inadequate care when they give birth. And as a result, childbirth remains a leading cause of death and injury to women worldwide.

65 Women rarely cause armed conflicts, but they always suffer their consequences. And when warring sides sit at one table to negotiate peace, women are often excluded, even though it is their future and their children's future that is being decided.

70 Though many countries have passed laws to deter violence against women, it remains a global pandemic. Women and girls are bought and sold to settle debts and resolve disputes. They are raped as both a tactic and a prize of armed conflict. They are beaten as punishment
75 for disobedience and as a warning to other women who might assert their rights. And millions of women and girls are enslaved in brothels, forced to work as prostitutes, while police officers pocket bribes and look the other way.

80 The status of the world's women is not only a matter of morality and justice. It is also a political, economic, and social imperative. Put simply, the world cannot make lasting progress if women and girls in the 21st century are denied their rights and left behind.

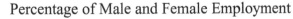

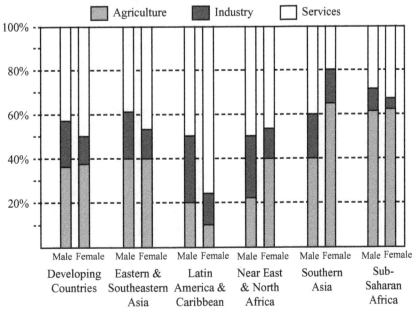

1. Over the course of the passage, the primary focus shifts from

   A) achievements made by audience members to goals set by a new generation of women.
   B) an explanation of the Fourth World Conference on Women to stereotypes that persist in developing countries.
   C) examples of progress in women's rights to examples of issues that still need to be addressed.
   D) the author's experiences in Beijing to her objectives for ending oppression.

2. As it is used in line 9, the word "call" most nearly means a

   A) social visit.
   B) summons.
   C) vocal cry.
   D) telephone communication.

3. It can reasonably be inferred from the passage that many members of the audience

   A) have dedicated much of the last fifteen years to helping oppressed women.
   B) were women who formerly lived in male-dominated countries.
   C) were not present at the Fourth World Conference on Women in Beijing.
   D) received insufficient medical care during childbirth.

4. Which choice provides the best evidence for the answer to the previous question?

   A) Lines 1-8 ("Fifteen . . . societies")
   B) Lines 9-12 ("For . . . realities")
   C) Lines 31-34 ("Now . . . peace")
   D) Lines 61-62 ("Women . . . birth")

5. The primary function of the third, fourth, and fifth paragraphs (lines 14-30) is to

   A) illustrate the advancements in women's rights that need to be replicated in the future.
   B) describe the type of opportunities that exist for women who live in developing countries.
   C) summarize the goals of the Fourth World Conference on Women.
   D) provide examples of the global progress that has occurred since the Fourth World Conference on Women.

Continue this passage on the next page.

6. An opponent of women's rights from a developing country claims that women around the world are offered the same chances for advancement as men but that women usually decline these offers. Which statement in the passage contradicts the opponent's claim?

    A) Lines 10-12 ("You . . . realities")
    B) Lines 27-30 ("And . . . developing")
    C) Lines 34-36 ("Women . . . lives")
    D) Lines 37-40 ("And . . . Beijing")

7. The sentence in lines 41-42 primarily serves which purpose in the passage?

    A) It challenges members of the audience to increase their participation in a cause.
    B) It makes a prediction about a claim made earlier in the passage.
    C) It refutes a common belief held by the speaker and the general public.
    D) It serves as a transition between the two main ideas in the passage.

8. Clinton uses the statement "It is, maybe, if we're really lucky, the end of the beginning" (lines 42-43) most nearly to mean

    A) women must be the authors of their lives.
    B) the ending of the story is yet unwritten and no one knows how it will conclude.
    C) there are several more planned sessions of the World Conference on Women.
    D) the initial phase of the women's movement has concluded but there is much more to be accomplished.

9. The author makes which of the following points about women?

    A) They comprise the majority of the global population living in poverty.
    B) They have contributed to social reform in much higher numbers than men.
    C) Few are allowed to participate in farming.
    D) They have attained nearly equal status as men in the United States.

10. According to Clinton, women are often left out of

    A) decisions about medical care.
    B) negotiations between countries in conflict.
    C) discussions about morality.
    D) policy making sessions about women's rights.

11. Which choice provides the best evidence for the answer to the previous question?

    A) Lines 59-60 ("Women . . . sick")
    B) Lines 66-69 ("And when . . . decided")
    C) Lines 80-81 ("The status . . . justice")
    D) Lines 81-84 ("It is . . . behind")

12. According to the passage, women still experience physical violence for all of the following reasons EXCEPT

    A) as a cautionary example for other rebellious women.
    B) as a strategy of war.
    C) as a punishment for a social impropriety.
    D) as a consequence of defiance.

13. According to the figure, in which two regions is the percentage of males employed in both industry and services higher than the percentage of females employed in these sectors?

    A) Eastern & Southeastern Asia and Latin America & Caribbean
    B) Latin America & Caribbean and Southern Asia
    C) Eastern & Southeastern Asia and Sub-Saharan Africa
    D) Near East & North Africa and Southern Asia

14. Which statement is best supported by the information in the figure?

    A) There are fewer industry jobs in Sub-Saharan Africa than there are in Latin America & Caribbean.
    B) Women have access to the same agricultural resources that men do in Eastern & South Eastern Asia.
    C) In most regions, women outnumber men in agriculture while men outnumber women in industry.
    D) Fewer women are employed in services in Southern Asia than women are employed in services in Latin America & Caribbean.

15. Do data in the figure prove Clinton's claim that women are the majority of the world's farmers?

    A) Yes, because the data indicates that there are more women farmers than men farmers in all but one of the regions.
    B) Yes, because the data provides evidence that women are more often employed in agriculture than in industry and services.
    C) No, because the data does not provide evidence of women in agriculture for all regions of the world.
    D) No, because the data is in percentages instead of in the numbers of women in agriculture.

Paired Passages Problem Set (Social Studies)

> Read the following passages and then answer the corresponding questions. Question 6 is a type of question that appears only on the SAT. If you are taking the ACT, you may choose to skip this question. Answers begin on page 378.

Passage 1 is from "Evaluating Online Learning: Challenges and Strategies for Success," US Department of Education, 2008. Passage 2 is from "Online Learning: One Teacher's Success Story," Tori Watts, 2016.

Passage 1

Online learning is a relatively new development in K-12 education but is rapidly expanding in both number of programs and participants. Given this expansion and
Line a dearth of existing research on the topic, it is critical to
5 conduct rigorous evaluations of online learning in K-12 settings to ensure that it does what people hope it will do: help improve student learning.

However, those undertaking such evaluations may well encounter a number of technical and methodological
10 issues that can make this type of research difficult to execute. For example, the scant research literature on K-12 online learning evaluation provides few existing frameworks to help evaluators describe and analyze programs, or tools, such as surveys or rubrics, they can
15 use to collect data or assess program quality. Another common challenge when students are studying online is the difficulty of examining what is happening in multiple, geographically distant learning sites. And multifaceted education resources—such as vast Web sites
20 offering a wide range of features or virtual schools that offer courses from multiple vendors—are also hard to evaluate, as are programs that utilize technologies and instructional models that are new to users.

Furthermore, evaluations of online learning often
25 occur in the context of a politically loaded debate about whether such programs are worth the investment and how much funding is needed to run a high-quality program; about whether online learning really provides students with high-quality learning opportunities; and
30 about how to compare online and traditional approaches. Understandably, funders and policymakers—not to mention students and their parents—want data that show whether online learning can be as effective as traditional educational approaches and which online models are
35 the best. These stakeholders may or may not think about evaluation in technical terms, but all of them are interested in how students perform in these new programs. At the same time, many online program leaders have multiple goals in mind, such as increased student engage-
40 ment or increased student access to high-quality courses and teachers. They argue that test scores alone are an inadequate measure for capturing important differences between traditional and online learning settings. And, like educators in any setting—traditional or online—they
45 may feel a natural trepidation about inviting evaluators to take a critical look at their program, fearing that it will hamper the progress of their program, rather than strengthen it.

Passage 2

With the sudden development and pervasion of online
50 learning programs in the last decade, it is no surprise that education authorities are slow to endorse such non-traditional learning outlets as online schools and supplementary programs. For one thing, online learning jeopardizes the very educational system that sustains
55 them; for another, it is new and unknown and still lacking impartial research and conclusive data. But as a former public school teacher, I can say with certainty that online high schools are much more effective in educating the majority of today's youth.
60 One advantage that an online school has over a traditional high school is accessibility. Students can replay the daily lesson in its entirety as frequently as needed and at their convenience. They also have access to supplementary content and materials for further exploration. A
65 student in a traditional learning environment has access to his teacher for only one or two hours a day and he must review the lecture by memory or by using simplified, and sometimes inaccurate, notes. Any additional research he conducts is done on his own, without
70 guidance or instruction. Another merit of online schools is that students are granted access to the best teachers in the world. Because there is no physical campus, administrators can recruit top educators from top colleges and top high schools without worrying about having to
75 relocate their recruits. An online campus also allows for a diverse student body, allowing students from all over the country to take advantage of an online school's ample websites and resources.

Online learning environments allow for optimizing
80 instruction in ways that a traditional classroom teacher just cannot accomplish. An online teacher can customize lessons and homework based on the skill level of each individual student. She can isolate particular weaknesses using the advanced computer programs, and then create
85 a curriculum tailored to that student's needs. Classroom teachers do not have the resources or time to design individualized lesson plans and homework assignments for upwards of one hundred and twenty students.

While opponents of online schools cite the lack of
90 student/teacher face time as a detriment to student achievement, evidence from my online classroom suggests otherwise. My current juniors are scoring 20% higher on their state standardized tests than the students I previously taught in a traditional classroom. State
95 officials have long defended the validity and necessity of our standardized tests, so why not put them to use in comparing online and traditional education settings? And while they are at it, they should evaluate my program and interview my students. Most students report that they
100 "see" me, their online instructor, many more hours a day than they ever saw their traditional classroom teachers.

1. Passage 1 is primarily concerned with the

   A) disadvantages of online learning.
   B) vastness of online learning tutorials.
   C) difficulties of evaluating online learning programs.
   D) superiority of online schools to traditional schools.

2. Which of the following situations is most analogous to the issues presented in lines 11-18 ("For example . . . sites")?

   A) An airline executive assesses an under-researched flight training program that is operating in many different cities.
   B) A biologist attempts to determine the different components of soil samples from all seven continents.
   C) A traditional classroom teacher fails to measure his students' progress with a standardized test.
   D) An author who is intimidated by technology handwrites her novels in a notebook.

3. In line 25, the reference to a "debate" suggests that

   A) programs are only funded if they meet certain political requirements.
   B) political agendas often influence the evaluations of online learning programs.
   C) a candidate's support or criticism of online learning programs weighs heavily in elections.
   D) online schools are more accessible to students than are traditional classrooms.

4. The comment between the dashes in line 44 primarily serves to

   A) explain a claim.
   B) clarify a term.
   C) express sarcasm.
   D) introduce a restatement.

5. According to Passage 2, education experts are hesitant to support online learning because

   A) the programs are insufficiently studied and a threat to traditional school systems.
   B) online courses developed quickly and then the programs stalled out.
   C) they have never served as public school teachers.
   D) traditional schools have many advantages over online schools.

6. Which choice provides the best evidence for the answer to the previous question?

   A) Lines 53-56 ("For . . . data")
   B) Lines 72-75 ("Because . . . recruits")
   C) Lines 75-78 ("'An online . . . resources'")
   D) Lines 94-97 ("State . . . settings'")

7. In line 83, "weaknesses" refers to

   A) low standardized test scores for traditional classroom students.
   B) the lack of resources and supplementary material available to public school teachers.
   C) the inability to effectively evaluate online learning schools.
   D) specific academic difficulties for a student.

8. If true, which of the following assertions about the author's current students detracts LEAST from her claim in lines 92-94 ("My current . . . . classroom")?

   A) They cheated on the test but the author's former students did not.
   B) They had a much higher average IQ score than the average IQ score of her former students.
   C) They participated in standardized test enrichment programs outside of school time but the former students did not.
   D) They had sophomore test scores that were lower than the sophomore test scores of the former students.

Continue this passage on the next page.

9. The primary purpose of Passage 2 is to

    A) to argue for stricter evaluation standards for online learning programs
    B) illustrate the advantages of online schools over traditional schools
    C) urge educators to supplement traditional classroom learning with online learning programs
    D) draw parallels between online learning and traditional classroom settings

10. The author of Passage 2 would most likely regard the concerns in lines 15-23 ("Another . . . to users") as examples of

    A) endorsements that threaten traditional school authorities.
    B) technological innovations.
    C) the advantages of online learning.
    D) the data that can be used to more effectively evaluate online schools.

11. The author of Passage 2 would most likely respond to the desires of the "funders and policymakers" (line 31) by asserting that

    A) online learning allows for more independent study than do traditional learning outlets
    B) research literature on online learning is nearly nonexistent
    C) online schools are able to reach students all over the globe
    D) state standardized tests already provide data comparing the performance of students in online and traditional schools

12. The "program leaders" (line 38) and the author of Passage 2 would disagree on which of the following points?

    I.   Online schools provide access to high-quality teachers.
    II. Standardized tests alone cannot compare student performance in online and traditional classrooms.
    III. Teachers are wary of having their program evaluated.

    A) I only
    B) II only
    C) I and III only
    D) II and III only

13. The authors of both passages would most likely agree that

    A) online learning has gradually evolved and expanded.
    B) online schools are more efficient and effective than traditional classrooms.
    C) it is difficult to evaluate an educational program without a central campus.
    D) there is a lack of reliable research evaluating online learning programs.

PROBLEM SETS AND REVIEW ANSWER KEY

Single Passages Problem Set 1 (Literary Fiction)—Page 346

1. (C) Prephrase: Simile (a comparison using *like* or *as*)

   Rhetorical Device Question:
   (A) an understatement: expressing an idea as less important than it really is
   (B) an allusion: a reference to a famous person, event, or work of art.
   (D) a cliché: an overused phrase.

2. (A) Prephrase: Flirting

   Facts and Details Question. She is flirting with the men she is dancing with, and Ethan thought she only used the gestures with him.

3. (A) Prephrase: Zeena would get rid of Mattie because of Ethan's feelings for her.

   Rhetorical Device Question:
   (B) Copycat: Uses the word *dull* from the first paragraph, but the entire second paragraph explains his fears.
   (C) True But Wrong/True to a Point: Ethan is worried that Mattie might marry, but he dismisses Denis Eady in line 80. Plus, this fear is discussed in the first paragraph and later in the passage. These are not the latent fears referred to in the second paragraph.
   (D) True But Wrong/True to a Point: Ethan is terribly worried about Mattie's departure, but it's because he cares for her, not because she takes care of Zeena. Plus, this fear is revealed in the later in the passage, not in the second paragraph.

4. (C) Prephrase: ability, interest in

   Words-in-Context Question:
   An inclination is a liking or preference.

5. (C) Prephrase: Difficult to prephrase.

   Rhetorical Device Question: Frome admits that Zeena needed the help of a stronger arm than the one which lay in his on walks home. He is referring to Mattie's arm, since he walked her home from the town socials at night.
   (A) True to a Point: Ethan is not convinced Zeena is as ill as she says she is; not the townspeople. In fact, Starkfield had always called her sickly.
   (B) Mattie and Ethan walked together after dances; *Zeena* and *each* make this answer wrong.
   (D) True to You? Ethan never says he feels guilty about his feelings for Mattie, so be careful not to put your own beliefs onto the character. Plus, this answer is about not being able to care for Zeena. It never says that he is incapable of this.

6. (C) Prephrase: Inability to keep house; "no natural turn for housekeeping"

   Facts and Details Question:
   (A) Not mentioned in the passage.
   (B) While Mattie does lack strength (line 22), but this is not in the same sentence as *defect*.
   (D) Not mentioned in the passage.

7. (A)   Prephrase: "she were to marry a man she was fond of" (line 28)

Facts and Details Question:
(B) Copycat: uses language from the beginning of the paragraph

8. (A)   Prephrase: Lines 27-31 if you found it prior to reading answer choices

Best Evidence Paired Question (Literal Comprehension)

9. (D)   Prephrase: Mattie will get in trouble with Zeena for her poor housekeeping

General Inference Question:
(A) Opposite: Zeena hopes that Mattie will marry Denis Eady
(B) True to You?
(C) Opposite: Zeena disapproves of Ethan when she catches him working at the churn.

10. (A)   Prephrase: Difficult to prephrase.

Facts and Details Question:
(B) Zeena is worried that others will think she stood in Mattie's way, not that Denis would think she disapproves.
(C) Not suggested in the passage.
(D) Opposite: Zeena indicates that Mattie will move out when she gets married.

11. (C)   Prephrase: Lines 67-70 if you found it prior to reading answer choices

Best Evidence Paired Question (Extended Reasoning)

12. (B)   Prephrase: Steadiness, hesitation (lines 72-24)

Facts and Details Question:
(A) While he reassures Zeena that Mattie is not leaving, Ethan is never tender with his wife.
(C) He avoids an immediate reply.

13. (D)   Prephrase: Impossible to prephrase

Facts and Details Question: Zeena is making faces at Ethan and comments about Mattie's work ability. She seems to antagonize her husband by predicting Mattie's departure and she notes that he is suddenly shaving every day. She is aware of the attention her husband is paying her cousin.
(A) Ethan's views on marriage are never presented or hinted at. Plus, if he did respect his marriage vows, it's unlikely he would work so hard to keep Mattie in his home.
(B) What was originally predicted? Without this information, you cannot prove this answer. Plus, nothing in the passage indicates this disease is rapid. She has always been ill.
(C) The passage indicates that Ethan has been neglecting the mill for the farm, but it does not state that he is in danger of losing his job. He may own the mill.

Single Passages Problem Set 2 (Social Studies/Humanities)—Page 348

1. (B)   Prephrase: The antagonism between Faulkner and Mississippi

    Main Idea Question:
    (A) True to a Point/Copycat: The first paragraph mentions *middle-class pretensions*, but Faulkner's criticism of the South involves many other factors.
    (C) True to a Point: Only one-half of the third paragraph deals with Faulkner's *escape*.
    (D) The last paragraph suggests that Faulkner eventually does *face* and *deal with* his culture, but that is only at the end; the rest of the passage is about his antagonism towards his culture.

2. (A)   Prephrase: Personification in *[Mississippi] swallowed hard and reacted negatively*

    Rhetorical Device Question:
    (B) an analogy: a comparison
    (C) symbolism: when an item stands for an idea
    (D) a parody: a work that imitates the style of another work for comic effect.

3. (D)   Prephrase: was not likely to hang his portrait or discuss his books

    General Inference Question:
    (A) This idea is not discussed in the passage
    (B) Copycat: This is never indicated in the passage, but the phrase *Civil Rights* is used.
    (C) Copycat: The passage says that official Mississippi would be more likely to burn Faulkner's books than to hang his portrait. This is an example of figurative language, where the author is exaggerating to get his point across.

4. (C)   Prephrase: The Civil Rights movement makes it easy to undervalue his personal struggle

    General Inference Question:
    (A) This idea is not indicated in the passage
    (B) Copycat: This answer plays on *laugh* in the sentence before the line reference.
    (D) Copycat: This answer plays on *emotions* in line 30, but is never stated in the passage. Plus, Faulkner did not expose racism, he simply commented on it.

5. (D)   Prephrase: his love of and commitment to his country, his very localness in Mississippi (lines 30-34)

    Reasons and Results Question:
    (A) True But Wrong: This is discussed in the following paragraph, but is not one of the reasons he is still read.
    (B) True to a Point: While he does criticize racism in Mississippi, this is not the reason the author indicates he is still read. Plus, *protest* would be hard to prove. He criticizes, but there is no evidence of him *protesting*.
    (C) True to a Point/Extreme: This is the most attractive wrong answer. The passage says Faulkner had a love of his country, but it's debatable whether the country is the United States or the rural countryside of Mississippi. Plus, love is not the same thing as *devout patriotism*. You can love the US without showing patriotism. This is an extreme phrase.

6. (B)   Prephrase: Lines 30-34 if you found it prior to reading answer choices

    Best Evidence Paired Question (Literal Comprehension)

7. (D) Prephrase: made it look bad; accused

    Words-in-Context Question: *to indict* means to accuse or to criticize, The context of lines 44-46 supports this definition.

8. (B) Prephrase: a state of mind that cannot admit that it loves what it hates or that it hates what it loves (lines 57-58)

    Facts and Details Question:
    (A) Copycat: Again, this answer is playing on the phrase *Civil Rights*.
    (C) Copycat: This answer plays on *laugh* in the second paragraph.
    (D) True But Wrong/True to a Point: Open antagonism (not veiled) existed between Mississippi and Faulkner, but that was not the conflict referred to in the line reference.

9. (D) Prephrase: large, heavy, intense

    Words-in-Context Question

10. (C) Prephrase: show that Faulkner felt the same way as Compson

    Purpose Question:
    (A) Extreme: We see one example of a character who portrays to his roommate his hatred of the South; *all* is extreme and unprovable.
    (B) Copycat: Again, this answer plays on *most famous* in line 56, but it's about the character, not the novel. We do not know what Faulkner's most famous novel is.
    (D) *Argue* is strong here since an argument is not being made. And remember, political changes are only one of the things that Faulkner indicts: he also detests middle-class pretensions and cultural backwardness (line 4).

11. (A) Prephrase: he needed to engage and understand his culture

    General Inference Question:
    (B) True to You? This might be a conclusion you have drawn, but it is not discussed in the passage.
    (C) While you might conclude that Faulkner realized he could work to change his culture, it does not indicate that he should work with Mississippi, nor that he would work to ease racial tension. His complaints include racism itself, not racial tension.
    (D) While Compson does echo Faulkner's personal feelings, the paragraph does not suggest that Faulkner eventually realizes this. He's likely known it all along.

Single Passages Problem Set 3 (Science)—Page 350

1. (B) Prephrase: look at the origins of Earth and other planets

    Purpose Question:
    (A) True But Wrong: This is discussed in the last two paragraphs, but is not the theme of the entire article.
    (C) True But Wrong: Legends are only provided in the first paragraph, not discussed in the entire article.
    (D) Nothing is *defended* in the passage.

2. (C) Prephrase: scattered

Words-in-Context Question: *interspersed* means scattered.
Pelted means struck repeatedly; *invigorated* means energized.

3. (C) Prephrase: how you go from a dust grain to a kilometer (lines 20-21)

Facts and Details Question:
(A) True But Wrong: This is a problem addressed in the passage, but it is not what is referred to in the line reference.
(B) Opposite: This is a widely accepted phenomenon, not something that scientists cannot figure out.
(D) Opposite: This is an accepted theory, not a piece of the story that is missing.

4. (B) Prephrase: Lines 20-22 if you found it prior to reading answer choices

Best Evidence Paired Question (Literal Comprehension)

5. (D) Prephrase: The amount of turbulence under the conditions of the solar nebula would prevent these gravitational instabilities from working (lines 28-30).

Reasons and Results Question:
(A) The seventh paragraph discusses the known composition of the sun.
(B) This is not discussed in the passage.
(C) True But Wrong: It is true that the isotopes are not proportional, but nothing about soil samples is mentioned in the passage.

6. (A) Prephrase: Lines 28-30 if you found it prior to reading answer choices

Best Evidence Paired Question (Literal Comprehension)

7. (B) Prephrase: The isotopes of certain elements (line 40)

Facts and Details Question:
(A) This is not discussed in the passage.
(C) Copycat: This answer uses *chemical processes* from line 44 to try to trick you.
(D) The passage never indicates that these two theories are the *leading* theories; plus, they are not the *differences* referred to

8. (A) Prephrase: This question is difficult to prephrase because there are many ideas in the sentence.

Facts and Details Question:
(B) True But Wrong: This is true in lines 59-60, but not in the line reference.
(C) The passage never states this.
(D) True to a Point: The passage states that the *atoms of the outer portion* are unchanged, not necessarily the entire sun.

9. (A) Prephrase: idea

Words-in-Context Question.

10. (C) Prephrase: This question is difficult to prephrase

General Inference Question:
(A) True to You? This is not stated or implied in the passage, but may be something you know.
(B) This is not stated in the passage.
(D) This is the most common wrong answer choice, but the ingredients that make up the sun are already known, as indicated by the hydrogen and helium mentioned in line 61.

11. (C) Prephrase: Impossible to prephrase

Rhetorical Device Question:
(A) Direct quotation appears in lines 20-22 (and others).
(B) Parenthetical reference occurs in lines 26-27.
(D) Rhetorical questions appear in lines 1, 53-54, and 70-71.

12. (D) Prephrase: positive, interested

Author's Attitude Question:
(A) It is *respectful*, but not *nostalgic*.
(B) A weak case could be made for *baffled*, but *sullen* is definitely wrong.
(C) The author is not *skeptical* of the research, nor is he *emphatic* about anything.

13. (D)

Charts and Graphs Location Question:
(A) If you reverse the axes and incorrectly look at a ratio of 5 for $\delta^{18}O$, you may erroneously select this answer as 0 is the ratio for $\delta^{17}O$.
(B) If you look at Mars instead of the carbonaceous chondrite meteorites, you will get this answer.
(C) If you look at the Earth instead of the carbonaceous chondrite meteorites, you will get this answer.

14. (D)

Charts and Graphs Conclusion Question:
According to the graph's explanation, "Cosmologists believe that planetary objects with ratios resulting in parallel slopes were created in a similar manner." Mars and the Earth have parallel slopes, and thus scientists must believe they have similar origins.

The other three answer choices are not stated or suggested by the graph.

Single Passages Problem Set 4 (Social Studies/History)—Page 354

1. (A) Prephrase: astonished (the term *somewhat* makes choice (A) an attractive answer)

Author's Attitude Question:
(C) Extreme
(D) Extreme

2. (B) Prephrase: lack, scarcity (opposite of *wealth* in line 1)

    Words-in-Context Question:
    (C) contingency: uncertainty
    (D) Poverty is most often associated with a lack of money, and thus this answer is attractive but wrong.

3. (B) Prephrase: the image of a sailor is not comparable to the images of soldiers

    General Inference Question:
    (A) This is not suggested.
    (C) This is not suggested.
    (D) Selecting this answer is inferring too much. We know the other two images were influenced by Bell I. Wiley, but we don't know if he is an author, an artist, or a historian. And this has nothing to do with Jack Tar.

4. (D) Prephrase: Impossible to prephrase

    General Inference Question:
    (A) Not stated in the passage; if anything, the army was more glorified than the Navy, since there is a lack of information.
    (B) True to You?
    (C) Extreme. *Few* makes this hard to defend, and actually the opposite was true in most cases. But neither side is indicated about African American sailors.

5. (C) Prephrase: Lines 25-33 if you found it prior to reading answer choices

    Best Evidence Paired Question (Literal Comprehension)

6. (B) Prephrase: Lines 34-36 if you found it prior to reading answer choices

    Best Evidence Support Question

7. (C) Prephrase: highlight a new term

    Rhetorical Devices Question.

8. (A) Prephrase: manual labor

    Purpose Question:
    (B) True to a Point: they are basic jobs, but the passage indicates they were performed by black enlistees.
    (C) The passage never states that these were daily chores. This answer tries to trick you because black men were assigned to small arms crews and to these menial chores; however, small-arms crews had their own jobs as listed in lines 52-54.
    (D) True to You?

9. (C) Prephrase: Difficult to prephrase.

    General Inference Question:
    (A) True to a Point: Lines 55-56 (outside of the line reference) indicate that white and black sailors exercised separately, but it never states that white sailors *refused* to exercise with other members.
    (B) Opposite: Line 51 indicates they were given small-arms.
    (D) Opposite: Outside of the line reference, in lines 65-73, we learn that the opposite is true.

10. (A) Prephrase: Impossible to prephrase.

Strengthen and Weaken Question: The argument is that black sailors served in inferior positions as laborers and servants rather than seaman.
(B) This neither strengthens nor weakens the argument (because it is about white sailors), and is in fact true, as indicated by lines 54-56.
(C) This neither strengthens nor weakens the argument (because it is about white sailors).
(D) This supports the idea that black sailors were discriminated against, which is not exactly the argument in the passage.

11. (B) Prephrase: rank

Words-in-Context Question.

12. (C) Prephrase: had seafaring skills that were discounted because he was black

Purpose Question:
(A) Copycat from line 30 and possibly True to You.
(B) Opposite.
(D) True to You? Dunbar's feelings are not revealed.

Single Passages Problem Set 5 (Science)—Page 356

1. (C) Prephrase: explain how viruses were discovered and discuss their origins

Purpose Question:
(A) *Examine* is an extreme word, as it means *to look closely*. Only one paragraph discussed the invention of the electron microscope, which allows scientists to see *viruses*, not only *microscopic particles*, as these had already been viewed with a compound light microscope.
(B) The second paragraph described the events (not just *experiments*) that led to the discovery of viruses, but this was held to only that paragraph. The purpose of one paragraph is not the purpose of the entire passage.
(D) Three common hypotheses were given in the fifth paragraph, but only the fifth paragraph. Again, the purpose of one paragraph is not the purpose of the entire passage, but this is a common wrong answer trap on primary purpose questions.

2. (A) Prephrase: Impossible to prephrase

General Inference Question:
(A) This is the correct answer based on lines 58-60.
(B) We are not informed why the filter was invented. Plus, the inventor, Chamberland, was not the scientist studying tobacco plants.
(C) This is an Opposite Answer. Bacteria is 100 times larger than viruses and can be viewed under a light microscope.
(D) Again, this is false. The three hypotheses each have proponents, but none has been accepted by all scientists. As direct proof this answer is wrong, lines 79-80 state that some scientists accept the third theory.

3. (C)   Prephrase: Ivanowski

Facts and Details Question:
(C) Lines 19 to 26 provide the answer, but specifically lines 23-26.

4. (D)   Prephrase: They were undetectable prior to the invention of the electron microscope.

General Inference Question:
(A) Not stated in the passage, although we learn that the more scientists learned about viruses, the more they were able to classify them.
(B) False. In line 18, the authors state that tobacco mosaic disease is a non-fungal disease, but nothing is implied about fungal diseases.
(C) True But Wrong. This is mentioned in lines 60-61 in reference to why current scientists do not know the exact origin of viruses, but it does not address a long-term lack of knowledge about viruses in general, as do lines 35-41.

5. (B)   Prephrase: Lines 35-41 if you found it prior to reading answer choices

Best Evidence Paired Question (Extended Reasoning)

6. (D)   Prephrase: made it possible

Words-in-Context Question

7. (C)   Prephrase: To show how little is still known about viruses in present day.

Purpose Question:
(A) This is the purpose of the last few sentences of the third paragraph.
(B) This is the purpose of the fifth paragraph.
(D) According to the fourth paragraph, viruses do not have fossil records because they cannot fossilize.

8. (B)   Prephrase: profession, study of science and viruses

Words-in-Context Question

9. (B)   Prephrase: 1) from free-living cells (line 71), 2) from escaped DNA and RNA molecules (lines 75-76), or 3) from self-replication (line 77)

Facts and Details Question:
(A) Not stated in the passage. This uses the word *escaped* from line 76 to trick you.
(C) This answer uses *free-living* from line 71 and *DNA and RNA* from line 76.
(D) This wrong answer takes plant pathogens from line 80.

10. (D)   Prephrase: Lines 77-79 if you found it prior to reading answer choices

Best Evidence Paired Question (Literal Comprehension)

11. (A)   Prephrase: are smaller (lines 35-37)

Comparison and Contrast Question

12. (D)   Prephrase: Impossible to prephrase

Facts and Details Question:
(A) This occurred third (lines 38-41)
(B) This occurred first (lines 23-26)
(C) This occurred second (lines 28-30)
(D) This occurred last (lines 49-52)

Single Passages Problem Set 6 (Social Studies/Great Global Conversation)—Page 358

1. (C)   Prephrase: examples of success to examples of problems that still exist

Purpose Question:
(A) The success stories are attributed to *women living in shanty towns, a group of church women,* and *a young woman.* We have no idea if these women are present in the audience.
(B) The passage does not explain the Fourth World Conference, nor stereotypes that persist.
(D) We do not know the author's experiences in Beijing (or even if she has been there).

2. (B)   Prephrase: request for action, plea for help

Words-in-Context Question
(B) summons: a request or demand to do something

3. (A)   Prephrase: Impossible to prephrase

General Inference Question:
(A) This is suggested in lines 9-12.
(B) This is not suggested.
(C) Opposite Answer. Clinton states that many people in the room heeded the call to action from the conference 15 years ago.
(D) This is not suggested. Many women do receive insufficient care during childbirth (61-64), but these people are not in attendance that we know of.

4. (B)   Prephrase: Lines 9-12 if you found it prior to reading answer choices

Best Evidence Paired Question (Extended Reasoning)

5. (D)   Prephrase: show examples of "the evidence of such efforts everywhere"

Purpose Question:
(A) True to a Point: These are advancements, but there is no indication that they need to be replicated.
(B) These are not necessarily opportunities for women, but rather progress that has been made. Only two of the examples are about women in developing countries: South Africa and Liberia. The third is in the U.S.
(C) The goals from the conference are not provided.

6. (C) Prephrase: Difficult to prephrase

Best Evidence Contradict Question:
(C) This answer contradicts the claim that women decline offers for opportunity, as it states that women continually seize opportunities.

7. (D) Prephrase: To change the subject; to show the other side of the issue.

Purpose Question:
(A) True But Wrong. The paragraph encourages people to participate elsewhere (lines 43-46), but not in the sentence referenced in the question.
(B) There is no prediction in this statement.
(C) The word *refutes* here may trick you into selecting this as the answer because of the word *but* in the sentence in lines 41-42. But the sentence is not refuting a common belief.
(D) This is the correct answer. The prior information in the text was about how far we've come since the conference; now she will talk about how far we still need to go. This is a transition between the two main ideas.

8. (D) Prephrase: Part is over but *there is still so much more to be done* (lines 43-44)

Words in Context Question (Statements):
(A) Don't let the word *authors* in the sentence trick you into picking (A)!
(B) Don't let the word *story* trick you into picking (B)!
(D) This is the correct answer. The following sentence says *There is still so much more to be done*, which helps give the statement context.

9. (A) Prephrase: Difficult to prephrase.

Facts and Details Question:
(A) Correct, from line 49.
(B) There is no comparison to men, nor any mention of the number of women who have participated in social reform.
(C) Opposite Answer. According to line 55, *women are the majority of the world's farmers.*
(D) This statement is not made in the passage.

10. (B) Prephrase: the *table to negotiate peace* (lines 66-69)

Facts and Details Question:
(A) True to You? Don't let lines 59-60 trick you into selecting this answer. Nothing is stated about women being left out of decisions.
(C) True to You?
(D) True to You? We get the sense this is true given how little rights women have in the second half of this passage, but it is never stated. This is a Literal Comprehension question, so the answer must be stated in the passage.

11. (B) Prephrase: Lines 66-69 if you found it prior to reading answer choices

Best Evidence Paired Question (Literal Comprehension)

12. (C)   Prephrase: Impossible to prephrase

Reasons and Results Question:
(A) Cited in lines 75-76 (*a warning to other women who might assert their rights*).
(B) Cited in lines 73-74 (*a tactic...of armed conflict*).
(D) Cited in lines 74-75 (*punishment for disobedience*).

13. (D)

Charts and Graphs Location Question:
(A) Eastern & Southeastern Asia: There are more females in services, so this is wrong.
(B) Latin America & Caribbean: There are more females in services, so this is wrong.
(C) Eastern & Southeastern Asia: There are more females in services, so this is wrong.
(D) Near East & North Africa: There are about 50% of men and 45% of women in service; there are about 28% of men in industry and 15% of women in industry.
    Southern Asia: There are about 40% of men and 20% of women in service; there are about 20% of men in industry and 15% of women in industry.

14. (C)

Charts and Graphs Conclusion Question:
(A) This is a very difficult question and an attractive wrong answer choice. While there is a lower *percent* of people employed in industry jobs in Sub-Saharan African than the percent employed in industry jobs in Latin America & Caribbean, we do not know the *number* of people employed. Sub-Saharan African can have a population of 100 million people, meaning several million people work in industry, but Latin America & the Caribbean may only have a population of 100 people, meaning that less than 100 people work in industry.
(B) Just because the percentages of men and women who work in agriculture in Eastern & South Eastern Asia are the same or nearly the same does not mean that the genders have access to the same resources.
(C) This is true. Only in Latin America & Caribbean do men outnumber women in agriculture, and men outnumber women in all regions in industry.
(D) Again, as in choice (A), it's impossible to know the *number* of women employed in either region. We only know the *percentage*.

15. (C)

Charts and Graphs Connection Question:
(A) True But Wrong. The data does indicate that the percentage of female farmers is higher than the percentage of male farmers in all but one region, but this does not include every region in the world. North America, South America, and Europe are just some of the regions missing from the figure, so it's impossible to draw a conclusion about the entire world.
(B) This does not address the percentage of women farmers vs. men farmers.
(C) This is the answer. See choice (A) for an explanation.
(D) Again, see choice (A).

Paired Passages Problem Set—Page 362

1. (C) Prephrase: The problems with evaluating online learning

   Main Idea Question:
   (A) Common wrong answer. Students assume that because Passage 2 supports online learning, Passage 1 must oppose it. But paired passages are not always "For/Against" arguments. The author of Passage 1 never says online learning is ineffective; he just cites problems with making those judgments.
   (B) True but Wrong: The author does state that there are vast websites (line 19), but this is not the central idea throughout the passage.
   (D) This would be the main idea of Passage 2, not of Passage 1.

2. (A) Prephrase: Impossible to prephrase, but you should note the line reference. It says that it is hard to evaluate a program without existing research and with learning taking place at different sites.

   Parallel Reasoning Question:
   (B) Nothing is noted about existing research in this situation.
   (C) Nothing is noted about existing research or distance learning in this situation.
   (D) Nothing is noted about existing research or distance learning in this situation.

3. (B) Prephrase: politics plays a part in evaluations and decisions about online learning

   General Inference Question:
   (A) Political requirements are not discussed, but this is the most common wrong answer.
   (C) True to You? If you selected this answer, you assumed too much from the reference.
   (D) True but Wrong: This is true in Passage 2, but not in Passage 1.

4. (B) Prephrase: explain the word *setting*. *Clarify* means *to explain.*

   Purpose Question:
   (A) No claim has been made yet in *And, like educators in any setting.*
   (C) There is no sarcasm in this article.
   (D) The words *traditional or online* do not restate anything from *And, like educators in any setting.*

5. (A) Prephrase: online learning jeopardizes the very educational system that sustains it and it is new and unknown and still lacking impartial research and conclusive data (lines 53-56)

   Reasons and Results Question:
   (B) True to a Point: The programs did develop quickly, but they did not stall out. Regardless, this is not why authorities are slow to endorse online learning.
   (C) If you chose this answer, you are assuming too much about the passage.
   (D) True But Wrong: This is the main idea of Passage 1, but not the answer to the question about Passage 2.

6. (A) Prephrase: Lines 53-56 if you found it prior to reading answer choices

   Best Evidence Paired Question (Literal Comprehension)

7. (D) Prephrase: students' weaknesses in school

   Facts and Details Question:
   (A) This sentence is about online students, not traditional students.
   (B) True but Wrong.
   (C) True but Wrong (from Passage 1).

8. (D) Prephrase: Impossible to prephrase

Strengthen and Weaken Question:
(A) If the author's new students cheated, then their scores could be the result of cheating, not from being enrolled in an online school.
(B) If the author's new students are smarter, then their scores could be the result of having more intelligence, not from being enrolled in an online school.
(C) If the author's new students have extra test training, then their scores could be the result of having more education, not from being enrolled in an online school.
(D) If the author's new students had lower sophomore scores, then this supports the argument that online schools are more effective than traditional schools, where students do not improve as much.

9. (B) Prephrase: show how online learning is better than traditional learning settings

Purpose Question:
(A) The author does not argue for stricter evaluation standards.
(C) The author is arguing in favor of online schools, not supplemented traditional schools
(D) While the author does draw some parallels, he does so to show how online schools are better.

10. (C) Prephrase: advantages of online learning (from lines 75-78)

Hypothetical Points of View Question:
(A) Copycat: uses language from the first paragraph of Passage 2.
(D) This answer takes an idea from Passage 2 and tries to trick you into selecting it.

11. (D) Prephrase: standardized tests would give them the data they want (line 96)

Hypothetical Points of View Question:
(A) True but Wrong: while the author of Passage 2 believes this, it is not a proper response to what the funders and policymakers want (which is data that shows online learning works).
(B) True but Wrong and somewhat Extreme: *nearly nonexistent* is much more extreme than *lacking* (line 56). And not a proper response to the desires of the stakeholders.

12. (D) Prephrase: Impossible to prephrase.

Compare and Contrast Question: Evaluate each Roman numeral statement.
I. They would agree on this (lines 40-41 and 73). So all answers with I are eliminated (A and C).
II. They would disagree on this (lines 41-42 and 96-97). Eliminate answers that do not include II (both B and D include II).
III. They would disagree on this (lines 45 and 98). The correct answer is (D).

13. (D) Prephrase: Difficult to prephrase, but there were two points of agreement that you might have caught: The first is that online learning is expanding rapidly (lines 2 and 49) and the other is that there is a lack of existing research (lines 4 and 56).

Compare and Contrast Question:
(A) Opposite: Both authors believe the opposite, as indicated in lines 2 and 49.
(B) True but Wrong: This is true in Passage 2, but not in Passage 1.
(C) True but Wrong: This is true in Passage 1, but not in Passage 2.

Chapter Sixteen
TEST READINESS

Are you ready to take the ACT and SAT? If so, follow these guidelines for your final preparation.

The Day Before the Test

The day before the test can be a stressful time. Try to relax as much as possible; read a book, see a movie, or play a video game. Engage in activities that will get your mind off of the ACT or SAT.

Take a Study Break

You should not study the day (or the night) before the test! Professional athletes call this "tapering." After weeks or even months of training for a competition, athletes take a day or two off before the race or the game to give their muscles a chance to rest and rejuvenate. Your brain works the same way. Cramming the day before the test can cause fatigue and poor performance on test day. So taper your "workout" the day before the ACT or SAT by skipping the study session. In doing so, you will be alert and mentally ready to tackle the multi-section test.

Eat Dinner

Approach the test the way athletes approach an important game. Trained athletes eat a meal containing complex carbohydrates the night before competition. Many high schools even prepare pasta dinners for their sports teams, because carbohydrates are stored by the athletes' bodies and used for energy the following day. But carbohydrates aren't just fuel for your muscles—they are fuel for your brain, too. You might want to make this fact known to your parents, because you will need to eat a dinner rich in complex carbohydrates, such as baked potatoes, bread, and pasta. A well-balanced meal the night before the test can help you stay sharp and focused on the day of the test.

Find the Test Center

Avoid any added stress on test day by finding the test center in advance. For most students, the test center will be their own high school. But if you are taking the test at another high school, find the test center and check out the parking situation ahead of time. Also make sure that you don't need to stop for gasoline in the morning. These two simple precautions will prevent you from arriving late and being denied admission on test day.

⬦ GRATUITOUS VOCAB
rejuvenate (vb):
to make fresh again

Confidence Quotation
"You have to have confidence in your ability, and then be tough enough to follow through."
-Rosalyn Carter,
First Lady of the United States

Gather Your Materials

Get your test materials organized in advance. Gather up everything that you need for the test the night before to avoid running around the next morning. Assemble the following:

- Your Test Admission Ticket: This ticket was mailed or emailed to you upon registration for the ACT or SAT. If you registered online, you can visit your ACT or College Board account to print out another copy.
- A Photo ID: You can use your driver's license or your school ID. For a more detailed list of acceptable identification, visit the ACT's or the College Board's website.
- Two No. 2 Pencils: Bring at least one spare pencil in the event one breaks during the test. You will not be allowed to sharpen your pencil. Mechanical pencils and pens are not allowed.
- An Eraser: Make sure that you use a fresh eraser to erase any mistakes or changes completely. Stray marks can be interpreted as wrong answers.
- Your Calculator: Make sure your calculator has fresh batteries. For a list of acceptable calculators, visit the ACT's or College Board's website.
- A Watch: You will need a watch to time each section. Testing centers may not have clocks or the clocks might be broken. Plus, it is easier and more efficient to glance at your wrist than search for a clock. Just make sure to turn off any alarms on the watch, or you may be dismissed for disrupting the testing room.
- A Snack: The entire test day takes most of your morning (and in some cases, part of your afternoon), so you may not be finished until after your normal lunch hour. There are short breaks during testing, at which time the proctors will allow you to eat snacks outside of the testing room. Take a granola bar or a bag of carrot sticks to avoid losing concentration when the hunger pangs arrive. Try to avoid a snack containing excess sugar.
- A Bottle of Water: You are also encouraged to drink water during each break. Take your own bottle of water in case the test center does not have drinking fountains.

Get a Good Night's Sleep

Go to bed early the night before the test. The entire testing experience is long and intense, and if you don't get a decent night's sleep, you are guaranteed to fade halfway through. Maybe you have a commitment that you cannot escape—like an athletic or musical event—but treat the evening like a school night and be in bed early. Skip the late movie, or the school dance, or the birthday party, or you might miss out on those very events at the college of your choice!

Mechanical pencils, pens, and highlighters are not allowed for use on the ACT nor SAT.

Getting an adequate amount of sleep the night before the test can help your concentration and stamina.

The Morning of the Test

After a great dinner and a good night's sleep, you should be ready to conquer the one little test that will help you gain admission to the school of your choice.

Eat Breakfast

It's a proven fact that breakfast increases your concentration, mood, and memory. Eat a healthy breakfast on the morning of the test. Many former test takers have complained about the distraction caused by grumbling stomachs—both their own and those of other students—so save yourself any embarrassment or discomfort by eating a breakfast and taking a snack.

Follow Your Normal Routine

If you wake up every morning and watch TV while you get ready for school, don't stop on account of the ACT or SAT! Similarly, if you've never had a cup of coffee, don't start on the morning of the test. Consistency in your routine will allow you to focus on your primary objective—acing the ACT or SAT.

Dress in Layers

The temperature of the room can have an effect on your test results. If you are too hot or too cold, you may have trouble concentrating. To help control the temperature, dress in layers; peel down to a t-shirt if you're warm or add a sweatshirt if you're cold.

Leave Your Cell Phone in the Car

If cell phones are seen or heard in the testing center, you will be asked to leave. Both the ACT and the College Board are very specific about this rule, and do not allow any electronic devices (music players, timers, cameras, etc.) in the test center. Avoid the temptation to text your friends or check your calls by leaving your cell phone and other electronic devices in the car.

Many of our students have reported test takers being dismissed due to cell phones ringing or vibrating during the test. Don't risk it! Leave your cell phone in your car.

Arrive on Time

Arrive at the test center by the time indicated on your admission ticket. Don't forget to bring all of the following:

- Your Admission Ticket
- Photo ID
- Two No. 2 pencils
- A fresh eraser
- A calculator with new batteries
- A snack
- A bottle of water

Students who arrive after the time on the admission ticket will not be admitted to the test center!

Believe In Yourself

Confidence can go a long way, and since you have read the *PowerScore ACT and SAT Reading Bible,* you should feel confident and able. As you wait at the test center, visualize yourself writing an exceptional essay and knowing the answers to all of the math, reading, and writing multiple choice questions. Many athletes use this same technique before a competition. Your performance will be a reflection of your own expectations.

At the Test Center

Upon entering the testing facility, test supervisors will ask to see your photo ID. Supervisors are instructed to deny admission to anyone who does not have valid ID or to anyone who does not match the photo on the ID.

You will be assigned a specific test center or room. You may be asked to sit in a specific seat or to avoid certain rows or seats. The test proctor may check your calculator to verify it is an approved model while waiting for the other students to arrive.

Once the supervisors instruct the proctor to begin, you will be asked to clear your desk and the test booklets and answer sheets will be distributed. The test booklet must remain closed until the proctor instructs you to open it. Anyone caught looking ahead before or during the test will be asked to leave.

GRATUITOUS VOCAB
biographical (adj): relating to a person's life

The proctor will lead you through the directions for filling out the biographical information on the answer booklet. Be sure to fill in the ovals for each letter or number. You may also be asked to copy a statement stating that you will not discuss the test until scores are returned.

The proctor will then tell you to turn to the first section in the test booklet and answer sheet, and testing will begin.

Snacks and drinks are allowed in the testing center, but must be consumed in the hallways during breaks.

If you engage in any misconduct or irregularity during the test, you may be dismissed from the test center. Actions that could warrant such consequences include creating a disturbance, giving or receiving help, cheating, removing booklets from the room, eating or drinking in the testing room, and using a cell phone.

If you encounter a problem with the test or the test center itself, report it to the proctor, and if possible, a test supervisor. Reportable problems include power outages, clock malfunctions, and any unusual disturbances caused by an individual or group.

If you feel anxious or panicked for any reason during the test, close your eyes for a few seconds and relax by taking a deep breath. Think of other situations where you performed with confidence and skill.

After the Test

At the completion of the final section, the proctor will collect the test booklets and answer sheets. You are not dismissed until the proctor gives you permission to leave.

You have a few days to cancel your SAT score by contacting the College Board. You must make this decision without the benefit of knowing how you scored. Since you are now able to choose which SAT scores are sent to colleges, we caution you to cancel your score only when necessary. Some valid reasons to cancel your score include becoming sick during the test or realizing that you incorrectly bubbled a section. Once a score is canceled, it cannot be reinstated and you do not receive a refund of your test fee.

It is more difficult to cancel an ACT score and the policies for doing so are not clearly outlined. The ACT also alerts potential colleges that your scores were canceled and does not specify a reason that they were canceled. But if you become sick during the test or experience some other emergency at the testing center, your best bet would be to cancel the scores with the proctor before leaving the room.

Scores are typically revealed online in your ACT or College Board account two to three weeks after the test. The official scores are mailed about a week after the online release.

It is extremely important to think positively about the test. Your thoughts dictate your actions.

Scores are released online about three weeks after the test.

Afterword

Thank you for choosing to purchase the *PowerScore ACT and SAT Reading Bible*. We hope you found this book useful and enjoyable, but most importantly, we hope this book helps you raise your ACT or SAT score.

In all of our publications we strive to present the material in the clearest and most informative manner. If you have any questions, comments, or suggestions, please do not hesitate to email us at act@powerscore.com or sat@powerscore.com. We love to receive feedback, and we do read every email that is sent to us.

Also, if you have not done so already, we strongly suggest you visit the website for this book at:

www.powerscore.com/readingbible

This free online resource area contains supplements to the book material, provides updates as needed, and answers questions posed by students. There is also an official evaluation form we encourage you to use.

If we can assist you in any way in your ACT or SAT preparation or in the college admissions process, please do not hesitate to contact us. We would be happy to help.

Thank you and best of luck on the ACT and SAT!

<u>Confidence Quotation</u>
"I can't believe it! Reading and writing actually paid off!"
-Matt Groening, creator of *The Simpsons*

Material recommended for review:

Test formats: pages 23-52

Scoring scales: pages 53-65

Preferred section order: pages 83-84

Active Reading: pages 91-94

Passage MAPS: pages 95-97

Line reference reading guide: page 139

Purpose Verbs: pages 230-233

Attitude Words: pages 237-240

Rhetorical Devices: pages 242-244

Literary Devices: pages 246-250

APPENDIX:
VOCABULARY: REPEAT OFFENDERS

The SAT changed its focus on vocabulary in 2015, removing many of the classic higher-level vocabulary words that had become associated with the SAT. The test makers are now choosing to concentrate on common academic words they have deemed "relevant" to college, which students will encounter in both Reading and Writing & Language questions and answers. The ACT uses most of these same words on their Reading tests, although to a lesser extent than the SAT.

The two tests also use common words that have two or more distinct definitions to assess whether students know the less common meaning. For example, the word *champion* is most often understood to be the noun meaning *winner* but it can also be a verb meaning *to support or defend*, which is how it would likely be tested on the ACT or SAT. And while the SAT claims to have done away with complicated vocabulary, take note that not all of the "obscure" words have disappeared. On released tests, we have found an occasional higher level word, including *egregious*, *didactic*, *ameliorate*, and *promulgated*.

It no longer makes sense, though, to study lists of 1000+ challenging words on the off chance that you will encounter ONE of these words on your test. For that reason, we have created a list of 300 academic text words that have frequently appeared on past tests. You may be quite familiar with some of these from your high school reading; in such cases, place a check mark next to the words to avoid redundant studying. Only study the words that are unfamiliar to you. On the final page of this chapter you will find a resource to help you comprehensively review vocabulary words.

↳ GRATUITOUS VOCAB
obscure (adj):
not clearly understood
egregious (adj):
extraordinarily bad
didactic (adj):
intended for education
ameliorate (vb):
to make better
promulgate (vb):
to make known

Vocabulary

- [ ] **abstract**: (*vb*) to draw or take away
Although Abby never mentioned her childhood, John abstracted from the conversation that she had a strict upbringing.
Word Forms: abstract (n.), abstractly, abstractness, abstraction

- [ ] **accommodation**: (*n*) something to fill a need; adaptation
The student received an accommodation on the ACT; he was given a large-print test booklet because of his poor eyesight.

- [ ] **acquire**: (*vb*) to come into possession of
The captive dolphin has acquired a taste for freshwater perch, a fish not found in its normal habitat.
Word Forms: acquirable, acquirability, acquirement   Related Words: acquisition

- [ ] **acute**: (*adj*) sharp
(1) *The patient complained of acute pain in his lower right abdomen, leading the doctor to test for appendicitis.*
(2) *The acute student quickly solved the difficult puzzle.*
Word Forms: acutely, acuteness

- [ ] **adhere**: (*vb*) to stick to; to follow through
Once you sign the athletic code of conduct, you must adhere to school rules in order to be eligible for the team.
Word Forms: adherable, adherence, adherent, adherer   Antonym Form: inadherent
Related Words: adhesive, adhesion

- [ ] **adversary**: (*n*) an opponent or enemy
The character's adversary plotted to embarrass her during the homecoming dance.
Word Forms: adversarial   Related Words: adverse, adversity, averse

- [ ] **advocate**: (*vb*) to argue in favor of
Adam advocated for longer lunch hours when he was elected class president.
Word Forms: advocate (n.), advocacy, advocatory, advocator

- [ ] **aesthetic**: (*adj*) relating to beauty
Alaina chose this church because of its aesthetic qualities; it was the most beautiful wedding chapel she had ever seen.
Word Forms: aesthetically, aesthetics (n.), aestheticize, aesthete, aesthetician   Antonym Forms: unaesthetic

- [ ] **allege**: (*vb*) to declare without proof
The teacher alleged that Allie cheated on the test, even though he had no proof.
Word Forms: allegeable, allegation, alleged, allegedly, alleger

- [ ] **alleviate**: (*vb*) to provide relief; to make easier
The medicine was created to alleviate headaches.
Word Forms: alleviation, alleviative, alleviatory, alleviator

- [ ] **allude**: (*vb*) to make an indirect reference to
Mrs. Alvarez alluded to a pop quiz on Monday, but would not confirm or deny its occurrence.
Word Forms: allusion, allusive, allusively

- [ ] **ambiguous**: (*adj*) open to more than one interpretation
Amber's ambiguous reply left me wondering where she had been all night.
Word Forms: ambiguously, ambiguousness, ambiguity   Antonym Forms: unambiguous, unambiguously, unambiguity

- [ ] **ambivalent**: (*adj*) having mixed feelings
Ambrose is ambivalent about attending college, which is why his applications still aren't completed.
Word Forms: ambivalently, ambivalence, ambivalency

- [ ] **analogous**: (*adj*) corresponding; similar
The analogous relationship between the brain and a computer has been the subject of many movies.
Word Forms: analogously, analogousness, analogy, analogue, analogize, analogic, analogically, analogist

- [ ] **anecdote**: (*n*) a short account of an amusing incident
The speaker used an anecdote about his dog to humorously illustrate why loyalty is important.
Word Forms: anecdotal, anecdotally, anecdotist
Related Words: anecdotage

388   THE POWERSCORE ACT AND SAT READING BIBLE

☐ **anomaly**: (*n*) an inconsistency; an oddity; a deviation from the norm
The yearly data showed an overall increase in sales, except for one anomaly; the month of July had an unexplained decrease in profit.
Word Forms: anomalous, anomalously

☐ **antagonize**: (*vb*) to provoke or display hostility
Annie antagonized her little brother by knocking over his tower of toy bricks.
Word Forms: antagonizable, antagonistic, antagonistically, antagonism, antagonist
Antonym Forms: protagonism, protagonist

☐ **application**: (*n*) the special use; the quality of being usable
The new computer has many applications: it can be used as a laptop or as a touch-screen tablet.
Word Forms: apply, applicable, applicably, applicant, applicator

☐ **apprehension**: (*vb*) fear or anxiety
April was filled with apprehension as she checked the mailbox for her report card.
Word Forms: apprehensive, apprehensively, apprehensiveness, apprehensible, apprehend

☐ **appropriate**: (*vb*) to take; to set aside
The county appropriated the land from the homeowners to use for the new highway.
Word Forms: appropriator, appropriative

☐ **apt**: (*adj*) 1. intelligent   2. likely
The apt student, who scored a 780 on the Math section of the SAT, is apt to attend a highly selective school.
Word Forms: aptly, aptness   Antonym Forms: inapt, inaptly, inaptness   Related Words: aptitude, inaptitude

☐ **articulate**: (*adj*) clearly pronounced; well-spoken
The articulate carpenter clearly expressed his concerns to the architect.
Word Forms: articulate (vb.), articulately, articulation, articulateness, articulator
Antonym Forms: inarticulate, inarticulately, inarticulation, inarticulateness

☐ **ascertain**: (*vb*) to make certain
The detective was able to ascertain the suspect's whereabouts on the night of the burglary through surveillance video.
Word Forms: ascertainable, ascertainableness, ascertainment

☐ **aspiration**: (*n*) a desire to succeed
The military medic had aspirations of becoming a doctor after his tour of duty.
Word Forms: aspirational, aspire, aspirer

☐ **assert**: (*vb*) to state confidently
Sam asserted his innocence when interviewed by the principal, swearing that he had nothing to do with the senior prank.
Word Forms: assertedly, assertion, asserter
Related Words: assertive

☐ **assume**: (*vb*) to accept as true without proof
Important Note: Assumptions made by an author are key components of reading questions. On the ACT and SAT, assumptions are unstated propositions that are accepted as true. You must be able to identify assumptions in order to form conclusions based on those assumptions. Consider the following sentence:
Mrs. Crawford will cancel the field trip next week if we continue to misbehave in class.
• Fact: We have previously misbehaved in class.
• Assumption: Field trips are fun.
• Assumption: Mrs. Crawford has the authority to cancel the trip.

☐ **austere**: (*adj*) 1. strict; disciplined; serious 2. simple; undecorated
Mr. Aston is the most austere teacher at school; he does not tolerate any talking nor does he accept late assignments.
Word Forms: austerely, austerity

☐ **authenticity**: (*n*) the quality of being real or genuine
Several critics questioned the authenticity of the politician's story about his tour of duty as a soldier.
Word Forms: authentic, authenticate, authentication, authenticator

Vocabulary

☐ **aversion:** (*n*) a feeling of intense dislike
Ava's aversion to dogs stemmed from an incident in her childhood when she was bitten by a stray terrier.
Word Forms: aversive, aversively, averse, aversely   Related Word: adverse, avert

☐ **belie:** (*vb*) to misrepresent
Her soft voice belies her aggressive demeanor.
Word Forms: belier   Related Words: lie

☐ **benevolent:** (*adj*) charitable; kind
The benevolent nun spent her entire life working with the poor.
Word Forms: benevolently, benevolence   Related Words: benefactor, benefit

☐ **bias:** (*n*) mental prejudice or tendency
The teacher was aware of her bias toward boys so she made it a point to call on girls more often.
Word Forms: biased, biasedly

☐ **bolster:** (*vb*) to support and strengthen
The manager hoped to bolster the morale of his sales team by creating an incentive program.
Word Forms: bolster (n.), bolsterer

☐ **callous:** (*adj*) insensitive; emotionally hardened
The senator's callous indifference to the suffering of the people in the war-torn country cost him reelection.
Word Forms: callously, callousness   Related Words: callus

☐ **catalyst:** (*n*) something that brings about change
The new teacher was a catalyst to the math department, ushering in welcome changes to the curriculum.
Word Forms: catalytic, catalytical, catalytically   Antonym Forms: anticatalyst, anticatalytic

☐ **censure:** (*n*) strong disapproval
High school teachers voiced their censure of the novel, citing several reasons for leaving it off the summer reading list.
Word Forms: censure (vb.), censurable, censurer   Related Words: censor

☐ **cerebral:** (*adj*) involving intelligence rather than emotions or instinct
Although Sarah was so angry that she wanted to quit her job, she decided to take a cerebral approach and weigh the costs before making a decision.
Word Form: cerebrally   Related Word: cerebrum

☐ **champion:** (*vb*) to support or defend
After her son was diagnosed with autism, Charla championed the opening of a school for students with special needs.
Word Form: championed   Antonym Form: unchampioned

☐ **characterize:** (*vb*) to mark as a quality or feature of
The movie was characterized as nostalgic teen romance and thus overlooked by the awards panel.
Word Form: characterizable, characterization   Related Word: character

☐ **chronicle:** (*vb*) to record
The reporter was hired by the army to chronicle the war; without his employment, we would never have known the true order of events during the conflict.
Word Forms: chronicler, chronically   Related Word: chronological

☐ **circumscribed:** (*adj*) restricted
Her driving privileges are circumscribed by the state; she is only allowed to drive at night if she is returning from work.
Word Forms: circumscribable, circumscriber   Related Word: circle, circumference

☐ **circumstantial:** (*adj*) dependent on conditions or circumstances
Whether or not we have school tomorrow is circumstantial to the weather; we'll need at least six inches of snow overnight to get the superintendent to issue a snow day.
Word Forms: circumstance, circumstantially

☐ **circumvent:** (*vb*) to go around; to avoid
I circumvented the construction on the highway by taking the bypass that goes around the city.
Word Forms: circumvention, circumventive, circumventer   Related Word: circle, circumference

☐ **clarify**: (*vb*) to make clear
The principal was asked to clarify his point about standardized testing, so he explained in detail how he plans to make changes to the way students are assessed in school.
Word Forms: clarification, clarifier   Related Words: clarity

☐ **cognitive**: (*adj*) relating to mental processes such as perception and understanding
To stimulate cognitive development in toddlers, expose them to numbers, letters, and other forms of print.
Word Forms: cognitively, cognition   Related Words: recognize, recognition

☐ **coherent**: (*adj*) clear and logical
Kobe began recycling when his daughter made a coherent argument about the money and energy he would save.
Word Forms: coherently, cohere, coherence, coherency   Antonym Forms: incoherent, incoherently, incoherence
Related Words: cohesive, cohesion

☐ **collaborate**: (*vb*) to work together
Colleen and Curtis collaborated on the book; Colleen wrote the stories and Curtis illustrated the scenes.
Word Forms: collaboration, collaborative, collaboratively, collaborator

☐ **colleague**: (*n*) a person that one works with in the same field or profession
The doctor was afraid that her colleagues would disagree with her diagnosis.
Word Form: colleagueship   Related Word: college

☐ **commend**: (*vb*) to praise
Corey was commended for returning the wallet he found at the mall.
Word Forms: commendable, commendably, commendation, commendatory   Related Words: recommend

☐ **commercial**: (*adj*) intended to make a profit; relating to the sale of goods and services
College football has become increasingly commercial, with major corporations paying for their names to appear on stadiums, uniforms, and the titles of bowl games.
Word Form: commercially, commercialism, commercialize, commercialization   Related Word: commerce

☐ **commonality**: (*n*) a quality held in common
Between the sports of tennis and badminton there are several commonalities, including the use of rackets and nets that separate opponents.
Related Words: common

☐ **competent**: (*adj*) capable; qualified
The competent driver maneuvered the congested and hazardous streets of New York City with ease.
Word Forms: competently, competence, competency
Antonym Forms: incompetent, incompetently, incompetence, incompetency

☐ **complacent**: (*adj*) contented to a fault with oneself or one's actions
After twenty years of teaching, Mr. Compton had become complacent, failing to keep up with new trends in education.
Word Forms: complacently, complacence, complacency

☐ **comprehensive**: (*adj*) including all
The book contains a comprehensive history of television in America, from the first broadcast in 1941 to the television shows that won this year's Emmy awards.
Word Forms: comprehensively, comprehensiveness   Related Words: comprehension

☐ **concession**: (*n*) the act of giving in or the actual thing that was given up
When the principal revoked our privilege to eat lunch off campus, she made a concession and allowed pizza to be delivered to the school once a week.
Word Forms: concessional, concessionary   Related Word: concede

☐ **concise**: (*adj*) expressing much in few words
Your essay should be concise; be sure to remove any unnecessary words or sentences.
Word Forms: concisely, conciseness, concision

☐ **condemn**: (*vb*) to express strong disapproval of
By 1800, slavery was condemned in many of the northern states.
Word Forms: condemningly, condemnable, condemnably, condemnatory, condemnation   Related Words: damn

VOCABULARY

u\

☐ **condescend**: (*vb*) to behave as if lowering oneself to an inferior level
Constance believed that her wealth permitted her to be rude and arrogant; she refused to condescend to speak to the bell boy at the upscale hotel.
Word Forms: condescending (adj.), condescendingly, condescension,
Related Words: descend

☐ **condone**: (*vb*) to excuse, overlook, or make allowances for
The honor code states that you condone cheating by not reporting it to a teacher.
Word Forms: condonable, condonation, condoner

☐ **conducive**: (*adj*) favorable; contributing to
Plenty of water and sunlight are conducive to a healthy garden.
Word Forms: conduciveness, conduce   Antonym Forms: inconducive
Related Word: conduct

☐ **conjunction**: (*n*) combination
The sorority, in conjunction with the disaster relief charity, is hosting a formal dance to raise money for the flood victims.
Word Forms: conjunctional, conjunctionally

☐ **consensus**: (*n*) agreement reached by a group as a whole
The town council members had to reach a consensus in order to pass the new ordinances.
Related Word: consent

☐ **conspicuous**: (*adj*) obvious
The realtor put the "For Sale" sign in a conspicuous spot in the front yard so that people in traffic could easily see it.
Word Forms: conspicuously, conspicuousness
Antonym Forms: inconspicuous, inconspicuously, inconspicuousness

☐ **constrain**: (*vb*) to hold back
The size of the small aquarium will constrain the growth of the turtle.
Word Forms: constrainable, constraint, constrainer   Related Words: strain

☐ **consummate**: (*adj*) perfect and complete
Constantine is the consummate host; he greets his guest, makes sure she is comfortable and enjoying herself, and introduces his new friends to everyone.
Word Forms: consummate (vb.), consummately, consummation

☐ **contempt**: (*n*) scorn or open disrespect
Connie was looked upon with contempt by her peers when she was discovered spreading rumors about them.
Word Forms: contemptible, contemptibility, contemptibleness, contemptuous, contemptuously, contemptuousness
Related Words: contemn

☐ **contradict**: (*vb*) to deny
The witness contradicted the defendant's alibi, saying that the suspect was in the pizza shop at the time of the robbery and not at work as he had stated.
Word Forms: contradiction, contradictable, contradictory

☐ **conventional**: (*adj*) following accepted customs and behaviors
Consuelo favored conventional wedding vows, while Callie wanted to break tradition and write her own.
Word Forms: conventionally, convention, conventionality, conventionary, conventionalize, conventionalist
Antonym Forms: unconventional, unconventionally, unconventionality

☐ **conversely**: (*adv*) the opposite of being true; on the other hand
The more expensive a product, the lower the demand; conversely, the less expensive a product, the higher the demand.
Word Forms: converse

☐ **convey**: (*vb*) to make known; to communicate
The novel conveys a sense of hope during a time in which desperation was the predominant emotion of the city.
Word Forms: conveyance

☐ **conviction**: (*n*) a firm belief
The teacher held fast to her conviction that all students could learn, despite opposition from the children themselves.
Related Word: convince

☐ **convoluted**: (*adj*) complicated
Connor was unable to finish the seventeenth-century novel due to the convoluted language of the period.
Word Forms: convolutedly, convolutedness   Related Words: involuted

☐ **corroborate**: (*vb*) to confirm or support with evidence
Coral's thesis was corroborated by three supporting paragraphs, each presenting an example that proved her main idea.
Word Forms: corroborated, corroboration, corroborative, corroboratively, corroboratory, corroborator
Antonym Forms: uncorroborated

☐ **counterargument**: (*n*) an opposing opinion
At the technology convention, the speaker asserted that tablets are valuable learning tools for children, but he was challenged by a member of the audience who brought up a counterargument: mainly, that "screen addiction" can be extremely harmful to young kids.

☐ **culmination**: (*n*) the highest point or final result
The best selling novel was the culmination of the journalist's long career.
Word Forms: culminate

☐ **curtail**: (*vb*) to cut short or restrict
The public service message is intended to curtail drinking and driving.
Word Forms: curtailment, curtailer

☐ **cynical**: (*adj*) distrusting and pessimistic
Cyndi's cynical attitude made it hard for her to believe in anyone's good intentions.
Word Forms: cynically, cynicism, cynic

☐ **dearth**: (*n*) a lack in supply
During the Second World War, the dearth of male baseball players led to the creation of a women's baseball league.

☐ **debunk**: (*vb*) to prove untrue
The reporter debunked the urban legend about the witch in the woods by revealing wild goats as the sources of the noises.
Word Forms: debunker

☐ **decisive**: (*adj*) deciding without dispute or hesitation
During the War, the lawmakers of Missouri cast a decisive vote to stay with the Union; they had no interest in seceding.
Word Forms: decisively, decisiveness   Antonym Forms: indecisive, indecisively, indecisiveness
Related Words: decide, decision

☐ **decry**: (*vb*) to express strong disapproval of
The politician decried the injustices suffered by the people of the nation.
Word Forms: decrier, decrial   Related Words: cry

☐ **deference**: (*n*) submission to another person
In deference to your wishes, I won't ask the restaurant employees to sing "Happy Birthday" to you.
Word Forms: defer, deferent, deferential, deferentially

☐ **delineate**: (*vb*) to outline
In her speech, Delilah clearly delineated her plans for changing several policies should she be elected class president.
Word Forms: delineable, delineative, delineation, delineator   Antonym Form: undelineated

☐ **denounce**: (*vb*) to openly speak out against
The sports reporter denounced the professional football team for raising ticket prices again.
Word Forms: denouncement, denunciation, denouncer
Related Words: announce, pronounce, renounce

☐ **depict**: (*vb*) to represent or show
The author depicts the historical figure as a charming but manipulative woman.
Word Forms: depictive, depiction, depicter   Related Words: depicture, picture

☐ **deplete**: (*vb*) to use up; to drain the supply
My energy was completely depleted after back-to-back football practices.
Word Forms: depletable, depletion, depletive

☐ **deride**: (*vb*) to ridicule
The unsupportive team captain derided Desiree's attempts to make the volleyball squad.
Word Forms: deridingly, derision, derisive, derider

☐ **derivative**: (*n*) something that came from an original
The Pilates exercise system is a derivative of the ancient Indian practice of yoga.
Word Forms: derivative (adj.), derivatively, derivativeness, derive, derivation

☐ **detract**: (*vb*) to take away
Although many found Detta beautiful, most would agree that her wickedness detracted from her good looks.
Word Forms: detractingly, detraction, detractive, detractor   Antonym Forms: attract, attraction, attractive
Related Words: distract, retract, extract

☐ **deviate**: (*vb*) to turn away from
The plot of the television series deviates from that of the novel when several characters who survive in the book are killed off on the show.
Related Word: deviant

☐ **devoid**: (*adj*) completely wanting or lacking
Devin is devoid of all social skills; she cannot even make eye contact or engage in small talk.
Related Words: void

☐ **differentiate**: (*vb*) to mark as different
It is easy to differentiate between the twins; Daisy has blond hair and Daphne has red hair.
Word Forms: differentiation, differential, differentially   Antonym Form: undifferentiated   Related Word: different

☐ **digress**: (*vb*) to wander away, especially from the main subject of writing or speaking
When Dr. Medrano was describing the symptoms of the flu, he digressed into a story from his childhood.
Word Forms: digression, digressional, digressionary, digresser   Related Words: progress, regress

☐ **diligent**: (*adj*) detailed and persistent
The diligent editor was praised for her ability to find errors in even the most difficult text.
Word Forms: diligently, diligence, diligency

☐ **diminish**: (*vb*) to decrease in size, extent, or range
The loud music from the party next door diminished after the police showed up.
Word Forms: diminishable, diminishment

☐ **diplomatic**: (*adj*) skillful in handling sensitive situations
When the two men got into a heated disagreement, Diana's diplomatic negotiation skills defused the situation.
Word Forms: diplomatically, diplomacy, diplomat

☐ **discern**: (*vb*) to perceive or understand with sight or other senses
The captain discerned another ship in the fog.
Word Forms: discernible, discernibly, discernment, discerner
Antonym Forms: indiscernible

☐ **disclose**: (*vb*) to reveal or uncover
The teacher disclosed to her class the winner of the Homecoming contest before the announcement was made.
Word Forms: disclosed (adj.), disclosure, disclosable, discloser   Antonym Forms: undisclose, undisclosed, undisclosable

☐ **discord**: (*n*) disagreement
The school board's refusal to accept the terms of the contract created discord among the administrators and teachers.
Word Forms: discordance, discordant, discordantly   Antonym Forms: concord, accord

☐ **discredit**: (*vb*) to cause to be distrusted or disbelieved
The prosecuting attorney was able to discredit the witness by proving he lied about the alibi.
Word Forms: discredit (n.), discreditable, discreditably, discreditor   Related Word: credit

☐ **discrepancy**: (*n*) a difference or inconsistency
I found a discrepancy with the balance of my checking account; the bank shows I have $50 less than I actually do.
Word Forms: discrepant, discrepantly, discrepance

☐ **discriminate**: (*adj*) able to judge quality; liking only things of quality
Divya had discriminate taste in shoes and preferred those that were cobbled in Italy.
Word Forms: discriminately, discriminate (vb.), discrimination, discriminative

☐ **disdain**: (*n*) a lack of respect accompanied by a feeling of intense dislike
The suspect was looked upon with disdain by the detectives who investigated the terrible crime.
Word Forms: disdain (vb.), disdainful, disdainfully, disdainfulness   Related Words: deign

☐ **disparage**: (*vb*) to belittle or criticize
My mom's feelings were hurt when I disparaged her cooking skills.
Word Forms: disparagement, disparaging (adj.), disparagingly, disparager

☐ **disparate**: (*adj*) different and distinct
The mixture of three disparate styles—jazz, rock, and country—created a unique sound and a diverse audience.
Word Forms: disparately, disparateness   Related Words: disparity

☐ **dispatch**: 1. (*vb*) to send out   2. (*n*) quickness
The dispatcher alerted the fire station to the emergency call with dispatch.

☐ **dispute**: (*vb*) to question the truth of
The church disputes the theory of evolution, instead citing religious sources of creation.
Word Forms: dispute (n.), disputable, disputant, disputation, disputer   Antonym Forms: indisputable, indisputably

☐ **doctrine**: (*n*) a belief that is taught, usually by a church or government
The religion's doctrine teaches that the good of the community is a higher personal priority than self-satisfaction.
Word Forms: doctrinal, doctrinarian   Related Word: indoctrinate

☐ **dubious**: (*adj*) doubtful; questionable
The candidate's dubious past came back to haunt her in the election.
Word Forms: dubiously, dubiousness, dubitable   Antonym Forms: indubious, indubiously   Related Words: doubt

☐ **earnest**: (*adj*) serious; sincere
The earnest student took the SAT seriously; he bought several study guides, and dedicated two hours a day to practice.
Word Forms: earnestly, earnestness

☐ **eccentric**: (*adj*) peculiar; odd
The eccentric woman often wore an angel halo and ballet tutu to the grocery store.
Word Forms: eccentric (n.), eccentricity, eccentrical, eccentrically

☐ **elicit**: (*vb*) to call or bring out
The woman elicits sympathy from her audience by telling the story of her difficult childhood.
Word Forms: elicitation, elicitor   Related Words: solicit
Note: *elicit* is often confused with *illicit*, which means *illegal*.

☐ **elite**: (*adj*) selected as the best
The elite college only admitted students with the highest SAT scores.
Word Forms: elite (n.), elitist, elitism

☐ **eloquent**: (*adj*) expressing oneself powerfully and effectively
The minister's eloquent sermon stirred the members of the church.
Word Forms: eloquently, eloquence   Antonym Forms: ineloquent, ineloquently, ineloquence

☐ **embellish**: (*vb*) to make better by adding details (especially false details)
When he saw the crowd losing interest in his tale, Emilio embellished the story by adding an adventure in a cave.
Word Forms: embellishment, embellisher   Antonym Forms: unembellished

☐ **emerging**: (*adj*) developing; coming into view
The country's emerging markets revealed an economy that was much further developed than the invading government originally believed.
Word Forms: emerge, emergent

☐ **eminent**: (*adj*) distinguished and prominent
The eminent professor has taught at distinguished colleges, which is why he is such a remarkable addition to the faculty.
Word Forms: eminently, eminence   Note: eminent is often confused with *imminent*, which means *about to occur*.

☐ **emit**: (*vb*) to give out; to discharge
The roses in the garden emitted a sweet smell that reminded me of my grandmother.
Related Word: emission

☐ **empathy**: (*n*) the understanding of another's feelings
Emma felt empathy for the victims of the earthquake, having lost her own home to a hurricane last year.
Word Forms: empathize, empathetic, empathetically   Antonym Forms: antipathy, antipathetic, antipathetically
Related Words: sympathy, apathy

☐ **emphatic**: (*adj*) expressed with emphasis
The teacher was emphatic about the project's due date; no late assignments would be accepted.
Word Forms: emphatically, emphaticalness   Antonym Forms: unemphatic, unemphatically
Related Words: emphasis, emphasize

☐ **empirical**: (*adj*) resulting from an experiment
As a scientist, Emmie relied on empirical data every day, which is why it was hard for her to trust her intuition.
Word Forms: empirically, empiricalness

☐ **encompass**: (*vb*) to surround or to include
The author's works encompassed nearly every genre, from poetry to theater to fiction.
Word Form: encompassment   Related Word: compass (vb.)

☐ **endow**: (*vb*) to fund; to provide with qualities or attributes
The young woman has been endowed with charm and keen insight, two qualities her father felt she needed to advance in the business world.
Word Form: endowment, endower

☐ **endure**: (*vb*) to continue despite difficulty
Enzo endured Mr. Smith's extremely boring lecture on photosynthesis.
Word Forms: enduring (adj.), enduringly, enduringness, endurance, endurer

☐ **engagement**: (*n*) the state of being involved or occupied
The level of engagement for the activities varies; in some, children will be grossly involved, but in others, they may only contribute a few ideas.
Word Forms: engage

☐ **enumerate**: (*vb*) to list one by one; to count
The author enumerated the three reasons that play-based learning is fundamental in preschool.
Word Forms: enumerable, enumeration, enumerative   Related Word: numeral

☐ **erratic**: (*adj*) unpredictable or inconsistent
Ericka's attendance was erratic; there was no clear pattern between the days she went to school and the days she missed.
Word Forms: erratically, erraticism

☐ **esteemed**: (*adj*) highly respected
The esteemed designer has been asked to participate in an exclusive fashion show to highlight his fall collection.
Word Forms: esteem (vb.), esteem (n.)

☐ **evoke**: (*vb*) to call forth emotions, feelings, or responses
Evan's stirring speech evoked a standing ovation from the audience.
Word Forms: evocable, evocation, evoker, evocator   Related Words: invoke, provoke, revoke

☐ **exemplary**: (*adj*) serving as a worthy example
The student's exemplary attendance record was recognized at the awards ceremony.
Word Forms: exemplarily, exemplariness, exemplarity, exemplar   Related Words: example, exemplify

☐ **exert**: (*vb*) to forcefully put into use; to strenuously apply oneself
The mayor exerted her influence in order to get her son accepted to the elite private school.
Word Forms: exertion, exertive   Related Words: invoke, provoke, revoke

☐ **expedient**: (*adj*) serving a purpose or personal interest
It was expedient to flatter Mrs. Jameson; it was rumored that the more compliments you paid her, the higher your semester grade would be.
Word Forms: expedient (n.), expediently, expedience   Antonym Forms: inexpedient, inexpediently, inexpedience

☐ **explicit**: (*adj*) clearly expressed or demonstrated
Mr. Jones left explicit directions for the substitute so he was surprised when they were not followed.
Word Forms: explicitly, explicitness   Antonym Forms: inexplicit, implicit, implicitly, implicitness

☐ **exploit**: (*vb*) to use for one's own advantage
The company was criticized for exploiting the workers by not paying a fair wage.
Word Forms: exploitable, exploitative, exploitive, exploiter   Related Words: exploit (n.)

☐ **extol**: (*vb*) to praise highly
The critic extolled the works of Shakespeare, citing them as the most important contribution to the English language.
Word Forms: extollingly, extolment, extoller

☐ **extravagant**: (*adj*) excessively high or expensive
The restaurant's extravagant prices attracted a wealthy clientele.
Word Forms: extravagantly, extravagantness, extravagance   Related Word: extravaganza

☐ **fabricated**: (*adj*) constructed to deceive
Fabian knew that he would be punished for going to the party so he told a fabricated story about studying at the library.
Word Forms: fabricate, fabrication, fabricator   Antonym Form: unfabricated

☐ **facilitate**: (*vb*) to make easier
The data about the number of cars through the intersection was presented to facilitate a decision about whether a traffic light is warranted.
Word Forms: facilitative, facilitator

☐ **feasible**: (*adj*) possible
Student loans are a feasible source of tuition for most incoming college students.
Word Forms: feasibly, feasibility, feasibleness   Antonym Forms: infeasible, infeasibly, infeasibility

☐ **flourish**: (*adj*) to do well or grow well
When I moved the plants to the windowsill, they suddenly began to flourish; the lack of direct sunlight must have really inhibited their growth.
Word Forms: flourish (n.)   Related Word: flower

☐ **foreseeable**: (*adj*) able to be known in advance
The accident was foreseeable by many members of the community, who urged the town council to install a light at the dangerous intersection.
Word Forms: foresee, foreseer   Related Word: foresight, foreshadow, foretell

☐ **formidable**: (*adj*) causing fear due to powerful strength
Forrest is a formidable opponent on the tennis court; he has not lost a set in his last twenty games.
Word Forms: formidably, formidableness

☐ **fortify**: (*vb*) to make stronger
The army fortified the area by adding security guards and a large chain link fence.
Word Forms: fortified (adj.), fortifiable, fortifyingly, fortifier   Antonym Form: unfortified

☐ **foster**: (*vb*) to encourage or care for
The arts foundation hopes to foster art education in the schools by donating supplies and materials.
Word Forms: fostered (adj.), fosteringly, fosterer

☐ **frame**: (*vb*) to conceive, plan, or formulate
The thoughtful student paused as she carefully framed her question so as not to offend the teacher.
Word Forms: frame (n.), framable

☐ **frivolous**: (*adj*) not serious; silly
The author's new novel is a frivolous look at life in the city; although it lacks the serious tones of his previous novels, it's a fun and enjoyable story.
Word Forms: frivolously, frivolousness, frivolity, frivol, frivoler

☐ **fundamental**: (*adj*) essential; basic
The fundamental principle of the educational theory is that all students can learn.
Word Forms: fundamentally, fundamentalism, fundamentalist

☐ **galvanizing**: (*adj*) spurring action or excitement
The country was galvanized by the first democratic election after centuries of an oppressive monarchy.
Word Forms: galvanize, galvanization, galvanizer

☐ **generalization**: (*n*) an opinion or conclusion formed from only a few facts or examples
Saying that freshmen are younger than sophomores is a generalization that is usually—but not always—true.
Word Forms: generalize, generalizable, generalizer   Related Words: general

☐ **gravity**: (*n*) seriousness
It took Grady a moment to understand the gravity of the situation when his father first told him about the missing money.
Related Word: grave

☐ **hasten**: (*vb*) to hurry
We must hasten if you're going to make it to school on time.
Word Forms: haste

☐ **hostile**: (*adj*) openly opposed; showing ill-will
Several hostile threats against the suspect's lawyer were made by unidentified callers.
Word Forms: hostilely, hostility

☐ **humble**: (*adj*) not arrogant or prideful; modest
The humble athlete preferred to talk about the team's accomplishments rather than his stellar individual contribution.
Word Forms: humbly, humbleness, humblingly, humbler   Related Word: humility

☐ **hypothetical**: (*adj*) supposed; based on a hypothesis
The medical students had to diagnose the actor's hypothetical illness based on the symptoms he pretended to have.
Word Forms: hypothetically   Related Word: hypothesis, hypothesize

☐ **idealism**: (*n*) the practice of seeing things in an ideal form
Even after all of the drama and conflict Ida witnessed, her idealism still remained; she still believed that she could bring harmony to the warring neighborhood.
Word Forms: idealistic, idealize, idealist   Related Word: ideal

☐ **illuminate**: (*vb*) to make clear; to supply light
The presentation on the artist was illuminating; I did not know that he was originally from China.
Word Forms: illumine, illuminatingly, illumination   Related Words: luminary

☐ **impart**: (*vb*) to communicate; to give
Teachers are hired to impart knowledge and guide students into adulthood.
Word Forms: impartable

☐ **imperative**: (*n*) a necessity; a command
Defending my brother against bullies is not just a family obligation, but a moral imperative.
Word Forms: imperative (adj.), imperatively

☐ **implicit**: (*adj*) implied though not directly expressed
Although we never mentioned the fight, there seemed to be an implicit agreement not to talk about it.
Word Forms: implicitly, implicitness, implicity   Antonym Forms: explicit, explicitly, explicitness

☐ **imply**: (*vb*) to suggest without directly stating
Important Note: Authors frequently imply information in the reading comprehension passages. These implications usually result in multiple choice questions designed to test a student's ability to understand such indirect suggestions. Consider an example:
When I arrived at school, I saw that all of the other students were wearing blue shirts too.
 • Fact: All of the other students are wearing blue shirts.
 • Implication: I am a student.
 • Implication: I am wearing a blue shirt.

☐ **imposition**: (*n*) the act of intruding; creating a burden
Ivan didn't normally mind his neighbor stopping by, but today her imposition prevented him from getting dinner on the table before the kids had to leave for practice.
Word Forms: impose, imposing, imposingly

☐ **inconsequential**: (*adj*) not important
The blown tire turned out to be inconsequential to the race results, as the driver still managed to come in first.
Word Forms: inconsequentially, inconsequent,
Antonym Forms: consequential, consequent, consequentially, consequentialness   Related Word: consequence

☐ **incontrovertible**: (*adj*) unquestionable; impossible to deny
Protesters demanded the release of the imprisoned woman, saying there was incontrovertible proof of her innocence.
Word Forms: incontrovertibly   Antonym Forms: controvertible, controvertibly, controvert

☐ **incredulous**: (*adj*) skeptical; not willing to believe
The incredulous car buyer did not believe the dealer's claim that the car was accident-free; he insisted on seeing a report on the car's history.
Word Forms: incredulously, incredulousness, incredulity   Related Word: incredible
Antonym Forms: credulous, credulously, credulousness, credulity

☐ **indictment**: (*n*) an accusation of wrongdoing
Ingrid made an indictment against Tony, claiming that he purposely miscounted the votes for Prom Queen.
Word Forms: indict, indictable, indictablly

☐ **indifferent**: (*adj*) showing lack of interest, concern, or bias
The writer produced an indifferent article about the two candidates by successfully suppressing her preference.
Word Forms: indifferently, indifference

☐ **indignant**: (*adj*) displaying anger due to unfairness
The seniors were indignant over their disqualification in the homecoming contest, claiming that the decision was unfair.
Word Forms: indignantly, indignation

☐ **induce**: (*vb*) to lead or bring about
The presence of the washed up jellyfish induced a panic in the beachgoers, few of whom dared to venture into the water.
Word Forms: inducible, inducement, induction   Related Words: conduce, produce, seduce

☐ **indulgent**: (*adj*) yielding; lenient; tolerant
The indulgent mother gave her child everything he wanted.
Word Forms: indulgently, indulgence, indulge

☐ **infer**: (*vb*) to conclude based on reasoning or evidence
Important Note: The ACT and SAT Reading sections will require you to make several inferences based on the passages. You must reach these conclusions through reasoning. Consider an example:
Malia had a hard time maneuvering on her crutches while carrying the open umbrella in the pouring rain.
  • Inference: Malia has an injury.
  • Inference: Malia is trying to avoid getting wet.

☐ **ingenious**: (*adj*) clever and inventive
Jeannie invented an ingenious device for the beach that combined a cooler, radio, and portable fan.
Word Forms: ingeniously, ingeniousness, ingenuity   Related Word: genius

☐ **inherent**: (*adj*) existing as a natural and essential characteristic
The abused dog had an inherent distrust of men, so only female volunteers at the shelter could get close to him.
Word Forms: inherently, inhere, inherence   Related Words: inherit

☐ **inhibit**: (*vb*) to limit; to hold back
Inez wanted to go camping with her friends, but she was inhibited by her fear of spiders and snakes.
Word Forms: inhibited (adj.), inhibition   Antonym Forms: uninhibited, uninhibitive

☐ **innate**: (*adj*) existing from birth; instinctive; being an essential part
The dog's ability to swim is innate; unlike a human being, he does not have to learn how to swim.
Word Forms: innately, innateness   Related Words: inherit

☐ **innovative**: (*adj*) creative or the condition of being something new and unseen
The first touch-screen computer was praised for its innovative monitor.
Word Forms: innovatively, innovate, innovation, innovator   Related Word: novel (adj.)

VOCABULARY

☐ **inquiry**: (*n*) an investigation; a question
If you have questions or concerns about the process, direct all inquiries to the head of security.
Related Words: inquire, query, inquisition,

☐ **insight**: (*n*) a clear understanding of a situation
Jane's insight into the computer problem was the result of years of working with the computer system.
Word Forms: insightful, insightfully, insightfulness

☐ **integrate**: (*vb*) to join together as a whole
The spine surgeon and the chiropractor integrated their practices to offer patients a more holistic medical experience.
Word Forms: integrative

☐ **inundate**: (*vb*) to flood
After the newspaper ran the controversial story, the editor was inundated with calls from hundreds of angry subscribers.
Word Forms: inundation, inundatory, inundator

☐ **invoke**: (*vb*) to summon into action or bring into existence
The psychic claimed that he could invoke the spirits in the house through an old-fashioned séance.
Word Forms: invocable, invocation, invocational, invoker   Related Words: evoke, provoke, revoke

☐ **irrelevant**: (*adj*) unrelated; not connected
We will address the issues with our health insurance; any other complaints are irrelevant and will not be discussed.
Word Forms: irrelevantly, irrelevance, irrelevancy   Antonym Forms: relevant, relevantly, relevance, relevancy

☐ **lament**: (*vb*) to express grief; to mourn
When Lamont left for college, his little sister lamented his absence for weeks.
Word Forms: lament (n.), lamentingly, lamentable, lamentably, lamenter

☐ **laud**: (*vb*) to praise, glorify, or honor
Landon was lauded for his achievements at the laboratory; he had made more progress in a year than most scientists had made in a decade.
Word Forms: laudable, laudably, laudative, laudatory

☐ **legitimate**: (*adj*) lawful; in accordance with accepted standards; genuine
Leah had a legitimate complaint when the dry cleaning company failed to remove the stain from her coat.
Word Forms: legitimately, legitimize, legitimation, legitimateness, legitimacy   Antonym Form: illegitimate

☐ **malice**: (*n*) a desire to make others suffer
Malika's sharp comment was delivered with malice; she knew that her words would hurt her mother's feelings.
Word Forms: malicious, maliciously, maliciousness   Antonym Form: unmalicious

☐ **malleable**: (*adj*) capable of being shaped or influenced
Mallory worried that her malleable son would learn inappropriate behavior from the older boys he played with at school.
Word Forms: malleably, malleableness, malleability   Antonym Forms: unmalleable, unmalleability

☐ **mandate**: (*vb*) to require (often by law)
The governor mandated school uniforms for all public school systems in the state.
Word Forms: mandate (n.)   Related Word: mandatory

☐ **marketable**: (*adj*) easy to sell
The new cell phone is quite marketable to today's teenagers because of its advanced technology.
Word Forms: marketability   Related Word: market

☐ **mediation**: (*n*) a negotiation or attempt to settle disagreements between parties
Megan and Melody went to peer mediation to settle their fight over the purple sweater.
Word Forms: mediator, mediate   Related Word: medium (n.)

☐ **meticulous**: (*adj*) extremely careful and precise with details
Miss Walter demanded meticulous essays; perfect spelling and punctuation were essential for a high grade.
Word Forms: meticulously, meticulousness, meticulosity

☐ **mimic**: (*vb*) to imitate or copy speech or actions
The parrot mimicked the pirate.
Word Forms: mimicker   Related Word: mimicry

☐ **mitigate**: (*vb*) to make less intense or severe
Mitch was grounded for a week when he broke curfew, but his mom mitigated his punishment by several days when she learned that he had been late because he was taking a sick friend to the hospital.
Word Forms: mitigable, mitigatedly, mitigation, mitigative, mitigatory, mitigator
Antonym Forms: immitigable, immitigably, immitigability, unmitigable, unmitigated, unmitigatedly

☐ **modest**: (*adj*) displaying a moderate or ordinary opinion of one's own talents or abilities
Although Moe was a gifted athlete, he was very modest; he acted as if his contribution was average at best.
Word Forms: modestly, modesty   Antonym Forms: immodest, immodestly, immodesty   Related Word: moderate

☐ **muse**: (*vb*) to think about
The author mused over the idea that money cannot buy happiness before presenting his counterargument.
Word Forms: muser, museful, musefully   Related Word: muse (n.)

☐ **myriad**: (*adj*) a great number of
The frozen yogurt shop has a myriad of toppings, from gummy bears to chocolate chips to sprinkles.
Word Forms: myriad (adj.)

☐ **naïve**: (*adj*) inexperienced and gullible
Nan was naïve in thinking that no one looked at her online social page except her friends; her father looked at it daily.
Word Forms: naïvely, naïveté

☐ **negligent**: (*adj*) careless and neglectful
The negligent babysitter was caught on the videotape ignoring the cries of the helpless infant.
Word Forms: negligently, negligence, negligible, negligibly   Antonym Forms: diligent, diligently, diligence
Related Word: neglect

☐ **nostalgic**: (*n*) having a desire to return to the past
When I revisited my childhood home, I was surprised by how nostalgic I felt.
Word Forms: nostalgia

☐ **novel**: (*adj*) new; fresh
Nova had a novel suggestion for improving worker morale: allow employees an extra day off each month.
Word Forms: novelty

☐ **objective**: (*adj*) not influenced by personal feelings or bias
It is important for a judge to be objective; he cannot let his personal beliefs affect his rulings.
Word Forms: objectively, objectivity   Antonym Forms: subjective, subjectively, subjectivity

☐ **obscure**: (*adj*) not clearly understood or expressed
Most of the movie audience did not understand the obscure reference to the other movie.
Word Forms: obscure (vb.), obscurely, obscurity

☐ **obsolete**: (*adj*) no longer in use
The typewriter became obsolete when the personal computer was made affordable for the general public.
Word Forms: obsoletely, obsoleteness, obsolesce

☐ **optimism**: (*n*) the tendency to look at the positive side of things
Oprah's optimism is contagious; many of her fans adopt positive attitudes after attending her shows.
Word Forms: optimistic, optimistically, optimist

☐ **ornate**: (*adj*) highly decorated
The ornate palace had colorful paintings and intricate wood carvings in every room.
Word Forms: ornately, ornateness   Related Word: ornament

☐ **overwhelming**: (*adj*) overpowering; intense
The stench of burning popcorn was overwhelming, forcing us to evacuate to the porch.
Word Forms: overwhelmingly, overwhelm   Antonym Forms: underwhelming, underwhelmingly, underwhelm

☐ **paragon**: (*n*) a perfect example
Parmida is a paragon of professionalism; she arrives on time, treats co-workers with respect, and refrains from gossip.
Word Forms: paragon (vb.), paragoned

☐ **paramount**: (*adj*) first in order of importance
No matter what your essay topic is, having a compelling thesis is paramount to receiving a good grade.

☐ **parenthetical**: (*adj*) characterized by the use of parenthesis
A remark in parenthesis is called a parenthetical remark, which is usually used to explain the sentence.
Word Forms: parenthetic, parenthetically, parentheticalness   Related Words: parentheses

☐ **partisan**: (*adj*) tending to favor one group or one way of thinking
Gun control is a partisan issue; one party favors government management while the other prefers individual authority.
Word Forms: partisanship, partisan (n.)   Antonym Forms: nonpartisan, bipartisan   Related Word: party

☐ **patronize**: (*vb*) to treat someone as if they are not as intelligent or important
Patrick was constantly patronizing me during the movie; he kept pausing it to explain what happened in a scene, even though I understood it as well as he did.
Word Forms: patronizingly, patronizer

☐ **penchant**: (*n*) a strong liking
Penny has a penchant for poetry; she has filled two notebooks with poems and poetic lines.

☐ **perceptive**: (*adj*) having keen insight or intuition
The perceptive secretary, who watched his boss cross the lobby, knew what she wanted just by the look on her face.
Word Forms: perceptively   Antonym Forms: imperceptive   Related Word: perceive

☐ **perpetuate**: (*vb*) to cause to continue
Pacey could stop the rumor by refusing to repeat it, or perpetuate it by passing it on to his best friend.
Word Forms: perpetual, perpetually, perpetuation, perpetuity, perpetuator

☐ **perplex**: (*vb*) to puzzle or confuse
Percy was perplexed by the complex puzzle and distressed that he could not find a solution.
Word Forms: perplexed (adj.), perplexingly, perplexity

☐ **pertinent**: (*adj*) relevant
The professor distributed a list of articles and books that were pertinent to the discussions in his course.
Word Forms: pertinently, pertinence, pertinency
Antonym Forms: impertinent, impertinently, impertinence, impertinency   Related Word: pertain

☐ **pervasive**: (*adj*) spreading or spread throughout
The pervasive odor of garlic quickly spread throughout the entire house.
Word Forms: pervasively, pervasiveness, pervade, pervasion,
Related Words: invade, invasive

☐ **phenomenon**: (*n*) an occurrence, often which is impressive or unusual
Echolocation is a sensory phenomenon that is used by some animals to locate objects in their environment.
Word Forms: phenomenal, phenomenally, phenomenalize, phenom

☐ **plausible**: (*adj*) believable
The teacher was upset with Imogene until the girl offered a plausible excuse for not arriving to class on time.
Word Forms: plausibly, plausibility   Antonym Forms: implausible, implausibly, implausibility

☐ **pragmatic**: (*adj*) practical; guided by practice rather than theory
When her bobby pin broke, Penelope found a pragmatic solution; she used a paper clip to hold back her stray hair.
Word Forms: pragmatically, pragmatism, pragmatist

☐ **precedent**: (*n*) an example that is used to justify similar occurrences at a later time
When I allowed Priscilla to leave early every day, I set a precedent that I could not deny to other employees.
Word Forms: precedented   Antonym Forms: unprecedented   Related Word: precede

☐ **preceding**: (*adj*) previous; coming before
The preceding chapter, which I read yesterday, provided the background of all the characters who begin their adventure on the ship in this chapter.
Word Forms: precede   Related Word: precedent

☐ **precipitate**: (*vb*) to bring about abruptly
Prescott's sudden move to a smaller apartment was precipitated by the loss of his job.
Word Forms: precipitate (adj.), precipitately, precipitateness, precipitative, precipitator   Related Word: precipitous

☐ **precision**: (*n*) accuracy; exactness
Pierce threw darts with precision, landing all three in the same red box on the dart board.
Word Forms: precise, precisely

☐ **predecessor**: (*n*) one who came before
On my first day at the new job, I cleaned out the items left in my desk by my predecessor.
Related Words: precede

☐ **prescribed**: (*adj*) set by a rule
Coming from a working class family, I felt out of place at the extravagant party, afraid I would break some prescribed social rule that only the richest members of society knew.
Word Forms: prescribable

☐ **presume**: (*vb*) to accept as true without proof
I presume that you are tired after your long drive today.
Word Forms: presumption, presumable, presumably, presumedly, presumptive, presumptuous, presumer
Related Word: assume

☐ **prevalent**: (*adj*) widespread; commonly occurring
Bass are the most prevalent species of fish in the lake, accounting for more than half of all fish caught by anglers.
Word Forms: prevalently, prevalence, prevail

☐ **principles**: (*n*) standard rules of conduct or management
The judge takes modern principles into account when applying long-standing laws to the people who come before her in her courtroom.

☐ **profound**: (*adj*) deep; intense
Her profound knowledge of electricity was showcased at the science fair, where she won first place for her project.
Word Forms: profoundly, profoundness, profundity

☐ **prolific**: (*adj*) highly productive
The prolific author had written over 60 books during her career.
Word Forms: prolifically

☐ **prominent**: (*adj*) important; noticeable
The senator is a prominent woman who is well-known for fighting unfair labor practices.
Word Forms: prominently, prominence

☐ **protagonist**: (*n*) the main character in a fictional work
The protagonist of the story is a young girl who returns home to find three bears in her bed.
Word Form: protagonism   Antonym Forms: antagonist, antagonism, antagonize:

☐ **provocative**: (*adj*) tending to rouse feelings of excitement, irritation, or anger
At the press conference, the boxer made provocative remarks intended to anger his opponent.
Word Forms: provocatively, provocativeness, provocation, provocateur   Related Word: provoke

☐ **prudent**: (*adj*) careful and sensible
Perry made a prudent decision when he chose not to ride home with his friend who had been drinking.
Word Forms: prudently, prudence, prudential, prude   Antonym Forms: imprudent, imprudently, imprudence

☐ **qualitative**: (*adj*) relating to the measurement of quality
The qualitative difference between the two phones is significant given that one has outdated technology.
Word Forms: qualitatively   Related Words: quality, quantitative

☐ **quantitative**: (*adj*) relating to the measurement of quantity
The cost of publishing a book is directly influenced by the quantitative requirements of your order; the fewer pages required and the more copies you order, the less money you pay per book.
Word Forms: quantitatively   Related Words: quantity, qualitative

☐ **quell**: (*vb*) to put an end to
The coach quelled the rumor that he was taking another job by signing an extension of his current contract.
Word Forms: quellable, queller

☐ **rebuke**: (*vb*) to sharply criticize or reprimand
The principal rebuked the three students who wandered away from their chaperone on the field trip.
Word Forms: rebuke (n.), rebukingly, rebukable, rebuker

☐ **rebut**: (*vb*) to prove false using evidence
The lawyer rebutted the witness's testimony by providing contrary evidence.
Word Forms: rebuttable, rebuttal, rebutter   Related Word: but (conj.)

☐ **receptive**: (*adj*) willing to accept new ideas or suggestions
The woman's father was not receptive to her boyfriend's marriage proposal.
Word Forms: receptively   Related Word: receive

☐ **reciprocate**: (*vb*) to give in return
When Mr. Reilly brought cookies, I reciprocated his kindness by returning the cookie tin full of freshly baked brownies.
Word Forms: reciprocal, reciprocity

☐ **redundant**: (*adj*) having ideas that are repeated unnecessarily
The first two months of sophomore French class seemed redundant, as we had already covered the material as freshmen.
Word Forms: redundantly, redundancy   Related Word: redone

☐ **refute**: (*vb*) to prove to be false; to deny as true
The senator refuted claims he was arrested for careless driving by publishing his flawless driving record in the paper.
Word Forms: refutable, refutably, refutability, refutal   Antonym Forms: irrefutable, irrefutably, irrefutability

☐ **reiterate**: (*vb*) to say again
Since you didn't hear me the first time, let me reiterate the rules of the game.
Word Forms: reiterable, reiterative, reiteration   Related Word: iterate

☐ **reminiscence**: (*n*) recalling of the past; a memory
Grandpa would often share his reminiscences at family gatherings, relating stories about Grandma when she was young.
Word Forms: reminisce, reminiscent

☐ **remiss**: (*adj*) careless and neglectful
Rebekkah was criticized for being remiss in her work; she had made many careless mistakes this week.
Word Forms: remissly, remissness

☐ **replication**: (*n*) the act of creating a copy
The illegal replication of brand name handbags remains an issue for authorities in the metropolis.
Word Forms: replicate, replicator   Related Word: replica

☐ **reproach**: (*vb*) to blame; to express criticism towards
The board of directors reproached the company president for falling profits and decreased revenue.
Word Forms: reproach (n.), reproachingly, reproachable, reproachableness, reproachably
Antonym Forms: irreproachable, unreproachable, reproachless   Related Word: reproachful

☐ **reproof**: (*vb*) an act or expression of strong disapproval
The politician seems to be above reproof; he was caught taking bribes from lobbyists and still won reelection.
Related Word: reprove

☐ **repudiate**: (*vb*) to reject
The celebrity repudiated claims that she had undergone plastic surgery.
Word Forms: repudiation, repudiator

☐ **reservation**: (*n*) a feeling of doubt
The bride had serious reservations about the wedding and wondered if it was too late to get back her rental hall deposit.
Related Word: reserve

☐ **resignation**: (*n*) unresisting submission
Once the suspect learned that his fingerprints were found at the scene, he confessed with resignation.
Word Forms: resign

☐ **resilient**: (*adj*) easily recovering or rebounding
Fire ants are resilient pests; even if you destroy their mound, they'll quickly rebuild just a few feet away.
Word Forms: resiliently, resilience, resiliency

☐ **resolute**: (*adj*) firm and determined
I faced a resolute opponent in my last wrestling match; he refused to lose.
Word Forms: resolutely, resoluteness   Antonym Forms: irresolute, irresolutely, irresoluteness
Related Words: resolution, resolve

☐ **restrain**: (*vb*) to hold back
I had to restrain myself from commenting on the article that was intended to create conflict.
Word Forms: restrainable

☐ **revere**: (*vb*) to regard with respect and awe
Paul Revere was one of many colonists who revered freedom and democracy.
Word Forms: reverable, reverent, reverently, reverence, reverential, reverer
Antonym Forms: irreverent, irreverently, irreverence   Related Word: reverend

☐ **rhetoric**: (*n*) skill in using language to persuade; empty talk
The real estate agent was well-versed in the rhetoric needed to sell the broken-down house.
Word Forms: rhetorical, rhetorically

☐ **rigorous**: (*adj*) rigidly accurate; strict
Roger started a rigorous weight loss program that consisted of a strict diet and an intense exercise schedule.
Word Forms: rigorously, rigorousness, rigor

☐ **sanction**: (*vb*) to approve
The school board sanctioned the new elementary school playground, so construction will begin next week.
Word Forms: sanction (n.), sanctionable, sanctioner   Antonym Forms: unsanctioned, sanctionless

☐ **satire**: (*n*) the use of ridicule; a work (such as an essay, play, or movie) intending to ridicule
The movie is a satire, making fun of all the teenage horror movies that came before it.
Word Forms: satiric, satirical, satirically, satirize

☐ **savvy**: (*adj*) knowledgeable; well-informed
Today's kindergartners are quite computer-savvy so they are given standardized tests on the computer.
Word Forms: savvy (n.), savviness

☐ **scorn**: (*n*) a lack of respect accompanied by a feeling of intense dislike
Steve knew he deserved the scorn of his teammates after he was caught cheating, but their reaction still saddened him.
Word Forms: scorn (vb.), scornful, scornfully, scornfulness, scorner

☐ **scrutinize**: (*vb*) to inspect carefully
Ruth scrutinized the classified ads, carefully reading each of the posted jobs.
Word Forms: scrutiny, scrutinizer

☐ **simulate**: (*vb*) to copy or imitate
The scientists simulated the conditions of the original experiment to see if they would get the same results.
Word Forms: simulated (adj.), simulation, simulative

☐ **sinister**: (*adj*) threatening evil or harm
The sinister villain threatened the hero in a climactic scene at the end of the movie.
Word Forms: sinisterly

☐ **skeptical**: (*adj*) having doubt
Skip was skeptical of the car dealer's promise of free oil changes, so he asked for the offer in writing.
Word Forms: skeptically, skepticalness, skepticism, skeptic

☐ **speculative**: (*adj*) based on careful consideration or contemplation rather than fact
Local theories about the girl's disappearance were all speculative; only she herself knew what really happened.
Word Forms: speculatively, speculativeness, speculate, speculation, speculator

VOCABULARY

☐ **stagnant**: (*adj*) not moving, flowing, or progressing
When the feeder creek ran dry, the small pond became stagnant; algae began to thrive in the motionless water.
Word Forms: stagnancy, stagnate, stagnation

☐ **static**: (*adj*) unchanging
Stacy was stuck in a static relationship; Stan was never going to propose marriage.
Word Forms: statically   Related Word: stasis

☐ **stipulate**: (*adj*) to require a condition in an agreement
In the lease, the landlord stipulated that pets were not allowed in the house.

☐ **subjective**: (*adj*) influenced by personal feelings or bias
Suzanne felt that her evaluation was unfairly subjective because it was clear her supervisor had a grudge against her.
Word Forms: subjectively, subjectiveness, subjectivity   Antonym Forms: objective, objectively, objectiveness, objectivity

☐ **subscribe**: (*vb*) to pledge; to approve
The anonymous donor subscribed a large sum of money for the construction of a new hospital.
Related Words: subscription

☐ **subsequent**: (*adj*) coming later; following in order
You will need to remember this basic arithmetic formula for subsequent assignments later this year.
Word Forms: subsequently   Related Words: sequel, sequence

☐ **substantiate**: (*vb*) to establish or strengthen
Her case against the insurance company was substantiated by other plaintiffs who suffered the same injustice.
Antonym Form: unsubstantiated   Related Word: substantial

☐ **subtle**: (*adj*) difficult to detect
The subtle irony throughout the novel is missed by most readers.
Word Forms: subtly, subtleness, subtlety   Antonym Forms: unsubtle, unsubtly

☐ **superficial**: (*adj*) on the surface; shallow; not significant
The officer was grazed by the bullet but luckily the wound was superficial and didn't require stitches.
Word Forms: superficially, superficiality,

☐ **suppress**: (*vb*) to stop; to control
The news anchor suppressed a smile when the reporter fell, but laughed hysterically as soon as she went off the air.
Word Forms: suppressible, suppressive, suppression, suppressor   Related Word: oppress, repress

☐ **sustain**: (*vb*) to uphold as valid
The critic sustained that the performance was superb, even though his peers thought it fell short of expectations.
Word Forms: sustainable, sustainability, sustainment   Related Word: maintain

☐ **synthesize**: (*vb*) to combine
The teacher synthesized her Writing and History lessons by creating projects that required students to write about historical topics.
Word Forms: synthesis   Related Word: synthetic

☐ **synthetic**: (*adj*) not real
The stadium uses synthetic grass on the field because it's easier to maintain than real grass.
Word Forms: synthetically   Related Word: synthesize

☐ **tact**: (*n*) consideration in dealing with others and avoiding giving offense
When breaking a commitment, such as a date or a dinner party, it is important to use tact to avoid hurting feelings.
Word Forms: tactful, tactfully   Antonym Forms: tactless, tactlessly, tactlessness, untactful

☐ **tangential**: (*adj*) slightly connected
While your story about the roller coaster is fascinating, it's only tangential to my point about the increasing price of amusement parks.
Word Forms: tangent

☐ **temperate**: (*adj*) moderate; not extreme
The plants prefer a temperate climate—not too hot and not too cold.
Word Forms: temperately, temperance, temper (vb.)   Antonym Forms: intemperate, intemperately

☐ **transcend**: (*vb*) to rise above or exceed the limits
Beethoven transcended his deafness to become one of the most famous composers of all time.
Word Forms: transcendingly, transcendence, transcendent, transcendental   Related Word: ascend, descend

☐ **transparent**: (*adj*) easily seen through
Tracy said the dog ate her homework, but it's a transparent excuse.
Word Forms: transparency

☐ **trivial**: (*adj*) small and of little importance
The documentary on poverty reminded me that my own financial issues are trivial compared to those of others.
Word Forms: trivially, trivialness, trivialize   Related Word: trivia

☐ **undermine**: (*vb*) to weaken
My argument for a soda machine in school was undermined by the ill-timed report on teenage obesity.
Word Forms: underminingly, underminer

☐ **underscore**: (*vb*) to emphasize
The recent dorm room fire underscores the need for fire extinguishers in every room.
Word Forms: underscore (n.)   Related Word: underline

☐ **undertake**: (*vb*) to commit to
Una had undertaken a job at the funeral home.
Word Forms: undertook, undertaken

☐ **unequivocal**: (*adj*) certain; having only one possible meaning
The politician's unequivocal speech about the environment let his constituents know exactly where he stood on the issue.
Word Forms: unequivocally, unequivocalness   Antonym Forms: equivocal, equivocally, equivocalness

☐ **validate**: (*vb*) to confirm
Valerie needed someone to validate her feelings: was it okay that she was so angry?
Word Forms: validation

☐ **viable**: (*vb*) capable of working; capable of living
Vivian proposed a viable alternative to burning fossil fuels.
Word Forms: viably, viability

☐ **vindicate**: (*vb*) to clear, justify, or prove
Vinnie's victory in court vindicated his actions; it proved he was allowed to build a privacy fence between the two houses.
Word Forms: vindication, vindicator   Related Word: vindictive

☐ **virtue**: (*vb*) moral excellence
Virgil risked his virtue when he failed to return the extra apple packed in the grocery bag by the cashier.
Word Forms: virtuous

☐ **warrant**: (*vb*) to authorize or justify
My dad says that my car accident warrants punishment; he's taking the car away for six months.
Word Forms: warrant (n.), warrantable   Antonym Forms: warrantless, unwarranted, unwarrantable

☐ **wary**: (*adj*) watchful; distrustful
The children were taught to be wary of strangers.
Word Forms: warily, wariness   Antonym Forms: unwary, unwarily

☐ **wistful**: (*adj*) expressing longing or yearning
Willie gave the car one last wistful look before he left the dealership; he wished he had the money to buy it.
Word Forms: wistfully, wistfulness

☐ **yield**: (*vb*) to produce; to give up
The field yielded enough bushels of corn for the farmer to buy a new tractor.
Word Forms: yield (n.)   Antonym Forms: unyielding

☐ **zealous**: (*adj*) enthusiastic and devoted
The zealous sports fan had a tattoo of his favorite team's logo on his ankle.
Word Forms: zealously, zealousness, zealot   Related Word: zeal

Strategies for Studying Vocabulary Words

1. **Write out the words and their meanings.**
   Transferring the words and their definitions to paper helps transfer the information into your long-term memory.

2. **Write new sentences for each word.**
   Similarly, using the word in context helps cement its meaning.

3. **Draw a picture representing the word.**
   Pictures can create a connection to the definition, and students who are visual learners are sure to prefer this method of vocabulary study.

4. **Type the words and definitions.**
   Type each word list into a word processing document or spreadsheet. Then try to define them without looking at the definitions.

5. **Write a short story using 10 or 20 vocabulary words.**
   Trying to create a context for each word is sure to help you remember its definition on test day.

6. **Read the word aloud and say it in a sentence.**
   Some audio learners find it easier to learn when they hear information. Record yourself for later playback.

7. **Analyze the roots, prefixes, and suffixes.**
   Can you find words that have the same suffix? If so, do they mean the same thing in both words? Learning to associate words with related words can help you solve even the toughest test questions.

8. **Group words by meaning.**
   Many SAT words have similar meanings. Organize your flashcards or your lists so that you associate a meaning, such as "lacking money" or "friendly" with all of the words in the group.

9. **Have someone quiz you.**
   Ask a friend or parent to quiz you using your flashcards.

10. **Write your own vocabulary quizzes.**
    Experts believe people learn best when they teach, so here is your chance! Write your own vocabulary quizzes and take them a week or two later.

INDEX

L

Line graph, 299
Line references, 126-128, 134-135, 138-139, 204, 286-287
Literal Comprehension, 203-226, 280-287
Literary fiction passages, 77, 113-118
Location questions (SAT), 306-310

M

Main Idea, 95, 99-102, 206-208
    questions, 206-208
MAPS, 95-98
Match an answer choice, 141-142
Materials, 10-11, 382
Math Test, 36, 45
    on the ACT, 36
    on the SAT, 45
Morning of the test, 383-384
Multiple viewpoints, 110-112
Myths, 130-131

N

Negative attitude words, 238-239
Neutral attitude words, 239
Non-fiction passages, 78-80, 95-97
Notate, 92-93, 116-118
    Active reading, 92-93
    Line references, 116-118
Number of attempts, 15-16

O

One Way words, 105
Openings, 99-103
Opposing viewpoint words, 106
Opposite Answers, 174
Order of passage subjects, 81-84
Organization (of passage), 253
Outlining, 234

P

Pacing, 74-75
Paired Passages, 155-168
Paired questions (SAT), 280-295
    Extended reasoning, 288-290
    Literal comprehension, 280-287
    Support and contradict, 290-295
Parallel Reasoning, 264-265
Paraphrase, 94, 137
    Active reading, 94
    Questions, 137
Passage introduction, 128-129
Passage MAPS, 95-98
Passage organization, 253
Passage openings, 99-103
Passage subjects, 76-80
    Order, 81-84
Patterns, 99-112
Pencils, 382
Photo ID, 382
Phrases in context, 192-195
Pictograph, 301
Pie chart, 301-302
Pivotal words, 104-108
Positive attitude words, 237-238
Power thoughts, 31
Predict (active reading), 91-92
Prephrase, 140-141, 174, 192, 205, 233, 257, 265, 266, 288, 294, 323, 328, 329
PreACT, 40
Primary purpose, 229-230
Proverbs, 100
PSAT, 49-50
Purpose, 96, 229-234
    Verbs, 230-233

Q

Question (active reading), 92
Question stem, 134-137
Quotation marks, 251-252

R

Reading speed, 89-90
Reading strategies, 87-124
Reading Test format, 68-70, 71-73
    ACT, 68-70, 156-157
    SAT, 71-73, 158-159
Reasons and Results, 214-217
"Refers to" questions, 211
Registration, 4
Relate (active reading), 94
Repeat Offenders, 387-408
Rephrasing questions, 137
Rethinking the ACT and SAT, 26-31
Return to the passage, 138-139
Review, 41, 51, 65, 86, 119, 148, 164, 188, 200, 221, 272, 334, 341-345, 386
Rhetorical devices, 242-252
Right answers, 170-172
Routine, 383

S

SAT to ACT Concordance, 65
Scatter plot, 300
Science passages, 77
Science Test (ACT), 37
Score report, 53, 55, 61
    ACT, 55
    SAT, 61
Scores, 53-65
    ACT scores, 54-58, 65
    Canceling, 385
    Concordance, 65
    Reporting policies, 16-18
    SAT scores, 59-64, 65
Sidebars, 92-93, 126
    Notating, 126
    Summary, 92-93
Single passages 125-154
Sleep, 382
Snacks, 382
Social Studies passages, 79

Statements in context, 196-197
Strengthen questions, 266-269, 290-293
Structure, 97
Study break, 381
Study schedule, 6-9
Style, 229-255
Subjects of passages, 76-80, 81-84
Supplemental material, 10-11
Synonyms, 170-171, 194

T

Tables (on the SAT), 302
Target score, 5-6
Test center, 381, 384-385
Test comparison, 24-25
Test dates, 39, 49
    ACT, 39
    SAT, 49
Test day, 13-15, 383-385
Test materials, 382 Test readiness, 381-385
Test registration, 2-4
Test schedule, 49
Test twins, 24-25
Time management, 74-75
Timers, 74
Tips and Tricks, 32
Toxic thoughts, 26-31
Trap answers, 174-184, 303
True But Wrong Answers, 178-179
True rhetorical devices, 242-241
True to a Point Answers, 180-181
True to You Answers, 181-182

U

U-Turn words, 104-105

V

Venn diagram, 301-302
Verbs (purpose), 230-233
Viewpoints, 106, 110-111
Visualize (active reading), 93
Vocabulary, 85, 387-408
    Repeat Offenders, 387-408
Vocabulary diagnostic, 151
Vocabulary strategies, 150
Vocabulary-in-Context, 267-274

W

Weaken questions, 266-269, 293-295
Websites, 21-22
Wristwatch, 382
Writing Test, 38, 46
    on the ACT, 38
    on the SAT, 46
Words-in-Context, 191-202
Wrong answers, 229-239